Political Power in
Birmingham, 1871–1921

ʃ∾ *Twentieth-Century America Series*

Political Power in

BIRMINGI

M, 1871-1921

By Carl V. Harris

THE UNIVERSITY OF TENNESSEE PRESS

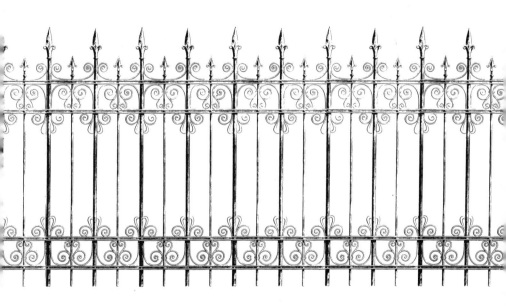

🙋 *Twentieth-Century America Series*

DEWEY W. GRANTHAM, GENERAL EDITOR

Publication of this book was assisted by grants from the Linn-Henley Charitable Trust and the Birmingham Metropolitan Study Project.

Library of Congress Cataloging in Publication Data

Harris, Carl Vernon, 1937–
    Political power in Birmingham, 1871–1921.
    (Twentieth-century America series)
    Bibliography: p.
    Includes index.
    1. Birmingham, Ala.—Politics and government.
2. Political participation—Alabama—Birmingham
—History. 3. Pressure groups—Alabama—Birmingham—History. I. Title.
JS598.2.H37   320.9′761′78106   77–1110
ISBN 0–87049–211–X

For my mother and father

Foreword

$\mathbb{B}$IRMINGHAM was the "Magic City" of the New South. Merely a gleam in the eyes of iron, coal, railroad, and real estate speculators in the 1870s, it had by the turn of the century a diverse economic base and ranked as a strong challenger to Atlanta's claim on supremacy in the Southeast. By that time, too. it possessed a more diverse white ethnic contingent than most southern cities, as well as burgeoning black ghettos which contained about one third of the total population. As in other places North and South, moreover, people, industry, and business spilled across the original municipal boundaries, creating the basis for city-suburban conflict and setting the stage for the great annexation drive of 1910 which yielded "Greater Birmingham," a sprawling municipality described by one modest booster as the "Magic City of the World, the marvel of the South, the miracle of the Continent, the dream of the Hemisphere, the vision of all Mankind." And like other places, rapid urban growth combined with technological and scientific innovations set off a sustained demand for improved and new municipal services which broadened the scope of local government. To a larger extent than many might imagine, and despite the assertion of the Magic City's uniqueness by its promoters, the history of Birmingham is the history of any late nineteenth- and early twentieth-century American metropolis.

This book should therefore command a broad audience. Americans in general and southerners in particular have for too long neglected the urban dimension of their past. That oversight was sad enough in 1970 when three-fourths of the nation lived in metropolitan areas and when it first became apparent that the most rapid urban growth was occurring in the "sunbelt" states. Now, when city-dwellers and suburbanites across the country are bedeviled by fiscal crunches, the specter of "stagflation," energy shortages, city-suburban animosities, and the persistence of race as a divisive element in places as distant and different as Boston, Louisville, and Detroit, that neglect is simply intolerable. Perhaps more than ever before we can now benefit from the balanced outlook on these and other metropolitan difficulties which only historical perspective can provide.

Citizens, students, scholars, and history buffs seeking relief from their amnesia about cities, however, will find their search confined to a narrow shelf of books. To be sure, the growing popularity of urban studies among historians since the urban crisis of the 1960s has helped redress the balance, and a few writers have even turned their attention to Dixie. As a result, we now know that the antebellum South urbanized at a more rapid rate than virtually all the rest of the Western world except the North and Great Britain. We know, too, that most of that growth took place on the periphery of the region; that it produced, by northern standards, relatively few small towns; that it created hostile environments for the "peculiar institution" of slavery; that it generated a strong and persistent stream of urban-rural conflict like that which characterized the North; and that ethnic conflict in the South's major cities in the 1850s disrupted urban politics below as well as above the Ohio River. Nonetheless, the study of urbanization in the Old South has only just begun.

Readers will find even less in print about southern cities after Appomattox. Published studies of Reconstruction typically concentrate on state and national developments, black communities, or race relations; and the standard account of the origins of the New South (1877–1913) handles cities only incidentally. And while the postbellum South had its share of urban machines and reformers, only Boss Crump of Memphis has attracted a full-scale recent study, and the region's vigorous municipal reform movement in the Gilded Age and Progressive Era has been the subject of but a handful of monographs. Equally disappointing, no one has yet produced an analysis of the rise of the South's varied interior cities.

Carl V. Harris' book is important in part because it touches on so many of these unexplored areas. Centering on the structure and distribution of political power, the approach is not only novel among historical studies but also applicable to other cities past and present. Harris contends that community power studies which ignore the historical process of decision-making are bound to be misleading. To demonstrate the case, he adopts a mode of analysis which divides the population into economic and social interest groups, indicates which issues each deemed most important, and reveals which groups most consistently got what they wanted. He explores first the extent to which various groups placed representatives in elective offices and whether that abetted the advancement of their interests. He then moves into struggles among the groups outside the electoral arena over taxation; the allocation of services; and social, economic, and utility regulation. Along the way he not only develops a critique of other community power studies, including such familiar targets as Floyd Hunter's on Atlanta and Robert Dahl's on New Haven, but he also lays bare the shifting complex of influence on the greasy pole of Birmingham politics under both the mayoral-aldermanic and commission forms of government.

This analysis comprises the heart of the book, and the findings challenge conventional wisdom at several points. While carefully and judiciously done, moreover, it is never arid. We learn, for example, that the cleavage in electoral politics was social rather than economic, and that in early contests between the "liberal" and "moral" elements over Sundays and saloons, liberals held their own, despite the use of the "black menace" by moralists as a rationale for tighter control over the liquor trade and more comprehensive regulation of the city's finely segregated Negro population. And though Harris concludes that the two top levels of economic groups controlled a preponderance of the city's wealth and exercised political power commensurate with that wealth, he also catalogues the conflicts between the top and middle ranks over such questions as downtown improvements, revenue policies, strikes, and corporation commissaries and paydays. In the end, Harris argues, the taxing, service allocation, and regulatory realms of local government each displayed a distinctive pattern of political power distribution, and neither the "power elite" nor the "pluralist" model explains sufficiently the dynamics of the urban political process.

This book, in short, is a sophisticated and readable contribution to the study of urban politics and history. Harris makes his case for Birmingham's respectability as the object of a case study in lively descriptive passages as well as with solid archival and statistical documentation. His discussion of the delicate and classic question of who did what to whom, how, and with what consequences is impressive. These issues have beguiled students of urban government since the days of Lord Bryce and Lincoln Steffens. Harris has advanced the art a significant notch by devising an approach useful to social scientists as well as historians and helpful to concerned citizens as well as urban professionals and politicians. Out of his research has come a distinctive and clearly written synthesis which deserves the attention of us all.

Cincinnati
June, 1976

Zane L. Miller
University of Cincinnati

Acknowledgments

$\mathcal{M}$ANY people and institutions have helped in the preparation of this study, and I am deeply grateful to each of them. Though only indirectly involved with this book, Professor Raymond L. Flory of McPherson College, McPherson, Kansas, stimulated my first interest in historical research, and the late Professor William B. Hesseltine of the University of Wisconsin inspired and guided my first forays into Southern history. Most directly involved with the book has been my dissertation advisor at the University of Wisconsin, Professor J. Rogers Hollingsworth. He introduced me to the political power debate; spent hours in patient but intense evaluation of my efforts to formulate an approach; and provided crucial encouragement and advice at every stage. Also, Professor Richard N. Current of the University of Wisconsin and the University of North Carolina at Greensboro gave vital support and valuable criticism from the inception to the conclusion of the study. The thoughtful suggestions of Professor Dewey W. Grantham, general editor of the Twentieth-Century America Series, have improved every page and chapter, and his encouragement has sustained me in the final stages of revision. I also benefited from the criticisms and suggestions of Professors Allan G. Bogue, Stuart D. Brandes, W. Elliot Brownlee, Alexander B. Callow, Jr., Peter R. Knights, Eric E. Lampard, Zane L. Miller, and David P. Thelen.

Vital financial support came from a Danforth Graduate Fellowship, 1962–68, from a 1970 Summer Faculty Fellowship granted by the University of California, Santa Barbara, and from research and travel funds granted by the Research Committee of the Academic Senate of the University of California, Santa Barbara. Portions of this book were published in the *Journal of Southern History* 38 (Nov. 1972), the *Alabama Review* 27 (July 1974), and the *Historical Methods Newsletter* 9 (Sept. 1976). I am grateful to the editors for permission to reprint them.

xi

Many librarians, government officials, and business representatives gave resourceful assistance. Miss Ruth Davis of the Wisconsin State Historical Society skillfully managed my voluminous interlibrary loan orders of microfilmed newspapers. During my research visits to Birmingham the late Mr. Fant H. Thornley, director of the Birmingham Public Library, Mr. Rucker Agee, donor of the excellent Agee Map Collection, and Miss Jessie Ham and her staff in the library's Department of Southern History and Literature were exceedingly generous in time and hospitality and made special arrangements to accommodate my research needs. More recently Mr. George R. Stewart, director of the library, and Miss Mary Bess Kirksey of the Southern History Department have assisted me greatly. I should also like to thank the librarians of the Business Library, Dun & Bradstreet, Inc., New York, New York; of the Alabama Department of Archives and History, Montgomery, Alabama; and of the Library of the University of Alabama, University, Alabama.

Among government officials I would especially like to thank the former city clerk of Birmingham, Mr. Judson P. Hodges, and his assistant, Mrs. Sarah Naugher, and her staff for providing access to city documents. At the Water Works Board of the City of Birmingham, Mr. T. H. Collins, general manager, and Mr. Orbie L. Mays, office manager, were especially accommodating in helping me locate and in giving me access to the records and letterbooks of the former Birmingham Water Works Company. The directors of several city departments and the staff of the Jefferson County Tax Assessor's office searched diligently through yellowing files and books to satisfy my unconventional requests for information long sunk in oblivion. In addition, the Louisville & Nashville Railroad, the Birmingham Realty Company, the Alabama Power Company, and the Southern Bell Telephone Company supplied specific information upon request. Since many citizens and officials who helped me unstintingly may disagree with my portrayal of their home town, I emphasize that I alone stand responsible for all interpretations presented in this volume.

Finally, my wife, Judy, has been a constant co-worker at every stage of research, statistical compilation, writing, revision, and typing. I cannot imagine how the book would have been completed without her devoted collaboration.

Santa Barbara   CARL V. HARRIS
September, 1976

Contents

Illustrations

xv

TABLES

Political Power in
Birmingham, 1871–1921

Introduction

I̲N Birmingham, Alabama, as in most nineteenth- and twentieth-century American cities, economic power was concentrated heavily in the hands of a very small minority composed of industrialists, corporation executives, bankers, and the wealthiest commercial and professional people, who together owned more than half the total wealth. High social status was limited to the few hundred prominent families who had entree to the shimmering circle of polite society.

But what about political power? Was it similarly concentrated in the hands of a small elite, or was it distributed broadly among the ordinary citizens—white-collar workers, small shopkeepers, artisans, clerks, wage earners, and servants, who made up the vast majority of the population and of the voters. What groups held most of the political offices? When the government levied taxes, provided services, and imposed regulations, whose opinions really counted? Who won and who lost? These questions are the central concern of this study of Birmingham, from its founding in 1871 to its fiftieth anniversary in 1921.

Citizens of Birmingham often discussed political power, sometimes in polemical language. In 1913, for example, the Birmingham *Labor Advocate* declared: "The governing power in the hands of such men as [Mayor Culpepper] Exum and his henchmen has proven to be the power of corporations, openly exercised for the corporations by the corporations, and has been used against the working men of the city to their detriment." But editor Frank P. Glass of the Birmingham *News*, also writing in 1913, disagreed. "The people alone rule," he said. Indeed, he believed that economic leaders exerted far too little political influence, and in 1915 he lamented: "The bulk of the businessmen are so absorbed in their own affairs . . . that they have taken no time for . . . the affairs of the community. This is part of the too common apathy in this busy bustling city as to the great business of good government."[1]

Questions about political power have long beguiled political observers, and in recent years political scientists and sociologists have generated an intense debate between a "power elite" school, which has found local political power concentrated heavily in the hands of economic and social elites, and a "pluralist" school, which has found local political power widely dispersed among groups from many economic and social levels, with no group really dominating urban government.[2] The two schools have been epitomized by two influential books: the power-elite school by Floyd Hunter's analysis of "Regional City" (Atlanta, Georgia), entitled *Community Power Structure: A Study of Decision Makers*, published in 1953;[3] and the pluralist school by Robert A. Dahl's *Who Governs? Democracy and Power in an American City*, a study of New Haven, Connecticut, published in 1961.[4]

For Atlanta, Hunter portrayed a stable pyramidal power structure presided over by a relatively permanent economic elite that made all significant community decisions. The elite operated mostly behind the scenes to defend and maintain long-established policies that served their interests. Their control of information enabled them to set the community agenda and decide which, if any, proposed departures from standing policy would be considered seriously.[5]

For New Haven, Dahl hypothesized that the power of any group or individual was likely to vary greatly from one type of issue to another. Studying three separate issue areas—urban redevelopment, education, and political party nominations—he found that most decision-makers were highly specialized in only one issue area, that leaders in different areas tended to come from different social strata, and that no general, all-controlling power elite existed. Political power was highly frag-

1. Birmingham *Labor Advocate*, July 18, 1913; Birmingham *News*, Feb. 28, 1913; Aug. 18, 1915.

2. The literature on the political power structure of American communities is extensive. The best annotated bibliography is Willis D. Hawley and James H. Svara, *The Study of Community Power: A Bibliographic Review* (Santa Barbara, Calif.: ABC-Clio, 1972). A useful anthology which surveys the development of the principal issues and reprints the major essays is Michael Aiken and Paul E. Mott, eds., *The Structure of Community Power* (New York: Random, 1970). A useful review essay is Wallace S. Sayre and Nelson W. Polsby, "American Political Science and the Study of Urbanization," in Philip M. Hauser and Leo F. Schnore, eds., *The Study of Urbanization* (New York: Wiley, 1965), 115–56.

3. (Chapel Hill: University of North Carolina Press, 1953; Garden City: Doubleday Anchor Books, 1963.) All page references are to the Anchor edition.

4. (New Haven: Yale Univ. Press, 1961.)

5. Hunter, *Community Power Structure*, 61–76, 91, 107–10, 238–42, 255–63.

mented and was exercised by many competing groups and government officials. Further, "economic notables" and "social notables" failed to participate in large numbers in any issue area and exerted little influence on decisions. Dahl concluded that little of the economic or social power of the notables translated into political power. The notables were not a ruling group at all; in fact, they had no more political power than did people from many other groups.[6]

Implicit in the disagreements between the two schools have been opposing assumptions, theories, and speculations about the historical development of community power structures and about the influence, or lack of influence, of past events and decisions in shaping power structures in the present.[7] Power elitists have tended to assume the existence of a long-standing, firmly entrenched, historically traditional structure of political power which quietly but effectively maintained established policies favored by a relatively permanent behind-the-scenes power elite.[8] Pluralists have seemed to be most impressed with the relative instability and impermanence of many power alignments, and in their analyses they have placed less emphasis on the influence of past decisions, of established structures, and of the behind-the-scenes influence of long entrenched leaders, and more upon chaotically shifting alignments in the present.[9]

Whatever their assumptions about the influence of the past, however, most students of community power have focused their actual research primarily upon the contemporary, post-World War II political systems

6. Dahl, *Who Governs?*, 63–84, 169; these findings are conveniently summarized in Nelson W. Polsby, *Community Power and Political Theory* (New Haven: Yale Univ. Press, 1963), 69–97.

7. For a more elaborate discussion of the contrasting assumptions about the influence of the past, see Carl V. Harris, "The Underdeveloped Historical Dimension of the Study of Community Power Structure," *Historical Methods Newsletter* 9 (Sept. 1976), 195–200.

8. Hunter, *Community Power Structure*, 91, 107–09, 240; Roland J. Pellegrin and Charles Coates, "Absentee-Owned Corporations and Community Power Structure," *American Journal of Sociology* 61 (Mar. 1956), 413; Delbert C. Miller in Howard J. Ehrlich, "Power and Democracy: A Critical Discussion," in *Power and Democracy in America*, ed. William V. D'Antonio and Howard J. Ehrlich (Notre Dame, Ind.: Univ. of Notre Dame Press, 1961), 101; Robert Presthus, *Men at the Top: A Study in Community Power* (New York: Oxford Univ. Press, 1964), 5; Terry N. Clark, "The Concept of Power," in Clark, ed., *Community Structure and Decision Making: Comparative Analyses* (San Francisco: Chandler, 1968), 79; Peter Bachrach and Morton S. Baratz, "Two Faces of Power," *American Political Science Review* 56 (Dec. 1962), 947–52.

9. Polsby, *Community Power and Political Theory*, 95–97, 112–21; Dahl, *Who Governs?*, 63–103.

of communities. Some scholars have provided brief sketches of the historical development of community power structures, but their methods of historical research have been much less rigorous and intensive than their methods of contemporary analysis. Some of the more intensive methods, however, can be adapted to historical data, and this case study of Birmingham attempts to modify the questions, concepts, and methodologies of the power structure debate and to employ them in more thorough analysis of the historical development of the political power structure of one middle sized, commercial-industrial city during the late nineteenth and early twentieth centuries.[10]

It was during this era, from the Civil War to World War I, that the modern American city emerged. Railroads tied the nation together, creating a national market and encouraging regions and cities to specialize. Industrialization and economic growth accelerated, and people migrated to cities in unprecedented numbers. Street railways and suburbs greatly expanded the urban areas, and within the spreading cities specialized commercial, industrial, and residential sectors emerged. City governments staggered under unaccustomed burdens, groping to meet overwhelming demands for new and more costly city services, struggling to come to terms with the emerging utility corporations, and often succumbing to corruption and boss-ruled machines. In response, a widespread municipal reform movement emerged, stressing honesty and efficiency and promoting new institutional structures.[11] Birmingham, founded in 1871, was a child of this formative era, and this book attempts to shed light on the dynamics of urban political power in the midst of turbulent growth and change.

Political power is defined here as the relative pressure that individuals or groups were able to exert in the city's governmental decision-making

10. Among historians Professor Samuel P. Hays has most directly confronted the question of the distribution of political power in the past, and in an influential study of municipal reformers in Pittsburgh, Pennsylvania, during the progressive era he urged that the political historian's most crucial task is the reconstruction of "the structure of the distribution of power and influence." See Hays, "The Politics of Reform in Municipal Government in the Progressive Era," *Pacific Northwest Quarterly* 55 (Oct. 1964), 160.

11. For accounts of these developments see Alfred D. Chandler, Jr., "The Beginnings of 'Big Business' in American Industry," *Business History Review* 33 (Spring 1959), 1–31; Blake McKelvey, *The Urbanization of America, 1860–1915* (New Brunswick, N.J.: Rutgers Univ. Press, 1963), 35–114; Charles N. Glaab and A. Theodore Brown, *A History of Urban America* (New York: Macmillan, 1967), 107–227; Sam Bass Warner, Jr., *The Urban Wilderness: A History of the American City* (New York: Harper, 1972), 85–112; Zane L. Miller, *The Urbanization of Modern America: A Brief History* (New York: Harcourt, 1973), 25–122.

process. Thus it refers to ability to shape government policies, to influence the outputs of the local political system. The political system is defined to embrace decisions about the actions, policies, and scope of government, but not to embrace community decisions that did not involve demands upon or decisions by and about local government. Thus the political system is viewed here as analytically separate from the economic system and the social system, but the political system did function within an "environment" created by the social and economic systems, it was open to influences and inputs from them, and it in turn had an impact upon them.[12]

For the analysis of political power, students of contemporary cities have developed three basic methods: positional, reputational, and decisional. Positional analysis (similar to the historian's collective-biography technique) consists of studying lists of a city's formal officeholders and their occupations or socioeconomic positions to discover which groups were most strongly represented among official decision-makers. This method, alone among the three, has been applied to historical data by some social scientists to reveal historical trends in the socioeconomic status of typical officeholders.[13] The reputational method, employed

12. The definition of political power employed in this study is similar to one suggested by Professor Lee Benson in "Political Power and Political Elites" in Lee Benson *et al.*, *American Political Behavior: Historical Essays and Readings* (New York: Harper, 1974), 287–88. This definition of the political system and its "environment" is congruent with the analytical scheme developed by David Easton in *A Framework for Political Analysis* (Englewood Cliffs, N.J.: Prentice-Hall, 1965) and in *A Systems Analysis of Political Life* (New York: Wiley, 1965). According to Easton's model, in most modern societies the political system is essentially the governmental system, in which "values are authoritatively allocated for a society." Its key distinguishing feature is that the political authorities have a monopoly on the use of legitimate physical coercion in society.
Some analysts of political power have found the Easton definition too narrow. For example, Robert Presthus has defined the "political process" to include "all community decisions that involve the allocation of important resources," whether or not the government authorities are involved. He believes that "our political and economic systems are inextricably bound together, and that the process by which each allocates desired values is essentially 'political.'" See *Men at the Top: A Study in Community Power* (New York: Oxford Univ. Press, 1964), 34. Presthus employed this broad definition in order to deal with the role of economic power in political decisions. But for precisely this purpose it is actually more useful to define politics more narrowly—to include only government decision-making—and then to ask to what extent demands and pressures from powerful members of the economic and social systems are able to shape governmental agendas and decisions.
13. Dahl, *Who Governs?*, 11–62; Robert O. Schulze, "The Role of Economic Dominants in Community Power Structure," *American Sociological Review* 23 (Feb. 1958), 3–9; Donald A. Clelland and William H. Form, "Economic Dominants and Community Power: A Comparative Analysis," *American Journal of Sociology* 69

mostly by the power-elite school, consists of interviewing a panel of community "knowledgeables," or "judges," who are asked to nominate lists of local men and women of reputed power and influence, especially people who do not hold formal offices. The investigator may then interview the nominees and study the sociometric patterns of inter-action among them to find the top leaders.[14] The decisional method is used mostly by pluralists. They eschew reliance upon "knowledgeables," who may be misinformed, and upon reputations, which may be distorted, and instead, through interviews, direct observations, government rec-ords, and newspapers, they study actual decisions as they are being made, seeking to determine who participates, who wins, and who loses. From such investigation, which focuses on actual behavior rather than shadowy reputation, the researcher constructs lists of those who wielded power.[15]

The historian engaged in a study of the late nineteenth and early twentieth centuries must select among and modify such methodologies, since he must rely primarily upon the surviving written record for data. The historical record provides ample data for positional analysis, which is employed in chapter 4. But since the historian cannot systematically interview the "knowledgeables," or inside dopesters, of the period, he can make little use of the reputational technique.[16] On the other hand, the historian can adapt the decisional method, since he can use govern-ment records and reports, financial statistics, tax records, newspapers, city directories, letters, and memoirs to reconstruct past decisions. Chap-ters 5 through 11 employ the decisional approach and reconstruct the major issues and decisions in all types of local government activity from the founding of Birmingham through its first fifty years.[17]

(Mar. 1964), 511–21; Donald S. Bradley and Mayer N. Zald, "From Commercial Elite to Political Administrator: The Recruitment of the Mayors of Chicago," *American Journal of Sociology* 71 (Sept. 1965), 153–67.

14. Hunter, *Community Power Structure*, 61–76, 255–63.

15. Raymond E. Wolfinger, "Reputation and Reality in the Study of Community Power," *American Sociological Review* 25 (Oct. 1960), 630–44; Polsby, *Commu-nity Power and Political Theory*, 95–97, 112–38; Dahl, *Who Governs?*, 64–72, 330–37.

16. One quasi-reputational approach available to the urban historian is content analysis of newspapers—tabulating the frequency with which men's names ap-peared, thus determining who had a newspaper reputation for power. But this can-not duplicate the most important alleged capability of the reputational interview technique—uncovering behind-the-scenes power figures who purposefully avoided public notice—and it will not be used here.

17. True, the historian sifting written records cannot gather as much detailed inside information as can the political scientist observing and interviewing partici-pants. But the method of the political scientist, which involves attending countless meetings while an issue unfolds, is so costly and time-consuming that usually he can

Individual issues will be grouped into three basic functions performed by local government: the *extraction* of money from citizens through taxes and fees; the *allocation* of services among citizens; and the *regulation* of some kinds of social and economic behavior. Within each function, more specific policy areas are defined as follows: extraction embraces the one policy area of municipal revenue; allocation, the two policy areas of general civic services and specific public improvements; and regulation, the three policy areas of social regulation, economic regulation, and regulation of utilities. Table 1.1 outlines the functions and the policy areas and details the content of the policy areas.[18]

In the reconstruction of issues, the focus will be upon the activity of economic and social interest groups. In chapter 3 the economic groups will be divided into upper-, middle-, and lower-ranking sets, according to the amount of local economic resources controlled by the typical firm in each group. The social groups will be characterized as to the predominant social status of their members.[19]

Separate chapters will tell the story of fifty years of interest-group contention in each of six policy areas, each chapter describing the pattern of policy that emerged over the decades, pointing out which groups considered the policy area important, and indicating which groups

---

afford to study only a very few issues, for a relatively short period in the present. This, perhaps, has led pluralist decisional investigators to neglect the weight of traditions, of abiding institutions, of past decisions, and of established policy patterns. The historian, using a lower-powered microscope, can focus on a broader field of issues, cover a much longer time span, and attempt to be more sensitive to the dynamics of the development of patterns of policy and power over time.

18. In developing this classification of government activities, I found helpful suggestions in Theodore J. Lowi, "American Business, Public Policy, Case-Studies, and Political Theory," *World Politics* 16 (July 1964), 677–715; in Lowi, *At the Pleasure of the Mayor: Patronage and Power in New York City, 1898–1958* (New York: Free Press, 1964), 140; in the discussion of political-system inputs, outputs, functions, and capabilities in Gabriel A. Almond and G. Bingham Powell, Jr., *Comparative Politics: A Developmental Approach* (Boston: Little, 1966), 25–41; and in Robert E. Agger, Daniel Goldrich, and Bert E. Swanson, *The Rulers and the Ruled: Political Power and Impotence in American Communities* (New York: Wiley, 1964), 195–201.

19. The focus on interest groups is a departure from the typical technique of both power elite and pluralist researchers, who have focused primarily on the power of individuals. But individuals come and go rather rapidly on the local political scene, while interest groups persist and provide a more stable unit of analysis for the historian. The focus on economic and social interest groups, ranked according to economic and social status, should be acceptable to the power elite school, which has emphasized the need to discover the social and economic bases of individual power, and also to the pluralist school, which has been primarily responsible for developing interest group analysis.

Table 1.1   **Three Government Functions and Six Policy Areas**

Extraction

1. Municipal Revenue

Allocation of Services

2. General Civic Services

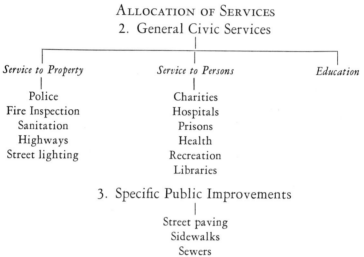

Service to Property	*Service to Persons*	*Education*
Police	Charities	
Fire Inspection	Hospitals	
Sanitation	Prisons	
Highways	Health	
Street lighting	Recreation	
	Libraries	

3. Specific Public Improvements

Street paving
Sidewalks
Sewers

Regulation

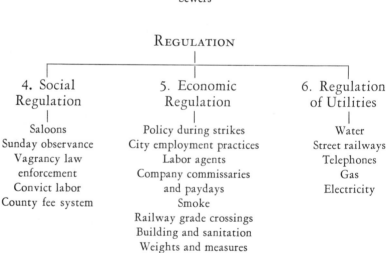

4. Social Regulation	5. Economic Regulation	6. Regulation of Utilities
Saloons	Policy during strikes	Water
Sunday observance	City employment practices	Street railways
Vagrancy law enforcement	Labor agents	Telephones
Convict labor	Company commissaries and paydays	Gas
County fee system	Smoke	Electricity
	Railway grade crossings	
	Building and sanitation	
	Weights and measures	
	Food and milk	
	Rent and food cost	

influenced it the most and which the least. A concluding chapter will compare the different policy areas and describe the general pattern of distribution of political power.

Birmingham is a convenient subject for such analysis because it grew quite rapidly and thus recorded, within the relatively brief span of fifty years, the entire story of a city from its origins as a brash boomtown to its emergence as a complex commercial-industrial metropolis of 200,000 population. While this new heavily industrialized southern city was not in all respects typical of American cities during the period, it did experience full force the benefits, problems, and political ramifications of rapid urbanization and industrialization. And it was not, as some observers have implied, simply a one-industry town or an overgrown company town. In 1943 when Chauncy D. Harris pioneered in the systematic classification of American cities according to economic function, he included Birmingham among those cities in which "both trade and manufacturing are well developed but neither is clearly dominant."[20] Thus Birmingham as a research site embraces articulate commercial and industrial sectors, distinct but interrelated, and both sectors contributed significantly to the remarkable growth that earned Birmingham the nickname, the "Magic City."

20. Harris, "A Functional Classification of Cities in the United States." *Geographical Review* 33 (Jan. 1943), 89, 91.

The "Magic City," 1871-1921

Ⓑ IRMINGHAM, Alabama, was born in 1871, a bold new boom town in an old cornfield. Its few hundred residents were mostly land speculators and gamblers, its streets were mud, its buildings were shacks, its railroad depot a boxcar. By the time of its fiftieth birthday in 1921, Birmingham had grown up to become the leading industrial city of the American South, its skyline dominated by imposing skyscrapers and industrial smokestacks, its incorporated territory stretching over fifty square miles of busy streets, sprawling streetcar lines, residential suburbs, and industrial plants. And in 1921 it had more than 180,000 inhabitants who produced coal, iron, steel, cast iron pipe, heavy machinery, and textiles, and who provided commercial, financial, and transportation services for the entire state of Alabama.

Coal, iron ore, and limestone lying near one another in the rugged wooded hills and valleys of northern Alabama formed the foundation for the economy of Birmingham. Until the Civil War no railroads reached the hill country, only scattered farmers settled the valleys, and the three minerals essential for making pig iron and steel lay virtually untapped. But during Reconstruction two railroads, the Alabama & Chattanooga and the South & North, built toward the district, aiming to intersect in Jones Valley, at the foot of Red Mountain, laden with iron ore, and within a few miles of the Warrior, Cahaba, and Coosa coal fields. In 1871 railroad developers and land speculators who were associated with the South & North Railroad organized the Elyton Land Company with $200,000 capital, bought 4,150 acres of farm land surrounding the proposed intersection, and began laying out and promoting a new "workshop town" to be called Birmingham.[1]

1. H.M. Caldwell, *History of the Elyton Land Company and Birmingham, Ala.* (Birmingham, 1892), 3-6; Martha Mitchell Bigelow, "Birmingham: Biography of

Jones Valley, roughly five miles wide and fifteen miles long, was one of many broad valleys formed by the ridged hills that trailed off southwesterly from the southern end of the Appalachian Mountains. Along the southern edge of the valley stretched rough, wooded Red Mountain, punctuated by occasional gaps that provided potential routes for railroads. The Alabama & Chattanooga Railroad, laying track from Chattanooga, ran northeast to southwest along the trough of Jones Valley. The South & North Railroad, laying track from Montgomery toward Nashville, entered the valley from the south through Gracie's Gap in Red Mountain, intersected with the Alabama & Chattanooga in the center of the valley, and exited to the north. The two railroads met on the western edge of the proposed city, ran parallel through a mile-long west-to-east railroad reservation along the equator of the Elyton Land Company property, and separated at the city's eastern edge. The Elyton Company and John T. Milner, chief engineer of the South & North, cooperated to lay out a checkerboard town, with avenues running parallel to the railroads and streets intersecting at right angles, with the main north-south street at the center of town becoming Twentieth Street.[2]

The Elyton Company's first president was a shrewd and experienced land promoter, James R. Powell. A former operator of a mail coach line, Powell had been an Alabama state senator, thereby acquiring the title "Colonel," though he restricted his Civil War activity to "manufacturing ice gratis in 1863 for the Confederate hospitals." After the war he had started a large cotton-land speculation scheme in Mississippi, but in 1871 he returned to Alabama because he saw in Jones Valley something "with millions in it." An aggressive and domineering figure, Powell resourcefully enticed northern and foreign ironmasters to visit Birmingham and he exuberantly advertised their pronouncements that the new city was destined to be the El Dorado of iron masters and the "manufacturing center of the habitable globe." For good measure he added that it was "a perfect Mahomet's paradise of lovely women." Operating out of a railroad section house, using wooden pegs to mark off streets in the corn stubble and mud, Powell began selling lots in

a City of the New South" (Ph.D. diss., Univ. of Chicago, 1946), 13–18; Ethel Armes, *The Story of Coal and Iron in Alabama* (Birmingham, 1910), 218–25, 234.

2. Bigelow, "Birmingham," 5–8; James R. Powell, "To the Stockholders of the Elyton Land Company," January 25, 1872, reprinted in *Birmingham City Directory, 1883*, 10–11.

June 1871. By the end of the year more than 100 houses and stores had sprung up, and more than 800 settlers had come, eager to buy in on the ground floor and share in the fortunes to be made from a "magical" increase in population and land values.[3]

In December 1871 the Elyton Land Company had its "Magic City" incorporated by the state legislature, enclosing a mere 1.4 square miles in the first city limits. The city charter provided for a mayor elected at large and a board of aldermen elected from wards, a system Birmingham would retain until 1911. By early 1873 the town had elected Powell mayor and dubbed him the "Duke of Birmingham," and he claimed to have 4,000 people in his domain. Next Powell prevailed upon the legislature to call a county election in May to decide whether the Jefferson County Courthouse should stay in the nearby village of Elyton or move to Birmingham. Determined to win, Powell provided an enormous free barbecue on the proposed new courthouse site in Birmingham, and he arranged excursion trains to bring hungry voters, black and white, "from the furthest confines of the County and perhaps beyond." The "Duke," brandishing a sword, handsomely mounted on a calico pony, personally marshalled his imported voters from depot to barbecue to polling place, and he had it whispered among the blacks that he was none other than General Ulysses S. Grant. By such methods bustling Birmingham cast a majority and captured the courthouse.[4]

Then in mid-1873 depression struck the nation, cholera smote Birmingham (killing 128 people), the predicted industries failed to materialize, and for a time the boom town's magic disappeared, as did much of its population. A disappointed Powell resigned and retired to his Mississippi plantation, and until 1880 Birmingham languished in the doldrums.[5]

It was a pattern to be repeated often in Birmingham history. The "limitless wealth of coal and iron" in the surrounding hills and the "unparalleled advantages of location" were indeed extraordinary, and they inspired great expectations of stunning ascent to "unrivaled" productivity and wealth. Birmingham did achieve remarkable growth, but never so rapid and magnificent as fantasized, and frequently the city suffered disappointing setbacks. Still, the partial fulfillment of past dreams always encouraged new visions, and during every slump there were promoters to preach, as did one in 1892: "Birmingham is now

3. Armes, *Story*, 224–27, 232, 234; Powell, "To the Stockholders," 12–14.
4. Powell, "To the Stockholders," 9; Caldwell, *History*, 8–10.
5. Caldwell, *History*, 10–13.

upon the eve of another forward movement towards that grand destiny which, so sure as day follows night, awaits her in the future." Birmingham developers, in short, were ever impatient with tantalizing but still unsatisfying successes, ever expectantly awaiting the dawn of the millennium, ever anxious about the threat of new devastating downturns.[6]

After 1873 the Elyton Land Company, under a careful and able new president, Dr. Henry M. Caldwell, concentrated less on attracting settlers and more on promoting development of coal and iron resources. In 1876 the Elyton Company and the Louisville & Nashville Railroad cooperated to finance a crucial furnace experiment in which, for the first time, pig iron was made from Alabama coke. (The small quantities of Alabama pig iron produced previously had been made with charcoal.)[7]

Still lacking was a ready supply of cheap, high-quality coking coal, and in 1878 railroad capitalist James Withers Sloss, mining engineer Truman H. Aldrich, and capitalist-prospector Henry Fairchild DeBardeleben formed the pioneer Pratt Coal and Coke Company to develop a coke supply. DeBardeleben, a dashing athletic figure of Hessian ancestry, was the son of a cotton planter in Autauga County. After his father's death, he had been taken into the family of Alabama's preeminent antebellum cotton textile manufacturer, Daniel Pratt of Autauga County. DeBardeleben superintended Pratt's cotton gin factory, married his daughter Ellen, helped manage his early ventures in northern Alabama railroads and iron, and, upon Pratt's death, inherited his capital and became "the one big-moneyed man" in northern Alabama. In the early 1870s, DeBardeleben caught the prospecting fever, saying later, "I'd rather be out in the woods on the back of a fox-trotting mule, with a good seam of coal at my feet than be president of the United States."

In 1878 DeBardeleben, Sloss, and Aldrich, later to be revered as the "captains of the Old Guard," found, explored and bought up a rich thick seam of uniformly high quality coking coal four miles northwest of Birmingham. Naming it the Pratt seam, DeBardeleben "put the whole power of his fortune, his credit, and his tremendous vitality for the advancement of the company." In February 1879 the new Pratt mines shipped their first coal; and soon in Birmingham, which had slept fitfully since 1873, "the sound of the hammer and the saw was heard again."[8]

6. *Ibid.,* 35.
7. Bigelow, "Birmingham," 24; Jean E. Keith, "The Role of the Louisville and Nashville Railroad in the Early Development of Alabama Coal and Iron," *Bulletin of the Business Historical Society* 26 (Sept. 1952), 165–74.
8. Armes, *Story,* 238–41, 272–74.

DeBardeleben, a persuasive promoter and relentless developer, turned his attention to iron. Obtaining from the Elyton Land Company a free twenty-acre site between the railroads just west of Birmingham, he persuaded Kentucky ironmaster Thomas T. Hillman to join him in building an iron furnace. In November 1880 the furnace, named Alice after DeBardeleben's daughter, went into blast. An immediate commercial success, it set off an iron boom, and Birmingham's prospects began rising. DeBardeleben later exulted: "There's nothing like taking a wild piece of land, all rock and woods, ground not fit to feed a goat on, and turning it into a settlement of men and women, making pay rolls, bringing the railroads in, and starting things going. There's nothing like boring a hillside through and turning over a mountain. That's what money does, and that's what money's for. I like to use money as I use a horse,—to ride!"[9]

Soon other industrial ventures, obtaining cheap or free sites from the Elyton Company, built a rolling mill and several foundries and iron pressure-pipe factories, and in 1881 James W. Sloss built two more iron furnaces on the eastern edge of the city. By 1883 the Alice Furnace employed 500 men, the Sloss Furnace, 600; the rolling mill, 450; other iron works, about 1,000; and the Pratt Coal and Coke Company, 1,000.[10]

After 1880 the pioneer companies expanded rapidly, many new companies began operation, and Birmingham production of coal and pig iron rose dramatically. In 1872 Alabama had produced only 17,000 tons of coal, but the development of the coal fields around Birmingham boosted Alabama's total to 4 million tons in 1890, 8 million tons in 1900, and 16 million tons in 1910. Similarly, in 1872 Alabama had produced only 11,000 tons of pig iron and ranked twentieth in the nation, but by 1890 the state produced 800,000 tons and ranked fourth in the United States. By 1900 Alabama produced more than 1 million tons; by 1910, nearly 2 million tons; and in 1917, nearly 3 million tons of pig iron. Not until after World War I did Alabama coal and pig-iron production level off.[11]

Because of the close proximity of coal and iron ore, Birmingham pig-iron companies enjoyed low transportation and assembly costs,

---

9. *Ibid.*, 343. See also *ibid.*, 283–85.

10. *Ibid.*, 284–89; *Birmingham City Directory, 1883*, 27.

11. William Battle Phillips, *Iron Making in Alabama*, 3d. ed. (University, Alabama, 1912), 187; U.S. Geological Survey, *Mineral Resources of the United States* (Washington, 1882–1921); U.S. Census, *Fourteenth Census, 1920*, X, *Manufactures*, 312, 315.

digging their own coal from their own mines, accommodating coal output to furnace needs. Birmingham industrialists relied on a large supply of Negro labor, which they could employ for low wages to perform the needed heavy, unskilled labor. As a result of these advantages, Birmingham companies produced America's cheapest pig iron, so inexpensive that it undersold English pig iron in England; and by 1898 Birmingham was the largest exporting point for pig iron in the United States and the third largest in the world. In 1900 three-fourths of the pig-iron exports of the United States came from Birmingham. The Alabama city also became a major coal supplier, with many commercial coal companies—some thirty-three by 1910—which produced no iron, but mined coal to sell to industrial plants, railroads, and city residents. The commercial coal companies (as distinguished from the iron furnace companies) ranged in size from million-dollar consolidated corporations to a few small independent companies with less than $10,000 capital.[12]

Once the Alabama capital of Pratt, DeBardeleben, and Sloss had kindled the fires of industry, capital from outside Alabama financed most of the dramatic coal and pig-iron development. And after the mid-1880s the absentee owners tended steadily to consolidate the many smaller companies into a few giant firms. In 1881 Tennessee industrialist Enoch Ensley and a group of Memphis capitalists bought out the Alabama founders of the pioneer Pratt Coal and Coke Company and the Alice Furnace, creating a sensation with the district's first million dollar deal. Then in 1886 the Tennessee Coal, Iron, and Railroad Company (T.C.I.), which until then had operated only in Tennessee, outmaneuvered Ensley on Wall Street, bought out his interests, and consolidated other companies to become Alabama's largest and most powerful coal and iron company.[13]

For a few years T.C.I. had a rival in the DeBardeleben Coal and Iron Company, formed in 1886 by the energetic Henry F. DeBardeleben with the support of Baltimore and London capitalists. DeBardeleben also consolidated smaller concerns, saying "I was the eagle and I wanted

12. U.S. Congress, Senate, *Report of the Committee of the Senate upon the Relations Between Labor and Capital,* 4 vols. (Washington, 1885), IV, 286–88, 292–97, 405–15; Bigelow, "Birmingham," 43; Victor S. Clark, *History of Manufactures in the United States,* 3 vols. (New York, 1929), III, 103–13; R.G. Dun & Company, *Reference Book (And Key) Containing Ratings of Merchants, Manufacturers and Traders Generally, Throughout the United States & Canada* (New York, 1910).

13. Armes, *Story,* 289–91, 361–62.

to eat all the craw-fish I could,—swallow up all the little fellows, and I did it." But in 1891 he confronted T.C.I. in a trading duel and reported ruefully: "a bigger eagle than I had ever been came along and swallowed me." T.C.I. absorbed DeBardeleben's holdings and recapitalized at $20 million, and the Birmingham *News* pronounced it "the grandest aggregation of capital and enterprise in the South."[14]

In 1900 the T.C.I. president's report documented the absentee ownership and control. Of 210,000 shares of T.C.I. stock, only 660 were owned by Alabamians. New Yorkers held 191,682 shares; residents of Massachusetts held 9,341 shares; other northern states, 4,750; other southern states, 2,040; and citizens of England, Ireland, and Germany, 1,527. In 1900 the T.C.I. board of directors included fourteen men in New York, two in Nashville, and one in Birmingham.[15]

Between 1887 and 1900 most of the other iron-furnace companies merged into three major corporations: the Sloss-Sheffield Steel and Iron Company, the Republic Iron and Steel Company, and the Woodward Iron Company. By 1912 only two other companies, with one furnace each, produced pig iron in Jefferson County. They were the Southern Iron and Steel Company (after 1913 the Gulf States Steel Company) and the Williamson Iron Company. By 1912 the six iron companies operated twenty-eight pig-iron furnaces in Jefferson County, fourteen of them owned by T.C.I., and the major iron corporations also operated extensive coal mines and coke ovens.[16]

Impatient boosters preached that Birmingham needed to launch steel production to achieve a still "more wonderful development," but not until 1895 did T.C.I. local managers overcome frustrating technological problems in converting Birmingham ore to steel. In 1899 T.C.I. built an open hearth steel plant in suburban Ensley, and on Thanksgiving Day made the first run of steel, greeted by the *News* as the dawn of the "Age of Steel" in Birmingham. The plant succeeded and expanded, producing 66,000 tons of steel in 1900 and 320,000 in 1907, and providing such high quality that in 1907 T.C.I. received an order for all the steel rails for the Edward H. Harriman railroads.[17]

14. *Ibid.*, 332–35, 423–24; Bigelow, "Birmingham," 37; Phillips, *Iron Making*, 160, 189–203.

15. *Annual Report of the Tennessee Coal, Iron and Railroad Company, For the Fiscal Year Ending December 31, 1899* (Birmingham, 1900).

16. Armes, *Story*, 298–301, 347–56, 443–47; Phillips, *Iron Making*, 160, 189–203.

17. Birmingham *State Herald*, Dec. 7, 1895; Birmingham *News*, Dec. 1, 1899; Armes, *Story*, 431–35, 463–66, 515.

But financially T.C.I. was insecure, its capital was limited, and its stocks and bonds were playthings on the New York market. In November 1907, during a financial panic, banker John Pierpont Morgan and the United States Steel Corporation suddenly bought nearly all the T.C.I. stock, deftly defending the coup, which gave them control of a strong competitor, as a sacrificial public service to save the bank that had owned the stock and thus to prevent the spread of the panic. Whatever the monopolistic advantages for U.S. Steel, Birmingham boosters hailed the advent of the giant corporation in their district, and predicted that Birmingham's population would triple in two years, that property values would rise 75 percent, and that the city would become "the largest steel manufacturing center in the universe."[18]

Again, prophecy far outran reality, but U.S. Steel did put T.C.I. on a firmer financial basis than ever before, steadily invested capital for new development, and provided much-needed technical resources and more vigorous management. The steel corporation installed a new T.C.I. president, George Gordon Crawford, who had been managing the National Tube Company, a major U.S. Steel subsidiary. Crawford, a native Georgian, an able chemist and engineer, and an "exacting, sober, and systematic" manager, immediately began rebuilding and expanding T.C.I. plants and equipment, inaugurating new methods, and increasing efficiency and production. He served twenty-three years as president, providing stability and, according to calculations by the Birmingham *News*, persuading U.S. Steel to invest $100 million in T.C.I. during his tenure in office.[19]

Still, the takeover by U.S. Steel was controversial, its impact on the development of Birmingham unclear. Alabama steel production did continue to grow, from 320,000 tons in 1907 to 530,000 in 1910 and 1,225,000 in 1916, and to U.S. Steel goes much of the credit. But production might have grown even faster had U.S. Steel not used a Pittsburgh base-price system that discriminated against the Birmingham subsidiary in order to protect investments in the older and larger Pittsburgh steel mills. Birmingham produced steel cheaper than did Pittsburgh, but beginning in 1907 even Birmingham customers buying T.C.I. steel had to pay the Pittsburgh base price, plus a phantom Pittsburgh-to-Birmingham freight charge, which in 1909 was replaced by

18. *News*, Nov. 5, 1907; Armes, *Story*, 507, 515–24.

19. Armes, *Story*, 525–27; Robert Jemison, Jr., "George Gordon Crawford, 1869–1936," in Miscellaneous Data from Robt. Jemison, Jr., Re. Developments and Personal References Re. a few Friends and Citizens of Birmingham, May 1965, TS, Birmingham Public Library. Hereinafter the library will be referred to as BPL.

a flat $3.00 per ton "Birmingham Differential." Thus U.S. Steel denied T.C.I. and steel-using manufacturers near Birmingham any competitive advantage from T.C.I.'s low steel-production costs. This price system, however, applied only to steel, not pig iron; and many other factors, such as the South's low degree of urbanization, late industrialization, and predominance of agriculture, helped hold the Alabama steel industry to a moderate growth rate. Abolition of the base-price system might have stimulated somewhat greater growth around Birmingham, but certainly it could not have brought the millennium that Birmingham boosters anticipated, futilely, at every turn.[20]

Besides producing coal, coke, iron, and steel, Birmingham industrialists began in the early 1880s to develop rolling mills, foundries, machine shops, railroad repair shops, and cast-iron pipe factories. Cast-iron pressure pipe became the city's leading manufactured product, and by 1921 such major Birmingham plants as the Dimmick Pipe Company and the American Cast Iron Pipe Company (ACIPCO) made Alabama the first-ranking state in the industry, producing 35 percent of the industry's national output. Another major Birmingham product was cotton-gin machinery. In 1897 two pioneer Birmingham companies combined to form the Continental Gin Company, which took control of smaller plants in six other cities and became the largest cotton-gin manufacturing company in the world. Other Birmingham products were wire, nails, bolts, chains, bridge works, stoves, and agricultural implements. [21]

In 1914 the Birmingham metropolitan district, which included Birmingham proper and two-thirds of the precincts of Jefferson County, contained eighty-five foundry and machine-shop establishments, with 3,959 workers and a yearly product valued at $7,694,718. In addition, the iron and steel blast furnaces, steelworks, and rolling mills comprised twelve establishments, with 5,732 workers and a product valued at

20. H. H. Chapman et al., The Iron and Steel Industries of the South (University, Univ. of Alabama Press, 1953), 371–75, 383–89, 415–16; George W. Stocking, Basing Point Pricing and Regional Development: A Case Study of the Iron and Steel Industry (Chapel Hill: Univ. of North Carolina Press, 1954), 7–8, 61–74; C. Vann Woodward, Origins of the New South, 1877–1913 (Baton Rouge: Louisiana State Univ. Press, 1951), 300–302, 315–17; News, Oct. 2, 1917; Birmingham City Directory, 1920–1921, preface.

21. William D. Moore, Development of the Cast Iron Pressure Pipe Industry in the Southern States, 1800–1938 (Birmingham, 1939), 28–36, 48; U.S. Census, Census of Manufactures, 1921, 337; Algernon L. Smith, Continental Gin Company and Its Fifty-two Years of Service (Birmingham, 1952), 37–57; Birmingham City Directory, 1903, 27–28.

$28,345,035. Combined, these industries accounted for 57.5 percent of the total value of the district's manufactured product and clearly formed the economic base of Birmingham.[22]

Beginning in the 1880s, however, the district had diversified into non-metal manufacturing as well, developing a major cotton-textile mill, a by-product gas plant, and numerous bakeries, printing companies, lumber mills, flour and grain mills, meat-packing plants, breweries, cotton-seed-oil mills, soft-drink and mineral-water companies, and factories producing brooms, furniture, paint, wagons, mattresses, fertilizer, cement, clay pipe, bricks, ice, soap, cigars, and boxes. By 1914 such establishments, together with railroad repair shops and coke ovens, which were inconveniently lumped with them in census reports, employed more than 10,000 workers and fabricated products valued at $26,675,857, or 42.5 percent of the district's total value of manufactured products.[23]

Rapid industrialization generated dramatic population increases, and Birmingham's urbanized area spread steadily. Real estate developers, who had founded and planned the original boom town, continued to play a major role in shaping the layout of the expanding city. In the 1870s most residences, boarding houses, and tenements clustered around the Twentieth Street business district immediately north of the railroads. But in 1884 the Elyton Land Company began a suburban movement, developing residential areas both north of the business district and south of the railroads. A full mile south of the business district, on rolling terrain along the foot of Red Mountain, the company developed South Highlands, which became the most fashionable residential area. During the booming years from 1883 to 1887 residential development paid off handsomely for the company, enabling it to declare annual dividends of 100, 95, 45, 340, and 2,305 percent on the original $200,000 capital stock.[24]

In the mid-1880s other speculators, inspired by such success, organized more than a score of new companies to engage in the "manufacture and sale" of lots in suburbs two to ten miles from the central city, outside the Elyton Company domain. In 1886 and 1887 the land companies rode the crest of a wild boom as excited speculators from all parts of the South converged upon Birmingham and bid prices 200 to 300 percent above realistic levels. "In many instances," recalled Henry

22. U.S. Census, *Census of Manufactures, 1914,* I, 24–26; *Thirteenth Census, 1910,* IX, *Manufactures,* 30–35.
23. *Birmingham City Directory, 1903,* 27–28; U.S. Census, *Census of Manufactures, 1914,* I, 24–26.
24. Caldwell, *History,* 16, 29.

M. Caldwell of the Elyton Land Company, "the purchaser would seize his receipt and rush out on the street and resell the property at a handsome profit before his bond for title could be executed." Suddenly in the spring of 1887 the land boom burst; many speculative land companies and projected suburban developments quietly collapsed; much unimproved property dropped in value, and the overextended Elyton Land Company itself fell into financial difficulty.[25]

Still, much of the growth of the 1880s was solid, and even after 1887 the coal and iron industry developed steadily and attracted new residents. In 1889 Birmingham annexed new residential areas, spreading its boundaries to encompass nearly three square miles, mostly within a one-mile radius of the original town center. In 1890 the population within these boundaries was 26,178, a 748 percent increase over the 1880 population of 3,086. Moreover, by 1890 approximately 20,000 people lived in urbanized areas immediately outside the city limits, in the Elyton Land Company's suburbs of North Highlands and South Highlands and in suburbs developed by the Smithfield Land Company and the Avondale Land Company, immediately west and east of Birmingham proper. During the 1890s these companies and half a dozen others that had survived the 1887 land collapse successfully promoted suburbs two to five miles from downtown Birmingham. To attract residents the developers had to provide street railways; and by 1890 streetcars, some pulled by mules, others by steam engines called "dummies," ran from the business district to most corners of the city proper. And during the 1890s land developers built street railway lines outward, east and west along Jones Valley to the growing suburbs. In 1891 some of the street railways began using electric power, and by 1903 electric cars had displaced all the mule cars and steam dummies.[26]

Industrialization and population growth attracted to Birmingham not only industrialists and laborers, but also mercantile and professional people eager to invest modest capital and resolute effort in the promising new town. Already in December 1871, when the six-month-old town was incorporated, it had fifty-two stores, seventeen constructed of brick. And many of the early merchants survived the 1870s and grew up with the town. One early grocer was Benjamin Franklin Roden. A DeKalb

25. *Ibid.*, 23–25; Hill Ferguson, "Avondale Land Company," TS, Hill Ferguson Collection, vol. 40, p. 20, BPL.

26. U.S. Census, *Eleventh Census, 1890*, I, *Population*, Pt. 1, 56; Ferguson, "Avondale Land Company"; J.P. Ross, "Notes on Birmingham Public Utilities," TS, Birmingham, 1932, pp. 8–21, BPL; Bigelow, "Birmingham," 64–66.

County farm boy, he had been wounded in the Civil War, serving after that in the quartermaster's department. After the war he worked his way through college in Texas, "paying his way by teaching the Choctaws in summer, up in Indian Territory." Returning to Alabama he set up a grocery and lumber business in Gadsden, and in August 1871, at age twenty-seven, he visited the new Birmingham settlement to sell shingles. "Finding more of a spirit of hustle in the Jones Valley camp than in other places," noted historian Ethel Armes, "he invested at once, put up a grocery store, and from that day forth built along with the town." By 1880 Roden had added a saloon and billiard parlor and was worth from $5,000 to $10,000, and by 1900 the B.F. Roden Company was a major wholesale grocery firm worth between $200,000 and $300,000.[27]

By 1880 downtown Birmingham had at least seven saloons, eighteen groceries, and thirty-eight merchants selling clothing, furniture, drugs, dry goods, hardware, and books; and they had a combined financial strength of approximately $200,000. During the 1880s the city's commerce expanded rapidly, and by 1887 the Birmingham *Iron Age* estimated that $3,279,000 was invested in Birmingham wholesale and retail food, clothing, and general merchandise stores. By 1900, when Birmingham's estimated gross volume of business in manufacturing and mining was $50 million, its estimated volume in wholesale and retail trade was $27 million; and by 1910 the wholesale trade alone had grown to $60 million.[28]

Growing population, commerce, and industry required banking services, and Birmingham became the financial center of Alabama. The first banker was Charles Linn, a former Swedish sea captain and Confederate blockade-runner who had become a wholesale merchant in Montgomery, Alabama. Going to Birmingham in 1871, he bought one of the first business lots and built the National Bank of Birmingham, a one-story frame building. In mid-1873, despite cholera and depression, Linn boldly built a new three-story brick bank "that overshadowed everything in sight." Despondent citizens dubbed it "Linn's Folly," but Linn, with a promoter's flair for confident ceremony, opened the bank with a New Year's Eve calico ball. Five hundred guests, a fourth of the town's population, came in bright calico garb and, by the light of hundreds of candles, danced away 1873 and some of the depression gloom.

27. R.G. Dun & Company, *Reference Book* for 1880, 1900; Armes, *Story*, 235–36.

28. *Birmingham City Directory, 1883*, 12; *ibid.*, 1903, 29; *ibid.*, 1910, 71; R.G. Dun & Company, *Reference Book*, 1880; Bigelow, "Birmingham," 34.

They had to wait until 1880 for real recovery and boom, but Linn's bank survived and he eventually prospered, as did many of the neighboring storekeepers and professional people who stuck out the depression with him. By 1887 Linn's bank had been joined by four others, and five years later the city had twelve banks with annual bank clearings of $27 million. By 1900 the bank clearings had grown to $43 million; by 1910, to $130 million.[29]

Birmingham's expanding commercial and financial activity stimulated downtown land values, and even after the 1887 real estate collapse, business-district values surged upward, eventually vindicating and making wealthy those early families that had bought lots and held onto them in persistent anticipation of magical returns. In 1871 the Elyton Land Company had sold its first downtown lots for from $75 to $100; and as late as 1882, with the industrial boom under way, the company had sold choice business lots for from $500 to $600. By 1892 such lots were worth $50,000 each, and by 1916 half of a downtown corner lot, originally purchased in 1871 for $37.50, sold for $200,000.[30]

Birmingham commerce and finance were aided by a proliferating web of railroad connections. By 1890 Birmingham's steadily growing tonnage of coal and iron freight had attracted three new trunk railroads, in addition to the two original lines, and by 1910 four more railroad lines entered the city. The nine trunk railroads provided excellent connections with major northern trade and manufacturing centers and with all nearby southern cities, and in the southeastern states Birmingham ranked second only to Atlanta as a transportation and distribution center.[31]

In sum, in Jones Valley a diverse urban system evolved, based on coal, iron, steel, and heavy manufacturing, but also performing regional transportation, trade, and financial functions, and developing varied sources of wealth and growth. As of 1900 any visitor who climbed Red Mountain to survey the spreading city 600 feet below would discover a

29. Armes, *Story*, 227; Bigelow, "Birmingham," 22; Birmingham *Age-Herald*, Jan. 1, 1899; Alabama Industrial Development Board, "An Economic Survey of the Metropolitan District of Birmingham," prepared by John A. Maguire, mimeo., Birmingham, 1932, BPL.

30. Caldwell, *History*, 32–33; *Age-Herald*, July 15, 1916; *Jemison's Sales Bulletin*, Nov. 1923, in Ferguson Collection, vol. 40, p. 61, BPL.

31. Warren Henry Manning, *Warren H. Manning's City Plan of Birmingham* (Birmingham, 1919), 18, 20; Rupert B. Vance and Sara Smith, "Metropolitan Dominance and Integration," in *The Urban South*, eds. Rupert B. Vance and Nicholas J. Demerath (Chapel Hill: Univ. of North Carolina Press, 1954), 114–34.

broad and varied panorama. He might have been struck first by the site's natural beauty. Heavy forests, partly deciduous, partly pine, covered the rugged rocky mountain and extended onto portions of the rolling hills of the valley. In the spring and summer profuse colorful wildflowers and the white blossoms of dogwood and magnolia brightened the green mountain and valley, and in the fall sumac turned the mountain burning red. The major man-made east-west axis was the Alabama & Great Southern Railroad (originally the Alabama & Chattanooga), which ran along the trough of Jones Valley parallel to the mountain crest; the major north-south axis was Twentieth Street, which ran perpendicular to the mountain crest and bisected the railroad at right angles in the middle of the downtown railroad reservation (see Map 1).[32]

Birmingham had extended its city limits in 1873, 1889, and 1893; and by 1900 the city boundaries formed a slightly irregular rectangle extending 2.3 miles along its base at the foot of Red Mountain, and stretching 3.2 miles in length north from the mountain. If the visitor atop Red Mountain looked down to the city's lower right corner he could see Highland Avenue, curving gracefully along the foot of Red Mountain. Along this spacious boulevard the city's wealthy businessmen and corporation managers laid out extensive estates and built imposing mansions, adorned with cupolas and columns. Boosters called it the most beautiful residential street in the South. Nearby streets in the rolling South Highlands accommodated moderately wealthy businessmen with comfortable homes.

Between South Highlands and the railroad tracks, residences clustered along the Twentieth Street axis, but the outer blocks, near the eastern and western boundaries, were largely open, undeveloped land. As Twentieth Street ran from the South Highlands toward the railroads, it moved progressively across areas of neat middle-class residences, then areas of modest workingmen's cottages, then across a three-to-five-block-wide belt dominated by Negro quarters, crowded with monotonous gray rows of narrow, unpainted shacks, blighted by smoke and coal

---

32. Manning, *City Plan*, 32. Neither axis ran exactly true to the points of the compass; the valley and mountain had a slight northeast-southwest tilt, and Twentieth Street ran 30 degrees west of true north. The following descriptions rely heavily on George B. Kelley, engineer, *Map of Birmingham, Alabama, and Adjacent Suburbs* (Birmingham, 1903); on *Map Showing the Lines Owned and Operated by the Birmingham Railway, Light and Power Co.* (Birmingham, c. 1905); and on *Birmingham City Directory, 1900.*

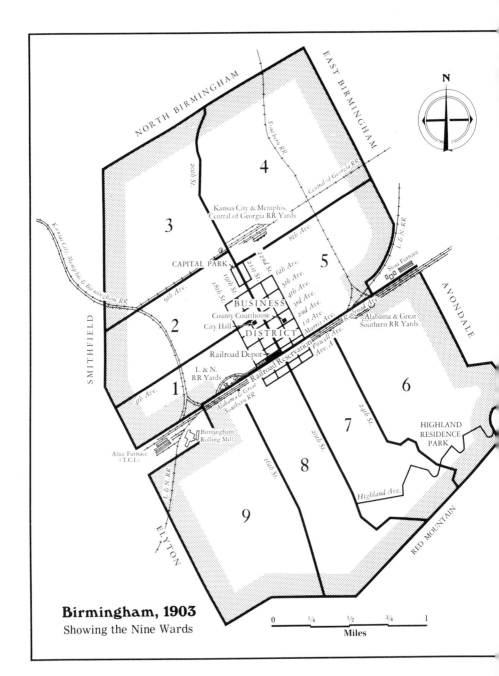

Birmingham, 1903
Showing the Nine Wards

North Birmingham

East Birmingham

Southern RR

Central of Georgia RR

L & N RR

20th St.

Kansas City & Memphis, Central of Georgia RR Yards

8th Ave.

Kansas City, Memphis & Birmingham RR

9th Ave.

CAPITAL PARK

22nd St.

21st St.

19th St.

18th St.

6th Ave.

5th Ave.

4th Ave.

3rd Ave.

2nd Ave.

1st Ave.

Morris Ave.

BUSINESS

County Courthouse

City Hall

DISTRICT

Railroad Depot

Railroad Reservation

Powell Ave.

Ave. A

Railroad Ave.

Alabama & Great Southern RR Yards

Sloss Furnace

AVONDALE

SMITHFIELD

L. & N. RR Yards

4th Ave.

Alabama & Great Southern RR

Birmingham Rolling Mill

Alice Furnace (T.C.I.)

L & N RR

ELYTON

16th St.

20th St.

24th St.

Highland Ave.

HIGHLAND RESIDENCE PARK

RED MOUNTAIN

N

3
4
5
2
1
6
7
8
9

0   1/4   1/2   3/4   1
Miles

dust from the nearby railroads and industries. At the eastern and western edges of the city the Negro shantytown extended north of the railroads and flanked the business district.[33]

Conspicuous at the edges of the city near the railroad reservation were the tall metal structures and smokestacks of the Alice and Sloss iron furnaces and the Birmingham Rolling Mill. By day the visitor atop Red Mountain could mark them by their pillars of smoke; by night he could see a continuous orange glow lighting the sky, with occasional spectacularly bright flashes from white-hot flame or streams of red-hot molten iron.[34]

Through the railroad reservation a maze of tracks formed a belt across the waist of the city, buckled by the depot next to Twentieth Street. Along Morris Avenue, immediately north of the railroads, stood the warehouses and markets of the major wholesale and produce merchants. The retail and financial district spread along Twentieth and Nineteenth Streets, between First and Fourth avenues north. The business district was dominated by three- and four-story red brick and white masonry department stores, banks, offices, and hotels, but was varied by smaller stores, artisan shops, livery stables, and boarding houses. West of the main business district a separate Negro business district was emerging between Sixteenth and Eighteenth streets.

A few blocks north of the business district, at Twentieth Street and Seventh Avenue, lay Capital Park, set aside by Birmingham's buoyant founders to accommodate the state capital whenever bustling Birmingham should wrest it from Montgomery. (Having failed to accomplish this by World War I, the city discreetly changed the name to Woodrow Wilson Park.) Between the business district and the park, from Fourth to Eighth avenues, were the original good quality residential areas, where business and professional people lived. Prominent corners were adorned by the edifices and spires of the oldest and largest congregations of the Baptist, Methodist, Presbyterian, and Episcopal churches. North of Capital Park were more railroad yards, and beyond on all sides lay much undeveloped potential residential area, punctuated by several new middle- and working-class neighborhoods.[35]

If, in 1900, the visitor atop Red Mountain looked to the right beyond Birmingham's eastern boundary, he could see the industrial suburbs of

33. Bigelow, "Birmingham," 67–68.
34. Manning, *City Plan*, 14.
35. *Birmingham City Directory, 1883*, 34.

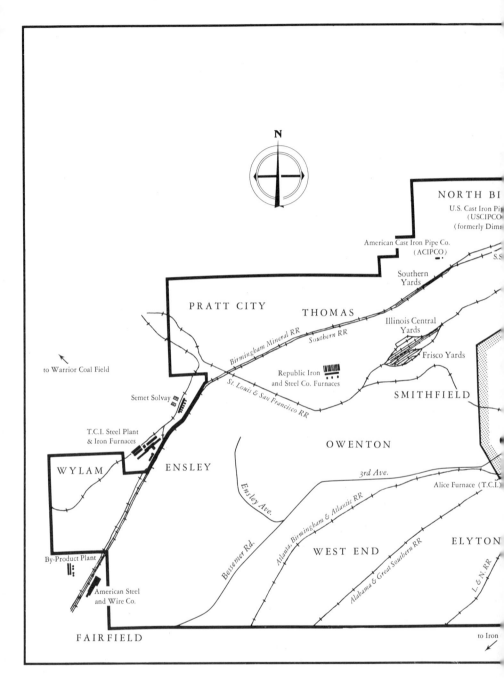

N

NORTH BI

U.S. Cast Iron Pi
(USCIPCO
(formerly Dimr

American Cast Iron Pipe Co.
(ACIPCO)

S.S

Southern
Yards

PRATT CITY

THOMAS

Illinois Central
Yards

Birmingham Mineral RR

Southern RR

Frisco Yards

to Warrior Coal Field

SMITHFIELD

St. Louis & San Francisco RR

Republic Iron
and Steel Co. Furnaces

Semet Solvay

T.C.I. Steel Plant
& Iron Furnaces

OWENTON

WYLAM

ENSLEY

3rd Ave.

Alice Furnace (T.C.I.)

Ensley Ave.

By-Product Plant

Bessemer Rd.

Atlanta, Birmingham & Atlantic RR

WEST END

ELYTON

American Steel
and Wire Co.

Alabama & Great Southern RR

L. & N. RR

FAIRFIELD

to Iron

28

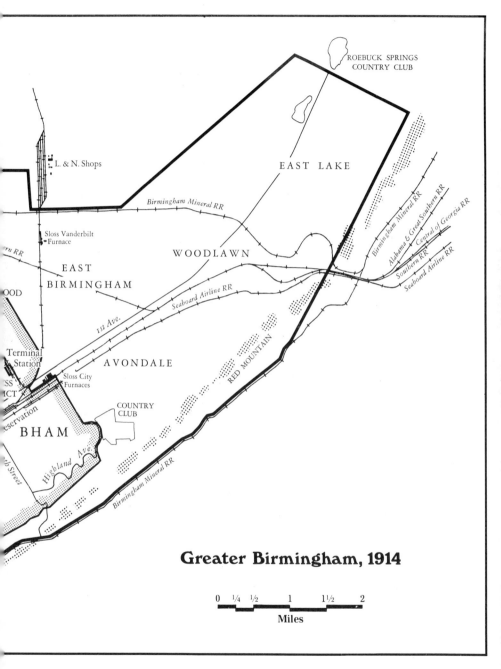

ROEBUCK SPRINGS
COUNTRY CLUB

EAST LAKE

L. & N. Shops

Birmingham Mineral RR

Birmingham Mineral RR

Alabama & Great Southern RR

Central of Georgia RR

Sloss Vanderbilt
Furnace

'rn RR

WOODLAWN

Southern RR

Seaboard Airline RR

EAST
BIRMINGHAM

OOD

1st Ave.

Seaboard Airline RR

Terminal
Station

AVONDALE

RED MOUNTAIN

SS
CT

Sloss City
Furnaces

servation

COUNTRY
CLUB

BHAM

Highland Ave.

h Street

Birmingham Mineral RR

Greater Birmingham, 1914

| 0 | ¼ | ½ | 1 | 1½ | 2 |

Miles

29

Avondale and East Birmingham, containing foundries, machine shops, railroad car works, a cotton mill, and streets lined with small drab one-story houses for workers. Further east along trolley tracks lay the sparsely settled residential suburb of Woodlawn, and beyond it, five miles from downtown Birmingham, lay East Lake, a middle-class residential suburb built around a popular wooded amusement park with a thirty-acre, spring-fed lake. Nearby was the pleasantly landscaped campus of Howard College, a Baptist liberal arts school with two hundred students.[36] (Map 2 shows these and the following areas as they were situated in 1914, after they were annexed into Greater Birmingham.)

To the north of Birmingham proper, five miles from Red Mountain, smoke rose continually from two iron furnaces and a pipe factory in the small industrial suburb of North Birmingham, at the far edge of Jones Valley. To the immediate west of Birmingham were the quiet residential suburbs of Elyton and Smithfield and the new wooded campus of Owenton College, a Methodist liberal arts school of two hundred students. Beyond Smithfield, streetcar tracks stretched one mile across open land to the northwest before reaching the town of Thomas, site of the Republic Iron and Steel Company's two iron furnaces. Northwest of Thomas, beyond another mile of open fields, lay the coal-mining town of Pratt City. Southwest of Pratt City, five miles from downtown Birmingham, stood the T.C.I. industrial suburb of Ensley. Nearby loomed the great smokestacks of the T.C.I. iron furnaces and steelworks, continuously belching dusty light-orange smoke that pervaded Ensley and permanently tinged its streets, trees, small stores, and straight monotonous rows of plain, narrow workers' houses. Finally, around the perimeter of Birmingham and all the suburbs ran the Birmingham Mineral Railroad, a giant oblong loop that connected the industrial plants, the trunk railroads, the iron ore mines atop Red Mountain, and the dozens of small coal-mining towns scattered over the Warrior Coal Field to the north and west of Birmingham.[37]

The basic outlines of city, suburbs, railroads, and industries persisted from 1900 to 1921, but, had the visitor of 1900 returned periodically to his Red Mountain vantage point, he would have seen striking change and growth within the abiding pattern. Major new industrial plants appeared, including several cast-iron pipe factories in North Birming-

36. Bigelow, "Birmingham," 270, 249.
37. *Ibid.*, 250; Graham Romeyn Taylor, "Birmingham's Civic Front," *The Survey* 27 (Jan. 6, 1912), 1467.

ham and the American Steel and Wire Mill built by U.S. Steel near
Ensley. All the suburbs spread, swelling outward from their nuclei and
filling in open land along the trolley lines. Within Birmingham proper
the elite South Highlands district began spreading up the slope of Red
Mountain onto terraces advertised as "almost equivalent to a health
resort . . . swept by cool breezes . . . high enough above the city to
be out of the zone of smoke, dust and soot." And in 1904 wealthy citizens
built the handsome half-timbered Birmingham Country Club and spacious golf links on vacant, low foothills near Highland Avenue.[38]

But vacant spaces between Red Mountain and the railroads filled
rapidly as the Birmingham Realty Company, successor to the Elyton
Land Company, systematically graded new lots, arranged street-paving
and utility extensions, and built houses to sell to middle- and working-
class buyers on the installment plan. Between 1901 and 1907 sales
ran from $300,000 to $500,000 per year. The company had similar
success with a major new middle-class subdivision, Norwood, built
along a winding boulevard on hilly terrain ten blocks north of the
business district.[39]

The downtown business district grew upward and outward. In 1900
at the main downtown intersection of Twentieth Street and First Avenue
venturesome developers built Birmingham's first steel frame and concrete "skyscraper," the ten-story Woodward office building, dwarfing the
surrounding three- and four-story banks and stores. Within ten years
two still taller office buildings—the slender, white sixteen-story Empire
and the massive sixteen-story Brown-Marx—rose at the same intersection, which boosters called "the heaviest corner on earth." And by 1910
four more tall steel-frame, fireproof office and bank structures, including
an elegant ten-story Chamber of Commerce building, had gone up on
nearby corners. The editors of the *American Architect* praised the design
of the buildings and declared that Birmingham, a "wide awake Southern
city," was "assuming an importance architecturally in keeping with the
progressive spirit of its citizens." Meanwhile, the business district pushed
outward as developers razed saloons, barber shops, lunch counters, and
residences around the edges and replaced them with spacious modern
department stores. And in 1909 eight of the trunk railroads opened the
massive new $2 million Terminal Station at a new location, Fifth
Avenue and Twenty-sixth Street, six blocks east of the business district.

38. Ferguson Collection, vol. 40, p. 126, BPL; Bigelow, "Birmingham," 256.
39. *News*, Jan. 15, 1903, Dec. 30, 1905, Apr. 8, 1908.

The L. & N. alone continued to use the original depot site on Twentieth Street.[40]

In 1898 Birmingham boosters began a movement to annex the suburbs into a Greater Birmingham, whose official population would truly reflect the size of the Jones Valley metropolis and win it the national rank and recognition it deserved. But opposition from industries and suburbs stymied the boosters, and to their dismay the official 1900 population of Birmingham reached only 38,451, excluding at least 40,000 in the nearby suburbs. "The city," lamented the *Age-Herald*, "stands before the world belittled by its cramped confines."[41]

From 1900 to 1910 boosters vigorously promoted annexation. In 1909 they finally pushed a Greater Birmingham bill through the state legislature, and the *News* exulted "MAGIC CITY COMES INTO OWN." On New Year's Day, 1910, Birmingham officially expanded to enclose forty-eight square miles, stretching fourteen miles from Ensley to East Lake, and measuring five miles at its widest point, from Red Mountain through the central business district to the tip of North Birmingham; these dimensions it would keep nearly unchanged for the next half-century (see Map 2). In November 1910 Birmingham held a Census Jubilee to celebrate its advent as a full-fledged metropolis, the third largest city in the former Confederate States, with 132,685 people, approximately 60,000 in Old Birmingham and more than 70,000 in the annexed suburbs. Since 1900 its corporate population had increased 245 percent, more than any other American city over 100,000, and Birmingham boosters gloried in nationwide publicity as the fastest-growing city in the United States. Few bothered to note that between 1900 and 1910 the actual increase in Birmingham's metropolitan population, in city and suburbs taken together, was a respectable but more modest 82 percent.[42]

As the Greater Birmingham movement approached fruition, municipal reformers launched a campaign to change from mayor-alderman government to the city commission plan pioneered by Galveston and Des Moines. With annexation the commission movement gained momentum because the expanded thirty-two member Greater Birmingham Board of Aldermen appeared unwieldy, inept, and corrupt. In a 1910 referendum, 88 percent of the Birmingham voters endorsed commission

40. *American Architect*, quoted in *News*, June 19, 1909. See also *ibid.*, June 13, 1900, Apr. 6, 1909; Bigelow, "Birmingham," 69–70.

41. *Age-Herald*, Oct. 14, 1900. See also *News*, Oct. 15, 1898.

42. *News*, Aug. 19, Dec. 16, 1909, Nov. 22, 1910; U.S. Census, *Twelfth Census, 1900*, I, *Population*, Part I, 58–59; *Thirteenth Census, 1910*, II, *Population*, 29–30.

government, and in 1911 Birmingham representatives got the state legislature to abolish the board of aldermen and replace it with a full-time, salaried, three-member city commission. Local reformers rejoiced, especially when former president Theodore Roosevelt praised Birmingham, the largest city yet to adopt commission government, for its "advanced step."[43]

From 1910 to 1920 the proud new metropolis continued to build, and new skyscraper bank and office buildings filled out the skyline. In 1914 citizens were especially delighted at the completion of the first-class, twelve-story Tutwiler Hotel, elegant enough, they hoped, that visiting U.S. Steel officials would no longer "insist on spending most of their time complaining of inadequate Hotel facilities." The demands of World War I brought increased production and prosperity to Birmingham, and steady population growth continued, though at the slower rate of 34 percent between 1910 and 1920.[44]

By 1921, its fiftieth birthday, Birmingham was approaching a population of 200,000 and boasted of being "The Biggest City in America For Its Age." Civic-minded citizens and school children prepared a stirring semicentennial celebration in October, with parades through gaily decorated streets, airplanes buzzing overhead, and band music and congratulatory speeches. For three evenings thousands jammed an open amphitheater in Avondale Park to see "The Magic City," a pageant of Birmingham, performed by a cast of 2,000. Six hundred dancers, accompanied by orchestra, chorus, narrative readings, and spectacular lighting effects, presented a romantic interpretation of the marvelous emergence of Birmingham. First, Indians roamed the valley and the Spanish explorer Hernando De Soto discovered Alabama. Then the industrialist, portrayed as a blacksmith, called forth coal, iron, and limestone, portrayed by dancers costumed in black, red, and white, to rise from the mounds where they were lying and intermingle to bring forth a beautiful female figure bearing the model of a sleek steel ship. At the proper moment Colonel James R. Powell, the duke of Birmingham, "reappeared" to proclaim Birmingham "the Magic City of the World, the marvel of the South, the miracle of the Continent, the dream of the Hemisphere, the vision of all Mankind."[45]

To climax the celebration, President Warren G. Harding arrived by

43. *News*, Mar. 10, 1911. See also *ibid.*, Apr. 10, 1911.

44. Robert Jemison, Jr., "The Tutwiler Hotel," in Miscellaneous Data from Robt. Jemison, Jr., BPL; U.S. Census, *Fourteenth Census, 1920*, I, *Population*, 336.

45. Birmingham *Labor Advocate*, Oct. 22, 1921; Birmingham *Post*, Oct. 24, 25, 1921; Wallace Rice, *The Pageant of Birmingham* (Birmingham, 1921).

special train to speak at Woodrow Wilson Park before "the largest crowd ever assembled in Birmingham." The president paid handsome tribute "to the marvelous achievement of a brief half century to which this city and its industries stand as a monument," and the crowd thundered applause. But unexpectedly he turned to the race problem and shocked and stunned his white listeners by urging political and economic equality between the races, though he carefully endorsed absolute separation in things social. "Let the black man vote when he is fit to vote; prohibit the white man voting when he is unfit to vote," declared Harding. The segregated Negro section of the crowd roared applause, but the larger white section turned suddenly cold and silent. The president, growing angry, "squared his jaw," pointed straight at the white section, and snapped: "Whether you like it or not, unless our democracy is a lie, you must stand for that equality." The "crowning event" of the celebration turned embarrassingly tense and sour, and the evening Birmingham *Post* headlined the "cool" response to the president's "Negro Speech." The *News* called the speech "bold" and "courageous," but saw "danger" in the "vociferous" response of Negroes, who might not have understood the carefully qualified equality suggested by the president. The *Post* more bluntly called it a "tactless address," a "blunder," a "violation of the proprieties of the circumstances of the president's visit," and an "untimely and ill-considered intrusion into a question of which he evidently knows little."[46]

Harding had appalled Birmingham by highlighting at its moment of most visible triumph its most tense and distressing social division. Ever since 1880 opportunities for industrial employment had attracted large numbers of blacks to Birmingham. By 1890 Negroes comprised 43 percent of Birmingham's population, and in 1910 and 1920 they made up 39 percent, the highest Negro percentage of any American city with more than 100,000 population. Most Birmingham whites, like most southern whites, were adamantly committed to a rigid white-supremacy caste system. They banned racial intermarriage, enforced an elaborate etiquette to define the superior position of whites in all personal relationships, strictly segregated Negroes in public accommodations, schools, churches, and housing, disfranchised them politically, and assigned them to low-status, low-skilled, low-paying occupations. And they bitterly resented "Yankee" meddling in racial matters, asserting that only southerners who lived with the racial situation could properly understand

46. *Post*, Oct. 26, 27, 28, 1921; *News*, Oct. 27, 1921.

and deal with it, and that northerners, like President Harding, had best let it lie "dormant."[47]

Another conspicuous social group in Birmingham were whites of first- and second-generation immigrant background. From the beginning, the city's coal and iron industry attracted workers of foreign background, many coming from northern industrial states where they had first settled, others coming directly from abroad. By 1890 first- and second-generation immigrants accounted for 13.4 percent of Birmingham's total population, and for nearly one-fourth (23.5 percent) of the white population. Though immigrant groups never influenced cultural and political life as much in Birmingham as they did in some northern cities, politicians and newspapers took careful notice of the Irish St. Patrick's Day parades, the national celebrations of the Italian Society, the attainments of the Schillinger brewery, built by three second-generation German brothers, and the cultural contributions of the Mendelssohn Club and the Mozart Musical Association, directed by Professor Benjamin Guckenberger, and of the Birmingham Choral Society, founded by the German Turn Verein. In 1890 the Germans were the largest "foreign" group, and the Irish second, with smaller groups of English, Russian, and Italian background. After 1890 Italians dominated foreign immigration to Birmingham and by 1910 they were the largest such group. But after 1890 heavy southern white migration to Birmingham reduced the total "foreign" percentage of the white population to 17.5 percent in 1910 and 15.1 percent in 1920.[48]

Men of immigrant stock concentrated heavily in the coal, iron, and steel industries, comprising in 1910 approximately half the white workers in those industries. Many of the skilled workers of the Birmingham Rolling Mill were first- or second-generation immigrants who gave a distinctly "foreign" atmosphere to the "rolling mill district" that

47. U.S. Census, *Thirteenth Census, 1910*, I, *Population*, 177–78; *Fourteenth Census, 1920*, II, *Population*, 49: Guion Griffis Johnson, "The Ideology of White Supremacy, 1876–1910," in *Essays in Southern History*, ed. Fletcher Melvin Green (Chapel Hill: Univ. of North Carolina Press, 1949), 124–56; *Birmingham City Directory* for 1883, 1887, 1890, 1900, 1910; U.S. Census, *Thirteenth Census, 1910*, Descriptions of the Enumeration Districts of the 9th Supervisor's District of Alabama, MS, available from the National Archives and Records Service, Washington, D.C.; *Post*, Oct. 28, 1921.

48. U.S. Census, *Eleventh Census, 1890*, I, *Population*, Pt. 1, 451, 674, 705, 709, 711, 713; *Twelfth Census, 1900*, I, *Population*, Pt. 1, 609; *Thirteenth Census, 1910*, II, *Population*, 60–63; *Fourteenth Census, 1920*, II, *Population*, 47, 50; Bigelow, "Birmingham," 186–89, 57–59.

covered two or three blocks immediately south of the mill. In the 1890s the mill workers were a significant political force, led by Sylvester Daly, proprietor of the popular Rolling Mill Saloon. Daly, born in England of Irish parents, had immigrated to Pittsburgh and served a rolling mill apprenticeship, then moved to Birmingham and worked as a rolling mill puddler until he saved enough money to open a saloon next to the mill. A large gregarious man with booming voice, blue eyes, red hair, and mustache, he regaled his customers and the Ancient Order of Hibernians and the Irish Democratic Club with Irish song and story, and he rode their votes to positions as city alderman and city and county jailer. When he died of liver ailments in 1901, nearly every prominent politician in the city attended the funeral at St. Paul's Catholic Church.[49]

In Birmingham a strong Protestant majority set the dominant tone of religious life, but significant minorities of Roman Catholics, Greek Orthodox Catholics, and Jews created a religious diversity which at times became a source of social division. Birmingham cultivated an image as a "city of churches," an image born in the 1870s when the Methodist, Baptist, Presbyterian, Episcopal, and Roman Catholic denominations built churches just north of the business district on prominent corner lots donated by the Elyton Land Company. These original congregations grew with the city, becoming the major downtown First Churches, with handsome stone and brick edifices and stained glass windows, and they were joined by neighborhood congregations that sprang up with every new suburb. By 1901 Edward W. Barrett, editor of the *Age-Herald*, declared: "Birmingham . . . is one of the best and most religious communities in America. . . . No city in the South has more church seating capacity compared to inhabitants—none has better preachers—and none better filled churches."[50]

By 1906 Birmingham had 6,604 Negro and 20,974 white church members. Most of the Negroes worshiped in segregated Negro Baptist and Negro Methodist congregations, and a tiny minority attended segregated Episcopal and Presbyterian churches. Of the 21,000 white church members in 1906, 58.8 percent were Protestant and 41.2 percent were non-Protestant. The non-Protestants, many of them first- and second-generation immigrants, were more numerous than in most southern cities. They included Roman Catholics with 38.0 percent of the total white church membership, Greek Orthodox Catholics with 1.4 percent,

49. U.S. Census, *Thirteenth Census, 1910*, IV, *Population*, 538–39; *News*, Jan. 16, 1901.

50. *Age-Herald*, May 12, 1901; Bigelow, "Birmingham," 200–207.

and Jews with 1.8 percent. Among the Protestants, the largest memberships belonged to the three evangelical Protestant denominations— the Methodists with 21.8 percent of all white church members, the Baptists with 9.8 percent, and the Presbyterians with 13.7 percent. The Protestant Episcopal Church, place of worship of many of Birmingham's social and economic elite, ranked next among Protestant denominations with 6.2 percent of the white church members. The final 7.2 percent of the white church members worshiped in small Protestant congregations of Disciples of Christ, Churches of Christ, the German Evangelical Synod, the German Lutheran Church, the Seventh-Day Adventists, the Congregational Church, the Christian Scientists, and the Salvation Army.[51]

Since the suburbs were much more heavily Protestant than was Old Birmingham, the creation of Greater Birmingham in 1910 greatly increased the Protestant portion among the city's white church members. By 1916 Birmingham had 50,000 white church members. More than 70 percent were Protestant, with nearly three-fifths (58 percent) of all white members belonging to the three major denominations: Methodist (34.2 percent), Baptist (16.6 percent), and Presbyterian (7.3 percent). The non-Protestant portion had been correspondingly reduced to 29.3 percent, with the Roman Catholic church embracing 24.9 percent of all white church members.[52]

Many members among the dominant evangelical Protestant churches continued the emotional evangelism and fervent personal piety of their southern rural background. They responded enthusiastically to stirring revivals, thousands turning out to hear such traveling evangelists as Sam Jones and Dwight L. Moody. And they sought to shape the moral climate of Birmingham according to their precepts of righteousness. To their intense dismay, however, gambling, prostitution, and rowdy saloons flourished, especially during the robust growth of the 1880s and 1890s, creating a frontier-town atmosphere and inspiring widespread newspaper headlines about "Bad Birmingham." Indeed, for several years in the late 1890s Birmingham had one of the nation's highest arrest ratios and gained a reputation as the "wickedest" town in the country. City officials said the ratio of arrests to population had been unfairly inflated by including suburban arrests but not the suburban population. Indignant pastors and editors demanded that the city be cleaned up and asserted

51. U.S. Census, *Religious Bodies: 1906*, Pt. 1, 380–407.
52. U.S. Census, *Religious Bodies: 1916*, Pt. 1, 29, 123, 364–66. The actual Roman Catholic proportions of the total white population were perhaps nearer 34 percent in 1906 and 22 percent in 1916, since only the Catholics counted baptized infants as members.

that the quiet upright majority of citizens were "building up and sustaining a righteous community," a "Better Birmingham." The conflicting images of Bad Birmingham and Better Birmingham persisted for years, and in 1921 churches and women's organizations were still crusading against "prevalent" vice to create a "cleaner Birmingham."[53]

This, then, was Birmingham after fifty years: a burgeoning young city based on heavy industry but diversified into trade, transportation, and finance. Like most other southern cities, its citizens were predominantly of native rural southern background, more than one third were Negro, and a strong majority of blacks and whites were Protestant. Yet Birmingham was distinguished from most southern cities by its newness; by its concentration on coal, iron, and steel; and by its more cosmopolitan population, with conspicuous communities of Germans, Irish, and Italians and with 30 percent of its whites worshipping in non-Protestant churches. Birminghamians themselves insisted that the spirit of their city was not typically southern; it had none of the easygoing Old South spirit, none of the drowsy languor of the quiet southern town. Birmingham, they said, was wide awake, "a progressive, energetic and active town," bustling with keen merchants, aggressive real estate promoters, enterprising industrialists, and sweaty workers. In 1912 Graham R. Taylor of *Survey Magazine* found Birmingham "a made-to-order city of our times," the "South's one big city which knows no heritage of civil war."[54]

And so it was, but Birmingham, for all its progress, had its share of problems and disappointments. The full measure of expected industrial grandeur never quite materialized; poverty, congestion, and crime were prevalent; and the race question, shared with all southern cities, was perennially troublesome. And the city, in its very newness and impetuous growth, was rough and unpolished. "Its makers," said Graham Taylor, had been "mining engineers, prospectors, ironmakers, not millwrights in town-building." Impatient promoters had often built thoughtlessly, with little imagination or plan, with little regard for amenities, and the city lacked "that dignity and ampleness" which were "so characteristic of the old South."[55]

Birmingham, in short, was an ambitious, grimy, gangling young giant, an unrefined but robust new metropolis of the New South.

53. Bigelow, "Birmingham," 209–15; *Age-Herald*, Feb. 10, 1901; *Post*, Sept. 23, 1921.
54. *Age-Herald*, Nov. 3, 1901; Taylor, "Birmingham's Civic Front," 1464.
55. Taylor, "Birmingham's Civic Front," 1464, 1468.

The Interest Groups

$\mathbb{T}$HE interests of the community," said the Birmingham *News* in 1903, "are wide and varied. They comprise the large corporations, the mercantile enterprises, the industrial concerns, the professional classes, the small property owner, the wage earner, and, in fact all spheres of human endeavor."[1] Endorsing a candidate for mayor and arguing that he would serve all groups, the *News* thus defined "interests" broadly. When discussion narrowed to particular issues, however, Birmingham politicians and journalists could also define interest groups narrowly, often according to specific organizations that represented functional sectors of the local economy: the Alabama Coal Operators Association (including iron companies), the Real Estate Association, The Board of Trade (merchants), the Jefferson County Medical Society, the Liquor Dealers' Association, the Retail Grocers' Association, and the Trades Council (labor). Such associations not only developed economic cooperation among their members, but also asserted the common interests of their members in politics. Other economic groups, such as utility companies and railroads, developed no specific local associations, but cooperated informally and put forward spokesmen, often company presidents or corporation attorneys, to assert their common political interests. Still other interest groups reflected, not common economic functions, but rather some common social characteristic, such as ethnicity or race, or some common attitude on a social issue, such as regulation of community morals. Among the associations of such social interest groups were the Anti-Saloon League, the Irish Democratic Club, the German-American Union, and the Negro Civic and Educational League.[2]

1. Birmingham *News*, Feb. 5. 1903.
2. This delineation of interest groups follows closely David B. Truman, *The Governmental Process: Political Interests and Public Opinion* (New York: Knopf,

Economic and social interest groups and their associations and spokesmen provide a useful analytical link between the economic and social systems, on the one hand, and the political system on the other. Because they defined and articulated the political policy aims and needs of their members, they can legitimately be viewed as the major protagonists in the political process. Of course, focusing on interest groups throws a strong spotlight on organized political activity, but consigns to the shadows the many citizens who belonged to no such organization, or whose membership was inactive. But other approaches to urban political history—whether through political parties and factions, or "reformers" and "bosses," or "Progressives" and "Conservatives"—also leave out many, or even most, citizens. Because the interest-group approach focuses on viable, vigorous associations and on spokesmen who undertook to ascertain and represent the wishes of social groups, occupational groups, and functional sectors of the economy, it probably is most capable of usefully reflecting the policy wishes of the entire spectrum of citizens.[3]

THE ECONOMIC INTEREST GROUPS

Sometimes during political campaigns or policy fights, Birminghamians spoke broadly of the "business" interests, and in Birmingham, as

---

1951). Truman defined an interest group as "any group that, on the basis of one or more shared attitudes, makes certain claims upon other groups in the society," and he considered such a group to be involved in the political process "if and when it makes its claims through or upon any of the institutions of government" (pp. 33, 37).

3. The interest group approach, like any other, involves some troublesome ambiguities. Association leaders, for example, might not always accurately represent the wishes of their rank and file constituents. But most local association leaders, serving voluntarily, elected annually from the rank and file, consulting frequently and informally with their many personal friends in the group, probably gave a more accurate representation of a more like-minded group than did either political leaders of parties, factions, and machines, or professional leaders of large bureaucratic state and national associations. Again, interest groups might have overlapping memberships; some businessmen, for example, invested in diverse economic activities. But the vast majority had one clear primary business interest whose policy concerns they most consistently supported. Finally, members of any business interest group were in fact everyday business competitors, and they might also compete, rather than cooperate, politically. But when group colleagues (merchants, for example) clashed over local government policy, the issue was usually some specific government favor or allocation (which street would get a new streetcar line?) rather than a question of basic policy (should the city encourage street railways to build from the business district to all suburbs?), which would affect most merchants similarly and generate cooperative lobbying.

in most cities, a broad general businessman's association—the Commercial Club from 1893 to 1909, thereafter the Chamber of Commerce —claimed to speak for the common interests of all business. The Commercial Club was founded in 1893 mainly by merchants; but the founders, seeking broad business cooperation, encouraged all businessmen to join, and soon the membership was quite diverse. The club leadership—some thirty to fifty officers, directors, and committee chairmen—reflected the diversity. Typically after 1900 merchants held one-fourth to one-third of the club's leadership positions; professional men 15 to 20 percent; realtors 20 percent; and coal, iron, railroad, utility, and manufacturing corporations and banks together one-fourth to one-third. Smaller businessmen, such as grocers, saloonkeepers, or artisans, were seldom club members and almost never leaders.[4] On some local issues the club was able to enunciate a policy on which such diverse businessmen could agree, but many issues divided businessmen so severely that the club could find no common position and remained silent. To avoid internal contention the club usually concentrated on general probusiness policies: advertising Birmingham's potential, attracting new capital and businesses, promoting public friendliness toward business, seeking more favorable freight rates, resisting the demands of organized labor, and seeking federal appropriations for nearby river and waterway improvements.[5]

In 1899 some merchants, wanting a more exclusively mercantile organization, founded the Birmingham Board of Trade. One of the founders explained that the Commercial Club had "ceased to be commercial" and that the purpose of the new Board of Trade was to deal with "every thing that affected in any way the interests of the merchant class." Thereafter on such issues as regulation of utilities, corporation commissaries, and railroad grade crossings, the Commercial Club, with its diverse membership and conflicting interests, equivocated and remained silent, but the Board of Trade, finding a consensus among merchants, took a firm and vocal position.[6]

Other specialized associations emerged rapidly. The retail grocers,

4. Birmingham *Age-Herald*, Jan. 14, 1893; *News*, Mar. 20, 1909. Leadership percentages are based on compilation of interest-group affiliations of all club leaders, 1895, 1900, 1905, 1910, and 1915.

5. *Age-Herald*, June 9, 1894, May 14, 1895; *News*, June 19, 1900, Feb. 11, 1911.

6. *Age-Herald*, Oct. 31, 1901. See also *ibid.*, May 25, 1899. Leaders of the Board of Trade also helped form the Merchants' Exchange and the Businessmen's League, whose main purpose was to attract more out-of-town trade to Birmingham. These organizations followed the lead of the Board of Trade on questions of local government policy. *News*, May 26, Oct. 7, 1905, Feb. 12, 1909.

most of whom ran small neighborhood stores in residential areas outside the main business districts, formed the Retail Grocers' Association and distinguished themselves from the downtown merchants in the Board of Trade.[7]

In 1900 Birmingham's commercial coal-mining companies and iron and steel furnace corporations organized the Alabama Coal Operators' Association to coordinate their efforts in wage-scale negotiations with coal miners. In 1908 the association members agreed to stop recognizing or negotiating with the miners' union, the United Mine Workers of America. The UMW struck, and the Coal Operators' Association coordinated successful efforts to break the strike and establish the open shop in Birmingham coal mines. It repeated this function in the 1917 and the 1919–1921 coal strikes, and throughout it also worked to keep tax assessments on mineral lands low and to prevent regulation of mining or of corporation commissary and payday policies.[8]

The Real Estate Association (later the Real Estate Exchange) provided cooperative realty appraisal and listing services and lobbied for realtors on such matters as tax assessment policy, regulation of housing conditions, and extension of city services to new residential areas.[9] The Master Builders' Association, or Builders' Exchange, and the General Building Contractors' Association fought the trade union movement and sought the aid of city government during strikes.[10] The Liquor Dealers' Association created an elaborate lobbying mechanism to meet the continuous threat of government regulation or prohibition of the liquor trade.[11] Truck and dairy farmers developed such organizations as the Dairymen's Association, concerned primarily with city regulation of the conditions under which they could market produce.[12] Small nonmetal manufacturers, such as bakeries, print shops, grain mills, sawmills, and manufacturers of fertilizer, glass, cigars, mattresses, ice, textiles, trunks, and furniture, organized the Birmingham Manufacturers' Association. The small manufacturers were concerned about local property and license taxes, but their main efforts went toward promoting the use of home-manufactured products, expanding the market for their products

---

7. *Age-Herald*, Jan. 4, 1902, Jan. 20, Feb. 22, 1915; *News*, Sept. 8, 1900, Jan. 19, 1905.

8. *News*, June 18, 27, 1900; *Labor Advocate*, Sept. 25, 1908; *Age-Herald*, Mar. 25, 1920, Jan. 23, 1921.

9. *Age-Herald*, Jan. 24, 1899, Oct. 25, 1901, Nov. 2, 1916, June 28, 1917.

10. *News*, May 19, 22, 1913.

11. *News*, Dec. 4, 1906, Oct. 29, 1907.

12. *Age-Herald*, Apr. 5, 1919; *News*, Mar. 22, 1900.

in Birmingham's hinterland, attracting new manufacturers to the city, and working for more favorable freight rates.[13]

Such economic interest groups as the utilities, the railroads, and the manufacturers of pipe, machinery, and foundry products embraced only a few large firms and found it unnecessary to create local associations. Rather, within each group the company presidents, managers, and attorneys cooperated informally and mobilized delegations to lobby for common taxation, annexation, or regulation concerns.[14]

A final business group, the banks, created the Birmingham Clearing House to handle transactions between local and out-of-town banks, but this was not a typical political-pressure association. In local politics, only a few problems, such as arranging enough city revenue to guarantee interest payments on city bonds, generated a clear-cut bankers' position. Most other concerns that might ally bankers, such as regulation of the money supply, interest rates, or bank practices, were national or state rather than local issues. Moreover, most banks invested in many types of local business, and bank boards of directors typically included merchants, realtors, professional men, industrialists, and utility executives. Banks, therefore, were often in a mediating position, similar to that of the Chamber of Commerce. On such issues as taxation, banks often played an integrative role, seeking to define a consensus program on which most businessmen could agree and then coordinating efforts to get local government to adopt it. Certainly the banks' resources and coordination gave their business allies important advantages over small businesses with few bank connections and over nonbusiness interest groups.[15]

The professional men of Birmingham had no single overall association, but several individual professions organized strong, politically influential associations. Physicians, for example, formed the Jefferson County Medical Society, which was the legally-designated county board of health, with authority to elect city and county health officers and to recommend quarantine, and which lobbied continually to improve health and sanitation facilities.[16] The bar association had great unofficial influence over nominations for city and county judgeships and often initiated changes in local court structure; it also maintained a law library

---

13. *News*, Mar. 27, 28, 1908.

14. *Age-Herald*, Feb. 4, 1903, Apr. 9, 1918; *News*, May 19, 1910.

15. *Age-Herald*, Jan. 15, 1902, Jan. 15, 1919. See the coordinating role of W.P.G. Harding, president of the First National Bank and of the Chamber of Commerce, during the tax-rate controversy of 1913 to 1915. *News*, Nov. 21, Dec. 5, 1913.

16. *News*, Jan. 10, Aug. 3, 1905.

in the courthouse.[17] Through the Birmingham Pastors' Union, clergymen worked continually for regulation of vice and liquor.[18] Public schoolteachers were slower to combine, having no organization until 1920, then splitting into two rival groups.[19]

Men from different professions, though they had no common professional association, often cooperated to promote certain common policy ideas. Sharing a respect for professional training and expertise, they advocated greater use of experts in local government to rationalize administration and to improve services and amenities. Being usually less tax conscious than business or labor, they constantly urged heavier expenditures to upgrade civic services.[20]

Roughly three-fourths of Birmingham's adult males were wage earners, a minority of them organized in labor unions, a majority unorganized. Wage earners varied in type from self-employed skilled artisans—barbers, blacksmiths, tinners, plumbers, photographers, bakers, shoemakers, painters, tailors, and watch repairers, many of whom considered themselves both small businessmen and trade unionists—to unskilled common laborers and servants. The skilled workers of Birmingham began forming craft unions early in the city's history, and in 1889 they founded the Birmingham Trades Council, a central body to which each member union sent delegates. In 1890 the weekly Birmingham *Labor Advocate* began publication and became the official organ of the Trades Council. The founders of the Trades Council included the iron molders, the ironworkers and steelworkers, the typographical union, painters, carpenters, tailors, and jewelers. During the depression of the 1890s the Birmingham labor movement suffered severe setbacks, and for a brief period in 1895 only the musicians' and printers' unions kept the Trades Council together. But by 1900 the council was reviving and the original trade unions had been joined by barbers, bricklayers, cigar makers, garment makers, and brewery workers. In succeeding years unions of electrical workers, railway workers, machinists, plumbers, retail clerks, bookbinders, broommakers, stage employees, postal employees, and various metal trades joined the council.[21]

Coal miners also participated in the Trades Council through their

17. *Age-Herald*, Dec. 27, 1890; *News*, Mar. 1, 1907.
18. *News*, May 6, Oct. 21, 1907.
19. *Age-Herald*, Jan. 15, 1920; Birmingham, Board of Education, *Annual Report of the Birmingham Public Schools*, 1920, pp. 124–27.
20. See, for example, *News*, May 23, 1911, Apr. 1, 1912.
21. *Labor Advocate*, Sept. 5, 1903, Jan. 7, 1910, Aug. 24, 1918, Jan. 24, 1920; *Birmingham City Directory* for 1890, 1900, 1910, 1920.

union, the United Mine Workers, whose membership in Birmingham rose and fell dramatically. Alabama coal miners first joined the United Mine Workers of America in 1890, but after losing a strike their organization dissolved. They created a state organization which fought an 1894 coal strike to a partial victory, and in 1897 they again affiliated with the national United Mine Workers. Organizing vigorously, by 1903 the UMW attained a membership of 11,500 in the entire mineral district. The union struck the iron-furnace companies from 1904 to 1906, and it struck both the iron-furnace companies and the commercial-coal companies in 1908 and 1919–1921. It lost all the strikes and after each defeat its membership declined drastically, in 1908, for example, falling from nearly 18,000 to 700.[22]

Always a larger proportion of Birmingham's white workers were organized than were its black workers, most of whom were employed as unskilled common laborers. But during several periods, especially 1897–1904, Birmingham unions, particularly the UMW, organized significant numbers of Negro workers. Since approximately one-half of Alabama coal miners were Negro, the UMW, if it was to unite coal miners, had to organize blacks and include them among its officers. From 1900 to 1904 the UMW organized approximately 6,000 black miners, and from 1900 to 1903 the Trades Council admitted black delegates from the miners' union and from several other Negro locals that together organized approximately 2,000 unskilled black workers. But in 1903 the Trades Council again drew the color line and the Negro locals were segregated in a Colored Central Labor Council. After 1904 many of the Negro locals collapsed, though the UMW continued to have several thousand black coal miners in its ranks until it was demolished by the loss of the 1908 coal strike.[23]

Though unions embraced only one-sixth to one-third of all wage earners in Birmingham and Jefferson County,[24] depending on whether

---

22. Robert Ward and William Rogers, *Labor Revolt in Alabama: The Great Strike of 1894* (University: Univ. of Alabama Press, 1965), 31–34, 51–53, 59; Paul B. Worthman, "Black Workers and Labor Unions in Birmingham, Alabama, 1897–1904," *Labor History* 10 (Spring 1969), 388–89, 403–404; *News*, June 10, 1907.

23. *News*, June 19, 22, 25, 1900, June 11, 1907; Worthman, "Black Workers," 378, 389–99.

24. These proportions were based on the total of all wage earners, including servants and washerwomen. If only industrial workers are considered, the proportion belonging to unions probably varied between one-fourth and one-half. *Labor Advocate*, Apr. 8, 1901, Aug. 2, 1902, Oct. 3, 1913; *News*, Apr. 23, 1900; U.S. Census, *Thirteenth Census, 1910*, Vol. IV, *Population*, 152–64.

coal miners were organized at the time, the leaders of organized labor claimed to speak for the general interests of all wage earners, unorganized as well as organized. The extent to which they actually did so is difficult to determine, since most unorganized wage earners had no effective way to articulate or record their policy preferences. Probably unorganized workers had little enthusiasm for such union organizational concerns as gaining permission for city firemen to join unions, or having city printing and construction done only by union employees, or stopping the protection of strikebreakers by police and deputies. And unorganized workers may have cared little for such union policy goals as the regulation of commissaries and the establishment of the two-week pay day. When, however, union leaders spoke for the workingman as a city resident of small means, concerned with taxation, provision of city services, and regulation of utilities, then surely they spoke too for most unorganized wage earners. Occasional referenda on taxation and on utility regulation indicate strongly that most workingmen endorsed the policy positions enunciated by leaders of organized labor.

A significant characteristic of economic interest groups is that they can be ranked according to the amount of local economic resources controlled by their typical, or median, firms. Citizens of Birmingham were accustomed to ranking economic groups informally according to their economic power; the editor of the *News* did so in 1903, for example, when he listed the "interests of the community" in rough descending order from the "large corporations" to the "wage earner." Such commonsense rankings corresponded rather closely with more systematic rankings of thirteen Birmingham business groups displayed in table 3.1, based on real and personal property tax assessments and credit ratings from the *Reference Books* of R.G. Dun & Company, a New York credit-rating agency. For each year each interest group's rank was determined by the financial strength of its median, or middle, firm. The rank order changed slightly at the top levels between 1890 and 1900. The utility companies did not move to their third-rank position until major consolidations in 1900–1901, and not until 1900 did the metal manufacturers move above the commercial-coal companies. But from 1900 through 1920 the rank order of business interest groups remained stable.[25]

25. Information on the financial strength of iron companies, metal manufacturers, coal-mining corporations, contractors, nonmetal manufacturers, merchants, saloons, grocers, and artisans came from the January volumes, 1890, 1900, 1910, 1915, and 1920, of the *Reference Book (And Key) Containing Ratings of Merchants, Manufacturers and Traders Generally, Throughout the United States & Canada*, published

Tables 3.2 and 3.3 show for each business interest group the distribution of all firms among seven categories of financial strength in 1900 and 1915, as well as the category in which the median firm fell. The four highest-ranking interest groups—the railroads, utility companies, iron companies, and banks—placed a majority of all their firms in the two highest categories of financial strength. The metal manufacturers and commercial coal-mining companies, which were closely associated with the iron and steel companies in economic function and in interest-group goals, had a smaller portion of firms in the two highest categories; and by 1915 each contained a few rather small companies. Still, a clear majority of their firms were in the top four categories, above $35,000. Therefore, the metal manufacturers and commercial coal-mining companies, along with the railroads, utilities, banks, and iron and steel corporations will be defined as the upper-ranking business groups—the groups with the greatest economic power.

At the other extreme, the business interest groups of saloons, grocers, and artisans placed a vast majority of all their firms in the lowest category of financial strength, below $1,000. These will be defined as lower-ranking business groups—the groups with the least economic power.

In between lay the real estate companies, contractors, nonmetal manufacturers, and merchants. The distributions of their firms, spreading across most or all categories of financial strength, were more diffuse than the distributions of either the upper- or the lower-ranking business

---

by R.G. Dun & Company of New York, available at the Business Library, Dun & Bradstreet, Inc., New York, New York. The books rated each firm in one of seventeen categories of "pecuniary strength," ranging from "Less than $500" to "Over $1,000,000." The ratings, based on regular detailed firm-by-firm reports from Dun Company agents in most major cities, including Birmingham, estimated all the economic assets that would affect a firm's credit standing. Ratings of some branch firms—only 3 to 5 percent of all Birmingham firms—could not be used because they were based on the assets of out-of-town corporation headquarters. This did not affect any major Birmingham manufacturing corporations, which Dun treated as subsidiaries and rated according to their local holdings.

The Dun Company did not rate banks, utilities, railroads, and real estate companies. Banks, therefore, have been rated according to their statements of capital and surplusses. The financial strength of utilities and of railroads was estimated from property-tax assessments, listed in the annual reports of the Alabama state auditor, and the strength of real estate companies was estimated from tax assessments listed in Merchant's Credit Association, *A List of Taxpayers of Jefferson County, Alabama; Showing Separately the Amounts of Real and Personal Property Assessed for the Year 1916, Together with the Post Office Address of Each Taxpayer or His Agent* (Birmingham, 1917), available in BPL. Since Birmingham property was assessed at approximately 30 percent of true market value, financial strength was estimated by dividing the assessments by .30. Such estimates were consistent with other available information about the capital of these companies.

Table 3.1 Rank Order of Business Interest Groups According to the Financial Strength of their Median Firms, 1890–1920

INTEREST GROUP	RATING OF MEDIAN FIRM (*In Thousands of Dollars*)				
	1890	1900	1910	1915	1920
Iron Companies	1,000+	1,000+	1,000+	1,000+	1,000+
Railroads	1,000+	1,000+	1,000+	1,000+	1,000+
Utilities	75–125	1,000+	1,000+	1,000+	1,000+
Banks	200–300	200–300	75–125	200–300	200–300
Mfg., metal	20–40	50–75	75–125	50–75	75–125
Coal-mining	125–200	50–75	50–75	35–50	50–75
Real estate	n/a	n/a	n/a	20–35	n/a
Contractors	10–20	10–20	10–20	10–20	5–10
Mfg., nonmetal	5–10	5–10	5–10	5–10	5–10
Merchants	5–10	3–5	3–5	3–5	5–10
Saloons	2–5	.5–1	—	—	—
Grocers	.5–1	.5–	.5–	.5–	.5–
Artisans	.5–1	.5–	.5–	.5–	.5–

Source: See n. 25, pp. 46–47.

Note: Those economic interest groups not included in the table are professionals, truck and dairy farmers, and wage earners.

n/a Not available.

groups. Still, for each of these four middle groups, the median firm and a majority of all the firms did fall above $1,000 (and thus above the majorities of all the lower-ranking interest groups) and below $35,000 (and thus below the majorities of all the upper-ranking interest groups). These four groups, therefore, will be defined as middle-ranking business groups—the groups with a middle amount of economic power.

Tables 3.1, 3.2, and 3.3, based mainly on Dun ratings in which the highest category was "Over $1,000,000," do not distinguish among the upper-ranking groups as clearly as does Table 3.4, based entirely on the 1916 property-tax assessments of those upper-ranking firms that owned property assessed at $50,000 or more. Table 3.4 shows clearly that, in terms of average and median Jefferson County assessments, the rank order of the top three groups, which towered far above all other groups, was: iron and steel companies, utilities, and railroads. Also, the total assessed valuation of the forty-one firms in Table 3.4 was $81,984, 607, which was 45.0 percent of the *total* assessed valuation of *all* property in Jefferson County ($182,250,312). Clearly the men who

Table 3.2 Percentage of Business Interest Group Firms in Each Category of Financial Strength, 1900

INTEREST GROUP	No. OF FIRMS (100%)	BELOW $1,000	$1,000 TO 10,000	$10,000 TO 35,000	$35,000 TO 75,000	$75,000 TO 200,000	$200,000 TO 500,000	OVER $500,000
Railroads	(7)							<u>100</u>
Iron Cos.	(4)						25	<u>75</u>
Utilities	(3)					33		<u>67</u>
Banks	(9)			11		33	<u>44</u>	11
Mfg., metal	(16)			44	<u>13</u>	13	31	
Coal-mining	(11)			27	<u>36</u>	27	9	
Real estate					No data			
Contractors	(5)		40	<u>40</u>	20			
Mfg., nonmetal	(44)	20	<u>39</u>	27	5	7	2	
Merchants	(240)	28	<u>45</u>	17	4	4	2	
Saloons	(43)	<u>56</u>	28	12	2	2		
Grocers	(160)	<u>89</u>	9	2	1			
Artisans	(28)	<u>86</u>	11	4				

Source: See n. 25, pp. 46–47.
Note: For each interest group, the percentage in the category in which the median firm falls is underlined.

Table 3.3 Percentage of Business Interest Group Firms in Each Category of Financial Strength, 1915

Interest Group	No. of Firms (100%)	Below $1,000	$1,000 to 10,000	$10,000 to 35,000	$35,000 to 75,000	$75,000 to 200,000	$200,000 to 500,000	Over $500,000
Railroads	(11)						9	<u>91</u>
Iron Cos.	(6)				17			<u>83</u>
Utilities	(5)					20		<u>80</u>
Banks	(9)				22		<u>33</u>	44
Mfg., metal	(23)		9	17	<u>30</u>	35		9
Coal-mining	(36)	3	17	28	<u>19</u>	6	17	11
Real estate	(204)	3	18	<u>37</u>	17	14	4	7
Contractors	(24)	21	21	<u>33</u>	8	13	4	
Mfg., nonmetal	(112)	27	<u>33</u>	17	14	5	2	
Merchants	(777)	37	<u>32</u>	19	7	3	1	
Saloons	(—)							
Grocers	(634)	<u>89</u>	9	1				
Artisans	(143)	<u>87</u>	12	1	0.3			

Source: See n. 25, pp. 46–47.
Note: For each interest group, the percentage in the category in which the median firm falls is underlined.

Table 3.4 Top Business Interest Groups, Arranged in Descending Order According to Average and Median Assessed Valuation of Firms with over $50,000 Valuation, 1916

Interest Group	No. of Firms	Total Assessment	Average Assessment Per Firm	Median Assessment
Iron Companies	5	$46,459,407	$9,291,881	$5,656,318
Utilities	4	12,567,236	3,141,809	1,794,673
Railroads	11	16,230,269	1,475,479	632,620
Banks	5	1,988,510	397,702	465,182
Coal-mining	8	3,086,551	385,819	371,722
Manufacturing, metal	8	1,652,634	206,578	178,620

Source: See n. 26, p. 51.

led the firms of the upper-ranking economic interest groups controlled more local economic resources than did the men who led the firms of either the middle- or lower-ranking groups.[26]

Three economic-interest groups—professional men, truck and dairy farmers, and wage earners—were not included in Tables 3.1 to 3.4, and since they were for the most part composed of individuals rather than firms, they are more difficult to rank. Still, they can be fitted into the rank order. Professional men fit most closely with the middle-ranking groups. To be sure, a few exceptional professional men, most of them attorneys, were paid spokesmen for other interest groups, such as iron and steel corporations, utility companies, or labor unions. Such men will be considered members of the groups that hired them, rather than of the broad professional interest group. As for the vast majority of Birmingham attorneys, clergymen, engineers, journalists, physicians, and teachers, however, they ranked far below the men who managed the upper-ranking firms, yet most of them probably ranked well above the lower-ranking saloonkeepers, artisans, and grocers. Most professional men, moreover, identified mainly with middle-ranking businessmen. The professions, therefore, will be included among the middle-ranking economic interest groups. The truck and dairy farms, many of them inside the 1910 city limits, were usually small one-family operations. Truck farmers frequently drove their vegetable wagons to the city-operated open market, or peddled on the streets, and many dairy

26. Merchant's Credit Association, *A List of Taxpayers of Jefferson County, Alabama; . . . 1916.*

farmers drove milk wagons to town daily, making deliveries at homes and neighborhood groceries. On the average the truck and dairy farmers probably ranked near the retail grocers and artisans, and they will be included among the lower-ranking groups.[27] Finally, wage earners, who comprised approximately 75 percent of Birmingham's population, clearly ranked at the bottom according to the amount of economic resources that was controlled by the typical interest-group member. The vast majority of wage earners stood as individuals, not even organized into labor unions. And the unions that did exist were not firms, but interest-group associations, and, in comparison with the associations of the business groups, the labor unions' economic resources were usually meager.

Table 3.5 shows the expanded rank order of sixteen business, professional, farm and wage earner interest groups, ranked according to the estimates of financial strength in the right-hand column, and divided into three sets. The set labels—"upper-ranking," "middle-ranking," and "lower-ranking"—refer directly to the right-hand column and to the amounts of local economic resources that were controlled by the typical members of the groups in each set, but not to the portion of Birmingham's population embraced in each set. Certainly the three sets did not embrace equal portions of Birmingham's population. Instead, as shown in parentheses in Table 3.5, the owners, officials, managers, and superintendents of the upper-ranking set of interest groups, most of them affiliated with firms worth more than $35,000, comprised only the top 1 percent of the population. The middle-ranking set of groups are so labeled because the worth of their firms typically fell in a middle range of $3,000 to $35,000, far below the corporation giants, but substantially above the typical members of the lower-ranking groups. But clearly the owners and managers of these firms of middle-range economic power did not cluster around the midpoint of Birmingham's population. Instead, they all stood just below the top 1 percent and within the next-highest 19 percent. Finally, the lower-ranking set of groups are so labeled because of the low amount of economic resources controlled by their typical members, and their membership embraced the entire lower 80 percent of the population.[28]

27. *News,* July 21, 1906, Sept. 24, 1913; Birmingham *Post,* Apr. 4, 1921.
28. The proportions of the population in each set of interest groups were compiled from the data on all persons ten years of age or over engaged in occupations, classified into 522 relatively precise occupational categories in the U.S. Census, *Thirteenth Census, 1910,* IV, *Population,* 152–64, 538–39. Since the inclusion of females and of males under twenty-one years of age would tend to overrepresent families of the

Table 3.5 Rank Order of Sixteen Economic Interest Groups, Arranged in Three Sets

Set and Group	Financial Strength of Median Member 1910
Upper-ranking Set (top 1 percent of population)[1]	
1. Iron and Steel Corporations	Over $1,000,000
2. Utility Corporations	Over $1,000,000
3. Railroads	Over $1,000,000
4. Banks	$75,000–$125,000
5. Manufacturers, metal	$75,000–$125,000
6. Commercial Coal Corporations	$50,000–$75,000
Middle-ranking Set (next highest 19 percent of population)[1]	
7. Real Estate Companies	$20,000–$35,000[2]
8. Contractors	$10,000–$20,000
9. Manufacturers, nonmetal	$5,000–$10,000
10. Merchants (except retail grocers)	$3,000–$5,000
11. Professionals (listed alphabetically)	middle
Attorneys	
Clergymen	
Engineers	
Journalists	
Physicians	
Teachers	
Lower-ranking Set (bottom 80 percent of population)[1]	
12. Truck and Dairy Farmers	Low
13. Saloons and Liquor Dealers	—[3]
14. Retail Grocers	Below $500
15. Artisans	Below $500
16. Wage Earners	Low
Skilled-craft laborers	
Clerical workers	
Coal miners	
Unskilled workers and servants	

[1]Proportion of adult male population, 1910. See n. 28, p. 52.
[2]1915 data.
[3]Prohibited in 1910.

THE SOCIAL INTEREST GROUPS

The social interest groups, organized around some common social characteristic or some common set of attitudes on a social issue, can also be crudely ranked according to the social and economic status of their typical members, though their ranking is even less precise than that of economic groups. Many social groups and organizations emerged in Birmingham, ranging from the top to the bottom of the social-status order, but few became politically active interest groups. The most important ones who did function politically were ethnic groups, Negro organizations, and the evangelical Protestant activists, who formed the core of the antisaloon movement. None of these represented a social elite.

Birmingham did have a social elite, but unlike older cities it had no "aristocracy" of old families that inherited prestige. In 1895 when the Tennessee Coal, Iron, and Railroad Company moved its headquarters from Nashville to Birmingham, company treasurer James Bowron observed: "I found on coming to Birmingham that to be in the iron trade was to be respectable; to be an officer of an iron making corporation was to have the entree to the best society; but to be the chief residential officer of the largest corporation was to carry the key to the Kingdom of Heaven." By contrast, said Bowron, "In Nashville ... I had never taken any commanding position in the social life of the city. In Birmingham I found it was not so much a question of what a man's grandfather had been, but the question was and still is, 'what does he do?' "[29] Thus social prestige came almost entirely from economic institutions, and Birmingham's social elite differed little from its economic elite.

The social elite had exclusive organizations—the Country Club and the Southern Club—which welcomed industrialists, prosperous commercial entrepreneurs, and professional people, but not Jews, no matter

---

lower-ranking occupations, all females and those males identified as under twenty-one were excluded from the estimates of population proportions. Two categories, "managers and superintendents (manufacturing)" and "manufacturers and officials" were subdivided into upper- and middle-ranking groups according to estimates from the Dun Company *Reference Books.* The "retail dealer" category was likewise subdivided into middle- and lower-ranking groups.

29. James Bowron, "Autobiography," 3 vols. TS, I, 363–64, Univ. of Alabama Library.

how prominent and successful.[30] The exclusive clubs were not lobbying associations and the social elite did not function as a coherent political interest group. Members of the elite were, to be sure, often active politically, and no doubt their status and influential contacts in the exclusive clubs gave them important advantages, but in political contention they usually represented their economic interests and acted through economic associations.

The ethnic and religious groups that did become politically active social interest groups embraced mostly people from the middle and lower social strata. This was clearly true of the evangelical Protestant activists, mostly Methodists, Baptists, and Presbyterians, who created such associations as the Anti-Saloon League and the Law and Order League to lobby for stricter government regulation of liquor, vice, and Sunday observance. Ably led by their ministers, who dominated the Birmingham Pastors' Union, the Protestant activists could, in the midst of their crusades, achieve great organizational unity and fervent mass support. Though the Protestant activists received some aid from social and economic leaders, any political success they scored must be attributed mainly to people of middle or lower social and economic status.[31]

Several ethnic minorities, embracing mostly lower- and some middle-status people, became politically active social interest groups. During the 1890s the Irish Democratic Club, the German-American Union, and the German-language newspaper, the Birmingham *Courier*, became influential units in city Democratic party politics, working effectively to place their members in political office and fighting against stricter government regulation of Sunday observance and saloons. The ethnic associations contained almost no members of Birmingham's social elite; the few ethnic leaders to attain economic prominence were German-Jewish bankers and merchants, who were strictly excluded from the elite social clubs.[32]

Birmingham Negroes faced severe caste prejudice and discrimination which paradoxically created, on the one hand, urgent common social concerns to stimulate interest group-unity and activity, and, on the other hand, debilitating disadvantages that undermined interest-group effec-

30. *Social Directory* (Birmingham, n.d. [*c.* 1909]); interview with John Beecher, Aug. 21, 1967.
31. *Age-Herald*, Aug. 30, 1899; *News*, July 14, Dec. 5, 10, 1900, Mar. 5, May 6, Oct. 28, 1907.
32. *Age-Herald*, June 25, 1892, May 27, 1899; Birmingham *Courier*, Nov. 13, 1902.

tiveness. After 1888 Birmingham whites used all-white Democratic primaries, and after 1901 Alabama whites used elaborate constitutional voting restrictions to deprive Negroes of the crucial political weapon of the vote, and racial discrimination kept most Negroes in the lowest-skilled, lowest-paid, least-organized occupations. A few Negro professionals and businessmen built a segregated Negro business section, but they were excluded from white business and professional associations. And their own racial associations, such as the Colored Citizens' League and the Negro Civic and Educational League, were weak and transitory. The strongest black organizations—the segregated Negro churches and fraternal orders—seldom operated as political interest group associations, though occasionally the Birmingham Preachers' Union and the Interdenominational Ministers' Alliance spoke for the race on local policy issues. Several Negro newspapers—the Birmingham *Hot Shots*, the Birmingham *Wide Awake*, and the Birmingham *Reporter*—helped articulate Negro needs and policy wishes, usually, however, presenting the point of view of the small Negro business and professional community.[33]

The social and economic interest groups as here defined and ranked will command the spotlight in the pages that follow. Chapter 4, employing the positional approach, will describe the extent to which members of the various groups sought and attained local elective office. Chapters 5–11, employing the decisional approach, will focus on interest-group contention over taxation, allocation of services, and regulation of economic and social life, and will seek to delineate the relative political power exercised by the groups of high, middle, and low economic and social rank.

33. Birmingham *Wide Awake*, Mar. 14, 1900; Birmingham *Reporter*, Aug. 4, 1917, Mar. 30, 1918; *News*, Mar. 15, 1914.

Position and Politics

$\mathcal{T}$HIS is a business town, and business men ought to dominate, not demagogues nor thin-pated, self-seeking theorists," declared Frank P. Glass, editor of the Birmingham *News*, in 1916. But to Glass, it seemed that business leaders did not in fact dominate city government, and to his dismay two city commissioners were indulging in most unbusinesslike demagogy against corporations. "It was in vain," he recalled, "that the *News* appealed to the businessmen of the city to get together, one year ago and elect a businessman as a candidate."[1] In his view, if businessmen were to dominate government, they had to get business leaders elected. If he was right, scholars could crudely measure the political power of various interests by discovering which groups got their members elected. And most social scientists who have empirically studied the historical development of community power structures have in fact relied almost exclusively on such "positional" analysis.

The positional method has distinct limitations, however, as editor Glass could have testified. The two demagogic city commissioners, for example, had both been businessmen themselves, and one of them had been Alabama's leading railroad attorney. At times the socioeconomic backgrounds of officeholders simply did not indicate reliably the trend of their decisions and actions in office. But the positional method can indicate lines of political cleavage in elections, it can show which groups were underrepresented or overrepresented in governing bodies, and it can reveal whether the same or different groups predominated in the city, the county, and the state agencies, all of which were often involved in local decisions. It can also help to reveal whether such municipal reforms as the adoption of city commission or city manager plans led to

1. Birmingham *News*, June 24, 1916.

the recruitment of officeholders from higher socioeconomic background, as reformers hoped.

VOTING RESTRICTIONS

Birmingham elected its officials by popular vote, but voting requirements prescribed by the state constitution, the legislature, or the city officials could severely affect the ability of Negroes and of poor and uneducated whites to vote. Birmingham was founded during the Radical Reconstruction of Alabama, and under the Alabama constitutions of 1868 and 1875 all male citizens over twenty-one years of age, including Negroes, were legally entitled to vote. In the 1870s approximately 30 percent of the registered voters in Birmingham city elections were black; and in the 1880s, from 45 to 48 percent. But in 1888 local white politicians established an all-white city Democratic primary to shut out Negroes, and in 1901 Alabama adopted a new constitution which used literacy and property requirements and a poll tax of $1.50 per year to disfranchise most Negroes.[2]

The advocates of Negro disfranchisement pledged publicly that the 1901 constitution would not disfranchise lower class whites, but many conservatives hoped privately that it would. Exact measurement of white disfranchisement is difficult, but Jefferson County voter participation data are suggestive. The percentage of Jefferson County white males over twenty-one who voted for governor or sheriff in all-white Democratic primaries was 59.0 in 1891, 40.1 in 1896 (when the real fight, with higher turnout, occurred in the general election), and 60.4 in 1900. After 1901 the percentages dropped to 25.4 in 1902, 29.2 in 1906, 33.7 in 1910, 38.1 in 1914, and 27.0 in 1918. Whether the 1901 constitution caused the drop in white-voter participation, and whether the decline occurred mainly among the poor and uneducated, is not certain. But the voting requirements, by their very nature, discriminated against the poor and uneducated, making it relatively more diffi-

2. Malcolm Cook McMillan, *Constitutional Development in Alabama, 1798–1901: A Study in Politics, the Negro, and Sectionalism* (Chapel Hill: Univ. of North Carolina Press, 1955), 201, 223, 255, 267–69; Birmingham *Iron Age*, Jan. 7, 1875, Nov. 15, Dec. 6, 1876, Nov. 23, 1882, Dec. 4, 1884, Nov. 25, Dec. 9, 1886; Birmingham *Weekly Independent*, Dec. 4, 1880; *News*, Nov. 9, 15, 16, Dec. 1, 4, 1888, May 1, 1899; Birmingham *Age-Herald*, Oct. 22, 1890.

cult for them to qualify as voters and burdening the lower-ranking interest groups with an undemocratic handicap.[3]

MAYORS AND ALDERMEN

Most of the nineteen mayors of Birmingham between 1871 and 1953 were businessmen who had worked their way up from small beginnings in Birmingham, and most, when elected, were affiliated with middle-ranking economic-interest groups, groups which stood in the top 20 percent of the population. No mayor came from the major upper-ranking manufacturing, mining, utility, or banking firms, the top 1 percent of the population, and no member of these firms ever even ran for mayor. On the other hand, only one mayor belonged to a lower-ranking group when elected. He was retail grocer David J. Fox (1893–1895), and Fox's grocery, rated between $10,000 and $20,000 by the Dun Company, was much larger than the typical grocery, which rated below $1,000.[4]

3. McMillan, *Constitutional Development*, 255, 266–69, 340–59. Number of male whites over twenty-one from U.S. Census, *Eleventh Census, 1890*, I, *Population*, Pt. 1, 754; *Thirteenth Census, 1910, Statistics for Alabama*, 603 (gives data for 1900 and 1910); *Fourteenth Census, 1920*, III, *Population*, 62; county election returns from *Age-Herald*, Dec. 31, 1891, Aug. 16, 1918; Birmingham *State Herald*, Apr. 19, 1896; *News*, Apr. 17, 1900, Aug. 29, 1902, Aug. 31, 1906, Apr. 5, 1910, Apr. 8, 1914.

4. Information on the mayors was compiled from *Birmingham City Directory* for 1883, 1887–1953; Birmingham, Alabama, Library Board and Works Progress Administration, "Alabama Biography: An Index to Biographical Sketches of Individual Alabamians in State, Local and to Some Extent in National Collections," TS, 1956, BPL; W.F. Teeple and N. Davis Smith (publishers), *Jefferson County and Birmingham, Alabama: Historical and Biographical* (Birmingham, 1887); Ethel Armes, *The Story of Coal and Iron in Alabama* (Birmingham, 1910); Birmingham *Ledger* (publisher), *The Book of Birmingham and Alabama* (Birmingham, 1914); George M. Cruikshank, *A History of Birmingham and its Environs: A Narrative Account of Their Historical Progress, Their People, and Their Principal Interests*, 2 vols. (Chicago, 1920); Lewis Publishing Company (publisher), *Birmingham* (Chicago, 1920); Thomas McAdory Owen, *History of Alabama and Dictionary of Alabama Biography*, 4 vols. (Chicago, 1921); John R. Hornady, *The Book of Birmingham* (New York, 1921); Blue Book Publishing Company (publishers), *Alabama Blue Book and Social Register* (Birmingham, 1929); Albert Burton Moore, *History of Alabama* (University: Univ. of Alabama, 1943); Florence Hawkins Wood Moss, *Building Birmingham and Jefferson County* (Birmingham, 1947); *Who's Who in America* for 1930–1953; R.G. Dun & Company, *Reference Book (And Key) Containing Ratings of Merchants, Manufacturers and Traders Generally, Throughout the United States & Canada* (New York, Jan. volumes, 1880–1920).

Table 4.1   The Mayors of Birmingham, 1871–1953

YEARS	MAYOR	OCCUPATION	RELIGION
1871–73	Robert H. Henley	Attorney, editor	n/a
1873–75	James R. Powell	Pres., Elyton Land Co.	Presb.
1875–78	William H. Morris (resigned, leaving unexpired term)	Merchant	n/a
1878–79	Henry M. Caldwell (appointed to fill unexpired term)	Pres., Elyton Land Co.	Presb.
1879–83	Thomas Jeffers	Merchant, lumber & coal	n/a
1883–89	Alexander O. Lane	Attorney	Presb.
1889–91	B. Asbury Thompson	Broker (former city treas.)	n/a
1891–93	Alexander O. Lane	Attorney	Presb.
1893–95	David J. Fox	Grocer	Presb.
1895–97	James A. Van Hoose	Wholesale grocer	Epis.
1897–99	Frank V. Evans	Broker (former city treas.)	Presb.
1899–1905	Walter M. Drennen	Merchant, dept. store	Meth.
1905–09	George B. Ward	Investment broker	Epis.
1909–10	Frank P. O'Brien (died in office)	Retired contractor	Cath.
1910	Harry Jones (filled unexpired term)	Head salesman, wholesale hardware co.	n/a
1910–13	Culpepper Exum	Mfg., fertilizer co.	Baptist
1913–17	George B. Ward	Investment broker	Epis.
1917–21	Nathaniel A. Barrett	Physician	Baptist
1921–25	David E. McLendon	County tax assessor	Meth.
1925–40	James M. Jones	Contractor, warehouseman	Meth.
1940–53	W. Cooper Green	Birmingham postmaster	Meth.

n/a Not available.

During three of Birmingham's first eight years the president of the founding Elyton Land Company doubled as mayor of the fledgling city. But in 1878 former Elyton president James R. Powell, seeking another term as mayor, met a tide of anti-Elyton sentiment and went down to bitter defeat. Never again was any city official or candidate so clearly connected with the Elyton company.[5]

5. *Iron Age*, Dec. 10, 17, 1874, Nov. 20, 1878; *Weekly Independent*, Jan. 4, Feb. 1, 8, 1879; Montgomery *Advertiser*, Jan. 26, 1879.

Instead, the mayors were typically young, aggressive downtown business or professional men who had demonstrated administrative skill by nurturing their own small firms to prominent success. From 1878 until 1940 every mayor but one had first arrived in Birmingham between his twenty-first and thirty-third birthdays, most of them coming from rural or small-town Alabama or from nearby southern states to seek their fortunes in the booming new industrial city. Three had started in Birmingham as industrial wage earners and had climbed into independent business positions. All the others had begun modestly in either the professions or small business and had quickly attained success. Most were relatively young when first elected mayor: four were in their thirties, seven in their forties, three in their fifties, and only one in his sixties. The median age when elected was 42.5.[6]

Between 1875 and 1921 the men who ran for mayor and lost were similar in background and economic affiliation to the men who won. Indeed, five of the winners also ran and lost at least once. Counting each man once for each race he entered, there were twenty-two winners, 95 percent of them from middle-ranking interest groups, and thirty-eight losers, 87 percent from middle groups. No winners came from upper-ranking groups, and only one, a grocer, from a lower-ranking group. Three losers were from upper-ranking groups, but none from major firms or corporations. Two were small savings bank presidents, and one was president of the small Birmingham Gas Company in 1888, before the days of utility consolidation. Two losers, a prolabor attorney and the founder of the local Musician's Union, represented the wage earners.[7]

The most common political stepping stone to the mayor's office was the board of aldermen, consisting of eight to thirty-two men elected from four to sixteen wards. Eight of the eleven mayors between 1878 and 1911 had first served on the board of aldermen, where they had established reputations for competence in handling city business. And the board of aldermen, like the office of mayor, was dominated by men from the top 20 percent of the population, men in the middle-ranking economic-interest groups. As Table 4.2 shows, during the forty years of the aldermanic regime, 1871 to 1911, middle-ranking groups supplied from one-half to two-thirds of the aldermen. Newspapers frequently intoned that the businesslike aldermanic tasks of preparing

6. Biographical information compiled from the sources cited in note 4.

7. Compiled from newspaper primary election returns and from the sources cited in n. 4.

Table 4.2 Economic Interest Group Rank of Birmingham Aldermen and City Commissioners, 1871–1950

| | ALDERMEN | | | | | CITY COMMISSIONERS | | | |
	1871–1879	1880–1888	1888–1898	1899–1910	1911–1920	1921–1930	1930–1940	1940–1950
Upper-ranking groups	7%	22%	20%	15%	15%	0%	0%	0%
Middle-ranking groups	68	53	50	68	85	91	100	100
Lower-ranking groups	12	25	30	14	0	9	0	0
Rank not known	12	0	0	3	0	0	0	0
Total	99	100	100	100	100	100	100	100
	(N=41)	(N=32)	(N=60)	(N=79)	(N=13)	(N=11)	(N=6)	(N=9)

Each election was counted separately, and men who were reelected were counted once for each election they won.
Source: See n. 4, p. 59.

budgets, contracting for city improvements, and enfranchising utilities should be handled by businessmen, "whose success in life has proven their fitness for a proper solution of the problems." And the dominance of businessmen among aldermen indicates that such ideas were widely accepted by voters.[8]

In aldermanic politics the lower-ranking groups, which embraced the lower 80 percent of the population, were always underrepresented on the board. They fared best in the late 1880s and early 1890s, when they supplied from one-fourth to one-third of the aldermen, but after 1898 their proportion declined as that of the middle-ranking groups rose. One reason was that before 1896 all aldermen were elected at large, though each was designated to represent a specific ward. Candidates for mayor customarily published "kite-tail" tickets containing one aldermanic candidate from each ward, balancing the ticket carefully between businessmen and workers. And mayors usually carried their entire ticket into office. But in 1895 a new law provided that voters in each ward would vote only for their own alderman, and by 1899 "kite-tail" tickets had disappeared, leaving each ward's candidates to run independently. Thereafter, fewer workingmen ran for office, and of those who did run, a smaller percentage won. Perhaps they lacked the prominence to run unsupported by a ticket; they may also have been hurt by the decline in voter participation after the 1901 constitution imposed the poll tax. The upper-ranking groups also won a smaller percentage of the seats after 1899, though they became candidates nearly as frequently as before. Perhaps their ability to attract votes declined when they were not on tickets that balanced them with workingmen.[9]

The cleavages in Birmingham mayoral and aldermanic politics did not usually follow economic-interest-group lines or political party lines; rather, increasingly from the early 1890s until 1911, they followed social-interest-group lines. Ethnicity and religion defined the social cleavage, and political conflict focused on the moral-cultural issues of the control of saloons and vice and the legal observance of Sundays. Neither election campaigns nor aldermanic voting patterns pitted economic interest groups or classes against one another or focused on economic class issues. With the partial exception of 1892, there were no significant workingmen's slates nor businessmen's slates, and only on rare occasions did campaigns produce economic class rhetoric. As Table

8. *Iron Age*, Oct. 5, 1882.
9. *Age-Herald*, Mar. 26, 1892, Nov. 13, Dec. 5, 6, 1894, Mar. 30, 1899.

4.3 shows, between 1888 and 1911 the defeated candidates for aldermen were collectively very similar to the successful candidates in their economic-interest-group affiliations, and this was true election by election as well. Opposing slates were often mirror images of each other, and opposing candidates from individual wards were often from the same economic group. Except for 1892, had the results of every aldermanic election been exactly reversed, it would have made little difference in the economic-interest-group representation on the board of aldermen.

Nor did Birmingham have competing local political parties. Like most Southern whites after Reconstruction, Birmingham whites affiliated overwhelmingly with the Democratic party. Republican Negro voters figured significantly in some elections in the 1880s and 1890s, but in local contests they usually aligned themselves with Democratic factions, and the Republican party did not become a significant organizing force in local politics. Nor did the fairly clear-cut factional divisions in the Alabama state Democratic party between Jeffersonian Democrats (Populists) and Conservatives, or between Silver and Gold Democrats, carry over consistently into city factions.[10] Rather, the competition in city elections was structured mainly by locally-oriented factions and leaders. Factional alignments often shifted rapidly, and in some periods they were shaped mainly by the personalities and cliques of leaders and by the mayors' pattern of awarding crucial aldermanic committee chairmanships.

Still, starting in the 1870s, several persistent issues helped to structure loose alignments of voters, candidates, and aldermen. In the 1870s two opposing factions aligned partially as pro-Elyton and anti-Elyton forces, but in addition they exuberantly dubbed one another respectively the "Puritans" and "the little whiskey ring." The Birmingham *Iron Age*, which sided with the Puritans, asked in 1877, "Why is it ... that every time a member of any of our churches offers for a municipal office, he is assailed with so much bitterness by some of the saloon keepers?" Further, the factions habitually charged each other with seeking, and making dishonorable deals to win, the Negro vote. In the late 1870s the so-called "whiskey ring," whose mayors and aldermen were actually respectable merchants, was probably more successful in winning Negro votes.[11]

10. See, for example, *Age-Herald*, July 6, 1892, on the expedient switch of the supporters of mayoral candidate David J. Fox from the Reuben F. Kolb to the Thomas G. Jones state faction.
11. *Iron Age*, Mar. 28, 1877. See also *ibid.*, Aug. 8, 1877, Dec. 6, 1876; Montgomery *Advertiser*, Jan. 26, 1879.

Table 4.3 Economic Interest Group Affiliation of Winning and Losing Candidates for Alderman, 1888–1910

Interest Group	1888–1898			1899–1910		
	Winners	Losers	Total Candidates	Winners	Losers	Total Candidates
UPPER:						
Iron	2%	0%	1%	1%	0%	1%
Utilities	2	1	1	1	5	3
Railroads	2	1	1	0	2	1
Banks	12	8	9	5	2	4
Mfg., metal	0	1	1	1	2	2
Coal Mining	3	2	3	6	1	4
(Subtotal)	(20)	(13)	(16)	(15)	(13)	(14)
MIDDLE:						
Real Estate	3	4	4	5	7	6
Contractors	3	7	5	3	6	4
Mfg., non-metal	3	7	5	6	5	5
Merchants	28	24	26	32	30	30
Professionals	12	9	10	23	15	19
(Subtotal)	(50)	(50)	(50)	(68)	(62)	(65)
LOWER:						
Saloonkeepers	8	3	5	5	7	6
Grocers	2	9	6	4	2	3
Artisans	0	2	1	0	3	2
Wage earners	20	18	19	5	10	8
(Subtotal)	(30)	(33)	(32)	(14)	(23)	(19)
UNKNOWN:						
Total	0	4	3	3	2	2
Total	100	100	101	100	100	100
	(N=60)	(N=92)	(N=152)	(N=79)	(N=87)	(N=166)

Because of rounding to the nearest percent, some columns do not add exactly to the subtotals shown.
Source: See n. 4, p. 59.

During the next decade, as Birmingham's industries took hold, bringing prosperity and growth, one man, Mayor Alexander O. Lane (1883–1889, 1891–1893), dominated city politics. He made vigorous improvements in city services and twice won overwhelming two-to-one reelection victories over opponents of similar background who could make no effective criticism of his record. Lane, an able attorney and a staunch Presbyterian, demanded strict law enforcement, but he had no sympathy with blue law piety or prohibition. His even-handed policy and firm, fair administration won respect on all sides and suppressed quarrels between "whiskey ring" and "Puritan" elements. He drew heavy support from white workingmen as well as businessmen. Moreover, Negro voters, praising his "fairness and justice," supported him strongly, and his broad popularity among whites neutralized the black vote as an issue.[12]

Lane epitomized the successful young middle-ranking men who would dominate the mayor's office for decades. The son of a small-town physician in rural Barbour County in southern Alabama, Lane attended and then taught in his hometown high school and studied law in the office of a family friend. Gaining admittance to the bar, he practiced law one year in a neighboring rural county; then in 1872, at age twenty-five, with only "limited means," he moved 150 miles upstate to the new Magic City of Birmingham. Within two years he entered a partnership with a leading senior lawyer, Colonel John T. Terry, and married the colonel's daughter. The law firm prospered, becoming associated with local merchants and realtors, and giving young Lane the prominence to launch a successful political career in 1882.[13]

In 1888 Lane declined to seek reelection, and political turbulence set in for a decade. The leading mayoral contenders, hoping to prevent the Negro vote from becoming a potent factor or an issue, organized Birmingham's first white Democratic party primary. The primary nominated B. Asbury Thompson, a carpenter's son who in Birmingham had risen from carpenter to iron works' foreman to city treasurer. In the general election Thompson turned back, by a two-to-one majority, the first and last Republican party challenge.[14] Thereafter in every election year through 1910 the white Democrats held a city primary, each pri-

12. *Iron Age*, Nov. 25, 1886. See also *ibid.*, Nov. 27, Dec. 4, 1884, Dec. 2, 9, 1886.
13. *Ibid.*, Sept. 4, 1884.
14. *News*, Nov. 2, 9, 15, 16, Dec. 1, 4, 1888; *Age-Herald*, Dec. 5, 1888.

mary organized by a City Democratic Executive Committee that had been elected in the preceding primary.

From 1888 to 1892 factions dissolved and shifted chaotically. Then in 1892 mayoral candidate David J. Fox, an alderman, enterprisingly mobilized a majority of the executive committee to call a surprise early primary (catching opponents unprepared) and to appoint mostly Fox men to be poll clerks and managers. Fox won handily, aided, allegedly, by wholesale ballot stuffing, and the executive committee, rebuffing witnesses who reported frauds, declared him the Democratic nominee.[15]

An irate "Citizens' Committee" and a "Citizens' League" proclaimed an independent ticket to oppose Fox in the 1892 general election, but they soon realized that their move was too late, and they withdrew, leaving Fox unopposed. Once Fox took office, however, the Citizens' League leaders plagued him with criticism, especially when his patronage "machine" awarded several of his executive committee supporters with city jobs. And Citizens' League leaders were instrumental in getting the state legislature to create a new separate police commission, stacked with Fox opponents, to appoint and control policemen, depriving a bitterly disappointed Fox of that patronage.[16]

The events of 1892 gave rise to a new more consistent factional alignment. In 1894 Fox chose his close ally Robert Warnock, the city tax collector, to succeed him, and he had the loyal executive committee call another early primary. The Citizens' League leaders, meanwhile, had created the Municipal Democratic Club, which boycotted the primary, allowing Warnock to be nominated unopposed. Then in the general election the Municipal Club fielded a Citizens' Reform ticket headed by James A. Van Hoose, who claimed to represent the "Best Element."[17]

Van Hoose had come to Birmingham at age twenty-four as pastor of the downtown Episcopal Church of the Advent, but because of poor eyesight he had given up the ministry in favor of a career as successful wholesale grocer and promoter of civic causes. He promised a "strictly business administration," opposed partisan patronage, and denounced "frauds upon the ballot." He especially pledged himself to clean up vice and to close saloons on Sundays, announcing that he personally

15. *News*, Sept. 2, 1890; *Age-Herald*, Feb. 25, Mar. 26, 29, 30, 31, Apr. 26, 1892.
16. *Age-Herald*, Nov. 15, 16, 17, 1892, Jan. 5, Mar. 7, 1893; *News*, Jan. 21, 1898; Alabama, *Acts, 1892–1893*, pp. 177–79.
17. *Age-Herald*, Feb. 22, Mar. 20, 25, 1894.

would sit as city court judge and would go "into every nook and crook and hole" and "prowl around the streets at night" to ferret out vice. Pastors urged the "good citizens" to mobilize behind the reform effort, while the regular Democrats warned that Van Hoose would "close the barrooms and open prayer meetings." The Irish Democratic Club and the German Citizens' Club, opposing blue law piety, voted near-ly unanimously to cast their several hundred votes for the regular Democrats.[18]

One other issue stirred great interest. Van Hoose candidly sought the Negro vote, speaking at large Negro rallies, promising a "fair and square ballot," effectively urging blacks to use their votes to help break up the city Democratic primary system that had shut them out of city elections. The Democrats, in response, recalled "the horrors of reconstruction and negro domination."[19]

On election day the white voters divided almost evenly, but the Negroes, with 37 percent of the registered voters, went solidly for Van Hoose, who won with 69 percent of the total vote, and presided over city government for the next two years.[20]

In 1896, at the end of one term, the Citizens dropped Van Hoose and nominated savings' bank president Christian F. Enslen for mayor. The 1896 election was largely a rematch between the coalitions of 1894, except that some Negro leaders, expressing "much disappointment" in the Van Hoose administration, switched to the Democratic nominee, Frank V. Evans, who openly welcomed their support and spoke at their rallies. Evans and the Democratic ticket won, receiving an estimated 60 percent of the white vote and 33 percent of the Negro vote. The defeated Citizens' Reform movement never again fielded a ticket against the nominees of the Democratic primaries, and the black vote disappeared as a factor and an issue. But the other issues and alignments generated by the Citizens' movement persisted as major factors within the Democratic primaries.[21]

The Citizens' movement, despite its business rhetoric and its claim to represent the "Best Element," had not polarized aldermanic politics sharply along class- or economic-interest-group lines, nor had it monopolized the support of businessmen. In the 1892, 1894, and 1896 elections combined, the Democratic and Citizen aldermanic tickets

18. *Ibid.*, Mar. 23, Apr. 1, June 5, Nov. 13, 15, 16, 20, 1894.
19. *Ibid.*, Nov. 25, Dec. 1, 1894. See also *ibid.*, Nov. 16, 20, 1894.
20. *Ibid.*, Dec. 5, 6, 1894.
21. *State Herald*, Oct. 7, Nov. 13, 14, 15, Nov. 24, 25, 28, Dec. 2, 1896; *News*, Nov. 20, Dec. 2, 1896.

were quite similar in economic-group representation. The Democrats nominated seven candidates from upper-ranking groups; the Citizens, five; the Democrats nominated sixteen from middle-ranking groups, the Citizens twenty. Only at the lower-ranking level did they diverge, with the Democrats nominating thirteen; the Citizens, seven. Among the lower-ranking candidates, nine wage earners were nominated by Democrats, only two by Citizens, and four saloonkeepers were nominated, all by Democrats, while five small retail grocers were nominated, all by the Citizens. Published lists of campaign committees showed both factions drawing similar portions of supporters from the upper- and middle-ranking groups, but Democrats drawing twice as many supporters from the lower-ranking groups, including twelve saloonkeepers who unanimously supported the Democrats.[22]

Social-interest-group membership and social rather than economic issues aligned most lower-ranking aldermanic candidates with the Democrats. All but three lower-ranking Democrats were listed as officers of either the German or the Irish political clubs. Three owned saloons, and another was the master mechanic in the local Schillinger brewery. Ethnic minorities were also represented on Democratic tickets by two Jews of middle economic rank. By contrast the Citizens' tickets included only two men of ethnic minority background, one a German merchant who had joined the Presbyterian church, and the other a German Baptist banker. Both men were exceptions that confirmed the pattern; their evangelical Protestant religious affiliation, rather rare among Birmingham Germans, ranged the two with the anti-saloon Citizens' faction, in sharp contrast to the vast majority of their countrymen. In 1896 the German Baptist banker, Christian F. Enslen, became the Citizens' candidate for mayor and went before the German-American Union to seek its support. The union heard him politely; but noting that it had placed two members, both saloonkeepers, on the Democratic aldermanic ticket, it voted unanimously to support the Democrats.[23]

During Mayor James A. Van Hoose's two-year Citizens' administration (1894–1896), the only issue consistently to align Citizens' aldermen against Democratic aldermen was a new tighter saloon-regulation proposal, sponsored by Van Hoose and a delegation of Baptist, Methodist, and Presbyterian ministers from the Birmingham Pastors' Union.

---

22. *Age-Herald*, Mar. 29, Nov. 15, 17, 24, 1892, Mar. 10, Apr. 7, Nov. 13, 14, 17, 1894; *State Herald*, Oct. 7, Nov. 12, 26, 1896; *News*, Nov. 10, 30, 1896; *Birmingham City Directory* for 1892, 1894, 896.

23. *State Herald*, Nov. 12, 1896.

Van Hoose and the Citizens controlled only a minority on the board of aldermen, and the majority Democrats, solid against the measure, defeated it. In 1896 Citizens' mayoral candidate Enslen, who had supported the saloon-regulation proposal, made it a major issue, asking "Why does Mr. Evans lead a ticket on which are three saloonkeepers and four men who voted openly for liquor" despite "the protest of the clergy?"[24]

No other issue created an even vaguely consistent Citizens'-Democratic split among aldermen. Both factions, for example, opposed a waterworks-company proposal to sell its plant to the city, because both found the price exorbitant. In December 1894 the bulk of both factions voted to perpetuate unchanged the regressive street tax of three dollars per adult male, a tax which labor unions fervently sought to reduce or abolish. The potentially class-oriented issue of school tuition came before the board of education rather than the aldermen, and three Democrats on the board reluctantly voted for elementary school tuition, while two Citizens opposed it. Elementary school tuition, which labor unions denounced, was actually imposed only once, in 1897, under the Democratic Evans administration. Finally, on the issue of convict labor, the Democrats charged in 1896 that Citizens' mayoral candidate Enslen planned, despite his firm denials, to begin leasing city convicts to coal-mining corporations, a program that would be an anathema to organized labor. Six months later the city did begin such a lease, upon the initiative not of Enslen but of Democratic Mayor Evans. In short, on the economic or potentially class-oriented issues before the board of aldermen, the regular Democrats, though they included more wage earners, were no stronger than the Citizens in supporting the goals of wage earners.[25]

After 1896 the Citizens' Reform organization faded away, but within the city Democratic primaries two much more loosely organized factions—the "Moral Element" and the "Liberal Element"—continued through 1921 to focus on the moral-cultural issues of saloons and Sundays and to provide some continuity of alignment and leadership. Leading the Moral Element, which often called itself the "Better Element," was the Birmingham Pastors' Union, aided by the Women's Christian Temperance Union, the Young People's Christian Union, the Christian

24. *News*, Nov. 27, 1896. See also *State Herald*, Dec. 31, 1895, Feb. 20, 1896.
25. On the waterworks, see *Age-Herald*, Nov. 13, 15, 1894. On the street tax, see *ibid.*, Dec. 27, 1894; *News*, Nov. 27, 1896. On tuition, see *Age-Herald*, Dec. 28, 1894; *News*, Feb. 19, 1897. On convict labor, see *News*, Nov. 27, 1896, Apr. 8, July 8, 1897.

Endeavor Union, and after 1906, the Anti-Saloon League. The Moral Element drew its support mainly from the more "pietistic," or evangelical, Birmingham churches, especially the Methodist, Baptist, and Presbyterian congregations. These congregations emphasized evangelism and the personal conversion experience, and they affirmed that personal religious belief should result in a life of pure moral behavior and in a concern for improving the morals of society. They placed less emphasis on formal creeds, liturgy, and church ceremony. In local politics their chief concern was to use the power of local government to enforce their moral precepts concerning vice, gambling, saloons, and Sunday observance.[26]

The Liberal Element, denouncing "Political Parsons," advocated the "orderly saloon," but opposed stricter regulation or Sunday blue laws. In 1902 the German-language Birmingham *Courier* reminded its readers that these were "Questions of greatest significance" which "affect you, the entire liberal citizenship, your children, and your manner of living [*Lebensweise*]." The Liberal Element drew strong support from other ethnic political groups such as the Irish Democratic Club, from many businessmen who deplored moralistic governmental meddling into business of any kind, and from Birmingham's more "liturgical," or ritualistic, churches, especially the Roman Catholics, Lutherans, Greek Orthodox Catholics, and Jews, and to some extent also the Episcopalians and some strongly calvinistic Presbyterians. The liturgical congregations emphasized formal creeds, liturgies, and sacraments, downplayed revivalism and emotional piety, and opposed state interference in matters of public morality.[27]

In 1906 a religious census revealed that, within the boundaries of pre-1910 Birmingham, the Moral- and Liberal-oriented religious groups were quite evenly balanced. Liberal-oriented Roman Catholic, Jewish, Greek Orthodox, German Evangelical, and German Lutheran congre-

26. *State Herald*, Dec. 31, 1895; *Age-Herald*, Mar. 4, May 4, Aug. 30, 1899; *News*, Dec. 5, 1900, May 6, Oct. 25, 1907, Oct. 19, 1915. This delineation of the religious traditions that supported the Moral and Liberal Elements has been informed by the perceptive analysis of Paul Kleppner, *The Cross of Culture: A Social Analysis of Midwestern Politics, 1850–1900* (New York and London: Free Press, 1970), 69–91, and Richard Jensen, *The Winning of the Midwest: Social and Political Conflict, 1888–1896* (Chicago and London: Univ. of Chicago Press, 1971), 58–68. Kleppner and Jensen distinguished between "pietistic" and "liturgical" (or "ritualistic") religious outlooks and argued that these divergent perspectives were basic to political conflict in the late-nineteenth-century Midwest.

27. Birmingham *Courier*, Nov. 13, 1902; *Age-Herald*, Nov. 16, Dec. 2, 1894, May 27, 1899; *State Herald*, Nov. 12, Dec. 2, 1896; *News*, Mar. 26, 1898, Jan. 24, Oct. 13, 1908; *Labor Advocate*, July 27, 1918.

gations together had 43.1 percent of white church members. Moral-oriented Methodist, Baptist, Presbyterian, Adventist, Congregationalist, and Disciples of Christ congregations had 50.1 percent of white church members. Episcopalians, with 6.2 percent of white members, tended to divide between the two, or to sway from one side to the other, favoring some Moral Element reforms but mostly opposing complete prohibition of saloons. Thus the Episcopalians and some less pietistic, antiprohibitionist Presbyterians, such as former mayor Alexander Lane, occupied the middle ground. This may have been one reason why Episcopalians and Presbyterians supplied so many mayors under the aldermanic regime.[28]

The Moral and Liberal elements were not quasi-political parties and did not provide rudimentary two-party competition. Although many local politicians aligned themselves definitely with one camp or the other, few actually bore the labels "Moral" or "Liberal" like party names, and some successful politicians skillfully posed as moderates, straddling the two, while others switched from one to the other when shifts in the balance of voters in their wards made it expedient. The two camps were indeed, as the contemporary term "element" implied, loose but persistent social-interest-group coalitions which provided the basic building blocks of city politics. As specific issues and personalities changed from one election to the next, the balance between the elements ebbed and flowed, and occasionally a nonmoral issue would temporarily derange the line between the elements. But only around the Moral and Liberal poles did local political currents persistently swirl.

From 1899 until the end of the aldermanic regime in 1911, the decisive city election was always the Democratic party primary, perfunctorily ratified in uncontested general elections. In 1899 Walter M. Drennen, son of a respected family that had moved to Birmingham in 1880 and built a $2,000 dry goods business into a five-story downtown department store, won the mayoral primary, defeating the incumbent Evans administration's handpicked candidate. Drennen, a Methodist but no blue-law enthusiast, shrewdly preempted the middle ground between the Moral and Liberal Elements, much as Alexander O. Lane had done in the 1880s. He promised to be much more vigilant than the incumbent Evans faction in enforcing existing saloon regulations, but he explicitly rejected a controversial new Pastors' Union proposal to close all saloons and allow liquor to be sold only by government-owned package-liquor dispensaries. On all other issues Drennen and the Evans candidate es-

28. U.S. Census, *Religious Bodies: 1906*, Pt. 1, 380–407.

sentially agreed, both fervently advocating better schools, lower license taxes, and more public improvements.[29]

Drennen won with 58 percent of the vote, but his board of aldermen, including many holdovers, leaned heavily to the Evans faction. Drennen, however, shrewdly distributed coveted committee chairmenships to flexible aldermen and soon gained control over patronage; and he worked smoothly with the board in building schools and a new city hall, paving streets, setting license taxes, determining budgets, and making appropriations. Only questions of disciplining the police who enforced saloon regulations divided the board along factional lines, and Drennen, holding to his middle ground and establishing a good record as an effective administrator, easily won reelection twice and served until 1905.[30]

During these years the City Democratic Executive Committee, composed of two members elected from each ward in each primary, was usually weighted toward the Liberal Element, but it established a tradition of fairness in setting primary dates, establishing rules and procedures for registration of Democratic voters, designating polling places, appointing polling managers and clerks, and supervising the vote count. The committee members elected in one primary seldom met until time to organize the next primary, two years later, and they did not function as a policy- or strategy-formulating group for the party or for any faction. Mayors and influential aldermen, rather than the committeemen, were the key factional leaders and strategists.[31]

During the six-year Drennen administration the continuing Moral-Liberal conflict focused primarily on a controversial police chief, Conrad W. Austin. Austin became chief in 1899 as a compromise dark-horse candidate appointed by a sharply divided police commission, but he quickly emerged as a moral crusader. Within weeks he had arrested, but failed to convict, a German newspaper editor and restaurant owner for selling beer on Sunday, and he had infiltrated alderman Sylvester Daly's Rolling Mill Saloon with a spy whose evidence led to the conviction of Daly's bartenders for selling beer on Sunday. An outraged Daly sought to disband the police commission, return the police department to the control of the aldermen, and depose Austin, but the commission and Austin survived. Austin's predecessor had averaged 8

---

29. *Age-Herald*, Jan. 15, Mar. 2, 3, 4, Apr. 4, 1899, Feb. 13, 1903; *News*, Mar. 24, 1900; *Labor Advocate*, Nov. 30, 1901.

30. *Age-Herald*, Apr. 7, May 18, 21, Aug. 9, 10, Sept. 8, 19, 20, 21, 1899, Jan. 1, Dec. 6, 1901, Mar. 3, 1903.

31. *Ibid.*, Jan. 1, 1901, Sept. 29, 1910; *News*, Jan. 18, 19, 25, 1907, June 19, July 21, 1908.

Sunday-law convictions per year, but in Austin's first year he arrested 142 and convicted 70 persons for Sunday violations, and he instituted vigilant raids on gambling rooms.[32]

In the 1900 Democratic primary the position of police chief, on the ballot for the first time, attracted more attention than all others. Two candidates with Liberal ties entered the race, each refusing to step aside, and Austin, supported by Moral Element leaders who urged churchmen to "vote as you pray," was reelected with a 42.1 percent plurality. He thereupon intensified his crusades and overreached himself, alienating many moderates and antagonizing many rank and file policemen. By 1903 Liberals and moderates united on a respected, noncontroversial police captain, William E. Wier, and elected him over Austin, whose vote dropped to 34.1 percent.[33]

By the next primary in late 1904 attention shifted to the race for a successor to Mayor Drennen, who did not seek reelection. Drennen endorsed a fellow merchant, but he lost to alderman George B. Ward, an able and dynamic young investment broker. Ward campaigned on a "good government" platform and he quickly built a reputation as an energetic, honest, progressive executive of the Theodore Roosevelt type. Continuing a trend begun by Drennen, he promoted stricter regulation and heavier taxation of utilities; he greatly increased the use of professional experts in health, sanitation, and inspection departments; and he launched cleanup and beautification drives.[34] Aldermen supported these reforms almost unanimously, but they divided sharply and blocked the one reform effort on which Mayor Ward, an Episcopalian, focused most intently: much stricter regulation (but not prohibition) of saloons. Seeking reelection in 1907, Ward declared: "The question is squarely before the people of Birmingham as to whether liquor interests and the sporting element shall gain control of your city government or whether conservative, law abiding citizens shall continue in possession."[35]

The Liberal Element resolutely challenged Mayor Ward, running their most prominent and respected leader, former sheriff and state legislator Frank P. O'Brien. O'Brien, an Irish Roman Catholic, had fought for the Confederacy and had cast his lot with infant Birmingham

32. *Age-Herald*, May 5, 6, 15, 17, Sept. 19, 20, 21, Oct. 6, 10, 1899; *News*, Dec. 24, 1900.

33. *News*, Dec. 5, 10, 1900; *Age-Herald*, Jan. 1, 1901, Feb. 6, 19, 22, Mar. 3, 8, 1903; *Labor Advocate*, Feb. 21, 28, 1903.

34. *Age-Herald*, Nov. 2, 17, 19, 20, 22, 23, 1904; *News*, Jan. 29, 1907.

35. *News*, Feb. 2, 1907. See also *ibid.*, July 6, Aug. 14, 1905, Aug. 8, 16, Dec. 6, 1906.

in 1871, gaining local renown as the contractor who built the first courthouse and rolling mill and as the proprietor of an opera house. Saloonkeepers heavily financed O'Brien's campaign, while the Pastors' Union crusaded for Mayor Ward.[36]

Mayor Ward won with a bare 51.7 percent majority, and thereupon he and the Pastors' Union proposed to restrict saloons to a narrow, heavily-policed, central saloon district and to charge them drastically higher license fees. During the summer of 1907 a determined majority of aldermen repeatedly defeated the proposal, provoking Mayor Ward to remove three of the opponents from powerful committee chairmanships and replace them with his supporters. Thereupon the majority Liberals, acting under provisions of a new Alabama municipal code, changed the board of aldermen into an aldermanic city council. The wards and aldermen remained the same, but the mayor was no longer allowed to preside or vote in council meetings or to appoint committees, though he did have a veto. The new council elected its own president, chosen by a Liberal caucus, to preside and to appoint committee chairmen, and he promptly deposed Mayor Ward's supporters from chairmanships, relegating several to the cemetery committee.[37] Mayor Ward, fortified with a pistol and a squad of loyal policemen, entered a council meeting from which he had been banned and sought, by ejecting the new council president, to undo the reorganization. But the courts upheld the new council and the Liberal caucus remained in control of it until the end of the aldermanic regime in 1911.[38]

The eighteen aldermen involved in the tumultuous factional politics of 1907 are described in Table 4.4. They were quite typical of Birmingham aldermen from 1901 to 1909; indeed these eighteen men together filled fifty-one of the seventy-two positions available on the four two-year boards sworn in between 1901 and 1909. The pro-Ward faction was all aligned with the Moral Element. The anti-Ward faction was a coalition of eight Liberal Element men and two prohibitionists who co-operated with the Liberals to defeat saloon reform, fearing that reform might undermine growing prohibitionist sentiment.

The nine wards that elected the aldermen were not congruent with socioeconomic neighborhoods. Each ward cut across several land-use zones or types of residential area, and each had a diverse population.

36. Armes, *Story*, 237; *News*, Jan. 21, Feb. 12, 19, 1907.
37. *News*, May 1, 4, 6, Aug. 13, 21, 22, 23, 24, 30, Sept. 9, 1907; *Age-Herald*, Aug. 23, 1907; Birmingham Minutes, of the Mayor and Board of Aldermen, L, 670 (June 5, 1907), 685 (July 3, 1907).
38. *News*, Oct. 2, 3, 4, 1907, Jan. 23, 1908; *Age-Herald*, Oct. 3, 4, 1907.

Table 4.4 Aldermanic Factions in Opposition to or in Support of Mayor Ward's Saloon Reform Program, August 1907

Ward No.	Percent of Foreigners in Ward[1]	Alderman	Economic Affiliation[2]	Business Rating[3] (in thousands of dollars)	Ethnic or Religious Affiliation[4]	Vote on 1908 Street Tax[5]	Listed in 1909 Social Directory[6]
Opponents							
1	24	Richard Burnett	Mer., whlsl. cigars	75–125	Presb.	yes	yes
2	37	Simon Klotz	Mer., tailor shop	35–50	Jew/Fr.	yes	no
7	20	Charles C. Heidt	Mer., coal & lumber	35–50	Presb.	yes	no
9	23	Adolph Stockmar	Contr., bldg. supply	20–35	German	no	no
2	37	John W. O'Neill	Mer., glass & tinware	20–35	Catholic	no	no
5	14	William R. Gunn	Mer., drugstore	5–10	Presb.	yes	yes
6	12	Frederick Fulghum	Atty. (Schillinger Brew.)	—	n/a	yes/no	no
1	24	John Greener	Saloonkpr., emp. BRLP	below $500	Catholic	yes/no	no

Prohibitionists (in tactical alliance with Opposition)

7	20	John L. Parker	Mer., drugstore, florist	35–50	Presb.	—	yes
8	18	Daniel A. Hogan	Grocer	n/a	Baptist	yes	no

Supporters

8	18	Harry Jones	Mer., slsmn., whlsl. hardware	300–500	n/a	yes	yes
4	13	John R. Copeland	Mfg., mattresses, bricks	75–125	Methodist	yes	no
4	13	Walter Moore	Pres., small coal co.	20–35	n/a	no	yes
3	13	Dick R. Copeland	Mer., produce co.	10–20	Methodist	yes	no
5	14	Blucher Cooper	Mer., furniture	5–10	Presb.	no	no
9	23	George H. Estes	Mgr., life ins. co.	—	Baptist	yes	yes
3	13	Richard Eggleston	Mgr., credit assoc.	—	n/a	no	no
6	12	John C. Forney	Attorney	—	Presb.	yes/no	no

n/a Not available.

[1] U.S. Census, *Thirteenth Census,* 1910, II, *Population,* 63.
[2] *Birmingham City Directory,* 1900–1910.
[3] R. G. Dun Company, *Reference Book,* 1905, 1910.
[4] Compiled from sources cited in n. 4, p. 59.
[5] *News,* Jan. 16, Feb. 6, 20, Mar. 5, 19, Apr. 2, 16, 1908.
[6] *Social Directory* [ca. 1909], BPL.

This was especially true of Southside Wards 6, 7, 8, and 9, which were long, thin, parallel rectangles set perpendicular to the railroad tracks (see map 1). In 1895 a board of "Citizen" and "Democratic" aldermen had designed these wards to disperse the Negro vote harmlessly by stretching each ward from the Negro section near the tracks, through white working-class sections, out to the middle and upper quality residential areas on the southern highlands near Red Mountain.[39]

Such wards were too heterogeneous to permit any precise detailed correlations between election returns and population characteristics. It was roughly true, however, that the wards with the highest percentage of first- and second-generation immigrants among their white voters were most likely to choose aldermen who aligned solidly with the Liberal Element, and vice versa (see Table 4.4). This "foreign" factor provides only a partial explanation of ward voting patterns, especially since no ward had a "foreign" majority among whites, and since several other factors influenced ward voting patterns. Still, Northside Wards 1 and 2, with the highest immigrant percentages, were the traditional Liberal strongholds. During the 1890s Ward 1 had typically elected saloonkeepers or skilled workers from the nearby Birmingham Rolling Mill, and in 1907 it was represented by saloonkeeper John Greener and by former saloonkeeper Richard Burnett, who had become a major wholesale cigar dealer, but who maintained close ties with saloons, his best customers. Ward 2, with 37 percent of its whites of immigrant background, typically elected downtown merchants of immigrant heritage.[40]

During the 1890s Ward 9 had been a Liberal Element stronghold, dominated by the rolling mill district at the northern end and bossed by Sylvester Daly of the Rolling Mill Saloon. After 1900 middle-class residential tracts spread rapidly over the southern foothills of Ward 9, and, after Daly's death in 1901, Adolph Stockmar emerged as the ward's key aldermanic politician. A prosperous building contractor, Stockmar could afford to live in the southern highlands, but, as a leader in the German-American Union, he maintained ties with many rolling-mill workers. In 1907 Ward 9 revealed its changing character by electing

39. U.S. Census, *Thirteenth Census, 1910,* II, *Population,* 63; *Age-Herald,* Nov. 27, Dec. 5, 1894; *State Herald,* Nov. 24, 1896; Alabama, *Acts, 1894–1895,* pp. 841–47.

40. Biographical data on aldermen compiled from sources cited in n. 4. Clearly the occupational make-up of wards also influenced voting patterns, but the census provided no occupational breakdowns by wards. The somewhat impressionistic occupational characterizations used here are based on contemporary accounts and on the *Birmingham City Directory.*

George H. Estes, a prominent anti-saloon Baptist layman, to be Stockmar's colleague. The other long thin Southside wards, as well as Northside Ward 5, were also closely balanced by 1907, often having one alderman in each camp. Finally, the two wards most consistently electing Moral Element aldermen, Northside highlands' Wards 3 and 4, each had only 13 percent first- and second-generation immigrants among its white population, the lowest such percentage, except for Ward 6 with 12 percent.[41]

Table 4.4 ranks the businessmen in each faction according to their financial strength, revealing a marked similarity between the two factions in their balance among occupations and their distribution of financial rankings. The sharpest contrast between the factions lay, not in economic characteristics, but rather in pro- or anti-saloon alignment and in ethnic and religious characteristics. Moreover, the sharply-defined pro-Ward and anti-Ward factions did not hold together consistently on such a class-oriented issue as the street tax. In 1905 the aldermen had unanimously abolished the street tax, but in 1908, during severe city financial difficulties, an aldermanic majority, drawn from both pro- and anti-Ward factions, three times ignored labor union protest and passed a new street-tax ordinance, only to have it vetoed each time by Mayor Ward (see Table 4.4).

Only one-third of the aldermen of 1907 had climbed into Birmingham's magic inner circle of social respectability—the 600 families listed in the city's first *Social Directory* in 1909 (see Table 4.4). Since polite society in Birmingham seldom accepted ethnic minorities, several very prosperous Liberal Element aldermen were excluded, but nonetheless the anti-Ward and pro-Ward factions each had three of the socially prominent aldermen.[42]

On the 1907 board the merchants, with nine of the eighteen positions, were the largest occupational group, as they were on most other boards. Only Jones and Burnett represented the 51 most prestigious downtown department stores and wholesale firms, those rated above $50,000 by the Dun Company. And Jones was not a proprietor or partner in his wholesale firm, but rather its head traveling salesman. The other seven merchant-aldermen in 1907, and the vast majority between 1901 and 1909, came from the 202 medium-sized stores, rated between $5,000 and $50,000. No aldermen came from the bottom 59 percent of the mer-

41. *News*, Jan. 16, 1901, Feb. 19, 1907; *Age-Herald*, May 27, 1899, Nov. 23, 1904.
42. *Social Directory* (Birmingham, n.d. [c. 1909]).

chants—the 363 firms (excluding retail grocers) rated below $5,000. All the merchant-aldermen were closely connected with the Board of Trade, the major interest-group association of downtown merchants. Indeed, five aldermen—Klotz, Heidt, O'Neill, Parker, and Cooper—served as president of the Board of Trade sometime between 1900 and 1910, and Gunn and Burnett held lower offices. The largest downtown mercantile firms, though they provided few aldermen themselves, probably felt that their more politically-oriented Board of Trade colleagues adequately represented their interests on the board of aldermen.[43]

In 1907 the other middle-ranking aldermen, typical of the pattern from 1899 to 1909, included four professionals, one nonmetal manufacturer, and one contractor, all of them closely tied to the downtown commercial community. The August 1907 board contained only one member of an upper-ranking economic group—Walter Moore, president of several small coal-mining companies. Until June 1907, however, the upper-ranking groups had filled two seats, a more typical proportion. The other seat had been occupied by Henry B. Gray, president of the small People's Savings Bank and Trust Company, but Gray had resigned in midterm to become lieutenant governor of Alabama. Both Moore and Gray were typical of the few upper-ranking aldermen in that both were heads of relatively minor firms within their interest groups. The major banks, industries, mining companies, and utilities never deigned to have their presidents, managers, or corporation attorneys run for aldermen. Occasionally a lower-level official of a major firm—a paying teller of a major bank or the station master of a railroad—became an alderman, but most aldermen from the upper-ranking groups were, like Moore and Gray, heads of minor firms.

On the other hand, the few aldermen from the lower-ranking economic groups usually came from the more skilled and prosperous levels of their rank. Typical of this pattern were 1907 aldermen John Greener, a saloonkeeper, and Dan Hogan, a prosperous grocer who had graduated from local Howard College. The wage earners who became aldermen, mainly during the 1890s, were usually foremen or skilled workers at the rolling mill, the machine shops, or the railroad yards. None of Birmingham's many unorganized unskilled wage earners ever ran for alderman.

43. R.G. Dun & Company, *Reference Book* for 1900, 1905, 1910; *Age-Herald*, June 6, 1901; *News*, June 7, 1900, June 5, Aug. 12, 1905, May 23, Dec. 12, 1907, June 15, 1910.

After 1907 the anti-Ward faction remained in firm control of city politics until the end of the aldermanic regime in 1911. In October 1907, however, the saloon issue lost salience in aldermanic politics because the voters of the entire county adopted prohibition, taking liquor regulation out of the hands of aldermen and making Birmingham legally dry even though a majority of city voters opposed prohibition. In the July 1908 primary, Mayor Ward did not seek reelection, and the Liberal Element again sponsored Frank P. O'Brien. Former Mayor Walter Drennen entered the race and gained Moral Element support when he urged tighter enforcement to give prohibition a fair trial. But in July 1908 Birmingham was in the midst of a bitter coal strike, and it came to light that Drennen owned stock in a small commercial-coal company that had signed a union contract rather than fight the strike. Drennen withdrew rather than bring the strike tensions into the campaign, and O'Brien became mayor unopposed, carrying in with him city council president Harry Jones, who defeated a strong Moral Element candidate. O'Brien and Jones cooperated closely, running the council through an efficient majority caucus, rewarding friends with patronage and using control of committees to channel city contracts to favored firms and banks.[44]

When Birmingham annexed the surrounding suburbs in 1910, the council created sixteen wards represented by thirty-two aldermen, most of them merchants and professional people tied to either the downtown or the suburban commercial communities. In the 1910 primary the Liberal Element reelected Harry Jones city council president; and for mayor it selected and handily elected Culpepper Exum, a manufacturer of chemical fertilizer and, though a Baptist, a prominent antiprohibitionist. And the Liberal Element continued to dominate the council until the advent of city-commission government in April 1911.[45]

THE CITY COMMISSION

Civic reformers deplored the favoritism and patronage payoffs of the aldermanic "ring," or "city hall crowd," and they advocated changing

44. *News*, July 6, 18, 28, Nov. 5, 1908, May 20, 1909, May 27, 1910, Mar. 2, 1911. Harry Jones had formerly been an alderman in the George Ward faction, but he gave higher priority to the financial and patronage operations of key committees than to moral issues, and he had expediently switched camps.
45. *News*, Apr. 27, May 4, 27, June 21, 1910.

to a city-commission form of government, which reformers were promoting in many American cities. Walker Percy, the general counsel for the Tennessee Coal, Iron, and Railroad Company, began the Birmingham commission movement, declaring in 1907: "The aldermanic position is one of minor importance; the honor does not, as a rule, appeal to the best class of our citizens." Therefore the city should abolish the unwieldy board of aldermen and replace it with an efficient, full-time, more prestigious three-man city commission, modeled upon the plan that had originated in Galveston, Texas.[46]

Soon both the Birmingham *Age-Herald* and the Birmingham *News* endorsed the commission plan. *News* publisher Rufus N. Rhodes, a long-time civic reformer who had supported the Citizens' Reform tickets in 1894 and 1896, the saloon reform plan of Mayor Ward, and then the prohibition movement, became a prime commission advocate, arguing that Birmingham could become a model city if only it could get its "strong, high class businessmen" to run the government. The theory of commission government, said the *News*, was that "A city is a business corporation in which the taxpayers are stockholders." And the city, like a corporation, should be run by a full-time board of directors. The trouble with aldermen was that most of them "do not have the business capacity, do not give the needful time to manage the public affairs, and are not paid for their services." Hence there was "neglect, extravagance and the practice of graft." The "remedy," said the *News*, was to be found "in a business-like commission form of government by which three or four or five experienced businessmen of character are entrusted with the management of the municipal affairs, [and] are paid fair salaries." The city commissioners would combine the powers of the mayor, aldermen, and police commissioners. They would sit together as the city legislative body, but each would also administer a city department. This would centralize power and make government more decisive and efficient. It would be "a long step in the city's industrial and commercial progress as well as in its moral uplift."[47]

In late 1908 evidence of aldermanic graft undermined public confidence in the aldermen and generated sentiment for change. In 1909 the reformers introduced a city commission bill in the state legislature. It was opposed by the so-called aldermanic "ring," by the merchants in the Board of Trade, which had close ties with the aldermanic regime, by the *Labor Advocate*, which considered an aldermanic government more

46. *Ibid.*, May 27, 1910, Mar. 2, 1911; *Age-Herald*, Oct. 24, 1907.
47. *Age-Herald*, Oct. 24, 1907; *News*, Dec. 7, 18, 1908.

democratic, and by Lieutenant Governor Henry B. Gray, who helped to kill the bill in the legislature.[48]

The *News* and Percy continued their commission campaign, gaining significant new strength in January 1910 when the city annexed all the surrounding suburbs into Greater Birmingham. Evangelical Protestants were much more numerous in the suburbs than in Old Birmingham, and they joined Moral Element leaders in supporting the commission plan in order to unseat the dominant Liberal-oriented aldermanic "ring," which they believed was not enforcing prohibition effectively. The Liberal aldermen clumsily provoked greater suburban distrust when they refused to give the suburbs equal representation on the board of aldermen and when the Liberal caucus appointed the first suburban aldermen, choosing men who would cooperate with it, rather than allowing the newly-annexed citizens to elect their first aldermen. Most suburbanites quickly concluded that a commission system, with three commissioners elected at large, would allow them to exercise their proper political leverage more effectively.[49]

Then in May 1910 Liberal Element leaders themselves abruptly dropped their opposition to the commission system when their ally, Emmet O'Neal, an antiprohibitionist, was elected governor. O'Neal had ridden a temporary statewide backlash against prohibitionism and had carried in an antiprohibition legislature, including an antiprohibition majority of the Jefferson County delegation. It suddenly seemed that Liberals could control the writing of a commission act and could have Governor O'Neal appoint Liberals to the first commission, entrenching them in powerful positions in the more centralized system. And this might give Liberals their best opportunity to retain power in Greater Birmingham, where evangelical Methodist, Baptist, and Presbyterian congregations accounted for 60 percent of the white church members, and where the Moral Element was bound to have a strong majority of voters.[50]

Aldermanic leaders therefore allowed the commission plan to be placed on the June 1910 primary ballot, and, with no organized oppo-

48. *News*, Oct. 10, 11, 12, 1907, Nov. 17, 21, 23, Dec. 1, 3, 4, 7, 18, 31, 1908, July 28, Aug. 10, 11, 12, 19, Dec. 16, 1909; *Labor Advocate*, Dec. 11, 1908, Jan. 8, 1909.

49. *Age-Herald*, Oct. 25, 1907; *News*, Sept. 22, 1908, Dec. 16, 1909, Jan. 28, May 4, 6, 10, 27, June 1, 2, 1910; Birmingham, Minutes of the City Council, N, 274–75 (Jan. 5, 1910).

50. U.S. Census, *Religious Bodies: 1916*, Pt. 1, pp. 123, 364–66; *News*, May 6, 7, 14, June 8, 9, 1910.

sition, it won an 88 percent endorsement. The T.C.I. attorney Walker Percy, a moderate on the saloon issue, had been elected to the state legislature on a city-commission platform, and he wrote and introduced a city-commission bill that would allow Birmingham voters to elect the first commission. But Henry B. Gray and Birmingham aldermanic leaders, going to Montgomery for a midnight hotel-room caucus with the antiprohibitionist Jefferson County legislators, worked out an amendment to have Governor O'Neal appoint the first three-man commission. Moreover, they concurred in recommending that O'Neal appoint incumbent mayor Culpepper Exum, incumbent city council president Harry Jones, and respected circuit court judge Alexander O. Lane, the moderate antiprohibitionist who had served four terms as mayor in the 1880s and 1890s.[51]

The *News* and other city commission reform leaders exploded in outrage. Judge Lane was a good man, they said, but aldermanic leaders Jones and Exum would team up against him, and "the same old political gang will be in control." Irate reformers urged Governor O'Neal to drop Harry Jones, "the peculiar creature and leader of the city hall crowd," and to appoint in his place former mayor George Ward. Governor O'Neal hesitated more than a month, then, in a political masterstroke, he appointed neither Jones nor Ward, but instead James M. Weatherly, a prominent corporation attorney, to join Exum and Lane on the first commission. The Liberal Element could not object to Weatherly because he was a prominent antiprohibitionist, but the commission advocates rejoiced because Weatherly brought to the commission exactly the preeminent social and professional standing and the devotion to civic improvement that they wanted to promote in city government.[52]

The first decade of city commission elections gradually revealed a new political balance created by annexation and the commission system. In 1913 commission president Exum, whose term expired, did not seek reelection, and a three-way race upset traditional Moral-Liberal lines. The candidates were Clement R. Wood, a Socialist attorney; Vassar L. Allen, a leader of the ardently prohibitionist Law and Order League; and former mayor George B. Ward, a moderate reform leader who had

51. *News*, Feb. 16, 17, 1911; Daniel J. O'Connell to J.H. Purdy, Feb. 18, 1911, B.W.W.C. Letterbooks.

52. O'Connell to Purdy, Feb. 25, 1911, B.W.W.C. Letterbooks; *News*, Mar. 2, 1911. See also *News*, Feb. 24, Apr. 4, 1911; telegrams from Jere King to Governor O'Neal, Feb. 24, Apr. 4, 1911, and telegrams from other Birmingham citizens to O'Neal, Governor's Office Records, Alabama Department of Archives and History, Montgomery, Alabama (hereinafter cited as ADAH).

never embraced prohibition, and who had built an image as an honest "progressive" businessman with a "social conscience." Wood spiced the campaign with sharp anticapitalist rhetoric, unusual in city politics, and he antagonized a self-styled "conservative element of organized labor," which opposed socialism and said it preferred to support a "clean-cut businessman." Wood nonetheless surprised politicians by capturing 22.2 percent of the vote, running best not in the traditional Liberal strongholds of Old Birmingham, but in such small outlying industrial suburbs as East Birmingham and Wylam, where he received over half the votes. In all the suburbs together he received 31.6 percent of the vote; in Old Birmingham, only 11.8 percent. The outright prohibitionist Allen ran a close third, with 22.0 percent, faring best in the suburbs. George Ward, emphasizing his moderate position between extremes, won easily with a 55.9 percent majority, sweeping 70 percent of the Old Birmingham vote and winning a 42.8 percent plurality in all the suburbs combined, though he ran behind Wood in several industrial suburbs.[53]

In 1914 commissioner James Weatherly, the former railroad attorney, came up for reelection, and Harry Jones, the aldermanic caucus leader who had almost been appointed to the commission in 1911, attempted a comeback against Weatherly. But Weatherly had gained immense popularity, even among workers, with his vigorous efforts to regulate utilities, and he captured an overwhelming 68 percent of the votes, 74 percent in the suburbs and 62 percent in Old Birmingham. Thereafter none of the old aldermanic Liberal Element leaders ran in city elections. Ironically, the annexation of the heavily Protestant suburbs, which Liberal city boosters had enthusiastically supported, had fatally undermined Liberal political power.[54]

All the early commissioners lived in Old Birmingham, however, in the best residential sections, and in 1915, when commissioner Alexander O. Lane ran for reelection, the lack of direct suburban representation became an issue. Lane's prohibitionist opponent, suburban druggist Arlie K. Barber, explicitly appealed to suburban discontent and received three-fourths of the suburban vote, enough to overcome a Lane majority in Old Birmingham. Also in 1915 the legislature expanded the commission to five members, and the suburbs captured one of the new positions, for a total of two. In both 1917 and 1921 the suburbs captured four of the five positions to dominate the commission, and for years

53. *Labor Advocate,* July 25, 1913; *News,* Sept. 14, 1913. See also *Labor Advocate* Aug. 8, Sept. 12, 1913; *News,* July 6, Sept. 7, 16, 19, 1913.
54. *News,* Sept. 13, 16, 22, 1914; *Labor Advocate,* Sept. 18, 1914.

thereafter they continued to do so. And nearly all the suburban commissioners were men of decided Moral Element sympathies.[55]

In 1917 the conflict between the suburbs and Old Birmingham intertwined with an extreme version of the traditional conflict over moral issues. Prohibition was considered a "closed issue" in 1917 because in 1915 the legislature had enacted statewide prohibition. But the Pastors' Union was campaigning for more stringent Sunday blue laws, including the closing of Sunday movies, and some key Moral Element leaders, such as Dr. A.J. Dickinson, pastor of the First Baptist Church, spiced this crusade with virulent anti-Catholic propaganda. Dickinson led a secret political anti-Catholic society called the True Americans, or T.A.'s, and in 1917 it publicly endorsed Dr. Nathaniel A. Barrett to oppose incumbent commission president George Ward, who had voted for Sunday movies. Barrett, a physician, a former mayor of the residential suburb of East Lake, and a prominent Baptist layman who had helped lead the attack on Sunday movies, welcomed the True American endorsement, and charged that Ward, an Episcopalian, was a tool of the Catholics. Barrett also campaigned as a representative of the suburbs, and he received 66 percent of the suburban vote, compared with only 25 percent for Ward and less than 10 percent for a minor third candidate. Ward, on the other hand, had strong support from the downtown business community and received 59 percent of the Old Birmingham vote. But Barrett's massive suburban majority swept him to victory. He immediately gratified the anti-Catholics by firing Birmingham's single Roman Catholic city official, police chief Martin Eagan, and replacing him with Thomas J. Shirley, a member of the anti-Catholic Ku Klux Klan that superseded the True Americans.[56]

The acrimonious 1917 campaign, in which George Ward boldly denounced the T.A.'s as bigoted "false Americans," bitterly divided Birmingham and split the Moral Element leaders, some of whom supported Ward and denounced T.A. anti-Catholicism. By 1921 the more moderate Moral Element leaders, reinforced by the active support of the League of Women Voters, were able to return the focus to their traditional concerns of control of gambling and vice. They charged that

55. *News*, Oct. 19, Dec. 14, 1915; *Age-Herald*, Oct. 16, 1917; Birmingham *Post*, Oct. 18, 1921.

56. *Age-Herald*, July 18, Aug. 1, 1916, Aug. 14, Sept. 19, 25, 26, 29, Oct. 6, 15, 19, 1917; *News*, Sept. 9, 15, 16, 19, 29, Oct. 2, 5, 6, 1917. Birmingham, Minutes of the Board of Commissioners, X, 394–95 (Nov. 6, 1917); Howard S. Shirley (son of Thomas J. Shirley) to Hill Ferguson, Sept. 8, 1958, in Hill Ferguson Collection, Personalities, vol. 48, BPL.

the Barrett administration, rather than cleaning up the city, had lethargically allowed prostitution and gambling to flourish, especially during the war years. And they neutralized Barrett's suburban appeal by supporting suburban challengers. Barrett again resorted to the anti-Catholic issue, but it was less resonant in 1921, and he and his entire administration were swept from power by new suburban crusaders who promised to clean up vice.[57]

The political patterns from 1915 to 1921 sorely disappointed Walker Percy, the *News,* and other civic reformers. They had promoted the city commission in hopes of placing a higher caliber of businessmen in charge of government. From 1911 to 1915 they found the commissioners quite satisfactory, and they rejoiced that the aldermanic Liberal Element had been shut out. But in 1915 and 1917 Alexander Lane and George Ward were defeated, and James Weatherly retired, and thereafter the commissioners diverged more and more from the *News'* ideal: "a thoroughly trained businessman, who is a demonstrated, recognized success—such a man as might be chosen for the presidency of a large bank, or the general manager of a large business."[58]

In 1915 the *News* called together sixteen "representative men," the "bone and sinew" of Birmingham industry and commerce, to form a businessmen's caucus, led by Walker Percy of T.C.I., to find, nominate, and elect the ideal businessman to the commission. But the caucus failed to find an appropriate businessman who would run and who had a chance to win, and it died without a candidate. The 1915 election was won by suburban druggist and anticorporation orator Arlie Barber, who in Walker Percy's view was a "dangerous man" and who in the *News'* view was "a narrow man of no demonstrated capacity for public service" whose election "would be a real calamity." Worse yet, soon after Barber won he announced himself a Socialist, though his socialism proved to be mainly an erratic brand of *petit bourgeoisie* anticorporatism. In 1917 the *News* organized another businessmen's caucus, but again failed to find the ideal businessman-commissioner and had to reconcile itself to the election of N.A. Barrett, the anti-Catholic candidate, whom the *News* described as "the narrow, bigoted, intolerant type, thoroughly incapacitated for the big task he seeks."[59]

57. *News,* Sept. 9, 1917; *Post,* Aug. 10, 18, Sept. 1, 2, 19, 23, 26, Oct. 12, 13, 18, 1921.

58. *News,* Aug. 15, 1915. See also *ibid.,* Apr. 4, May 1, 1911.

59. *Ibid.,* Oct. 12, 14, 1915, Oct. 8, 1917. See also *ibid.,* Aug. 22, Sept. 5, 12, 1915, Sept. 21, 22, Oct. 4, 1917; *Age-Herald,* Oct. 31, 1915, Aug. 14, Oct. 5, 1917.

Actually, once the prominent men of 1911 and 1913 retired, the city commission was run by men of approximately the same economic status as those who had typically dominated the board of aldermen before 1911. The major change in economic rank was that after 1915 men from the middle-ranking groups, all in the top 20 percent of the population, still further increased their dominance of city government (see Table 4.2). On the commissions between 1911 and 1950 only corporation attorney James Weatherly (1911–1917) came from an upper-ranking group, and only labor organizer William L. Harrison (1921–1925) from a lower-ranking group. Harrison had supported women's suffrage in the 1919 state legislature, and in gratitude the Birmingham League of Women Voters gave him enthusiastic and probably decisive support in the 1921 commissioners' race, the first Birmingham city election in which women voted.[60] The post-1915 commissioners differed from the old aldermen mainly in their suburban residence and their Moral Element orientation. And they were more often professional men and less often merchants, perhaps because professional men could more easily interrupt their careers for a term as a full-time government official.

In 1921 the new commission president was David E. McLendon, who as a young man had been secretary of a rural Farmers' Alliance Store, who had come to Birmingham in 1890 and worked his way up from express-company agent to deputy county-tax assessor to head tax assessor, but whose success had been tarnished by ventures in two small manufacturing firms that had gone bankrupt by 1921. McLendon's fellow commissioners were a salesman for the Proctor and Gamble Soap Company, a woman schoolteacher (wife of an undertaker), the principal of a suburban school, and a labor leader. Not one fit the *News'* image of the ideal businessman-commissioner. Nor were the men elected between 1925 and 1953 much different. After 1925 there was little turnover on the commission, and Birmingham was governed by a contractor and warehouse owner who had been a leader of the True Americans and a comptroller in the anti-Catholic Barrett administration, a former clerk of the county court of misdemeanors, an assistant city editor of the Birmingham *Post*, a radio station vice-president, a real estate broker who had become postmaster, and, finally, a furniture salesman and radio sportscaster (T. Eugene "Bull" Connor) who in 1933 had been selected by *Sporting News* as the outstanding radio sports announcer of the United States. All the men elected after 1921 were

60. *Post*, Aug. 1, 19, 1921; *Labor Advocate*, Aug. 27, 1921.

classified with middle-ranking economic groups, and all had made modest beginnings and achieved moderate business or professional success in Birmingham.[61]

THE BOARD OF EDUCATION

Men from the top 20 percent of the population—the middle- and upper-ranking economic groups—thoroughly dominated the separate board of education. The board, established in 1884 by the legislature, was appointed by the board of aldermen or the city commission. Of the thirty-six board members between 1890 and 1920, 83 percent came from middle-ranking groups, 14 percent from upper-ranking groups, and only 3 percent from lower-ranking groups. Professionals provided 50 percent of the members and merchants 25 percent. Although organized labor took an intense interest in local school policy and often urged the appointment of specific union leaders, their school board nominees were never chosen. The one member from the 80 percent of the population in the lower-ranking groups was Mayor David Fox, a retail grocer.[62]

COUNTY ELECTIONS

Birmingham was the county seat of Jefferson County, and on many vital issues the center of decision-making was the county courthouse rather than the city hall. Birmingham voters cast a percentage of the total county vote roughly commensurate with their proportion of the county population: slightly less than 30 percent before the annexation of 1910, slightly less than 60 percent after 1910. Since most county primaries featured at least three or four candidates for every position, with only a plurality necessary to win, rural areas might theoretically have united on one "rural" candidate and elected him even if he received almost no urban support, or vice versa. But the cleavages did not run sharply along urban-rural lines; both city and county precincts scattered their votes among many candidates, and in nearly all county elections

61. Compiled from sources cited in n. 4 and from Jefferson County, Tax Assessment Books, 1921, Jefferson County Courthouse.

62. List of school board members from Birmingham, Board of Education, *Annual Report of the Birmingham Public Schools, 1925*, p. 9. See also *Labor Advocate*, Aug. 23, 1912, May 30, 1913; *Age-Herald*, Dec. 9, 1901.

the successful candidates demonstrated roughly equal appeal to city, suburban, and outlying rural voters.[63]

THE COUNTY SHERIFFS

The elected decision-makers of Jefferson County came, as did the city officials, predominantly from the upper fifth of the population in the middle-ranking economic interest groups. Between 1890 and 1920 the eight county sheriffs were a grocer-farmer, a wholesale druggist, the proprietor of the Birmingham Opera House, a bailiff in the county criminal court, a wholesale fruit merchant, the clerk of the county circuit court, the president of a seed company, and an incumbent deputy sheriff. All but the first came from middle-ranking groups; four were moderately successful businessmen, and three were professional government bureaucrats. Their opponents were men with similar careers and economic status.[64]

THE COUNTY COURT OF COMMISSIONERS, OR BOARD OF REVENUE

The county legislative body—the court of county commissioners before 1899, the board of revenue thereafter—drew nearly two-thirds of its members from the middle-ranking economic groups. Fewer than one-tenth came from upper-ranking groups, and slightly more than one-fourth from lower-ranking groups. In county elections as many as sixty-eight candidates vied for the four or five board positions, and choices were usually poorly defined, with no party labels, factional tickets, or public positions on issues to clarify the chaotic campaigns. In all elec-

---

63. Based on tabulations of county election returns in *Age-Herald*, Dec. 25, 31, 1891; *State Herald*, Apr. 19, 1896; *News*, Apr. 27, 1900, Sept. 18, 1906, Apr. 5, 1910, Apr. 8, 1914. Available returns of the 1918 primary are too fragmentary to be of use. Population data from U.S. Census, *Fourteenth Census, 1920*, I, *Population*, 336; II, *Population*, 50.

In only three county elections, which involved exceptionally strong ideological alignments, did winners receive significantly heavier support from one area than from others. They were the 1896 general election for sheriff, contested by a Populist and a Democrat; the 1894 legislative election, contested by Jeffersonian and Democratic tickets; and the 1914 legislative election, contested by Prohibition and Local Option tickets.

64. Compiled from sources cited in n. 4.

tions except 1920 some men won with a plurality of less than 25 percent. Only organized labor regularly published endorsements for board candidates, but until 1920 not one labor endorsee was elected, though some had placed as high as seventh in a field of twenty-five, or tenth in a field of sixty-eight. In 1920, however, labor, displaying new organizational and political strength, endorsed four and elected two.[65]

The Birmingham *News* typically deplored what seemed to it the low caliber of men on the board. In 1912, for example, it urged "the heavy taxpayers, the representative citizens of the County" to "form some sort of an organization, to pick out five or more candidates as distinctly capable and worthy men for the duties of the Board, and to recommend them to the people." But the *News* found businessmen "too busy, or too indifferent" to nominate a slate, and most men elected to the board failed to measure up to the *News'* standards. Rather, typical board members were small-time merchants, small real estate dealers, road construction contractors, or professional county government bureaucrats (tax assessor, clerk of court). Between 1890 and 1920 the board included only one lawyer and only one downtown Birmingham merchant, a furniture and liquor dealer on the outer edge of the business district. Clearly the leading citizens of Birmingham did not sit on the county board.[66]

THE COUNTY DELEGATION TO THE STATE LEGISLATURE

Both the city and county governments were creatures of the state legislature, dependent for their powers and their very existence upon legislative acts. Indeed, the legislature could abolish any local government body and replace it with a new agency and new officials. It did so in 1899 when it replaced the court of county commissioners with a board of revenue, and in 1911 when it replaced the mayor, aldermen, and police commission with a city commission. And in both county and city decision-making, local officials and interest groups frequently had to ask the legislature to approve decisions, to grant more power, or to

65. The percentages are based upon thirty-seven of the forty-seven men who served. The other ten were not listed in city directories and probably came from rural sections of the county. *Age-Herald*, Dec. 25, 31, 1891, May 13, 1916, Apr. 3, May 15, 1920; *State Herald*, Apr. 19, 1896; *News*, Apr. 27, 1900, May 25, 1908, Apr. 6, 1912; *Labor Advocate*, Apr. 7, 1900, Apr. 7, 1900, Apr. 16, 1904, Mar. 29, 1912, Apr. 10, 1920.
66. *News*, Mar. 28, 1912.

remove restrictions. The official local channel of access to the state lawmakers was the Jefferson County legislative delegation, composed of one state senator and several delegates to the state House of Representatives (two before 1892, six from 1892 to 1901, and seven after 1901). All the delegates were elected by the county at large; Birmingham had no separate representatives. Still, after 1892 at least four and often five or six of the legislative candidates who carried the city precincts were among the final county winners.[67] But as late as 1920 only Jefferson, Mobile, and Montgomery counties had cities of at least 25,000 population, and these urban counties, containing 21 percent of Alabama's population, were underrepresented in the legislature, holding only 13 percent of the seats in the House and 9 percent in the Senate. Rural representatives who had no ties to large cities dominated the legislature.[68]

Between 1890 and 1921, 69 percent of the sixty-seven Jefferson County delegates to the House came from middle-ranking economic groups. Only 8 percent, including corporation attorneys, came from upper-ranking groups; and 16 percent, including labor attorneys, from lower-ranking groups. The rank of 7 percent could not be determined. Only 13 percent were merchants, but 45 percent were professionals, most of them attorneys associated with the downtown business community.[69]

The only economic group to endorse legislative candidates regularly was organized labor, which often supported a prominent union leader, a well-known labor attorney, or a business "friend" of union labor. Between 1890 and 1920 five of sixteen union candidates were elected, as were four of the five labor attorneys and six of the twelve friends of labor.[70]

In addition to the house delegation, Jefferson County was represented by a single state senator, who usually, according to a custom of

67. Precinct returns in *Age-Herald*, Dec. 25, 31, 1891; *State Herald*, Apr. 19, 1896; *News*, Aug. 29, 1902, Sept. 19, 1906, Apr. 8, 1914.

68. Hallie Farmer, *The Legislative Process in Alabama: Legislative Apportionment* (University, Ala.: Bureau of Public Administration, 1944), 33–36; U.S. Census, *Fourteenth Census, 1920*, I, *Population*, 336; II, *Population*, 117.

69. *Alabama Official and Statistical Register* for 1903–1919. Included in the upper rank, rather than among professionals, were corporation attorneys Walker Percy, Augustus H. Benners (three terms), John B. Weakley, and Alexander T. London. Included in the lower rank were labor attorneys Sam Will John (two terms), John J. Altman, and Isadore Shapiro.

70. *Age-Herald*, Dec. 12, 1891, Mar. 1, Apr. 8, 1894; *State Herald*, Mar. 31, 1896; *Labor Advocate*, Mar. 5, Apr. 2, June 4, 1898, Aug. 9, 1902, June 9, 1906, Apr. 29, 1910, Apr. 17, 1914, Aug. 24, 1918, Apr. 5, 1919.

senatorial courtesy, was allowed by other senators to dictate passage or defeat on all local bills applying only to his own county. Corporations liked to control the key senate seat. In 1906, for example, Birmingham Water Works Company superintendent Daniel J. O'Connell wrote: "We are in better shape if we can have the Senator from this County on our side, as we do not have to trouble over so many men as we have in the House." And between 1890 and 1920 the office of state senator was the only one filled predominantly by the top 1 percent of the population in the upper-ranking groups. Six senatorial terms, stretching uninterruptedly from 1888 to 1914, were served by corporation friends, and two terms, after 1915, by members of the middle groups. The senators were John T. Milner (1888–1896), pioneer developer and owner of the Milner Coal and Railway Company; Dr. Russel M. Cunningham (1896–1900), T.C.I. prison physician; Hugh M. Morrow (1900–1905, 1910–1914), attorney for the Birmingham Railway, Light, and Power Company and the Sloss-Sheffield Steel and Iron Company; Nathan L. Miller (1906–1910), sometime attorney for the Birmingham Water Works Company; Thomas J. Judge (1915–1919), attorney with no corporation affiliation; and Charles R. West (1919–1921), a schoolteacher and "friend of labor."[71]

Corporation domination of the one office they sought suggests that they could win when they wanted to and that their failure to hold other offices reflected their lack of interest in the offices rather than an inability to win. For the senate the corporations were careful to sponsor attractive candidates with broad local family and political ties. For example, Senator John T. Milner, who served two terms, was the railroad engineer who in 1871 had chosen the site of Birmingham and who had subsequently developed vast coal lands. The aura of respect that surrounded pioneer developers helped sweep him to overwhelming victory when he ran for office. The other corporation man to serve two terms, Hugh M. Morrow, was the son of a highly respected old Jefferson County farming and mercantile family. At the University of Alabama he was the star baseball pitcher and the valedictorian of his class, and he then served as secretary to the university president while getting a law degree. Upon graduation he was immediately taken into one of the leading firms of corporation attorneys, and they quickly discovered that

71. O'Connell to J.H. Purdy, June 12, 1906, B.W.W.C. Letterbooks; *Alabama Official and Statistical Register* for 1903–1919; *News*, July 11, 1906, July 27, 1908, Aug. 2, Oct. 5, 1911; *Age-Herald*, Sept. 7, 1915.

his obvious ability, his attractive personality, and his wide local family connections made him an easy winner in senatorial campaigns.[72]

During some years, when a popular anticorporation candidate ran, the corporations resorted to heavy campaign contributions. In 1906, for example, Charles P. Beddow, a popular labor and damage-suit lawyer, ran for the Senate and superintendent O'Connell of the waterworks told his general manager: "it will never do for us to have him in the legislature." Therefore, "The corporations about here, who are interested in legislation, expect to have a man by the name of John H. Miller make the race, and of course they are expected to stand the expense." This "may cost us as much as $250.00," he added, "but it will be money well spent." However, the corporations soon dropped John H. Miller, who seemed too unpopular to defeat Beddow, and they finally settled for a second choice, Nathan L. Miller, who was not a full-time corporation attorney, but who had handled cases for the waterworks. A former clerk of the county court, Nathan Miller had political visibility and alliances which made him a more viable candidate. According to the News, it was "a matter of common notoriety" that the corporations gave Miller a vast campaign fund, and Miller squeezed past Beddow by 50 votes out of 9,000 cast. The corporations could not buy the senatorship for any friend; they had to consider popularity and sometimes they had to go with a second choice; but in such a close race their campaign funds probably made the difference.[73]

From 1914 to 1921 no more corporation friends were elected senator from Jefferson, and in 1914 attorney Thomas J. Judge, who did win, was quite unacceptable to the corporations. In the 1915 legislature however, the corporations had many friends from other counties. In 1914 the Alabama Anti-Saloon League, determined to enact prohibition, cooperated closely with corporations, and included corporation friends on the prohibition tickets of many counties. The prohibitionists won control of the 1915 legislature and quickly enacted statewide prohibition; then they cooperated closely with the corporations on other issues. Thus the flexibility of corporation leaders, who had originally opposed prohibition in 1907, and their ability to arrange statewide alliances with

72. *News*, Aug. 18, 1898; *Age-Herald*, Dec. 31, 1891; biographical sketch of Hugh Morrow in "Miscellaneous Data from Robt. Jemison, Jr., Re. Developments and Personal References Re. a few Friends and Citizens of Birmingham," TS, 1965, BPL.

73. O'Connell to Purdy, June 12, 1906, and Aug. 29, 1906, B.W.W.C. Letterbooks; *News*, July 14, 1906. See also *News*, July 25, Aug. 13, 25, 31, 1906; *Labor Advocate*, Aug. 25, 1906.

rural groups, gave them legislative strength that did not always depend on being able to win elections in Jefferson County.[74]

In sum, however, local elective offices in Birmingham were dominated by moderately successful local businessmen in the interest groups possessing a middle range of economic power. These overrepresented groups, whose members were in the top 20 percent of the population, had attained recognition in the eyes of voters as legitimate governing groups, and it would seem probable that when their spokesmen appeared before government officials, they found greater understanding and sympathy for their policy demands than did spokesmen from other groups. Still, the groups that provided a majority of officeholders may not have dominated decision-making. The officials may have developed peculiar officeholders' interests of their own, or the economic power of the top 1 percent of the population in the upper-ranking groups or the voting power of the 80 percent of the population in the lower-ranking groups may have prevented officials from favoring the middle-ranking groups in all decisions. Only analysis of the entire spectrum of actual decisions made by the elected officials can reveal which interest groups exercised the greatest power over political outcomes.

74. *Age-Herald*, Jan. 15, Sept. 7, 26, 1915; *News*, Sept. 27, 1915; *Labor Advocate*, Mar. 18, 1916.

V

Municipal Revenue, 1871-1911

$\mathbb{I}$N municipal government, finance overshadows every other problem," observed Birmingham mayor George B. Ward in 1905.[1] Revenue always fell short of meeting even the most pressing needs, and the city's efforts to extract more revenue were hindered by tight tax restrictions in the state constitution as well as in the city charter, which had been enacted by the rural-dominated state legislature. The city property tax, in particular, was limited by state-prescribed tax rates and assessment procedures and by the reluctance of the legislature to approve annexation of new taxable property. Such constraints forced Birmingham to rely heavily on its second major source of general revenue—the license tax, levied as a fee for the privilege of doing business in the city—and to extract as much income as possible from such minor revenue sources as street taxes, school tuition, fines, and convict labor.[2] (Statistical data on all Birmingham's sources of yearly general fund revenue, from 1873 to 1922, are presented in the appendix.)

From 1890 to 1911 Birmingham struggled to find a proper balance between the property tax and the license tax. In 1890, in comparison with ninety-five other American cities in the 20,000 to 50,000 popula-

1. Birmingham *News*, May 4, 1905.

2. Other minor sources of revenue were street repair payments, inspection fees, and such miscellaneous items as interest, donations, rent, franchise payments, and poll taxes. The general revenue as defined here did not include specific assessments for paving streets and sidewalks or for building sewers, which will be discussed in chapter 8, and it did not include money borrowed by the city, which will be considered in chapter 7. Nor did general revenue include income from municipal industries, since Birmingham owned no utilities.

Another local government, Jefferson County, extracted revenue from Birmingham citizens, and reference will be made to county finance when it is relevant to the main issues in city finance. But since county records were unsystematic and incomplete and the county tax structure was simpler and less variable, the main focus will be on city revenue.

tion class, Birmingham received an extraordinarily heavy proportion (36.0 percent) of its revenue through the license tax on business and liquor, and an unusually small proportion (34.3 percent) from the property tax. The other ninety-five cities of similar size received only 9.4 percent of their revenue from license taxes, and 77.9 percent from property taxes. Thirteen cities of similar size in the southeastern states received 14.5 percent of their revenue from license taxes and 69.5 percent from property taxes. Per capita revenue figures revealed the same pattern. From the license tax Birmingham received $3.59 per capita, the southeastern cities $1.35, and the other eighty-two cities $0.82. From the property tax Birmingham received $3.43 per capita, the southeastern cities $6.47, and the other eighty-two cities $7.74.[3]

Birmingham's unique pattern had emerged early in its history and it persisted through 1920 and beyond. In its second and third fiscal years, 1873 and 1874, Birmingham received 36.9 percent of its revenue from license taxes and only 33.3 percent from property taxes. By 1881 the proportions were 48.3 percent from the license tax, 22.4 from the property tax; by 1885, 38.2 percent from the license tax and 31.2 percent from the property tax (see appendix). By 1920 Birmingham had grown into the 100,000 to 300,000 population class, and had moved toward the more typical city pattern, but the influence of its early pattern persisted. In 1920 it received 27.0 percent of its revenue from license taxes, 57.4 percent from property taxes. Five other southeastern cities in the same size class reported corresponding percentages of 10.4 and 73.1; and for all other American cities of that size the percentages were 2.8 and 88.0.[4] Census reports indicated that all cities in the most rural states, especially in the South and Far West, relied on unusually heavy business license taxes, and Birmingham, pinched by Alabama's particularly severe constraints on city revenue, had developed an exaggerated version of the southern and far western pattern.[5]

3. Compiled from U.S. Census, *Report on Wealth, Debt, and Taxation at the Eleventh Census: 1890*, Vol. 15, Pt. 2, *Valuation and Taxation* (Washington, D.C., 1895), 560–79. Some census categories were reclassified. Revenue from special assessments, public services, and municipal industries was excluded. Property tax revenue includes all taxes on real and personal property and all county and state aid to education, which usually came from taxes on local property. The license tax includes both business- and liquor-license fees. Although the census attempted to separate business and liquor fees, its classification was inconsistent and inaccurate, and only the total license-tax figures are useful.
4. U.S. Census, *Financial Statistics of Cities Having a Population of Over 30,000: 1921* (Washington, D.C., 1922).
5. *Ibid.: 1918*, p. 59.

During the 1890s merchants, bankers, insurance agents, professional men, saloonkeepers, artisans, and grocers, who were subject to the comparatively high license taxes, protested continually against the heavy tax burden on "business," as compared with the light burden on "property." Businessmen, of course, paid property as well as license taxes, but they complained much more about the license taxes, which many found more burdensome. Especially unhappy were the lower-ranking businessmen—saloonkeepers, artisans, neighborhood storekeepers—because the license tax schedules were heavily regressive. Not until 1897 were license fees graduated according to the size of businesses, and even thereafter the fees for small merchants represented a larger percentage of inventory value than did the fees for larger merchants. In 1895 most lower-ranking businesses owned property assessed at less than one thousand dollars and paid a yearly city property tax of less than five dollars, but their license fees ranged from ten to twenty-five dollars, and grocers who handled uncured meats paid an additional fifty dollars.[6]

Most businessmen probably shifted the bulk of their license tax onto customers, but they complained nonetheless. At best the tax, which had to be paid in lump sum at the beginning of each year, was a nuisance. Annual license fee increases forced the merchant to raise prices slightly without netting any additional income, and during the depression of the 1890s merchants may have found it difficult to raise prices in proportion to rising license fees. Most businessmen considered the license tax an onerous burden and earnestly demanded that it be reduced.[7]

The city property tax was more broadly based than the license tax, being levied directly on all owners of homes and businesses, and indirectly, through the rent, on families and businessmen who rented homes or stores. Technically city property tax revenue was raised through two separate procedures. First, as of 1890 the city levied a direct tax of five mills, or fifty cents on each $100 assessed valuation. Second, the county and state levied an education tax on Birmingham property and allocated a portion of it back to the city as "aid to education." Since the total property tax from these two procedures was exceptionally low, in comparison with other cities, from 1890 to 1911

6. City license schedules in Birmingham *Age-Herald*, Dec. 21, 1894, and *News*, Dec. 23, 1896: Jefferson County, Tax Assessment Books, 1904 (earliest year available), Jefferson County Courthouse, Birmingham, Ala.

7. *Age-Herald*, Nov. 20, Dec. 18, 1890, Jan. 5, 26, 1895, Jan. 25, 1899, Nov. 28, 1901.

Birmingham's mayors and aldermen sought, with some success, to increase property tax revenue by raising city property tax rates, by annexing more taxable property, and by increasing assessed valuations.

THE PROPERTY-TAX RATE

After 1875 city property tax rates were severely limited by the Alabama state constitution. In 1874 Conservative Democrats "redeemed" Alabama from Radical Republican Reconstruction, and Democratic propaganda, exaggerating the tax and debt increases under the Radicals, built public distrust of government taxing power. In 1875 the "conservative agrarian-minded" Redeemers wrote a new constitution. Displaying even more parsimony than Redeemers in other southern states, they restricted tax rates to the extremely low levels of 7.5 mills (75 cents on $100 assessed valuation) for the state and 5.0 mills (50 cents on $100 valuation) for counties and cities. And they even prohibited special local taxation for schools.[8]

Such restrictions severely hampered the government of rapidly-growing young Birmingham, and from the beginning forced it to rely on an unusually high license tax. By the late 1880s and early 1890s city political leaders and editors were demanding that the constitutional restriction be revoked. The depression of the 1890s further crippled city revenue and intensified their demand.

In 1893 Birmingham officials got the state legislature to pass an amendment that would increase the city's property tax rate from 5.0 to 7.5 mills (75 cents on $100 assessed valuation); and as required by the constitution, the legislature submitted the amendment to a statewide referendum.[9]

The strongest support for the amendment came from bankers and investment brokers who wanted the city to be able to maintain uninterrupted bond interest payments, and from businessmen who thought it

8. Malcolm Cook McMillan, *Constitutional Development in Alabama, 1798–1901: A Study in Politics, the Negro, and Sectionalism* (Chapel Hill: Univ. of North Carolina Press, 1955), 176, 181, 202, 210–14, 232, 317, 329; Horace Mann Bond, *Negro Education in Alabama: A Study in Cotton and Steel* (Washington, D.C.: Associated Publishers, 1939; New York: Atheneum, 1969), 37, 55–60; Walter L. Fleming, *Civil War and Reconstruction in Alabama* (Chicago: S.J. Clarke Pub. Co., 1906; New York: Peter Smith, 1949), 571–82.

9. McMillan, *Constitutional Development*, 234; Birmingham *Iron Age*, Nov. 4, 1886; *Age-Herald*, Aug. 2, 1894.

crucial that the city maintain its credit standing. But not all businessmen agreed, and the Commercial Club equivocated. First it voted to remain neutral, but later, after a thorough investigation of the city's critical financial condition, it endorsed the amendment. The Birmingham *Age-Herald* urged that "property should bear its share of the burden" so that "active business" might be relieved of the "enormous drag net license tax," but many merchants remained opposed. They believed that any tax increase was inappropriate during the depression, and they probably doubted that the straitened city would really reduce the license tax, even if the property tax rate increased.[10]

All major Birmingham real estate and land companies opposed the property-tax-rate increase, preferring, with good reason, that the city continue to rely more heavily on the license tax. For example, the Elyton Land Company, with property assessed at $1,300,000, paid a yearly city property tax of $6,500 and would face an increase of $3,250 if the amendment passed, but the license tax cost the company only $25 per year for each agent.[11]

With Birmingham citizens confused and divided, the amendment had little chance of obtaining the required approval of a majority of all voters in a statewide election, especially since it appeared on the ballot of a hotly-contested 1894 gubernatorial general election pitting Populists against Conservative Democrats. A majority of voters simply failed to mark the amendment portion of their ballots, and their abstentions counted against the amendment, and it lost.[12]

In Birmingham itself only 39.1 percent of the electorate voted yes, the rest either voted no or abstained. Since Birmingham had only four precincts for state elections, precise analysis of sources of support is impossible, but comparisons with the gubernatorial vote are suggestive. In 1894 Ruben F. Kolb was the Populist-Jeffersonian gubernatorial candidate. He was an anathema to Birmingham businessmen of all types, but he had the avowed support of coal miners and of much of organized labor. And in Birmingham the strongest Kolb-Populist-labor precincts were the weakest amendment precincts, and vice versa. Two precincts that gave Kolb only 17.6 and 13.5 percent gave the amendment 57.2 and 57.1 percent majorities, respectively, while two precincts

10. *Age-Herald*, July 31, 1894. See also *ibid.*, Dec. 24, 1893, July 24, 25, 28, 29, Aug. 2, 3, 1894.
11. *Ibid.*, Apr. 27, Aug. 2, 30, 1894.
12. *Ibid.*, Aug. 12, 1894.

that gave Kolb 49.3 and 44.2 percent gave the amendment only 35.1 and 18.7 percent, respectively.[13]

Within two weeks of the defeat of the tax-rate amendment, the board of aldermen and the board of education declared that to keep the schools open they would have to charge tuition in all grades, rather than just in the high school. Four months later the aldermen significantly increased the scope of the license tax, which they could do without state approval.[14]

Such actions spurred advocates of a property tax increase to new efforts. The Commercial Club, the school officials, and organized labor, seeking to circumvent the constitutional prohibition on a city school tax, got the Jefferson County legislative delegation to obtain passage of a two-mill *state* school tax that would apply only to Birmingham. Birmingham collected the unusual school tax in 1896 and 1897, but many large property owners refused to pay it, and in 1897 the Southern Railway got the state supreme court to declare it unconstitutional.[15]

In 1897 the aldermen again raised license tax rates sharply, and Mayor Frank V. Evans declared, "An equalization of taxes is most necessary." The "present 'dragnet' known as our license schedule, imposes an undue burden upon every branch of business in the city," he added, but "this must be imposed in the absence of power to place equal burden upon real estate owners." Reminding his aldermen that "the organic laws of your State, to which organism you and I bow in submission," prohibited higher city property taxes, Evans launched a campaign for a new Birmingham Tax Amendment to the constitution, this time to double the city's property tax rate from five to ten mills ($1.00 on $100). The amendment pledged the new tax exclusively for payment of interest on city bonds, an item which had been absorbing so much of the city's declining revenue that in 1895 the aldermen had been forced to defer interest payments for five years. The German-Jewish owners of the Steiner Brothers Bank had financed the deferred interest payments and bought many of the below-par bonds, and they enthusiastically supported the new tax amendment, rallying Liberal Element friends to it. Most Birmingham merchants endorsed the amendment, after obtaining a clear promise that if it passed the license tax would be reduced.

13. *Ibid.*, Robert David Ward and William Rogers, *Labor Revolt in Alabama: The Great Strike of 1894* (University: Univ. of Alabama Press, 1965), 124–29.

14. *Age-Herald*, Aug. 15, 16, Dec. 15, 21, 1894.

15. *Ibid.*, Jan. 2, 3, 4, 5, 22, Apr. 4, Dec. 24, 1895, July 3, 1897; *Alabama vs. Southern Railway Co.*, 115 Ala. 250 (1896).

The daily newspapers favored the amendment, as did spokesmen for organized labor, who had been promised that if it passed the school tuition would be abolished. For a workingman with three children in school, the tuition could amount to fifty-four dollars a year; for only one child in the first grade it was nine dollars a year. By contrast, the property tax increase on a one-thousand-dollar home would be five dollars per year, paid either directly or through the rent, and many workingmen's homes were valued at far less.[16]

In 1897 Evans and an aldermanic committee persuaded a sympathetic Jefferson County legislative delegation to put the amendment through the legislature and submit it to another statewide referendum. Determined not to lose because of abstentions, they persuaded the legislature to place the words "For Birmingham Amendment" on the ballot and to instruct the voter to leave the words intact to vote yes, or scratch them out to vote no. This assured an amendment victory, which occurred in August 1898. By 1898 the economic picture was brightening and Birmingham opposition to a higher property tax had declined since 1894. No separate 1898 referendum totals were recorded for Birmingham, but Jefferson County as a whole cast only 384 negative votes, while recording 5,150 affirmative ones, including abstentions. By contrast, on the 1894 tax amendment Jefferson had cast 1,676 definite no votes and another 4,801 abstentions, which had counted against it. In 1898 some large property owners opposed the amendment and challenged the constitutionality of the voting procedure, but the court upheld it. Thus the city doubled its property-tax rate. The new five-mill bond tax assured payment of the yearly interest on city bonds, which promptly rose to par, and the Steiner Brothers Bank turned a neat profit for its patriotic aid to the city.[17]

From 1890 to 1898 total Birmingham revenue had increased only 0.7 percent, and property-tax revenue had actually declined 7.8 percent. Only a 12 percent increase in license-tax revenue had kept the city solvent. In 1898 the license tax provided 39.0 percent of city revenue; the property tax, only 36.7 percent. Between 1898 and 1900 the new five-mill bond tax boosted property tax revenue 93 percent, but this

16. *News*, Jan. 7, 1897; Birmingham, *Message of the Mayor and the Annual Reports of the Officers of Birmingham, 1897*, p. 8. See also *Age-Herald*, Dec. 23, 1896, Jan. 25, 1899, Nov. 22, 1901, Feb. 6, 7, 14, 19, 1915; Birmingham *State Herald*, Apr. 24, 1896; *News*, Feb. 18, 19, 1897, July 23, 30, 1898, Jan. 20, 1900; Birmingham *Labor Advocate*, July 16, 1898.
17. *Age-Herald*, Aug. 12, 1894, Aug. 8, 1898; McMillan, *Constitutional Development*, 247–48; *News*, Feb. 18, 1897, Aug. 3, 1898, Aug. 10, 1900.

did not lead to the promised license-tax reduction. In 1900 the license-tax rates were identical with those of 1897, and greater business activity had boosted actual license revenue by 42 percent. The license tax continued to provide 34.6 percent of the city's revenue, compared with 44.4 percent from the property tax. Mayor Evans sadly acknowledged that the promise of license reduction had not been kept, but he said the "onerous" license schedule remained "necessary under present conditions." At least elementary school tuition was abolished as promised, but the high school continued to charge two dollars per month.[18]

In 1901 Alabama held a new constitutional convention, mainly to disfranchise Negro voters. Many Birmingham officials, acutely aware of Birmingham's growing need for more revenue, hoped the convention would remove the strict constitutional limits on city tax rates, limits which the *Age-Herald* called "unreasonable and often times harmful." But the state Democratic party leaders had promised the property-tax-conscious rural voters that the new constitution would not relax any limitations on tax rates, and the convention delegates adhered inflexibly to the pledge. The best the Birmingham delegates could do was to incorporate the 1898 Birmingham bond-tax amendment in the new constitution, thereby retaining the new ten-mill rate.[19]

Birmingham educators, labor leaders, and daily newspapers, and many Alabama educators urged the convention to allow local school districts to levy special local school taxes on property, *in addition* to the regular municipal tax. Since Birmingham city constituted a local school district, this would have enabled it to circumvent the tax-rate limitation, but the rural-dominated convention rejected the idea. As a gesture, the convention did allow each county to levy a meager one-mill special school tax, in addition to one-half mill already authorized for counties, and it pledged three mills of existing state tax to be apportioned among the counties for schools. The *Age-Herald* labeled this pure buncombe, totally inadequate, and certainly it allowed Birmingham no new flexibility in setting its own property tax rate.[20]

During the remaining ten years of aldermanic rule, Birmingham did not seriously seek to increase its property-tax rate. Approval seemed unlikely so soon after doubling the rate in 1898. Had the aldermen been authorized to adjust the rate upward slightly year by year, property-tax

18. *Age-Herald*, Jan. 25, 1899; also see Appendix.
19. *Age-Herald*, Sept. 3, 1900. See also *ibid.*, June 9, 1901; McMillan, *Constitutional Development*, 255, 327.
20. *Age-Herald*, Feb. 2, 6, Mar. 10, Aug. 18, 1901; McMillan, *Constitutional Development*, 238–40, 324–27.

revenue could have grown gradually with the demand for services. But local politicians would not propose a difficult and costly constitutional referendum until the tax rate had become hopelessly inadequate, and even then they would hesitate, knowing that the necessarily large proposed increase would provoke resistance. After 1898, therefore, the city property-tax rate remained the same for nearly twenty years. In 1904 the county did increase the county school tax from .5 to 1.5 mills, as allowed by the new constitution, and it allocated approximately .75 mill back to Birmingham as county school aid, but this slight increase did not begin to keep pace with the city's growing demand for services. Again Birmingham leaned heavily on other revenue sources, chiefly the business-license tax, to make up the difference.[21]

The long-run impact of the 1875 constitutional tax limit illustrated how an outcome early in a city's history could, if frozen into a constitution or charter, continue to have a profound influence on policy and on the success or failure of interest groups long after the particular reasons behind the original outcome were forgotten. Birmingham, of course, was not entirely a passive victim of the state-imposed constraint. Important elements within the city—especially large landowners and to some extent small property owners—fought to keep the venerable tax limit, because it constantly enhanced their ability to maintain an attractive low-tax policy. But other elements—especially merchants— found that the persisting state constraint prevented them from having an impact on tax policy commensurate with their usual influence with city officials.

ANNEXATION OF PROPERTY

During the 1880s the industrialists who built Birmingham's first iron furnaces and rolling mills prevailed upon the aldermen to pledge not to annex and tax the plants for at least fifteen years. But by 1892 a majority of the aldermen decided that the most painless way to increase property tax revenue would be to annex the industries and several residential suburbs, and they sent the legislature a bill to do this. The Tennessee Coal, Iron, and Railroad Company, which owned the Alice iron furnace, urged aldermen to keep their promises and "encourage manufacturing enterprises." The president of the Birmingham Rolling Mill, James G. Caldwell of Louisville, announced that the mill, which

21. Birmingham, *Message of the Mayor, 1906*, pp. 5–8.

was "an immense feeder to the trade of this city," was "unwilling to pay a municipal tax." And while his company "naturally would dislike very much to leave your city," yet "we can produce letters wherein we are offered lands, free water and no taxes in our own state of Kentucky if we will move."[22]

A few downtown spokesmen believed that the city, which needed to attract more industry, should honor and extend its exemption pledge. But most aldermen, most spokesmen for the downtown merchants, most suburban residents who were about to be annexed, and Mayor David Fox all believed that the industries should come in and help carry the city tax burden, and in early 1893 they got the legislature to pass the bill bringing in the suburbs and industries.[23]

But by summer 1893 depression had struck Birmingham and the nation. On July 1 the Birmingham Rolling Mill closed down. The management intimated that it proposed to move away and further implied "that the fact of its being brought in had much to do with the shutting down." By January 1894 Mayor Fox, the aldermen, and the Commercial Club reversed themselves and promised the rolling mill people that the city would ask the next legislature to alter the city boundary to exclude the mill, if the mill would start up again. One month later the mill fired up.[24]

When the legislature met again in January 1895, the aldermen proposed to shift the city boundaries to run inside the rolling mill, the Alice Furnace, and Sloss Furnace. But the Commercial Club and a new mayor, wholesale grocer James A. Van Hoose, tried to delay and amend the bill. They agreed to exclude the rolling mill, but not the furnace companies and their commissaries, which competed with local merchants. Suddenly the rolling mill, which bought its pig iron from the T.C.I. and Sloss furnaces, closed its puddling department, throwing five hundred men out of work. It announced that it had been offered extraordinary inducements to move from Birmingham, and that some stockholders favored the move because "they feel discouraged at the prospects of adverse legislation at Montgomery and failure of our Birmingham citizens to unite in an effort to relieve them of city taxation." Without taking time for amendments, the Jefferson County legislative delegation rammed through the new city limits bill, making neat indentations to exclude the rolling mill and the Alice and Sloss furnaces. On February 6 the

22. *Age-Herald*, Nov. 24, Dec. 6, 1892.
23. *Ibid.*, Jan. 24, 27, 30, 1893; Alabama, *Acts, 1892–1893*, pp. 323–26.
24. *Age-Herald*, Jan. 4, 1894. See also *ibid.*, Jan. 10, Feb. 13, 1894.

governor signed the bill, the rolling mill ordered all its men back to work, and the *Age-Herald* proclaimed: "THAT BILL DID IT."[25]

The annexation question soon became more complex as industries, streetcar lines, and residential suburbs sprawled far beyond the 1895 boundaries. In 1898 city boosters within Birmingham began a "Greater Birmingham" movement to annex all the surrounding suburbs so that Birmingham's "true population" would go on record in the 1900 census. A larger, more visible city would attract more capital investment, they said, and its people and government could borrow money for improvements at lower interest rates. They also saw an urgent need for a unified sanitation system for the entire urbanized area, and they continued to consider annexation of industries and suburbs a convenient way to expand the city property-tax base. Soon the Birmingham mayor and board of aldermen, the Board of Trade, and the Commercial Club were coordinating an intensive campaign for Greater Birmingham, and they gained the support of nearly all citizens and interest groups *inside* the city. By 1908, when a referendum was held on Greater Birmingham, 93 percent of the voters inside Birmingham were for it.[26]

Winning the support, or acquiescence, of residents and interest groups outside the city was much slower and more difficult. When Greater Birmingham was first proposed in 1898, suburban residents, who came mostly from middle- and lower-ranking interest groups, stoutly opposed annexation. But many gradually changed their minds, believing that improved city services would make the higher city taxes worthwhile and would perhaps enhance the value of their property. At first organized labor opposed annexation, but by 1903 the *Labor Advocate* had strongly endorsed Greater Birmingham. Suburban workingmen were probably divided, but many hoped that a Greater Birmingham could provide better schools and sanitation and firmer control of utility corporations.[27]

Some owners of large suburban tracts of vacant land opposed annexation, as did most farmers who might be included. However, the development-oriented Birmingham Realty Company, successor to the Elyton Land Company, supported annexation, even though it continued to own much vacant land both outside and inside Birmingham; and by 1909

25. *Ibid.*, Feb. 3, 7, 1895. See also *ibid.*, Jan. 12, 13, 17, 19, 22, 26, 1895; Alabama, *Acts, 1894–1895*, pp. 841–47.

26. *Age-Herald*, Jan. 26, Feb. 2, 1899, Sept. 26, 1900; *News*, Oct. 15, 1898, Sept. 8, 1905, July 18, 1906, Jan. 2–6, 1908; Birmingham, Minutes of the City Council, M, 191 (Jan. 9, 1908).

27. *News*, Oct. 22, 31, Nov. 1, 2, 5, 7, 1898, May 28, 1907; *Labor Advocate*, Dec. 17, 1898, Sept. 12, 1903, Aug. 4, 1906.

the booster-minded Birmingham Real Estate Association unanimously and enthusiastically endorsed Greater Birmingham.[28]

In the Greater Birmingham referendum of 1908 suburbanites were still divided, but 58.6 percent of them voted for annexation. Of the ten suburbs which voted, six favored Greater Birmingham by majorities ranging from 54 to 72 percent, but the four most industrial suburbs of East Birmingham, North Birmingham, Pratt City, and Fairview opposed it, by majorities of 51 to 58 percent. Ensley did not participate in the referendum.[29]

The strongest opposition to Greater Birmingham came from industrialists whose plants lay interspersed among the suburbs and who sought either to keep their plants from being annexed, or failing that, to get tax exemptions. The Sloss-Sheffield Steel and Iron Company had furnaces just east of the city and in the suburb of North Birmingham. The Republic Iron and Steel Company had furnaces in the suburb of Thomas, three miles northwest of Birmingham, and T.C.I. had a vast installation of iron furnaces and steel plants at Ensley, six miles northwest of Birmingham. A complex of iron foundries and machinery manufacturing companies lay immediately east of Birmingham, and the major cast-iron pipe and cotton-gin manufacturing companies clustered in the suburb of North Birmingham.[30]

Greater Birmingham promoters found it difficult to devise an annexation formula that would satisfy enough suburbanites and industries to gain passage by the legislature. For example, in early 1899 a compromise bill to annex several suburbs and industrial plants seemed near passage. But before the final vote, railroad and corporation attorneys got the measure amended to make "little slice[s] of country" into the new boundaries to exclude each big industry. This shattered the tenuous compromise that had united a majority of the Jefferson representatives. Unable to annex the industries and fearful of suburban anger if only industries went free, the representatives allowed the bill to die. Again in the 1903 legislature, Greater Birmingham boosters seemed near success, only to have Jefferson County's single state senator, corporation attorney Hugh Morrow, invoke senatorial courtesy to kill the bill, saying it would force industrial plants away from the city.[31]

In the next legislative session, in 1907, two rival Greater Birming-

28. *News*, Dec. 16, 1907, Jan. 2–6, 1908, July 14, 1909; Ira J. Sandefur to Governor Braxton Bragg Comer, July 31, 1907, Governor's Office Records, ADAH.
29. Birmingham, Minutes . . . Council, M, 191 (Jan. 9, 1908).
30. *News*, June 20, 1907.
31. *Age-Herald*, Jan. 31, Feb. 11, 18, 19, 21, 1899, Mar. 19, Oct. 1, 1903.

ham bills appeared. Attorney E. J. Smyer of the Jefferson County Sanitary Commission, eager to bring the entire urbanized area under city sanitary jurisdiction, sought to neutralize opposition by drafting an annexation bill that exempted mining and manufacturing plants from city taxes for fifty years. But the city attorneys of Birmingham and of several of the suburban towns objected to such tax "discrimination." Legislative representative, Jere C. King, a suburbanite, said that if the suburbs were to come in and pay higher taxes, so should the industries; and he and the city attorneys drafted a bill to annex nearly all suburbs and industries without any tax exemptions.[32]

Both bills passed the House, but in the Senate Jefferson County's Nathan L. Miller, a part-time corporation attorney, endorsed the Smyer bill and attempted to invoke senatorial courtesy to kill the King bill. Ordinarily other senators would have honored his request. But in 1907 the lieutenant governor, who presided over the senate, was former Birmingham alderman Henry B. Gray, president of a small downtown savings bank. Knowing Birmingham's revenue problems first hand, Gray denounced industrial tax exemptions and vigorously promoted the King bill. And he used his power over committee appointments to line up a bare majority of one, including his own tie-breaking vote, to break all precedent and override senatorial courtesy, reject Senator Miller's crippling amendments, and pass the King bill.[33]

The bill's fate then depended on Governor Braxton Bragg Comer, also from Birmingham. Comer had run on a railroad regulation platform and had cultivated a "Progressive," anticorporation image, but he himself was an industrialist, the owner of the Avondale Cotton Mill, which would be annexed. He had always urged Birmingham to use tax exemptions to attract new industries, and he had favored the Smyer bill. But when the King measure came to the fore, Comer's old associates in the Birmingham Commercial Club and Board of Trade pressured him to sign it. These clubs had been the political base from which Comer had launched the railroad-rate crusade that had carried him to the governorship, and they had provided vital political and financial support for his entire legislative program. Bowing to their insistent demand, he reluctantly signed the King measure.[34]

The King Act provided for a Greater Birmingham referendum,

32. *News*, July 19, 25, Sept. 20, 1906, Feb. 12, May 28, June 20, 25, 1907.
33. *Ibid.*, July 17, 24, 26, 30, 1907.
34. *Ibid.*, Aug. 11, 13, 1906, Feb. 12, Aug. 5, 6, 8, 9, 1907; James F. Doster, *Railroads in Alabama Politics, 1875–1914* (University: Univ. of Alabama Press, 1957), 146–56; *Age-Herald*, Mar. 7, 1903.

which carried: 3,496 for annexation, 900 against. But opponents attacked the constitutionality of the act and found enough technical imperfections that the courts declared it null and void.[35]

In 1909 Representative King reintroduced his measure in a fortuitous special session of the legislature, called mainly to enact statewide prohibition. He and Gray again pushed the bill through both houses, but attorneys from the three major iron and steel corporations prevailed upon a house committee to make neat incisions in the new boundaries to exclude the Sloss furnaces in North Birmingham, the Republic furnaces in Thomas, the entire suburb of Ensley, and all the T.C.I. industrial plants and iron and steel furnaces.[36]

Again crucial decisions lay with Governor Comer, who had the authority to make executive amendments and demand that the legislature include them before he would sign the bill. And the governor received many suggestions for changes. Residents and town officials of many suburbs wrote that they were willing to come into Greater Birmingham only if Ensley and the iron furnaces came in too. Suburban Woodlawn city attorney R. Dupont Thompson denounced the attempt "to tax the little fellows to exclusion of larger ones." Six foundries and manufacturers of pipe and machinery telegraphed to request that Comer exclude their plants from the city, especially since the iron furnaces were to be left outside. But Comer's political allies from the railroad regulation movement, including his staunchest supporter, the Birmingham *News*, urged him to keep all the manufacturers in and to bring in the iron furnaces as well. The *News* wanted "no class legislation and discrimination" and said the industries "enjoy privileges for being in this territory and it is hard to see any fair reason why they should be exempt from their just part of the responsibilities of running the government."[37]

Comer sided with his downtown allies and sought to live up to his anticorporation image. He left all the foundries and pipe machinery

35. *Ibid.*, July 30, 1907, Dec. 28, 30, 1908; Birmingham, Minutes . . . Council, M, 191 (Jan. 9, 1908).

36. *News*, Aug. 5, 6, 9, 10, 13, 1909.

37. R. Dupont Thompson to Comer, Aug. 17, 1909; Mayor N.A. Barrett and East Lake aldermen to Comer, Aug. 17, 1909; telegrams to Comer from American Casting Company, Payne & Joubert Machine & Foundry Company, The East Birmingham Iron Roofing & Corrugating Company, Birmingham Machine & Foundry Company (which claimed to speak for eighteen industries), Southern Sewer Pipe Company, and American Cast Iron Pipe Company, Aug. 14–16, 1909; Frank S. White to Comer, Aug. 6, 1909, Governor's Office Records, ADAH; *News*, Aug. 10, 1909.

manufacturers inside the new boundaries. By executive amendment, which he got the legislature to approve, he also included all the Sloss and Republic iron furnaces, the T.C.I. coke ovens at Pratt City, and the town of Ensley, where T.C.I. owned much real property. But he excluded the T.C.I. iron furnaces and steel mill, which stood one block from downtown Ensley. Comer's new boundaries included Sloss property valued in 1911 at more than $664,000, Republic property valued at $872,567, and T.C.I. property valued at $504,180, including real estate in Ensley. But T.C.I. equipment, iron furnaces, and steel plants located immediately outside Ensley and valued at $3,778,239 escaped annexation.[38]

The behind-the-scenes considerations that enabled T.C.I. to escape are not entirely clear, but an interesting clue appeared in a 1911 letter from T.C.I. president George Gordon Crawford to W.P.G. Harding, president of the First National Bank in Birmingham and an important adviser to Governor Emmet O'Neal. In 1911 T.C.I. was seeking to prevent the appointment of an unfriendly tax commissioner, and Crawford argued that T.C.I.'s vast plans for expansion and development depended on appropriations from the directors of the parent United States Steel Corporation, appropriations which must be won in competition with the managers of the U.S. Steel plants in Pittsburgh, Pennsylvania, and Gary, Indiana. "I have secured appropriations for the Birmingham District," wrote Crawford in 1911, "largely upon the representations which I have made that the people of this section were sufficiently enlightened to realize the benefits which would accrue through the investment of capital, and that it would be encouraged and treated fairly if it were put here." He continually had "to encourage our New York people in everyway" about Birmingham, because "it is far from their headquarters and it is difficult for me at best to keep them favorably inclined towards this Southern development." Therefore, he warned, any "unfair treatment of corporate enterprises" would "excite suspicions in the minds of the financial people in New York who control our company, to a degree that would make any efforts to obtain additional capital to carry on these developments very much more difficult and possibly unsuccessful."[39]

This basic argument, much more credible, flexible, and repeatable

38. *News,* Aug. 19, 1909; Alabama, *Local Acts, 1909,* pp. 393–95; Jefferson County, Tax Assessment Books, 1911.

39. Crawford to Harding, Jan. 30, 1911, Governor's Office Records (Emmet O'Neal administration) ADAH.

than a crude threat to move to another city, apparently impressed government authorities and helped T.C.I. maintain its tax-exempt status outside the city limits. In 1917, for example, city commissioner Arlie K. Barber proposed that Birmingham annex the T.C.I. plants and force them to pay their share of the city taxes. City commission president George B. Ward quickly cited a T.C.I. proposal to invest $25 or $50 million in the district and said the annexation idea would do "injury to the proposed development." The rest of the commission agreed with Ward and quickly dismissed the idea of annexing T.C.I.[40]

Although T.C.I. largely escaped the 1910 annexation, the Sloss and Republic companies, the pipe and machinery manufacturers, and the foundries suffered a major and unexpected defeat. And it soon turned out that including the industries had been crucial to the financial success of Greater Birmingham. For several years the entire annexed area cost the city approximately as much for services as it paid in taxes. Although the industries actually added less to the tax base than did the residential suburbs, the industrial plants paid more in taxes than they cost the city for services, and some of their tax revenue paid for services in the work-ing-class suburbs they had generated, thus sparing the city from a financial deficit from its annexations.[41]

Analysis of the annexation goals and achievements of the upper-, middle-, and lower-ranking economic groups reveals interesting patterns of power. It is significant, first, that on this issue no single unified "power elite" controlled Birmingham and automatically dictated decisions. In-deed, by 1907 the issue provoked intense conflict between industrial and commercial leaders. Moreover, all groups involved in the struggle displayed some real leverage and ability to help shape the final outcome. The lower-ranking wage earners were not a unified bloc. Those inside Old Birmingham were generally for annexation, but they took little part in the struggle aside from voting in the 1908 referendum. Wage earners in the suburbs remained hesitant and divided to the end, but because they were numerically strong and because they were the party being courted by the expansionist downtown interests, they exercised considerable leverage. They won some concessions and guarantees about civic services and schools, and after annexation the quality of their services did improve significantly. They also impressed Governor Comer

40. *Age-Herald*, Jan. 24, 1917.
41. *News*, Aug. 21, 1909; Jefferson County, Tax Assessment Books, 1911; re-ports of the city comptroller in *News*, Mar. 2, 1913, and *Age-Herald*, July 22, 24, 1915.

with their strong belief that it would be unfair to annex them without the industries.

From 1890 to 1910 the downtown commercial and professional men of the middle-ranking groups experienced continual frustration on the annexation issue. They were well organized, they dominated the board of aldermen, and they mobilized all the mayors for annexation, but their local political power was not sufficient to win the necessary legislative approval. They finally succeeded in 1907 and 1909 only through unique and almost fortuitous political circumstances that placed two Birmingham citizens, Governor Comer and Lieutenant Governor Gray, in positions where they could break the legislative power of the industries.

Over the twenty-year annexation struggle the upper-ranking industrialists enjoyed considerable success in translating economic power into political power. The Birmingham Rolling Mill and the Alice and Sloss furnaces fought off annexation in 1895, and all the industries avoided city taxes for another fifteen years. Industrialists had much political success with the argument that all Birmingham citizens would suffer if the city burdened the crucial industries. Industrialists also used influence at legislative bottlenecks to block annexation. When finally in 1910 many industries did experience defeat, the biggest corporation still got away, and the one that got away weighed more in terms of assessed valuation than did the two iron and steel corporations that got caught. Arguments about not handicapping industrial development with taxes remained potent.

ASSESSED VALUATION OF PROPERTY

The low assessed valuation of Birmingham property was a third factor that constrained property-tax revenue. State law prescribed and county officials executed an assessment procedure that virtually guaranteed low assessments, and mayors and aldermen, complain as they might, had no ability to change it. As of 1890 each property owner assessed the value of his property himself and reported it, under oath, to the county tax assessor, who reported it to the court of county commissioners. The assessor and the court had the right to inspect property and correct unreasonably low assessments; but they lacked a staff and budget for such work, and they seldom made corrections, especially on returns which were equal to or slightly higher than the returns of the previous year.[42]

Between 1896 and 1900, however, Governor Joseph F. Johnston revised the assessment machinery. Johnston had been a prominent Birmingham attorney, banker, and industrialist; but as a politician he had developed an anticorporation image, and in 1896 he was elected governor as a "half-Populist" free-silver Democrat. Though Johnston believed corporations to be valuable economic institutions, he also believed that they and all property owners should contribute more to government revenue, so that government would have the means to provide more services and to play a more dynamic role in promoting economic development. In 1897 Johnston persuaded the legislature to create the new position of county "back-tax commissioner." The commissioner was to examine all assessment returns and to recommend raises, and he was to receive a commission of 10 percent of the taxes on the raises that the county court approved. Corporations considered this a defeat because the commissioners, seeing the prospect of large commissions, would probably concentrate on making major raises on big corporations.[43]

The locally elected court of county commissioners still set the final assessments, however, and in 1897 Jefferson County's court granted almost none of the raises recommended by the back-tax commissioner. In fact, in 1897 Jefferson County's total assessment declined. Even so, the activity of the back-tax commissioner was distasteful to the corporations, because he publicized their low assessments and aroused anticorporation sentiment. In 1898 Governor Johnston investigated the Jefferson County court and found that they had maneuvered to keep some proposed corporation raises off the docket and had made deals to keep all corporation raises very small. The governor promptly had the legislature abolish the county court and replace it with a board of revenue, the first board appointed by him. In 1899 the back-tax commissioner and Johnston's new board of revenue concentrated on corporations and jolted the major utility and iron-furnace companies with

42. U.S. Census, *Report on Wealth, Debt, and Taxation at the Eleventh Census: 1890*, vol. 15, Pt. 2, *Valuation and Taxation*, p. 103; *Age-Herald*, Mar. 10, 1892; *Birmingham City Code, 1890*, pp. 40–41.

43. Sheldon Hackney, *Populism to Progressivism in Alabama* (Princeton: Princeton Univ. Press, 1969), 13, 137–44; *News*, Jan. 27, 1897; Alabama, *Acts, 1896–1897*, pp. 521–31, 1489.

raises ranging from 48 to 150 percent of their original assessments.[44]

But in 1900 Governor Johnston left office, and his successor, who was much less vigorous in promoting state revenue and services, appointed back-tax commissioners who essentially let the system revert to self-assessment by owners. By 1907 Mayor George B. Ward estimated that commercial property in central Birmingham was assessed at 18.5 percent of market value and residential property at 20 to 35 percent. In 1907 the state tax commission found Birmingham property assessed at 22.5 to 28 percent of market value. And as of 1905 the railroads' assessed valuation per mile, which was set by a state board, had not changed significantly since 1895.[45]

In 1907 Braxton Bragg Comer, another prominent Birmingham industrialist with anticorporation leanings, became governor, sweeping in a sympathetic legislature and seeking to regulate railroad and utility rates and to force the companies to pay much heavier taxes. Like Johnston, Comer wanted the state to have enough revenue to become a dynamic instrument for economic growth. Comer's legislature created a new state tax commission to raise all assessments in the state from their estimated level of approximately 30 percent of market value to 60 percent. And for railroads and utilities the legislature added a new "intangible property" tax on stocks and bonds.[46]

Under the Comer program Birmingham railroads and utilities experienced heavy tax increases. Between 1905 and 1910 the "tangible" assessed valuation on Jefferson County railroads increased by 22 to 50 percent per mile of track, and the new "intangible" assessment added another 19 to 22 percent to the total railroad assessed valuation. Utility

44. *News*, Aug. 23, 24, 31, Sept. 23, 1897, July 6, 1900; *Age-Herald*, Jan. 22, 27, Feb. 18, Aug. 27, 1899.
Some assessment raises made by the 1899 board of revenue were:

Corporation	Assessment Proposed by Company	Assessment Set by Board of Revenue	Percent Raise
Birmingham Gas Co.	$ 80,000	$ 200,000	150.0
Consol. Elec. Lt. Co.	128,130	200,000	56.1
Birmingham Railway & Elec. Co.	196,270	375,000	91.1
T.C.I.	2,200,309	3,250,000	47.7
Sloss Steel & Iron	551,395	1,000,000	81.4
Pioneer Mining & Mfg.	316,443	600,000	89.6

Source: *Age-Herald*, Aug. 16, 26, 1899.

45. *Age-Herald*, Feb. 28, 1901; *News*, May 1, 17, 1907; Alabama, *Annual Report of the State Auditor* for 1895–1907.
46. Hackney, *Populism to Progressivism*, 311–14; Alabama *Acts, 1907*, p. 372.

assessments advanced even more sharply. The Birmingham Railway, Light, and Power Company (B.R.L. & P.) had been compromising with the board of revenue for relatively small yearly assessment increases. But in 1907 its proposed "tangible" assessment of $1,768,000 was suddenly raised to $2,500,000, and then the state tax commission added a new "intangible" assessment of $2,750,000. The final B.R.L. & P. assessment of $5,250,000 had been raised 196 percent over the company's original 1907 return and 437 percent over the company's total 1905 assessment.[47]

Industrialists also received special attention in 1907. The new state tax commission demanded that Jefferson's back-tax commissioner and board of revenue push county assessments up to 60 percent of market value. And Jefferson's new back-tax commissioner Frank S. White, an ally of Governor Comer, focused energetically on the corporations. He proposed raises of $17,000,000, half of that amount on the county's nine largest corporations. The corporations fought the raises before the board of revenue and finally compromised for significant but smaller raises. For example, a proposed 79 percent T.C.I. raise was compromised at 41 percent, and a proposed 172 percent Sloss raise was settled at 45 percent.[48]

The assessments and raises of such iron corporations as T.C.I. were usually the county's largest, but critics argued that they were far too small. The critics did not dispute the assessments on company plants and equipment but rather the assessments on reserve mineral land. The 1907 raises on T.C.I. pushed its plant and equipment assessment to approximately 25 percent of the company's reasonable book valuation of $8 million; and despite the efforts of Governor Comer's tax commission, 25 percent of true value remained the norm for assessments throughout the county and state. But critics questioned the methods of assessing T.C.I.'s 150,000 acres of reserve coal and iron land in Jefferson County. In 1907 the company assigned the land a book value of approximately $11,250,000, or $75 per acre, a value based apparently on prices at which the company had originally purchased the land from the federal government, railroads, and farmers. And the 1907 assessed value of the land was roughly 25 percent of the T.C.I. book value.[49]

47. Alabama, *Annual Report of the State Auditor* for 1905, 1910; *News*, Aug. 17, Nov. 15, 1907.
48. *News*, July 5, 1907; Jefferson County, Tax Assessment Books, 1907.
49. In 1907 T.C.I. listed its land, property, and construction as worth $44,815,951. In 1906 it had set the cost of plants and equipment at $11,211,872 (including approximately $3,000,000 for the subsidiary Alabama Steel and Shipbuilding Company,

But experienced Birmingham mining engineers estimated the actual royalty value of T.C.I. iron ore in Jefferson County lands to be thirty-five cents per ton, or $133,360,395, and the royalty value of the coal to be $84,116,902. This made the land worth $217,477,315, or roughly $1,450 per acre, for mineral rights alone, exclusive of surface rights. The total 1907 T.C.I. tax assessment of $4,750,000 for both plants and lands was only 2.2 percent of this royalty estimate for mineral lands alone.[50]

Moreover, John Moody of *Moody's Magazine*, Frank A. Munsey of *Munsey's Magazine*, and Richard H. Edmonds of *Manufacturers' Record* said that U.S. Steel officials privately considered their Alabama iron ore worth not thirty-five cents but rather one dollar per ton, which would have made a total value of $381,146,602 for iron ore.[51] This valuation plus the $84,116,902 royalty value of coal would have made the reserve mineral land worth $465,146,602, or roughly $3,100 per acre. The total T.C.I. tax assessment for both plants and lands was only 1.0 percent of that estimate.

Of the three methods of estimating the value of reserve mineral land, the Jefferson County board of revenue almost unquestioningly accepted the first and lowest—T.C.I.'s own book value—and it never seriously considered surveying the lands to estimate tonnage value. (In 1914 the state tax commission did briefly seek to estimate tonnage value. See chap. 6.) The county had no authority or funds to hire an engineering staff. Moreover, in practice it customarily based real estate assessments upon current income production rather than upon market value. In assessing rental property, for example, the board often ignored the actual market price of the property and estimated true value to be roughly 6.5 times the annual gross rent currently earned by the property. It then set the assessed valuation at approximately 25 or 30 percent

---

whose tax assessments were calculated separately, and $8,000,000 for T.C.I. plants). This left $33,604,079 as the book value of 447,423 acres of mineral lands. Of these, 149,893 acres, or 33.5 percent, were in Jefferson County. Therefore a very rough approximation of the T.C.I. book value of Jefferson County mineral lands would be 33.5 percent of $33,604,079, or $11,257,366. This is $75.10 per acre. See U.S. Congress, House of Representatives, *Hearings Before the Committee on Investigation of United States Steel Corporation*, 8 vols. (Washington, D.C., 1912), II, 1127, 1230–31, VI, 4687; Jefferson County, Tax Assessment Books, 1907.

50. U.S. Congress, House, *Hearings . . . United States Steel Corporation*, II, 974, 991–1022, 1034–40; the royalty value, which varied with the quality and accessibility of the minerals, was the amount per ton which a company would have to pay for mining from land which it leased rather than owned.

51. *Ibid.*, 1129–35; Edmonds' editorial quoted in Ethel Armes, *The Story of Coal and Iron in Alabama* (Birmingham 1910), 522. He believed T.C.I. should actually consider the ore worth two dollars per ton.

of the estimated true value. Therefore, in dealing with reserve mineral lands which earned no current income, the board did not think it appropriate to consider the market or royalty value of minerals. Rather, seeking to apply the income-production guideline to corporate property, it defined corporation interest and dividend payments as the income, and it therefore considered the official capitalization or book value upon which the company paid the interest and dividends to be a reasonable measure of the company's income-producing property. In 1907, therefore, the board accepted T.C.I. book value of seventy-five dollars per acre for mineral land, and it set the assessed valuation at approximately 25 percent of that, or nineteen dollars per acre. Since this was more than the average assessment of farm land, it seemed consistent.[52]

The board's use of this procedure affected Birmingham revenue, even though most of the reserve mineral land was outside the city limits. Had the board chosen to assess much higher, according to tonnage estimates, the city would have benefited through an increase in the county education tax and through an accompanying rise in county aid to Birmingham schools.

The board's principle of estimating value according to current income production also benefited major real estate developers and individual owners of large amounts of real property. As of 1907 land companies such as the Birmingham Realty Company (successor to the Elyton Land Company) held many vacant blocks of property for future sale, blocks both inside Birmingham and within half a mile of the city limits. Since such blocks produced no current income, the board of revenue allowed the companies to assess them for very low amounts, often only 2 to 5 percent of a reasonable market value. Realtors defended this practice, intoning that the only logical measure of the value of idle property was indeed income production. But their position was inconsistent. Developers holding idle land were actually discounting future income, and any estimate of true value should have taken into account both present and speculative future income. Such income was best indicated by the current market value of similarly situated land, and according to law, that market value should have been the basis of assessments. By convincing the board to ignore current market value and to base assessments of idle land solely upon current income production, the speculative land developers achieved a major tax break. When the developer finally sold the land, the tax assessment promptly rose to 25 or 30 percent of the sale price, but then the new owner paid the tax and the

52. *Age-Herald*, Aug. 27, 1899; Jefferson County, Tax Assessment Books, 1907.

developer paid no tax on the speculative income earned by his land.[53]

The assessment machinery also allowed real estate companies to defeat most proposed increases on downtown commercial buildings and residential rental houses. In 1907 the Jefferson County back-tax commissioner, under heavy pressure from Governor Comer's state tax commission, proposed significant raises on the realty companies and large property owners, the first such raises since 1900. The Birmingham Real Estate Association promptly hired a battery of lawyers who would represent any taxpayer whose property assessment had been raised more than $5,000 and who would pay the association one-tenth of 1 percent of the taxes he had paid in 1906. The association's lawyers found legal flaws in the procedures of the back-tax commissioner and forced a major delay in the hearings before the board of revenue. And most large property owners, taking advantage of the delay and uncertainty, were able to compromise on small raises. In 1907 the total raise finally achieved by the back-tax commissioner on all Jefferson County property, far from boosting the average assessment to 60 percent of market value, was barely enough to nudge it to 30 percent.[54]

In summary, as of 1910 Birmingham officials were stuck not only with a frozen property-tax rate, but also with a stagnant level of assessment. The system's greatest beneficiaries were the corporate owners of reserve mineral lands, all ranking economically in the top 1 percent of the population, and the speculative owners of valuable vacant real estate, all ranking in the upper levels of the next highest 19 percent of the population. But all real estate owners, whether they held downtown commercial property, residential rental property, or individual owner-occupied residences and workingmen's cottages, appreciated and helped to perpetuate the system which kept their assessments low. The assessment system, it should be noted, did not uniformly protect all high-ranking groups. In 1907 it dealt sudden sharp raises to the railroads and the utilities, whose quasi-public status made them vulnerable to rising anticorporation sentiment.

THE LICENSE TAX

When the constraints upon the property tax brought Birmingham to financial crisis, the mayors and aldermen had no choice but to exercise

53. *News*, Aug. 23, 1897, May 21, 24, 1907; *Age-Herald*, Aug. 27, 1899; Jefferson County, Tax Assessment Books, 1905–1910.
54. *News*, June 5, 28, July 10, Aug. 12, 26, 1907.

more severely their unhampered authority to levy business license fees. During the city's dire depression crisis of 1895–1897, for example, when proposed increases in the property-tax rate failed, the aldermen extended the license schedule to much previously untaxed merchandise, such as books, clothing, crockery, dry goods, furniture, glassware, hardware, stoves, tinware, and other household furnishings. And in 1897 the aldermen for the first time graduated the license fees according to the merchant's maximum inventory value during the previous year. Thus, in 1894 a merchant with an $8,000 inventory of hardware had paid no hardware license fee; in 1895 he paid $15; and in 1897 he paid $50. In 1897 the graduated fees went as high as $150 for stock worth $25,000 or more, but they were still regressive, averaging 2 percent of a $250 inventory, but only 0.6 percent of an inventory ranging from $5,000 to $25,000.[55]

The sharp 1897 boost in the license tax spurred merchants to support the 1898 Birmingham tax amendment, in return for a promise of license-tax reduction. The amendment passed, but the revenue-hungry city officials could not bring themselves to reduce an established flow of revenue, and they left the promise unfulfilled.[56] In 1901, therefore, when the Alabama constitutional convention reaffirmed the strict limits on the property-tax rate, the merchants of Birmingham sent the attorney of the Board of Trade to tell the convention: "If it is important to fix a limit on the power to levy a property tax, why is it not equally important to put a limit on the power to levy a privilege [license] tax? The privilege tax in the past has been more abused than the direct or property tax." But Birmingham Mayor Walter M. Drennen, a department store owner himself, opposed any constitutional limit on city license taxes, and argued that the flexibility of the license tax—the one major source of revenue regulated solely by the aldermen—was essential to city solvency. The merchants obtained no license-tax restriction; the new constitution provided tax-limit restrictions only upon the property tax.[57]

Until 1907 the license tax on merchants remained quite stable. Then the adoption of prohibition by Jefferson County, over the vigorous opposition of a majority of the city aldermen, dried up the $113,000 liquor-license tax, which was 13.7 percent of the total city revenue. This

---

55. License ordinances in *Age-Herald*, Dec. 21, 1893, Dec. 21, 1894; and Birmingham, Minutes of the Mayor and Board of Aldermen, G, 145 (Dec. 21, 1896).
56. *Age-Herald*, Jan. 25, 1899, Nov. 28, 1901.
57. *Ibid.*, June 17, 1901. See also *ibid.*, June 14, 15, 16, 1901.

forced the aldermen to increase the merchant license-tax rates from 30 to 50 percent on all items and all sizes of inventory. Mayor Ward recommended that they simultaneously adjust the graduated scale so that the larger merchants would pay a fee proportional to that paid by smaller merchants, but the aldermen ignored him. The new fees varied from 3 percent of the inventory value of the smallest merchants to just below 1 percent for the largest. These rates persisted through the final years of aldermanic government.[58]

The utility corporations suffered proportionately still greater license tax increases. As of 1900 utility license taxes had been relatively low, nearly the same as in 1890. The railroads paid $500 each; most utilities paid from $100 to $500 each; and the waterworks paid $1,000, but was contesting half of it in court. In 1905 Mayor Ward declared that the city should boost the utility license fees to 2 percent of gross company receipts, and the aldermen began voting dramatic increases against the unpopular utility corporations. Between 1904 and 1907 the Birmingham Railway, Light and Power Company (street railway, gas, electricity, and steam heat) saw its license tax rise 289 percent, from $9,000 to $35,000 a year. Between 1904 and 1907 the waterworks' license tax rose 1,500 percent, from $1,000 per year to $15,000, which was 3.7 percent of gross annual receipts; and each railroad's license tax increased from $500 to $1,750 per year. By 1907 the utilities and railroads were contributing 30.5 percent of the city's business-license revenue, compared with 18 percent in 1895.[59]

For several years the utilities were unable to resist the increases. In 1906 waterworks superintendent Daniel J. O'Connell sought to coordinate a protest by several companies, but he learned to his disappointment that the street railway president thought the "best thing to do" was "to pay it and say nothing more about it." The street railway probably took this attitude, said O'Connell, because "they are constantly wanting new franchises and rights to use the streets." And certainly all the utilities, which frequently needed to negotiate new rights with the city, and which had provoked the hostility of most voters, were more vulnerable, even, than merchants when the aldermen raised license taxes. At the same time the utilities and railroads were bearing the brunt of Governor Comer's program to boost property-tax assessments, and con-

58. *News*, Dec. 5, 1907; Birmingham, *Message of the Mayor, 1907*, p. 13; Birmingham, Minutes . . . Council, M, 155 (Dec. 18, 1907).

59. *News*, Aug. 17, Nov. 25, 1905, Nov. 15, Dec. 5, 1907; Birmingham, Minutes . . . Aldermen, H, 217–18 (Dec. 6, 1899), L, 533–35 (Dec. 19, 1906); Birmingham, *Message of the Mayor, 1907*, p. 12.

sequently they suffered the sharpest tax increases of any groups in Birmingham.[60]

The financial statistics of 1907 revealed Birmingham's continuing heavy reliance on the license tax, which provided 38.7 percent of total city revenue, while the property tax provided 39.7 percent. By 1910 the loss of liquor license revenue and the annexation of suburbs and industries had reduced the license tax to 25.6 percent of total revenue and raised the property tax to 59.4 percent. Even so Birmingham still relied far more heavily on license taxes than did any of the other five southern cities in the 100,000 to 300,000 population class. The corresponding percentages in Louisville were 12.2 and 83.9; in Atlanta 11.8 and 76.9; in Memphis 4.5 and 90.0; in Nashville 3.8 and 86.7; and in Richmond 7.8 and 81.3. No other Alabama city was in Birmingham's size class, but the influence of Alabama's severe state constraints on city property-tax revenue could be seen in the revenue patterns of Mobile, which received 27 percent of its revenue from the license tax and 65 percent from the property tax, and of Montgomery where the percentages were 28 and 63.[61]

MINOR REVENUE SOURCES

In addition to the two major revenue sources, Birmingham had several minor sources, the most important being the street tax, the fines and earnings of convicts, and the school tuition.[62] These tended to hit hardest at the poor, and in periods of intense revenue shortage aldermen consciously sought to squeeze more than usual out of these sources.

The Birmingham city charter said the city could require every male between the ages of eighteen and fifty to work several days each year on the streets. As a substitute, the city charged a street tax of three dollars per adult male. Since everyone paid the same amount, regardless of his property or income, it hit the poor hardest. And in 1894 the *Age-Herald* said "The very object of the street tax law is to make people who would otherwise contribute nothing pay a small sum toward the support of the

60. O'Connell to J.H. Purdy, Jan. 3, 1907, B.W.W.C. Letterbooks.
61. U.S. Census, *Financial Statistics of Cities* for 1907, 1910, 1911. The statistics of all the cities have been reclassified to make the categories consistent. See n. 3 above.
62. Other minor and less significant sources of revenue were street-repair payments by corporations, inspection fees, interest, donations, rent, franchise payments, and the poll tax.

city government. In this way the negro is made to furnish something."
But labor unions denounced the tax as inequitable, and large industrial
corporations found it a nuisance, especially when the street-tax collector
issued wholesale garnishment proceedings against the wages of many
workers. During the depression of the 1890s the aldermen encouraged
the tax collector by temporarily offering him a 9 percent commission
on all street taxes, and he more than doubled street-tax revenue by cor-
nering Negroes and white day laborers who had previously dodged the
tax. But in 1898, when the property tax rate increased, labor leaders
and several sympathetic aldermen began a determined drive to abolish
the street tax. In 1899 they persuaded the aldermen to reduce it to two
dollars per male, and in 1905 to abolish it completely, to the delight
of organized labor and the industrial corporations.[63]

Birmingham voters and aldermen believed that convicted lawbreakers
should provide enough revenue, either through fines or hard labor, to
cover the cost of maintaining the police and prison systems, without
burdening the taxpayers. City convicts who could not pay their fines
were sentenced to the chain gang to work out the fine at fifty cents per
ten-hour day cleaning and repairing streets. Between 80 and 90 percent
of the chain gang prisoners were Negro, but, until 1915, whites who
could not pay their fines were chained along with Negroes. Often in
department reports the police chiefs totaled the fines and convict earnings and proudly noted how close they came to covering the costs and
payroll of the police department. In 1896 the Birmingham *State Herald*
reported that the police commissioners "were of the opinion that the
police department is a source of revenue to the city."[64]

In times of special financial distress the city intensified law enforcement to increase revenue. During the depression year 1897, the aldermen went to the unusual length of leasing all prisoners with sentences
of more than sixty days to the coal mines of the Sloss-Sheffield Steel and
Iron Company, in return for maintenance and seventeen cents per day
per prisoner. Mayor Frank V. Evans claimed that the system served
"to diminish crime in our midst, curtail expenses, [and] increase reve-
nues." Among the first sixty-nine prisoners sent to the mines, 90 percent
were black, including 25 percent who were black women. The sixty-
nine had committed such crimes as vagrancy, larceny, assault and battery,
gambling, and prostitution. Organized labor, especially coal miners,

63. *Age-Herald*, Dec. 1, 1894, Nov. 16, 1899; *News*, Nov. 17, Dec. 22, 1898,
Dec. 7, 1905.
64. *State Herald*, Feb. 12, 1896; *News*, June 26, Sept. 12, 1900.

denounced the city for "placing punishment at the limit whereby crime may be made a source of revenue for the city," and both daily newspapers opposed the system. By 1898 the city, confident that the property-tax-rate increase would pass, did not renew the lease.[65]

The city, however, continued to view its prisoners as a source of revenue. In 1899 Police Chief Connie W. Austin, a reform-minded, antiliquor, antigambling crusader, proudly announced that his frequent raids and strict enforcement had boosted fines and convict earnings so high that "the city clears about $800 per month out of the police department." This, he boasted, made Birmingham "one of the few cities of the country whose police force is more than self sustaining."[66]

From 1897 through 1910 the city depended almost entirely on the convict gang to clean and repair streets and sewers. Labor leaders endorsed this use of convict labor and suggested that convicts also collect garbage. City street commissioner John M. McCartin, who took charge of the 90- to 125-man street gang in 1901, believed the police department should consistently supply him with enough convicts to accomplish the necessary street work. In 1905, according to the *News*, McCartin complained to the mayor that he had only one hundred convicts and needed "one hundred more men to accomplish the work on the streets that is expected of his department," and he specifically urged stricter enforcement of the vagrancy law to produce the needed workers. During the next few years vagrancy enforcement did intensify, and in 1907 approximately 193 men per day served on the street gang. That year fines plus the value of convict labor totaled $80,000, which exceeded by $4,000 the total cost of the police department, and which accounted for 9.7 percent of the city's entire general revenue. By 1911, after annexation had greatly increased the property tax revenue, fines and convict labor still accounted for 7.0 percent of Birmingham's general revenue. Most other southern cities of similar size extracted less than 1 percent of their revenue from fines and convict labor, and Nashville 2.4 percent. Only Atlanta, at 6.2 percent, approached Birmingham in reliance upon convicted lawbreakers as a source of revenue.[67]

In Birmingham one other city department—education—at times

65. *News*, July 8, 1897 (Mayor Evans), Mar. 31, 1897 (coal miners), Apr. 8, 1897, Feb. 19, 1898; *State Herald*, Jan. 17, 1896.

66. *Age-Herald*, Oct. 28, 1899. See also *News*, June 26, Sept. 12, 1900.

67. *Labor Advocate*, Apr. 16, 1898, May 18, 1901; Birmingham, *Message of the Mayor, 1897*, pp. 7–12, 25–26; *ibid.*, 1898, p. 41; *Age-Herald*, Mar. 15, Oct. 28, 1899, Apr. 4, May 26, 1901, Jan. 28, 1902; *News*, June 26, 1900, Sept. 26, 1905, Feb. 14, 1908; U.S. Census, *Financial Statistics of Cities* for 1907, 1910, 1911.

extracted significant amounts of revenue from its patrons. As of 1890 the elementary grades were tuition free, but high school students paid two dollars per month, which covered 73 percent of high school costs. During the mid-1890s the aldermen, failing to increase the property tax, resorted to charging elementary school tuition. This caused 25 percent of the white and 38 percent of the black school children to drop out the first month. Many working-class people supported the 1898 property tax amendment in the hope of eliminating tuition, and in 1898 the board of education did drop the elementary, but not the high school tuition. Year after year the Trades Council petitioned to abolish the high school tuition, but the board of education sadly announced that it must again levy the eighteen-dollar-per-year tuition, which accounted for 2 percent of the city's total revenue. Finally in 1910 the aldermen and board of education, buoyed by the increased property tax revenue following annexation, agreed to abolish all tuition, and the *Labor Advocate* celebrated the realization of a long-sought reform.[68]

REVENUE PATTERNS, 1871–1911

From 1871 to 1911 rural-oriented state constraints squeezed and shaped Birmingham's revenue pattern. The constraints enhanced the ability of industrialists and real estate interests to maintain favorable tax policies, but they frustrated the efforts of merchants, small manufacturers, professional men, artisans, and grocers to reshape the tax structure. Thus the very middle-ranking commercial and professional interests that dominated city governing bodies found it necessary to impose the heaviest direct revenue burdens on their own groups. Only by doing so could they provide the basic civic "housekeeping" services which downtown businessmen considered absolutely essential.

Lower-ranking groups—the bottom 80 percent of the population— also felt the pressure created by state constraints. The city used intense law enforcement to squeeze extra revenue from politically impotent Negroes. It penalized small grocers and saloonkeepers with a regressive license tax, much of which was probably shifted to wage earners. And for years it relied to an unusual extent upon the street tax and school tuition, which were especially obnoxious to workingmen. Still, wage earners, whether buying or renting houses, liked the low property tax

68. *Age-Herald*, Aug. 26, 1894, Aug. 13, Sept. 7, 1899; *News*, Sept. 25, 1897, June 11, 1900; *Labor Advocate*, Mar. 1, 1907, Jan. 7, June 24, 1910.

and were reluctant to see the rates or the assessments rise. Although the machinery that kept the property tax low bestowed its greatest advantages upon the largest landholders and the major industrialists, it also provided some immediate benefit for small taxpayers, and their low-tax attitudes helped maintain the system.

With the partial exception of the utility corporations, Birmingham's upper-ranking groups—the top 1 percent of the population—benefited greatly from the state constraints and from legislative bottlenecks that made tax increases difficult. Between 1890 and 1910 some of the constraints were weakened or removed, but the political configurations that made such changes possible were quite uncommon. The only important tax defeats imposed upon Birmingham's upper-ranking groups —the establishment of the back-tax commissioner in 1897, the increased assessments on railroads and utilities in 1907, and the annexation of 1910—were accomplished through the legislature, which alone had sufficient authority. And they occurred only after the crucial intervention of Governors Joseph F. Johnston and Braxton Bragg Comer. Both governors had rallied a majority of Alabama's rural population against specific corporations and had helped to create "anticorporation" legislatures that would act against upper-ranking groups. The conjunction of issues and leadership to produce such legislatures occurred only twice between 1890 and 1910; more often the legislative configuration and the traditional state revenue structure served to shield upper-ranking groups from increased taxation.

VI

Municipal Revenue, 1911-1921

$\mathbb{B}$IRMINGHAM revenue patterns shifted sharply with the annexations of 1910 and the advent of commission government in 1911. The annexation added less new business than new property, and thereafter the property tax produced twice the revenue of the license tax. But license taxes remained high and continued to provide an unusually large portion of city revenue. In 1911 the new city commission adopted more businesslike accounting methods which revealed that the aldermen had been running large annual operating deficits and funding them with long-term bonds. The commission retrenched severely but deficits persisted. Most citizens believed that license taxes had reached their upper acceptable limits and that only the property tax could provide additional revenue. But the procedures for raising the property tax were unwieldy, especially since citizens disagreed sharply over who should shoulder the increased burden.[1]

THE LICENSE TAX

The 1910 annexation brought many unhappy suburban merchants under the high license tax. One grocer with an inventory of $1,000 found his yearly license tax tripled, from $51 in the suburbs to $151 in Greater Birmingham. His property tax on residence, store, and merchandise doubled, but even so was only $30 per year. The license schedule discriminated heavily against small neighborhood grocers and general stores. Those with approximately $1,000 inventory paid a fee of 7.5 to 15 percent of the value of their inventory, but merchants with inventories of $3,000 to $50,000 paid 1.0 to 1.5 percent, and the major

1. Birmingham *News*, Apr. 11, 1911, Mar. 11, 1913.

merchants with inventories of $100,000 to $150,000 or more paid only 0.3 or 0.4 percent. In 1916 the small merchants and retail grocers mobilized to demand license fee "equalization." The city commission, responding probably to suburban voting strength in 1915, revised the fee schedule to 1.0 to 1.5 percent of inventory at the lower and middle levels, and 0.6 to 0.9 percent at the upper levels. Merchants with $150,000 inventory were appalled to see their license fee rise 200 percent from $500 to $1,500. They sent a Board of Trade committee to protest, and it hammered out a compromise that left the new lower rates intact at the lower inventory levels, but that reduced the rates for inventories above $100,000 to 0.4 or 0.5 percent. Thus large merchants who had paid $500 in 1915 finally paid $600 to $800 in 1916. The compromise rates were still regressive, but less oppressively so.[2]

Under the new rates license tax revenue continued to grow absolutely and to provide roughly 22 to 27 percent of total city revenue. After 1913 most merchants, hoping to reduce the license tax, supported a movement to increase the city property tax. By 1920 they succeeded and obtained a 20 percent reduction in mercantile licenses, the first such cut in thirty years. City commission president N.A. Barrett said, "Local business men have had to labor under the handicap [of high license taxes] for practically as long as Birmingham has been a city. It has always been the intention of the city to cut the licenses as soon as it is practicable, but never until now has it been at all possible."[3]

In 1920, before the reduction, the license tax provided 27 percent and the property tax 57.4 percent of general revenue in Birmingham, as compared with 10.4 and 79.8 percent, respectively, of the combined general revenue of the five other southeastern cities in the 100,000 to 300,000 population class: Louisville, Atlanta, Memphis, Nashville, and Richmond. By 1922, Birmingham's new balance was 18.2 percent from license taxes and 71.3 percent from property taxes, as compared with 9.9 and 80.5 percent in the other five cities.[4]

From 1911 to 1921 the utility license tax also stirred controversy. By 1910 the street railway paid approximately 2 percent and the water-

2. T.H. Friel to Governor Braxton Bragg Comer, Aug. 14, 1909, in Governor's Office Records, ADAH; license ordinances in Birmingham, Minutes of the Board of Commissioners, V, 440–61 (Dec. 16, 1914), V, 369–88 (Dec. 28, 1915), W, 421–45 (Dec. 29, 1916); Birmingham *Age-Herald*, Jan. 1, 7, 8, 11, 18, 1916.

3. *Age-Herald*, Dec. 21, 1920.

4. U.S. Census, *Financial Statistics of Cities Having a Population of Over 30,000: 1921* (Washington, D.C., 1922); *ibid., 1922* (Washington, D.C., 1924).

works 3.3 percent of gross receipts, and waterworks superintendent Daniel J. O'Connell feared "almost a hopeless fight" to keep aldermen from raising his fee to $20,000, or 3.7 percent of gross receipts. In 1911 the utility companies, fearing that Birmingham's revenue-hungry officials and corporation-hating voters would relentlessly force the utility license rates ever higher, turned to the state legislature and induced it to limit city license taxes on utilities to 2 percent of gross receipts.[5]

After the legislature adjourned, citizens suddenly discovered, to their great dismay, that an extra "joker" clause, mysteriously added during the last-minute confusion, provided that a utility company's city license tax should be reduced by an amount equal to the city property tax it paid on its intangible assessment. This in effect canceled the entire license tax on Birmingham utilities. Most Birminghamians blamed the "joker" clause on Representative Walker Percy, an attorney for the waterworks. But private correspondence indicates that neither the waterworks officials nor Percy had any prior knowledge of the "joker" clause, and that they were happily surprised to discover that some unknown legislative friend of utilities—perhaps a corporation attorney from another county—had secretly provided a large tax break for utilities. For the next four years the Birmingham Water Works Company, citing the "joker" clause, refused to pay any of its yearly $18,000 license fee. But the Birmingham Railway, Light, and Power Company, less eager to take advantage, agreed in 1911 to "donate" to the city the full license fee of $50,000, and in 1912 half the fee, or $25,000. Waterworks superintendent O'Connell wrote privately that the B.R.L. & P. did so because it had many city contract negotiations pending and wanted "to keep peace in the family" until the contracts were settled.[6]

When the 1915 legislature met, the waterworks officials were resigned to repeal of the joker clause, which quickly occurred. Indeed, they feared passage of a proposal to require four years' retroactive payment, but they defeated it. Then they supported a drive by Jefferson County representative John B. Weakley—a major stockholder in another county's waterworks—to reduce the limit on city utility license taxes from 2 percent of gross receipts to 1 percent. Weakley, who held key committee positions, appeared likely to succeed, despite energetic opposition from Birmingham city officials. But then the B.R.L. & P. Com-

5. O'Connell to J.H. Purdy, Nov. 30, 1910. See also *ibid.*, Apr. 8, 15, 1911, B.W.W.C. Letterbooks; *News*, Dec. 15, 1910; Alabama, *Acts, 1911*, pp. 188–89.

6. O'Connell to Purdy, Dec. 26, 1911. See also *ibid.*, Apr. 8, 15, Dec. 30, 1911, B.W.W.C. Letterbooks; *News*, Nov. 14, 25, 1911, July 23, Oct. 21, 1912; *Age-Herald*, Jan. 9, 1915.

pany informally let it be known that it "cared little for the proposed reduction" because "the people would become outraged" and the "company would prefer to retain the good will of the people rather than to incur their enmity." This strengthened legislators who preferred a 2 percent limit and they kept it in force for the remainder of the decade.[7]

The episode of the "joker" clause probably did as much as any single event to convince Birmingham citizens that corporations pulling backstage wires really ran Birmingham politics. But the reaction of the B.R.L. & P. Company and the repeal of the "joker" clause in 1915 demonstrated that anticorporation outrage could be an effective political force and that such a blatant special favor to corporations was a fluke that could not long survive. The episode's key outcome, however, was the acceptance on all sides of the original utility proposal—a stateimposed limit of 2 percent of gross receipts. Companies with little local defense against popular anticorporation actions had found an effective backstop in the state legislature.

THE STREET TAX AND SCHOOL TUITION

After 1910 Birmingham relied less heavily on its minor sources of revenue, especially since it had abolished the street tax in 1905 and the high school tuition in 1910. Only once, in 1916 when a lawsuit temporarily froze 30 percent of the city's property tax, did the financial situation become so critical that officials resorted briefly and reluctantly to the unpopular street and tuition levies. In 1916 labor unions protested fervently and got the commission to make the levies less onerous than originally proposed. Industrialists also opposed the new street tax and maintained constant pressure to drop it, especially since they blamed it, in part, for a 1916 exodus of Negro workers from Birmingham to the North. By mid-1917 the revenue situation had brightened and the city commission promptly repealed the street and tuition levies, which for one year had provided approximately 4 percent of city revenue. Though labor leaders had been unable to forestall the taxes in a crisis, they were able, with the political help of industrialists, to insist that the city use them no longer than absolutely necessary.[8]

7. *Age-Herald*, July 30, 1915. See also *ibid.*, July 21, Aug. 5, 1915; H.H. Horner to A.M. Lynn, Sept. 10, 13, 1915, B.W.W.C. Letterbooks.

8. *Age-Herald*, Jan. 20, Aug. 26, 1915, Jan. 29, Feb. 2, July 19, 1916, Jan. 10, June 27, 1917.

FINES AND CONVICT LABOR

Throughout the decade, however, fines and convict labor continued to contribute significant revenue. In 1913 the city commission adopted a new accounting procedure: the actual yearly cost of maintaining the prisons was divided by the number of man-days worked by convicts during the year to arrive at a "cost per head per day" for convict labor. The city comptroller charged the street and sanitation departments this cost— 93.2 cents in 1914—for each convict they used. In 1914, with a convict gang of approximately 140 men per day, these departments accomplished all their work without employing nonconvict labor except for foremen and wagon drivers. The departments, which otherwise would have had to pay workers $1.25 or $1.50 per day, benefited; and besides, the city recovered the cost of maintaining the prisons. The labor of the able-bodied convicts even covered the maintenance of convicts who could not work.[9]

Between 1914 and 1920 reform-minded city commissioners sought to ameliorate some of the inhumanity of the chain gang. They shortened sentences of well-behaved convicts, reduced the use of shackles, forbade corporal punishment, and stopped using white prisoners on the streets. City commissioner James D. Truss, who was in charge of the streets, denounced the reforms because they reduced his street force, and in 1917 he declared: "I cannot think, under existing conditions, how the streets of Birmingham can be economically maintained. . . . This comes as a consequence of having made our city prison a boarding house instead of a house of correction." Truss exaggerated, but convict revenue did drop from more than $30,000 in 1915 to $16,000 in 1918 and $20,000 in 1920. One factor that contributed to this reduction was a tough 1915 prohibition law that markedly reduced arrests. However, it also reduced the cost of prison maintenance, and in most years convict earnings continued to cover prison costs. In 1920 convict earnings and fines accounted for more than 6 percent of city revenue. Thus Birmingham continued to extract a larger portion of its revenue from convicted lawbreakers than did any other city of similar size.[10]

9. Birmingham, Committee of One Hundred, *Report of Sub-Committee to Investigate Expenditures of the City of Birmingham* (Birmingham, 1915), 21–22.
10. Truss statement in *Age-Herald*, Jan. 9, 1917. See also *ibid.*, May 16, 1915, Nov. 9, Dec. 13, 1916, July 28, 1917, Dec. 5, 1919; *News*, Apr. 19, 1911; U.S. Census, *Financial Statistics of Cities, 1921.*

THE PROPERTY TAX

Between 1911 and 1921 most interest groups agreed that Birmingham must increase its property tax revenue, but they clashed over how to do it. Annexation of industrial property had been popular in previous decades, but only the Tennessee Coal, Iron, and Railroad Company plants remained outside and there were no serious proposals to annex them. Therefore most proposals for increasing property tax revenue focused on one of three alternative strategies. The first was to raise the assessed valuation of property, especially that of wealthy groups whose property, allegedly, was greatly underassessed. The second was to make Birmingham a separate county, so that all county taxes collected inside the city would be used for city rather than rural services. The third was to raise the city property-tax rate.

The First Strategy: Assessment Equalization. The first strategy, raising the valuation of underassessed property, was proposed solely by spokesmen for wage earners and small property owners. They knew that most property was assessed at far less than the lawful 60 percent of market value, and they believed that their small pieces of residential property were assessed much nearer 60 percent than were industrial, commercial, and large blocs of idle real property. Studies by the state tax commission and the county back-tax commissioner supported their belief, and they contended that a scientific equalization of all assessments at 60 percent would dramatically increase city revenue at little cost to workingmen and small property owners. And during the first half of the decade they stubbornly opposed any tax-rate increase until such equalization had occurred.[11]

The Birmingham *Labor Advocate*, alone among Jefferson County interest-group spokesmen, praised the back-tax commissioner's large assessment increase proposals, denounced the board of revenue for adopting so few of them, and in 1912 supported the governor and the state tax commissioners, who intervened to try to boost Jefferson County assessments. Labor leaders proposed two basic changes in assessment procedure. First they urged the state to create boards of expert tax appraisers to make assessments scientifically instead of letting the locally

11. *News*, May 22, June 1, 1912; Birmingham *Labor Advocate*, Apr. 5, 12, Nov. 1, 1912, Dec. 25, 1914.

elected board of revenue, which was subject to political pressures, set assessments. Second, they denounced the custom of assessing improvements and improved land at a higher percentage of market value than unimproved land. Indeed, they urged the opposite, proposing that vacant unimproved urban land and reserve mineral land be assessed at 75 percent of market value and improvements at 25 percent. In 1916 the Trades Council took the lead in organizing a labor Tax Reform League to work for this policy.[12]

Most other groups, especially those whose property tended to be relatively underassessed, opposed any major increase in assessed valuations in Jefferson County. The Birmingham Real Estate Association led the opposition, and in most conflicts it was joined by the iron furnace corporations, utilities, banks, manufacturers, and merchants. By 1913 all these groups acknowledged that the city needed more property tax revenue, but they proposed to provide this by increasing the city tax rate, which would raise only their city taxes, rather than increasing their assessed valuations, which would raise their county and state taxes as well.[13]

The opponents of assessment increases argued that all Jefferson County property was already assessed higher than property in other Alabama counties, and that the other counties should be equalized up to Jefferson's level before any Jefferson assessments were raised. They argued accurately that the back-tax-commissioner system discriminated against large rich counties like Jefferson, where high potential commissions spurred commissioners to energetic efforts to raise assessments, and that it favored small rural counties, where potential commissions were so small that the office of tax commissioner often stood vacant or was filled by a perfunctory performer.[14] Moreover, the opponents charged that the governors and state tax commissions, reluctant to raise assessments on voters throughout the state, instead "raided" rich Jefferson County, a "luscious peach on a low-hanging bough." This, said the opponents, was why the state tax commission intervened in 1912 "over the heads" of the Jefferson board of revenue to propose raises of $41 million, in addition to $25 million proposed by the back-tax commissioner. Such raises would have increased Jefferson's assessed valuation

12. *Labor Advocate*, Apr. 5, 1912, July 24, 1914, Apr. 23, 1915, Jan. 15, 22, Oct. 7, Nov. 4, 1916.

13. *News*, May 22, June 3–13, 1912, Nov. 21, 1913; *Age-Herald*, Dec. 22, 1914.

14. *News*, Aug. 19, 1912, Mar. 25, 1914; Alabama, *Report of the State Tax Commission, 1914*, p. 12.

58 percent, but large taxpayers successfully fought the raises in court, and Jefferson's final 1912 valuation was only 7 percent higher than the 1911 valuation.[15]

In 1914 opponents of assessment increases were appalled when the state tax commission established a special Birmingham office to collect technical data and construct detailed maps to provide a basis for more accurate assessment of coal and iron ore lands. The state commission pointed out that the local board of revenue, lacking the staff and budget to gather mineral land data, had no choice but to accept the corporations' book values as the basis of assessment. "Manifestly these lands, particularly those of a mineral character, are greatly under assessed," said the state commission, and they "can never be properly and fairly assessed without such accurate data as it is the object of this office to supply." The commission noted that in Minnesota the collection of technical data had in six years increased the assessment of mineral lands from $65 million to $250 million, and it anticipated an increase of similar magnitude in Alabama.[16]

In 1914 the Birmingham Real Estate Association and Chamber of Commerce played a leading role in organizing a County and State Tax Reform League to seek legislative changes in assessment machinery. Their low assessment preferences were congenial to the rural interests that dominated the legislature, and in 1915 they prevailed upon the legislature to enact all essential points of their program. The new law abolished the position of back-tax commissioner; scuttled the Birmingham mineral assessment office; deprived the state tax commission of its power to intervene in county assessments; assigned complete control of county assessments to a county equalization board of three local real estate agents; and provided that assessments, once set by this board, were to stand unchanged for four years, rather than being reconsidered every year. The low-assessment advocates believed, accurately, that if local rather than state authorities set final assessments, taxpayers would suffer few significant assessment increases. Jefferson officials would sympathize with the argument that Jefferson already had higher assessments than other counties and that it paid an excessive portion of state taxes. Equalization boards in other counties would also underassess competitively,

15. *News*, Aug. 19, 1912. See also *ibid.*, May 15, June 3–13, July 1, 22, Aug. 22, Sept. 24, Dec. 18, 1912, Mar. 26, 30, Apr. 24, 1913; Alabama, *Annual Report of the State Auditor of Alabama* for 1911, 1912.

16. Alabama, *Report of the State Tax Commission, 1914*, pp. 7, 46–50.

and if no state agency had authority to intervene, few large raises would occur anywhere.[17]

The sponsors of the new system effectively advertised it as an equalization plan, claiming that the expert equalization boards, appointed rather than elected, would promptly equalize assessments at 60 percent of market value. But the machinery of the plan practically guaranteed that this would not happen, and it did not. To boost the 1915 Jefferson County assessment from the existing 30 percent to the proposed 60 percent of market value, the assessors would have needed to raise assessments 100 percent on the average. In fact, in 1916 the new Jefferson County Board of Equalization proposed raises only one-third that large. The Real Estate Exchange found even this exorbitant, and in apparent amazement, denounced the new board as "tax raiders." But the equalization board quietly settled for modest raises, and the total 1916 county assessment was only 12.8 percent larger than the 1915 assessment. The level of assessment was still below 35 percent of market value.[18]

Under the new plan, the 1916 assessment stood practically unchanged until 1920, though during World War I Birmingham experienced an economic boom and steep inflation. From 1916 to 1920 local bank clearings increased 583 percent, and from 1917 to 1920 the cost of housing rose 68 percent and land values soared. But property tax assessments reflected none of this, increasing less than 3 percent between 1916 and 1920. During the same period license-tax revenue, which did respond somewhat to the boom, increased 85 percent, even though the rates remained the same. The National Industrial Conference Board estimated that by 1920 the assessed valuation in Alabama was only 19.3 percent of market value.[19]

The state legislature met again in 1919, and Governor Thomas E. Kilby, eager to increase state revenue and services, overcame intense opposition and pushed through a measure that centralized tax assessment procedures in state hands. State-appointed and state-controlled

17. *News*, Mar. 25, Sept. 25, 29, Nov. 5, Dec. 1, 1914, June 1, 1916; *Age-Herald*, Dec. 13, 17, 1914, Feb. 7, July 17, 30, Oct. 21, 1915; Alabama, *Report of the State Tax Commission, 1914*, p. 11; Alabama, *Acts, 1915*, pp. 413–31.

18. *Age-Herald*, Apr. 8, 1915, May 25, 26, June 1, 22, 28, 29, July 24, Nov. 10, 11, 1916; Alabama, *Annual Report of the State Auditor* for 1915, 1916.

19. Alabama Industrial Development Board, "An Economic Survey of the Metropolitan District of Birmingham," prepared by John A. Maguire, mimeo, Birmingham, 1932, BPL; Institute for Government Research of the Brookings Institution, *Taxation of the State Government of Alabama*, vol. 4, pt. 3 of *Report on a Survey of the Organization and Administration of the State and County Governments of Alabama* (Washington, D.C., 1932), 150–52.

county tax adjusters were to set all assessments, which were to stand unchanged only two years, and the state tax commission was to have the power to audit personal or corporation records. Kilby also proposed that assessment appeals should go to special nonjury district tax courts, but to get his basic plan enacted, he had to agree instead to retain the right of appeal to locally elected boards of revenue or to local jury courts.[20] In 1920 the new state-appointed tax adjuster in Jefferson County, even though restrained by the threat of appeals, raised the county assessment 26 percent, the largest increase in at least thirty years. It was, however, the first raise in four years, and it did not offset inflation.[21]

In 1923 the legislature completely reversed itself, repealing Kilby's new centralized assessment machinery and returning the assessment process to locally elected officials. The Brookings Institution studied the resulting system and concluded: "The procedure amounts in most cases to self-assessment by the taxpayers." During the early 1920s the ratio of assessed valuation to market value of property in Alabama was estimated at 19.3 percent by the National Industrial Conference Board, at 31.4 percent by the federal census, and at 33 percent by the Detroit Bureau of Governmental Research. In other words, the groups who had sought scientific equalization of assessments at 60 percent of market value had fallen far short.[22]

The Second Strategy: A Separate County.   A second strategy for increasing city property-tax revenue was to make Birmingham a separate county which could use both city and county taxes for city services. As of 1914 Jefferson County levied a seven-mill property tax, which brought in $987,500, and two-thirds of it, or $668,800, came from property inside Birmingham. The county apportioned back to the city only $144,200 ($122,700 for schools and $21,500 for streets). County officials claimed that they employed much of the remaining $524,600 which came from city taxpayers to finance county hospitals, charities, and courts that city residents used. But even the county's calculations, which exaggerated its expenditures on city services, revealed that prop-

20. *Age-Herald*, July 9, Aug. 12, Sept. 6, 11, 1919; Alabama, *Acts, 1919*, pp. 308–27.

21. Alabama, *Annual Report of the State Auditor, 1921.*

22. Brookings Institution, *Taxation*, 126–36, 151, 225; *Labor Advocate*, Jan. 31, 1920; U.S. Census, *Wealth, Debt, and Taxation, 1922*; C.E. Rightor (Detroit Bureau of Governmental Research), "Commentary upon the Comparative Tax Rates of 177 Cities, 1923," *National Municipal Review* 12 (Dec. 1923), 719–28.

erty inside the city paid at least 2.4 mills of tax from which city residents received no benefit. Thus if the city became a separate county the 2.4 mills plus the savings from government consolidation would add the equivalent of three or four mills of property tax to city revenue, without any actual increase in the taxes paid by city residents.[23]

In 1912 and 1913 merchants, professional people, the merchant-oriented Birmingham *News*, the Birmingham *Ledger*, and city commission president Culpepper Exum seized upon the separate-county idea as a seemingly painless way to augment city revenue and perhaps to reduce license taxes. Exum had agonized over a growing deficit that was impairing city credit with local banks. Finally, he invited Birmingham's economic leaders—five iron and coal corporation officials, four bankers, two utility company officials, three daily newspaper publishers, four major real estate company presidents, six leading merchants, two physicians, and one labor leader—to a "Financial Problem Dinner" at the country club. There he described the revenue crisis and presented a detailed, carefully prepared, separate county plan as the best solution.[24]

The meeting impressed the economic leaders with the urgent need to augment city revenue, and they asked the Chamber of Commerce to appoint a special committee to find the best method. The committee considered Exum's separate county plan, but it found the iron and coal companies adamantly opposed because they believed they "would be too greatly victimized by tax gatherers." Perhaps they feared that the new city-county assessors would raise industrial assessments; perhaps they feared that if the rural portion of Jefferson County were deprived of Birmingham revenue, the rural assessors would raise mineral land assessments. Publicly the corporations emphasized that the expense of keeping a separate corps of lawyers for each county would be too great. The Chamber of Commerce finally sided with the major corporations and rejected the separate county idea in favor of a city tax rate increase.[25]

But in 1915 Jefferson County legislator Isadore Shapiro, whose strongest support had come from inside Birmingham, sponsored separate county legislation. *Age-Herald* reporter Hugh Roberts predicted that Shapiro's bills would die "a-borning" because legislators, "impressed"

23. *News*, Feb. 28, Mar. 16, 1913; *Age-Herald*, July 18, 24, 1915; Birmingham, Board of Education, *Annual Report of the Birmingham Public Schools, 1914*, pp. 16–17.

24. *News*, July 18, 19, 20, 1912, Feb. 26, 28, 1913.

25. *Age-Herald*, Aug. 15, 1915. See also *ibid.*, Dec. 20, 21, 1914; *News*, Mar. 11, 20, May 25, June 4, Oct. 23, 31, 1913.

with the "big voices" of Birmingham corporations, were "rendered timid," and as a result, would not act. The bills did die in committee. Whether the "big voices" of the corporations caused the death was less clear. In any case, the corporation voices were seconded by Jefferson County officeholders, who might lose their positions, and by most rural Jefferson voters, who opposed letting wealthy Birmingham secede from the county. In the legislature the separate county advocates could not override that coalition.[26]

During the 1919 session of the legislature Birmingham city commissioner Henry P. Burruss and assistant city attorney Jere C. King (author of the 1909 Greater Birmingham Act) led another fight for a constitutional amendment to make Birmingham a separate county. King asserted, that "if the taxpayers of Birmingham spent their money where they pay it, we would have good streets." Burruss calculated that "at the present time we are making a free gift of over $500,000 annually to the upkeep of the county." The Chamber of Commerce sponsored a debate in which Burruss spoke for the separate county, and Augustus H. Benners, T.C.I. attorney and state legislator, spoke against it. The chamber voted 102 to 21 against the separation and lobbied against it in Montgomery. A second T.C.I. attorney, Borden Burr, made daily speeches around the county to build sentiment against division of "Imperial" Jefferson County. In a close vote the legislative house defeated the separate county amendment, with five Jefferson representatives against it and two (a labor organizer and a delegate from Bessemer) for it. At the end of the decade, the advocates of a separate county, like the advocates of increased assessments, had experienced only defeat.[27]

The Third Strategy: A Tax-Rate Increase. By the time the separate county plan came before the legislature in 1915 and 1919, most merchants no longer supported it. In 1913 and 1914 they had followed the lead of the Chamber of Commerce in rejecting the separate county plan in favor of the third strategy—a tax rate increase. In 1913 the president of the Chamber of Commerce was W.P.G. Harding, president of the First National Bank, which had close ties with the major corporations. From October to December 1913 Harding orchestrated a civic campaign of newspaper articles, editorials, and mass meetings to publicize the

26. *Age-Herald*, Aug. 15, 1915. See also *ibid.*, Dec. 13, 1914, July 17, 18, 1915; *News*, Dec. 14, 16, 1914.
27. *Age-Herald*, Aug. 23, 1919. See also *ibid.*, Aug. 22, 27, 29, Sept. 4, 1919.

advantages of a tax-rate increase over an assessment increase or a separate county. But a tax-rate increase required a constitutional amendment approved by the state legislature and the state electorate, and the legislature was not scheduled to meet until 1915. In November 1913 sixty-eight determined industrialists, merchants, bankers, and professional men, convened by Harding, commissioned twelve prominent men to plead with Governor Emmet O'Neal to call an immediate special session of the legislature to pass an urgently needed tax rate amendment. Governor O'Neal listened sympathetically but decided against a special session, forcing the civic leaders to wait until 1915.[28]

In 1914 Harding turned the Chamber of Commerce presidency over to Paschal G. Shook, a prominent iron and coal dealer. Shook continued to mobilize sentiment for a tax-rate increase, and in December 1914 he and city commission president George B. Ward, an investment broker, appointed a prestigious "Citizens' Committee of 100" (actually 159), in which representatives of the top 1 percent of the population in the upper-ranking interest groups held 17 percent of the positions, representatives of the top one-fifth of the population in the middle-ranking groups held 79 percent of the positions, and representatives of the bottom four-fifths of the population in the lower-ranking groups held 4 percent of the positions. These men held highly publicized hearings; and in January 1915, right before the legislature convened, the committee reported unanimously that a city tax rate increase was the only possible revenue solution. Most leading Birmingham merchants signed the report, though as late as December 1914 some of them had still favored the separate county plan.[29]

As of 1915 Birmingham's city property tax rate was still limited by the 1901 constitution to ten mills ($1.00 for $100.00 assessed valuation). In addition Birmingham received the equivalent of approximately 2.5 mills of property-tax revenue from county and state aid to education. (The county levied a 1.5-mill school tax and in 1914 apportioned back to Birmingham 91 percent of the amount paid by Birmingham property, and the state levied a 3.0-mill school tax and apportioned to Birmingham 46 percent of the amount paid by Birmingham property.)[30]

28. *News*, Oct. 19, 23, Nov. 16, 21, Dec. 5, 1913.
29. Committee listed in *Age-Herald*, Dec. 18, 1914; report Jan. 19, 1915; Birmingham, Committee of One Hundred, *Report of the Sub-Committee on Permanent Financial Relief for the City of Birmingham*, (Birmingham, 1915); *News*, Dec. 14, 16, 1914.
30. Birmingham, Board of Education, *Annual Report*, 1914, pp. 16–17. County

In July 1915 the leaders of the Committee of 100, lobbying skillfully, prevailed upon the legislature to submit to a statewide referendum a "home rule" constitutional amendment. It would authorize Birmingham to boost its property tax rate from ten to fifteen mills, if a city referendum approved. Civic leaders campaigned for the amendment throughout the state, and they bombarded Birmingham with "home rule" arguments. Opponents, most of them spokesmen for workingmen's suburbs and the suburban business districts, demanded equalization of assessed valuations before any tax rate increase, but they lacked the resources for an elaborate campaign. Still, the low-tax sentiment of rural voters gave the opponents a powerful advantage. In the December 1915 referendum the rural voters turned the amendment down, and, more important, so did the middle- and working-class suburbs of Birmingham. The percentages for the amendment were 40.8 statewide, 34.5 in Jefferson County, 37.4 in Greater Birmingham, and 61.4 percent in the four precincts of Old (pre-1910) Birmingham, the only Birmingham precincts that endorsed it. Nine of the thirteen annexed suburbs gave it less than 25 percent. Even if the state had approved the amendment, the antagonistic workingmen and suburban residents would probably have blocked the rate increase in the necessary local referendum.[31]

The united upper- and middle-ranking economic groups, the top one-fifth of the population, had met unexpected defeat on a major revenue issue. "That Birmingham itself would refuse to vote home rule for itself was never considered," exclaimed the *News* in disbelief. "Truly patriotism is measured in Birmingham by the thimbleful." But the *News* vowed to "awaken" the city through "teamwork."[32]

Instead of teamwork the promoters of a tax rate increase experienced more frustration, and within six months another stunning reversal actually reduced Birmingham's effective property tax rate for a time. Five mills of the existing ten-mill city rate stemmed from the 1898 Birmingham Tax Amendment, which had been incorporated in the 1901 constitution. It pledged the five mills for interest and sinking funds for bonds "heretofore issued" or "now authorized by law to be issued." The city, interpreting this liberally, had used most of the five mills for

---

and state aid to education included small amounts of other miscellaneous revenue, including poll taxes.

31. Alabama, *Acts, 1915*, pp. 674–77; *Age-Herald*, Jan. 1, July 21, 23, 24, Sept. 17, Nov. 3, 7, Dec. 26, 28, 1915, Jan. 11, 1916; *Labor Advocate*, Dec. 25, 1914, Nov. 5, 1915.

32. *News*, Dec. 28, 31, 1915, Jan. 2, 1916.

bonds issued after 1901. But in June 1916 Thomas C. McDonald, a large property holder, alleged in a lawsuit that the five mills must be used exclusively for pre-1901 bonds. If that were done, the pre-1901 bonds could soon be retired, and then, said McDonald, the city must drop the 1901 five-mill bond tax. To the surprise and consternation of the city commissioners, McDonald won in the city court and in the state supreme court. Only two of the five mills had been going to pre-1901 bond payments; the other three were being used for post-1901 bonds. The decision froze those three mills in an unneeded sinking fund for pre-1901 bonds, and forced the city to dip into other revenue to meet payments on the post-1901 bonds. For practical purposes, the already straitened city had lost the use of three mills of its ten-mill tax rate.[33]

The civic leaders who had sought to raise the city tax rate were near despair, but one other legal possibility emerged, and they seized upon it. The 1915 legislature had approved another constitutional amendment, subject to a November 1916 state referendum, to allow both counties and local school districts to levy special three-mill school property taxes, in addition to the regular property taxes. After the McDonald decision the *Age-Herald* said the school tax amendment might save Birmingham finances and urged a "massive education campaign" to get voters to pass it "overwhelmingly."[34]

Birmingham civic leaders organized a committee of one thousand and mobilized one hundred "prominent men" to carry out a "heavy speaking schedule" for the amendment. They discovered to their delight that the school tax amendment inspired far greater enthusiasm statewide and locally than had the "home rule" amendment. Across the state, school boards and educators campaigned for it. In Birmingham most people in the lower four-fifths of the population desired improved free school facilities and wanted to end the emergency school tuition and street tax that the city commission imposed immediately after the McDonald decision. The annexed suburbs urgently needed new school buildings and more teachers. And labor unions, which had equivocated on "home rule," unanimously and enthusiastically endorsed the school tax and held "educational" rallies to promote it.[35]

33. Alabama Constitution, 1901, Art. XI, Sec. 216, in Francis N. Thorpe (comp.), *The Federal and State Constitutions, Colonial Charters, and Other Organic Laws*, 7 vols. (Washington, D.C., 1909), I, 219; *Age-Herald*, June 8, July 11, 17, 1916; *News*, Jan. 17, 1918.

34. *Age-Herald*, Aug. 18, 1916.

35. *Ibid.*, July 18, 19, 24, 1916; *Labor Advocate*, Aug. 12, 1916.

The 1916 school tax campaign provoked much less demand for prior assessment equalization than had the 1915 "home rule" campaign. Enthusiasm for better schools overrode concern with assessments. Also the Real Estate Exchange had quite successfully advertized the 1915 assessment law as an effective equalization device; and in the spring of 1916 it had, by daily protests and mass meetings against "enormous" equalization raises, created the erroneous impression that painful equalizing changes were being made. Though the final 1916 assessment was far short of an equalized 60 percent of market value, many people apparently believed that essential equalization had taken place. Even if not, the 1916 assessments were frozen for four years, making it futile to advocate major assessment increases before 1920.[36]

In November 1916 convincing majorities of 59 percent in Alabama and 79 percent in Jefferson County approved the school tax amendment. In January 1917 a three-to-one majority in Jefferson County approved a new three-mill county school tax. Birmingham would receive its portion as county aid to education, and had in effect increased its property tax rate by three mills. But three old mills were still frozen by the McDonald decision. In March 1918, therefore, the city commission proposed that the voters of Birmingham, which comprised a local school district, approve an additional special three-mill district school tax, as allowed by the 1916 amendment. If that carried, promised the commission, it would immediately stop levying the three mills of the 1901 tax that were piling up money in a frozen sinking fund. Again a school tax proved politically popular, gaining enthusiastic endorsements from labor and from suburban leaders, and on election day it rolled up a 79 percent majority.[37]

In approving the tax-rate increases in the form of school taxes, the wage earners and suburban residents had at least earmarked the new taxes for education, the city service which was most important to them. The city commission promised that "every dollar" of the 1917 county school tax and "every cent" of the 1918 district school tax would go to schools. But when the city board of education received the 1917 county school tax, the city commissioners immediately diverted some city funds from education to other city services, and school income actually rose by only 70 percent of the new tax revenue. In 1918 the city commission

36. *Age-Herald*, May 25, 26, June 1, 29, 1916.
37. *Age-Herald*, Nov. 11, 1916, Jan. 31, 1917, Mar. 1, May 1, 7, 1918; *Labor Advocate*, May 4, 1918; *Code of Alabama, 1923*, I, 429.

applied $200,000 of the new $300,000 district school tax to interest payments on post-1901 bonds, in replacement of the frozen three mills of the 1901 tax, and the schools actually gained only $100,000, or 33 percent of the new revenue. Still, education gained more than did any other department, and wage earners rejoiced when this put an end to tuition.[38]

By 1919 the civic leaders who in 1913 had set out to raise the city property tax rate from ten to fifteen mills had in fact, after waging three strenuous tax campaigns, merely overcome the McDonald suit loss and raised the rate three mills. Critical revenue deficiency persisted, and the economic leaders continued to resist a large assessment increase or a separate county arrangement. In 1919 they mobilized the Chamber of Commerce to help rebuff commissioner Henry Burruss' separate county proposal in the legislature. Then they worked with three other Birmingham city commissioners, John R. Hornady, John E. Brown, and John H. Taylor, and with officials from forty-two other financially troubled towns, to have the legislature submit to the voters a new "home rule" city tax-rate constitutional amendment. In the referendum campaign the amendment promoters, having noted the popularity of the 1916 school-tax amendment, stressed the school needs of the cities. But a municipal "home rule" tax generated much less enthusiasm than a clear-cut school tax, and the 1919 amendment mustered a bare majority of 52.5 percent in Alabama, a slight majority (percentage not available) in Birmingham, and it actually lost with 49.5 percent in Jefferson County.[39]

The amendment authorized any city to increase its tax rate as much as five mills if it obtained local referendum approval. Another provision, which received almost no pre-election publicity, in effect overthrew the McDonald decision and specifically freed all five mills of Birmingham's 1901 bond tax for any existing or future bonds. Therefore the city commission, which in 1918 had suspended three mills of the 1901 bond tax and replaced them with the district school tax, could, after 1919, reinstate and use the three mills, thereby increasing the tax rate through common ordinance that required no voter approval. The commission desired a five-mill increase. For schools it needed two mills, which it

38. *Age-Herald*, Jan. 31, 1917, Mar. 1, 1918; U.S. Census, *Financial Statistics of Cities* for 1918, 1919; Birmingham, *Financial Report of the City of Birmingham, Alabama* for 1918, 1919.

39. *Age-Herald*, Sept. 27, Oct. 23, Nov. 14, Dec. 21, 1919, Jan. 18, Feb. 21, 1920.

was sure voters would approve, and for improvements in police, fire, and street services it needed three mills, which it feared workingmen and suburbanites might oppose out of suspicion that they would not reap commensurate service improvement. Therefore, for the police, fire, and street improvements the commission reinstated, by ordinance, the three mills of the 1901 bond tax. For the schools it submitted a two-mill tax to the voters, who in May 1920 gave it 90.5 percent approval. This time at least the schools received all the new school tax revenue.[40]

Thus between December 1915 (when the first home rule amendment failed) and May 1920, the actual Birmingham property tax rate rose eight mills. The school tax issue had been the battering ram that broke down initial voter resistance to a higher tax rate, because all eight new mills won their necessary local referendum approval under an explicit "school tax" label. But the eight-mill increase in "school" taxes boosted school expenditures the equivalent of only five mills, and approximately three mills of the new revenue financed improvement in other services.[41]

The increased property tax rate made possible a 20 percent reduction in the merchant license tax in 1921, and it rendered Birmingham's pattern of license and property taxes more like that of other cities. But this did not mean that Birmingham property had become heavily taxed in comparison with property in other cities. In 1922 Birmingham received only $16.09 per capita from property taxes, compared with $23.35 per capita in the southeastern cities of Louisville, Atlanta, Richmond, Memphis, and Nashville combined, and compared with $32.94 per capita in all other American cities in the 100,000 to 300,000 population class. Accurate comparisons of tax rates in different cities are difficult, especially because the data do not reveal the rates of taxes paid to counties and states and then returned to cities. But in 1923 the National Municipal League compiled total city, county, and state tax rates for all 165 American cities with more than 30,000 population. Birmingham's total property tax *rate* ranked 104th among the 165

40. *Ibid.*, Feb. 21, 25, Apr. 6, 1920; Alabama, *Acts, 1919*, pp. 899–903; Birmingham, Minutes . . . Commissioners, Z, 362 (May 11, 1920); Birmingham, Board of Education, *The Birmingham School Survey, 1923* (Birmingham, 1923), 155.

41. In 1915 Birmingham had spent the equivalent of 5.7 mills of property-tax revenue on education, including 3.2 mills from general city funds and 2.5 mills from the state and county aid to education provided by the 1901 constitution. By 1922 the city spent the equivalent of 10.4 mills of revenue on education, including the "old" state and county aid of 2.5 mills and the new 8 mills. The 3.2 mills of general funds had been released to other services. U.S. Census, *Financial Statistics of Cities* for 1916, 1920, 1922; Birmingham, *Financial Report* for 1915, 1920, 1921.

cities, but its estimated ratio of assessed valuation to market value (33 percent) ranked 162d, and its total property tax rate when adjusted for level of assessment ranked last among the 165 cities.[42]

REVENUE PATTERNS, 1911–1921

Between 1911 and 1921 the upper- and middle-ranking groups, the top one-fifth of the population, gradually united upon a revenue remedy —a property tax-rate increase—and eventually obtained its adoption, meanwhile sidetracking alternate remedies—a separate county or an increased assessed valuation—which lower-ranking groups and, originally, some middle-ranking merchants had favored. But the leaders of the upper- and middle-ranking groups had discovered that even when they were united and highly mobilized, as they were in 1915 in the Committee of 100, they could not simply dictate or readily control revenue decisions. Constitutional restrictions, legislative bottlenecks, and referendum requirements enabled many groups to delay or veto unwelcome revenue proposals and thus to help shape final outcomes. Still, it was a measure of the power of the upper-ranking economic leaders— the representatives of the top 1 percent of the population—that only they had the resources to seize the initiative, to mobilize the middle-ranking groups behind their proposal, and to overcome constitutional, legislative, and referendum obstacles. They had time and money to organize prominent committees, to obtain expert formulation of realistic but self-serving proposals, to hire skilled attorneys, and to arrange helpful alliances in the state legislature. They also had the support of the daily press, which enabled them to set the agenda for public discussion, to neutralize the assessment equalization issue by giving the impression that equalization had taken place, to use the "school tax" label even when it was misleading, and to obscure the fact that the 1919 state tax amendment would allow the Birmingham city commission to restore the three-mill 1901 bond tax without a referendum. Exploiting these advantages, they finally prevailed.

Birmingham wage earners and suburbanites demonstrated considerable leverage on revenue decisions, but in the end, especially when the free public school system seemed endangered by revenue shortage, they were reduced to approving the revenue alternative they had op-

42. U.S. Census, *Financial Statistics of Cities*, 1922; Rightor, "Comparative Tax Rates," 719–28.

Birmingham City Hall, at Nineteenth Street and Fourth Avenue, North, was built in 1901–1902. *Courtesy Birmingham Public Library.*

Above: The Alice Iron Furnace, built by Henry F. DeBardeleben in 1880, was the first of several industries that sparked Birmingham's boom during the 1880s. *Below*: Workers handle "pigs" of iron at the Sloss-Sheffield Steel and Iron Company, 1907. *Courtesy Birmingham Public Library.*

A horse and wagon carry a load past the office buildings at Twentieth Street and First Avenue, North, *c.* 1910. *Courtesy Birmingham Public Library.*

The Birmingham Skyline, as seen from the northwest in 1914, featured the Tutwiler Hotel (flying flags), the framework of the uncompleted Roden Hotel, the twenty-five story Jefferson County Savings Bank, and "the

heaviest corner on earth" at Twentieth Street and First Avenue. In the foreground are workers' houses at Fourteenth Street and Sixth Avenue, North.
Courtesy Alvin W. Hudson Collection, Birmingham.

Above: The house in the foreground was built in 1886 by Robert Jemison, Sr., part owner of the street railway, at the corner of Twenty-first Street and Sixth Avenue, north of the business district. *Below*: Workers pose at the entrance to the Birmingham Coal and Iron Company's Red Ore Mine on Red Mountain in 1909. *Courtesy Birmingham Public Library.*

The downtown view from the Brown-Marx Building in 1907 was punctuated by the tower of the Jefferson County Courthouse in the center and by St. Paul's Roman Catholic Church to the right. *Courtesy Birmingham Public Library.*

Above: Along the foothills of Red Mountain, Birmingham's wealthiest entrepreneurs built homes on fashionable Highland Avenue, shown here in 1907. *Below*: Victorian Greek Revival houses stand near a modern apartment building at the juncture of Highland Avenue and Twentieth Street, South, *c.* 1907. *Courtesy Birmingham Public Library.*

The intersection at Twenty-first Street and First Avenue, North, where the Steiner Brothers Bank was erected in 1890, had such heavy traffic by 1915 that a traffic director was required. *Courtesy Birmingham Public Library.*

The Louisville & Nashville Railroad Passenger Station and train shed was built in 1887 at Twentieth Street and Morris Avenue. *Courtesy Birmingham Public Library.*

The concrete Twenty-Second Street Viaduct, flanked by warehouses, ran across the main railroad reservation toward Red Mountain. It was completed in 1929. *Courtesy Birmingham Public Library.*

Above: The Birmingham City Hall (far left) and Fire Station (adjacent to City Hall) stood at Nineteenth Street and Third Avenue, North, in 1881. *Below*: Twentieth Street runs north through the business district as it was during World War I. On the right is the First National Bank Building at Second Avenue, North. *Courtesy Birmingham Public Library.*

"The heaviest corner on earth," at Twentieth Street and First Avenue, was weighed down (left to right, counterclockwise) by the American Trust Building, the Brown-Marx Building, and the Empire Building. The Woodward Building on the fourth corner is hidden by the Brown-Marx. c. 1915. *Courtesy Alvin W. Hudson Collection, Birmingham.*

The Sloss-Sheffield Iron Furnace, eight blocks from downtown Birmingham, lights the night sky in 1916. *Courtesy Birmingham Public Library.*

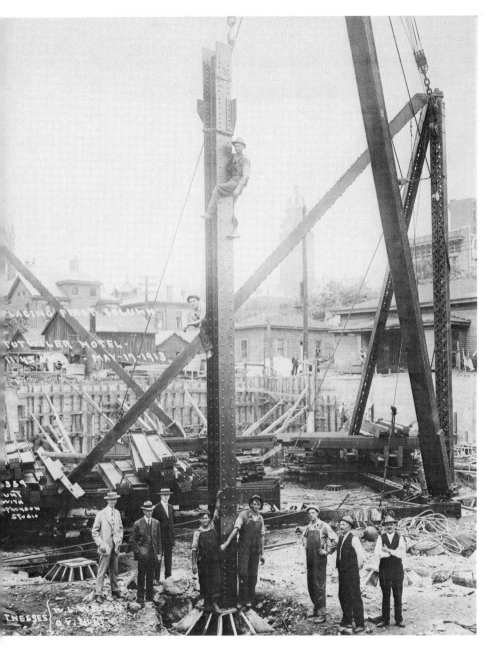

In May 1913 workers erected the first steel column of the new twelve-story Tutwiler Hotel at Twentieth Street and Fifth Avenue, on the northern edge of the business district. *Courtesy Birmingham Public Library.*

Above: The Paul Hayne elementary school, shown in 1907, was built as the new "Southside" school at Twentieth Street and Fifth Avenue, South, in 1887–1889, and was named in honor of the southern poet Paul Hamilton Hayne. *Below*: The fifty-five foot iron statue of the ancient god Vulcan, symbol of Birmingham, stood watch over the Alabama State Fairgrounds in 1910. Cast in 1903 by Guiseppe Moretti, Vulcan was mounted atop Red Mountain in 1937.

posed. Still, they forced advocates of a higher tax rate to go through awkward channels and to earmark the new tax money for education. Though the voters were partially misled about the ultimate division of the earmarked money, the education department did become the major beneficiary of the tax-rate increases. After 1917 the suburbs dominated the city commission, influenced allocations, and used the new revenue to upgrade their schools dramatically. And education expenditures grew faster than did those of other departments.

Throughout the property tax struggle the city continued to extract an unusually large revenue through fines, convict earnings, and license taxes, but even this did not bring its total general revenue up to par with similar cities. In 1920 Birmingham's total general revenue was $16.22 per capita, which was 61.3 percent of the $26.47 per capita in Atlanta, Louisville, Richmond, Nashville, and Memphis combined, and only 52.1 percent of the $31.12 per capita in all other American cities in the 100,000 to 300,000 population class. By 1922, with its new property-tax revenue, Birmingham still had only 77.9 percent as much revenue per capita as the five southeastern cities and 60.9 percent as much as the other American cities. The constraints and patterns of influence that had long depressed Birmingham revenue continued to have their effect.[43] And Birmingham's persistent difficulty in performing the function of extraction of revenue inevitably set constraints upon its performance of another function—the allocation of services.

43. U.S. Census, *Financial Statistics of Cities* for 1921, 1922.

VII

General Civic Services

To Mayor Frank V. Evans, addressing the board of aldermen in 1898, the dilemmas of allocating scarce revenue were cruel. "The cry of retrenchment," he acknowledged, was popular in general, "but undertake it specifically, in the police department, and you bring about inadequate protection to our homes and firesides; in the department of fire protection, and you are met by double insurance rates; in the department of health, and 'pestilence walketh at noonday'; and in the department of schools and you rob us of our greatest pride."[1] Still, Birmingham, with its singularly low general revenue, had to neglect some essential services, and the patterns of allocation and neglect helped to reveal the distribution of political power.

This chapter will focus on the general departmental services which the city included in its yearly operational budget and financed from general tax revenue. A second type of service—constructing streets, sidewalks, and sewers—was not included in yearly operational budgets. The city made such improvements in only a few specific locations each year, and financed them through direct special assessments on the owners of adjacent property, rather than by general taxation. They will be the focus of chapter 8.

Birmingham's ten departments of general civic services can be grouped into three categories: services to property, services to persons, and education (see table 7.1). The services to property were the essential housekeeping services necessary to maintain urban property. They protected property from fire and theft, maintained access by keeping streets clean, lighted, and repaired, and cleared property of refuse and garbage. Of course, such services also aided the persons who occupied

1. Birmingham, *Message of the Mayor and the Annual Reports of the Officers of Birmingham, 1897*, p. 11.

Table 7.1 Birmingham per Capita Departmental Expenditures as Percentage of Combined per Capita Expenditures of Five Other Southern Cities, 1910, 1920

	1910	1920
TOTAL, ALL DEPARTMENTS	89.8%	63.3%
EDUCATION		
Schools	110.4	81.0
SERVICES TO PROPERTY		
Police	94.1	49.4
Fire	123.6	82.8
Inspection	166.7	67.7
Sanitation	55.2	63.8
Highways	66.2	52.5
SERVICES TO PERSONS		
Health	86.7	32.3
Charities, Hospitals, Prisons	36.5	16.6
Library	18.8	56.7
Recreation	17.4	43.4

Source: U.S. Census, *Financial Statistics of Cities, 1910, 1911, 1920*. Birmingham "1910" figures are from the 1911 census report.

Note: The five other cities were Louisville, Atlanta, Memphis, Richmond, and Nashville. In 1910 they were the only southern cities besides Birmingham in the 100,000 to 300,000 population class. Departmental per capita expenditures for the individual cities are given in the Appendix, Table A.3.

the property, but the city allocated the services and measured their adequacy in terms of property values and property maintenance rather than in terms of assistance to persons. To perform each service, city employees physically visited (or in the case of fire, were prepared to visit) each piece of property they served. The services to persons, on the other hand, focused primarily on the preservation and enrichment of human lives, and could not be distributed or measured in terms of property. City employees made health, hospital, welfare, library, and recreation services available at some central facility, and persons who used the services visited the facility (in the case of prison, involuntarily). Education was a special type of service to persons, placed in a separate category here because its expenditures followed a unique pattern and because by 1920 it alone accounted for nearly 40 percent of city operating expenditures—four times more than any other single department. (Data on Birmingham's yearly departmental operating expenditures appear in the appendix.)

As Table 7.1 shows, Birmingham's intensifying scarcity of general revenue dictated that by 1910 it spent only 89.8 percent as much per capita for civic services as did other southern cities of similar size, and by 1920 only 63.3 percent as much.[2] (And the southern cities spent far less per capita than did northern cities of similar size.) In the face of these conditions, which services did city officials emphasize and which did they allow to suffer neglect? Which services did they deem so vital that they granted them per capita appropriations equal to the standard set by more affluent city governments?

Table 7.1 suggests that Birmingham's education and fire departments were most consistently able to resist the downward pressure of revenue scarcity. In 1910 both spent more per capita than did the corresponding departments in the other five southern cities combined, and by 1920 they still spent approximately 80 percent as much, even though by then Birmingham was spending only 63 percent as much per capita for all civic services. By 1920 the other services to property had moved close to or below this 63 percent level, and ranged between 49 and 67 percent. Each of the services to persons, however, fell well below 50 percent in either 1910 or 1920. And in 1910 "library" and "recreation" and in 1920 "charities, hospitals, and prisons" fell below 20 percent. In 1920 the total per capita departmental expenditures of the other five southern cities combined were $20.24 while Birmingham spent $12.82, leaving a difference or shortfall of $7.42. Of this shortfall, 47.7 percent was accounted for by the five departments of services to property, which together embraced 45.6 percent of the total Birmingham budget. Education, with 38.9 percent of the Birmingham budget, accounted for only 15.8 percent of the shortfall, while the four departments of services to persons, with only 7.7 percent of the Birmingham budget, accounted for

2. Table 7.1 deals only with the yearly operating expenditures, not with capital outlays for new equipment or buildings. In the city's annual accounts, the cost of the capital outlays showed up in yearly interest payments on long-term bonds. Since the interest payments came from general-fund revenue, Birmingham's capital outlays, like its yearly expenditures, were severely constrained. Capital outlay patterns were quite similar to yearly expenditure patterns, favoring fire and education, and neglecting charities, hospitals, and prisons. The following analysis focuses mainly on yearly operating expenditures, with some attention to the capital outlays of a few departments.

31.0 percent of the shortfall. In general, the services to persons suffered the most, but education the least, from the revenue shortage.[3]

SERVICES TO PROPERTY

All citizens benefited from services to property and most interest groups supported at least the minimum level of service essential to the "self preservation" of the city. But downtown businessmen found first-rate services to downtown property absolutely crucial, and they exerted constant pressure to keep those particular services far above the minimum and as near as possible to the standard set by other cities. Only top quality fire and police protection could guarantee the safety of stores and merchandise and keep insurance costs down. And first-rate street maintenance, lighting, sanitation, and traffic control would maximize the drawing power of the business district, making it attractive, safe, and efficient. Significantly, the businessmen generally succeeded in persuading the city to maintain good property services downtown, even when the scarcity of revenue dictated quite inadequate property protection for the city as a whole. Precisely in the allocation of civic services did Birmingham's middle-ranking groups receive the greatest benefit from their domination of local bodies of government. To the great advantage of the business district, the business-oriented city officials operated upon the apparently unquestioned assumption that they should allocate protective services according to the property values of sections of the city, rather than according to population density. Therefore the protection of the visibly-valuable downtown property commanded top priority.

The pattern of police protection illustrated these priorities. In 1900 the police commission used the entire police force to patrol fourteen beats, nine in the central business district, five in the immediate outskirts of the business district, and none in residential areas. Despite this the Board of Trade, speaking for the merchants, said that the downtown force was "not sufficient to protect the business portion of the city, as each patrolman has four blocks on his beat." But the board did acknowledge that "the residence portion has no protection at all." The police commission urged the appointment of more policemen, saying: "We should have men in the residence part of the city at all times, and especially at night if same cannot be furnished in the day time, but we

3. General administration and miscellaneous costs, with 8 percent of the budget, accounted for the remaining 6 percent of the shortfall.

haven't a man in the residence part at all. They are wholly unprotected, and at times the calls from this part of the city come so fast that we are unable to answer them and give them the attention that they should have." The board of aldermen gradually added more policemen, but police department reports and the complaints of citizens attested that the pattern of "business streets . . . not patrolled as well as they should be" and residential streets "almost wholly unprotected" persisted through the years. In 1914 police chief Martin Eagan noted that as a result: "Burglaries have been numerous in residence and thinly populated districts of the city, where more policemen are badly needed. In the business district burglaries have been few."[4]

The allocation of fire protection illustrated still more clearly the influence of the middle-ranking downtown business community. Merchants considered first-class fire protection absolutely crucial, because inadequate protection led the insurance-rate-setting agency, the South-eastern Tariff Association (S.T.A.), to impose much higher yearly fire insurance premiums on both buildings and merchandise, significantly increasing business costs. The S.T.A. examined fire department efficiency and loss records and placed each city in a class, from first to fourth. The class established the city's basic insurance-premium rate, though within the city the rates varied according to type of building.[5]

In 1891 Birmingham bought enough new fire-fighting equipment to climb from second to first class, but revenue scarcity continually threatened its ability to stay there. In the depressed 1890s and again in 1904 it temporarily slipped back into second class, causing 50 percent increases in insurance premiums on merchandise. Both times the major downtown merchants, with the blessing of the board of aldermen, negotiated directly with S.T.A. over the necessary improvements, and both times they persuaded the aldermen to find enough money to comply with the S.T.A. first-class requirements.[6]

When Birmingham lost its first-class rating in 1904, Mayor Walter M. Drennen reported that it cost the merchants "almost $100,000 per year additional insurance on their stocks of merchandise and build-

4. Birmingham *News*, July 6, 1900, Jan. 18, 1900, Oct. 9, 1914; Birmingham *Age-Herald*, Oct. 21, 1899. See also *ibid.*, Mar. 22, 1899, Sept. 22, 1919; Birmingham, *Message of the Mayor, 1897*, p. 65; Birmingham *Labor Advocate*, Jan. 30, 1904, Oct. 13, 1911, Oct. 24, 1913; *News*, Feb. 14, 1908.

5. *Age-Herald*, Jan. 15, 1893.

6. *Ibid.*, Jan. 15, 1893, Mar. 26, 1895, Apr. 9, Aug. 3, 1899, Feb. 10, 12, 14, 21, 22, 26, 1901; *News*, Sept. 13, 1900; Birmingham, Minutes of the Mayor and Board of Aldermen, I, 324–25 (Feb. 25, 1901).

ings in the congested district of the city." The S.T.A. told the Board of Trade that Birmingham, which had one fire plug per block in the business district, must increase them to two per block, and that in the residential section, which had one plug every two to five blocks, there must be one per block. The city also needed more firemen, alarm boxes, trucks, engines, and building inspectors. Aldermen estimated that the S.T.A. proposal would cost $48,000 in immediate outlay and an additional $87,000 per year for maintenance, doubling the yearly fire department expenditure. The Board of Trade recognized that the S.T.A. demands were "entirely beyond" the means of the board of aldermen. Therefore, in January 1905 the Board of Trade and the aldermen, meeting jointly, agreed to "do those things necessary to put the 'congested' district—where the great values are—on a first-class basis," and let the residence area remain on a second-class basis. This would cost only 23 percent as much ($11,000) in immediate outlay and 29 percent as much ($25,000) in yearly maintenance expenditures. A committee of the Board of Trade worked out the details with S.T.A., and the aldermen ratified the agreement, which doubled fire plugs and protection in the business district and returned it to a first-class rating. Residential areas received no new protection and remained in second class. The merchants said it was a good bargain; the city spent $25,000 more per year and the merchants saved $100,000 per year in premiums.[7]

This basic pattern persisted for the next fifteen years, and in 1910, with the annexation of more residential areas, it intensified. Residential areas in Old Birmingham remained in second class, and the newly annexed suburban areas varied from second to fourth class. Studies in 1909, 1911, and 1913 by the National Board of Fire Underwriters documented in detail a persistent pattern of "good" spacing of hydrants "in the congested value district," while "in most residential and minor mercantile districts the spacing is far too wide and double the present number of hydrants are needed."[8]

7. Birmingham, *Message of the Mayor*, 1904, p. 12; *News*, Jan. 18, 1905. See also *ibid.*, Feb. 8, 9, Mar. 15, 1905, Feb. 27, Mar. 7, 1906, Jan. 29, 1907; *Age-Herald*, Oct. 5, 12, 1904.

8. *News*, Mar. 18, May 26, 1910, Sept. 6, 1911, Mar. 21, May 6, 1913; Birmingham, *Message of the Mayor*, 1906, p. 9; National Board of Fire Underwriters, Committee on Fire Prevention, *Report on the City of Birmingham, Ala.* (New York, 1909), 13. A map of fire hydrant locations, compiled from the minutes of the board of aldermen by Judith H. Harris, revealed that by 1911 the city had complied with the National Board of Fire Underwriters' downtown recommendation of two hydrants at each intersection and one between intersections, but that it was not close to complying with the residential recommendation of two hydrants at each intersection, nor

The city commission did improve suburban fire protection, replacing some volunteer stations with small full-time suburban departments. And in 1911 it motorized most of the downtown department, decreasing yearly operating costs while increasing efficiency and providing quicker protection to suburbs. Still, downtown protection remained far superior, and in 1912 fire chief A.V. Bennett reported, "Naturally the greater part of the equipment is centered in the city proper. About six square miles of densely populated territory must be protected from fire, the business district, representing many millions of dollars, being included in this area." Clearly, he continued to assume that his first obligation was to the high-value business district. In 1913 the National Board of Fire Underwriters found the apparatus and manpower for the central city "sufficient," but "in the outlying districts . . . the total strength is insufficient and protection inadequate."[9]

By 1915 the suburbs were exhibiting more electoral strength, and when the 1915–1916 revenue crisis dictated a temporary retrenchment in fire expenditures, the suburbs challenged the fire chief's downtown point of view. New chief S.A. Middleton proposed to drop all suburban firemen, returning those stations to volunteer service, but to keep the main downtown stations at full strength. The suburban leaders protested and persuaded the city commission to make across-the-board reductions of men in downtown and suburban stations, keeping a few full-time men at each substation. As soon as the revenue crisis subsided all stations returned to their previous strength, but the suburbs had demonstrated some increased leverage on allocations.[10]

Birmingham's upper-ranking industrial groups showed less interest in and exerted much less influence upon the allocation of fire protection than did the middle-ranking commercial groups. A fire hydrant map reveals that the city placed no extra hydrants near industries, and none

---

even with a stopgap emergency residential recommendation of one hydrant per intersection. *Ibid.*, pp. 9, 11, 33, 35; *Supplement, 1911*, pp. 3, 10, 11; *Supplement, 1913*, p. 13.

9. *News*, May 22, 1911, Nov. 17, 1912; National Board of Fire Underwriters, *Report on the City of Birmingham, Ala., Supplement, 1913*, pp. 7–8. For several years after 1911 Birmingham suffered a high fire-loss record, despite its efficient motorized department. The Southeastern Underwriters' Association (successor to S.T.A.), did not blame the fire department, but rather the widespread use of wooden shingles in congested low-grade residential sections. S.T.A. temporarily placed a 15 percent penalty increase on many Birmingham premiums, but exempted better business buildings. By July 1916 Birmingham's fire-loss record had greatly improved, and the 15 percent penalty was removed. *News*, May 17, 1912, Mar. 20, 1913, July 17, 1914, July 2, 1916.

10. *Age-Herald*, July 15, 16, 21, 24, 25, 1915.

at all inside industrial plants. Before 1910, of course, most heavy industries were outside the city limits and rented their own private fire hydrants from the Birmingham Water Works Company and located them throughout their grounds. Even after annexation the companies rather than the city maintained and paid the annual rental on all hydrants inside the plants. Also, according to fire underwriters' reports, "A few manufactories maintain fire pumps and have fire brigades for their own protection." Even such nonmetal industries as the Avondale cotton mill maintained their own water supply, fireplugs, and sprinkling system. Indeed, some industrialists cited their independence from city fire protection as one reason why they should not have to pay city taxes. In short, in the allocation of fire protection, only the downtown business district received favored treatment.[11]

Birmingham's allocations for street maintenance showed a similar pattern. In 1897, after nearly all downtown streets had been paved, but when street improvement in residential areas was just beginning, city engineer Julian Kendrick reported: "In the way of street repairs, the first object has been to try and maintain the improved streets to such an extent that the large amount of money spent in their original construction would not be lost by neglected repairs. The second object has been to afford as much relief as possible to those sections of the city lying along the streets where no permanent highway improvements have been carried on."[12] These common-sense priorities, which favored the business district, persisted. City engineers and street commissioners reported that maintaining good repair of "paved," hard surface streets required much less expenditure per mile than did maintaining "unpaved" streets of light macadam, gravel, and dirt. Yet in 1920, in a pattern similar to several previous years, the city budgeted approximately $150 per mile for repairs of paved streets and only $72 per mile for repairs of unpaved streets. As a result, the 80 miles of paved streets, concentrated in the business districts and better residential suburbs, were adequately maintained, but the 70 miles of gravel streets and the 700 miles of dirt streets, located mainly in the outlying residential areas, were in terrible condition, many being scarcely passable. According to the *Age-Herald*, city commissioner Henry P. Burruss estimated that for the unpaved streets

11. National Board of Fire Underwriters, *Report on the City of Birmingham, Ala.*, 1909, pp. 24, 33; *News*, May 23, 1912. The fire hydrant map was plotted from city minutes.

12. Birmingham, *Message of the Mayor, 1897*, p. 26. The yearly highway allocations did not include outlays for original street-paving, which were financed separately through special assessments. See chapter 8.

"it will take an easy $350,000 [$450 per mile] to get them in shape and keep them in shape for awhile."[13]

The city used some street maintenance funds to sweep the paved downtown streets every night and a few paved access streets once a week, but residential streets went unswept. And the city also sprinkled downtown streets exclusively. In 1904 street commissioner John M. McCartin reported, "The merchants unanimously recognize that their stocks of goods have been greatly protected from the damage by dust. The public appreciates the fact that it has been much more comfortable to live and do business in the districts sprinkled than elsewhere in the city." And he warned the aldermen, "The demands from citizens outside of the area sprinkled for extensions to the sprinkling limits are increasing daily, but . . . I do not see how any relief can be extended to them unless your honorable body will consent to an increase of appropriation for the enlargement and maintenance of the sprinkling equipment." Such increases were not forthcoming, and by 1911 the *News* said, "No pretense is made by the city of sprinkling any except downtown streets, and if the [dust] evil is to be removed the people themselves must take the initiative," using their garden hoses. During the summer of 1921 city commissioner Henry P. Burruss declared: "I realize conditions on unpaved streets that are traveled to any extent are deplorable," but "the department has no funds for extra sprinkling," and "I am recommending to the people that they pray for rain."[14]

Street lights, which consumed a final portion of street maintenance funds, also clustered heavily in the business district. In 1907 a visitor found the business district well lighted but was surprised that so many residential streets were dark. Even so, merchants wanted more light downtown, and in 1911 they launched a campaign to have the city install a "Great White Way" on the main business streets. The *News* editorialized: "In communities where the streets are brilliantly lighted, the thoroughfares are thronged with people at night. Men and women enjoy walking about looking into the show windows . . . and making plans for shopping, if the downtown section of the city is made attractive. But they will not come out if the thoroughfares are dark. Result: no business is done at night in the city without lights, and the merchants lose half the advertising value of their well arranged windows." In this

13. *Age-Herald*, Feb. 21, 1920. See also *ibid.*, Feb. 9, Mar. 7, 17, 1920; *News*, Sept. 28, 1913.

14. Birmingham, *Message of the Mayor, 1904*, pp. 140–41; *News*, May 16, 1911; Birmingham *Post*, June 9, 1921.

instance the city commission, citing financial stringency, denied the merchants' request. But so essential did the merchants consider attractive lighting that they installed and maintained the larger lights themselves.[15]

The department of sanitation—the final service to property—also gave top priority to the business district. In 1905, for example, Mayor Ward, reporting on the street and sanitation departments, declared: "At present the business district is kept in such condition as to invite the praise of visitors and residents"; but he could only promise vaguely that "the increased equipment being added to the department from time to time will result in all parts of the City being taken care of." Refuse and garbage removal in residential areas improved only gradually until the summer of 1907, when a small typhoid epidemic frightened citizens. Suddenly the unsanitary Negro "quarters" loomed as a "menace" to the entire city. Sanitary inspector E.M. Duncan assigned an extra force to keep the Negro sections cleaner, saying, "it is here that our cooks, servants and washerwomen come from and if these quarters are filthy they will bring the filth into our homes and thereby cause sickness." Soon the sanitation department devoted more time and effort to outlying poor areas than did any other department.[16]

Again in 1916 Birmingham suffered a typhoid epidemic and physicians blamed it mainly on the many outdoor toilets, or "dry closets," in the Negro sections, where there were no sanitary sewers. Federal health expert L.L. Lamsden warned that not only humanitarian reasons, but "just cold business reasons" demanded more attention to this problem, and the city developed a weekly dry-closet scavenger service for areas without sewers. It charged a 35-cent monthly fee, however, to force poor whites and Negroes, who supposedly paid few taxes, to underwrite the new service.[17]

Sanitary facilities and services in Negro sections were not yet on a par with those in the white sections, and the downtown area still commanded more attention than residential areas; but since poor sanitation anywhere threatened the entire city, the sanitation department continued to pay some special attention to outlying residential areas and Negro sections. From 1916 to 1920 sanitation department expenditures showed a larger percentage increase than did those of any other department and made more gain toward the level of expenditure of other cities (see table 7.1 and appendix).

15. *Age-Herald*, July 22, 1907; *News*, Sept. 5, Dec. 7, 1911.
16. Birmingham, *Message of the Mayor*, 1905, p. 17; *ibid.*, 1907, pp. 162, 169.
17. *Age-Herald*, July 21, 1916. See also *ibid.*, July 3, 1916, June 7, 13, 1918.

In sum, Birmingham's services to property suffered from the scarcity of revenue but city officials, giving first priority to the business district, maintained downtown services at an adequate level, and caused the residential areas, especially outlying areas and Negro sections, to bear most of the adversities of inadequate property services. To build this pattern the businessmen's associations mobilized steady pressure on sympathetic city officials. And this provoked no organized protest. True, individual residents did frequently complain about dark streets, inadequate fire or police protection, or irregular garbage pickups, but no "residential" association aggregated such complaints or mustered consistent pressure on decision-makers. City officials quelled the most vehement complaints by making piecemeal changes, such as adding a fire hydrant or a streetlight, changes which did not affect the overall distribution of property services. The pattern did not change after 1915, when the annexed suburbs began electing commissioners and influencing service allocations, because the suburban demands were usually articulated by suburban businessmen, and their goal was to spread the pattern of downtown favoritism among the several suburban business districts, not to favor residential areas over commercial ones.

Few residents actually advocated taking services away from the business district, where some worked, where many shopped, and where visibly higher values and congestion created an obvious need for more protection than in residential areas. But few citizens were aware of precise definitions, such as those provided by the S.T.A., of the proper ratio between "first class" business and "first class" residential protection. When residential areas slid to second class while the business district climbed back to first class, few realized it, and soon most residents considered the new ratio normal, since it still corresponded roughly to the pattern of fire danger. So also with the entire pattern of giving the downtown top priority, while skimping on residential services. The pattern was created gradually by the continuous well-organized efforts of groups with a strong common interest in maintaining high standards where they did business, and through precedent the pattern became widely accepted as normal.

SERVICES TO PERSONS

Services to persons—charity, hospitals, institutional homes, prisons, libraries, recreation, and the department of health and vital statistics—

suffered most from Birmingham's revenue shortage (see table 7.1). Taxpayers deemed such services less essential to the physical functioning and survival of the city, and when revenue scarcity forced retrenchment, officials reduced these services first, or even, in extreme crisis like 1916, temporarily eliminated them. Three of the services—charity, hospitals and institutional homes, and prison maintenance—tended to redistribute money from property owners and taxpayers to the poorest citizens, many of them Negroes. Many taxpayers argued that redistribution of wealth was not a legitimate function of local government and they sought, therefore, to hold such services to a minimum. But three other services—library, recreation, and the health department—were used by citizens of all classes, and, while they might have a mild redistributive tendency, they were probably used and supported most by the taxpaying middle class.

From 1882 until 1916 the city government's expenditures for charity payments to poor individuals—one of the three more redistributive services—were channeled almost entirely through voluntary charity associations, such as the United Charities, or, after 1909, the Associated Charities. Prominent members of the middle- and upper-ranking economic and social groups founded and led these organizations and raised $1,000 to $3,000 per year through private donations. The city added supplementary appropriations varying from $600 to $1,200 per year. The city and the businessmen who organized the charity associations aimed primarily "to give material relief when necessary but to eliminate as far as possible all street begging." Material relief—food, schoolbooks, clothing, coal, rent payments, medicine—should go to the "deserving poor" who had suffered genuine emergency, such as fire or the loss of a breadwinner. Even for these families, work, rather than gifts, should be provided for anyone considered able to work. Businessmen and city officials expected the charity associations "to maintain a registration bureau to which applicants for charity may at any time be referred for investigation" to screen out all "unworthy objects" and to discourage the unsightly nuisance of street begging. So important did city officials consider the elimination of begging that in 1914, as in most previous years, they matched their $600 yearly appropriation to the Associated Charities with a $693.17 "Direct Relief" fund, which city hall itself used "largely for buying railroad tickets to get destitutes out of town."[18]

18. Quotations from Associated Charities' statement of purpose, *News*, April 28, 1909; and Birmingham, Committee of One Hundred, *Report of the Sub-Committee to Investigate Expenditures of the City of Birmingham* (Birmingham, 1915), 72–73.

In mid-1915 the city commission, retrenching severely to meet the intense revenue crisis, completely eliminated charity appropriations from the 1916 budget. The Associated Charities, already faltering for lack of funds, collapsed under this blow and urged the city to take direct charge of charity work. In 1916, when city financial prospects began improving, the city commission did so, creating a new Relief and Corrections Department, with $3,000 for direct family relief and for operation of the central card file on relief applicants. A small but conscientious staff struggled desperately to provide the most urgently needed material aid, often referring needy families to churches because the department's appropriations were inadequate. By 1924 civic leaders created a new voluntary organization, the Community Chest, and the city commission, declaring that "voluntary contributions have made it unnecessary to burden the taxpayers" for relief work, promptly abolished the Department of Relief and Corrections and turned its entire work, including the central registration bureau, over to the Community Chest.[19]

A second redistributive service to persons—support of hospitals and institutional homes—was from 1874 to 1915 channeled entirely through private organizations. Until 1900 Birmingham had only one private hospital, the Hillman, to which the city appropriated approximately $25 to $100 per month to supplement private donations and support charity patients. But often, reported the *Age-Herald* in 1891, "poor patients have not been able to secure admission" because "the management was obligated to take all pay patients possible to make the institution pay expenses." In 1900 the Roman Catholic church opened the larger St. Vincent's Hospital, which did more charity work. Still, in 1902 the *News* said that neither hospital "enjoys the endowment or public appropriations necessary to make them purely charity hospitals," and added, "It does seem that Birmingham has grown large enough to establish and maintain a city hospital. . . . There are few cities in the country so large as Birmingham without a city hospital and a city ambulance corps." By 1906 the aldermen appropriated $100 per month to each hospital to maintain a few charity beds for indigent patients, but voted down a proposal to double the appropriation, and

See also *News*, Jan. 21, 1897, Feb. 8, 1900, Oct. 21, 1909, Dec. 9, 1910; *Age-Herald*, Dec. 12, 1894; Bessie A. Brooks, *A Half Century of Progress in Family Welfare Work in Jefferson County* (Birmingham, 1936), 2–5.

19. *Age-Herald*, July 13, 28, 1915; Birmingham, Minutes of the Board of Commissioners, X, 445 (Nov. 30, 1917), Z, 76 (Oct. 30, 1919); Brooks, *A Half Century*, 7–8, 12–13, 22–28.

certainly considered the establishment of a city hospital far beyond their means.[20]

Gradually after 1900 the city initiated regular appropriations to other institutions—a mercy home, a girls' home, a free milk depot, an orphans' association, an old folks' home, a Salvation Army home, an anti-tuberculosis association, and the Pisgah rescue home—and by 1914 such appropriations reached a peak of approximately $18,000 per year. But when the 1915–1916 financial crisis terminated all appropriations for hospitals and charities, the institutions were left, in the words of the *Age-Herald*, to "rely on a generous public to help them keep their doors open." Moreover, when financial prospects began improving, the city renewed none of the appropriations, choosing instead to channel its entire new, much lower, charity expenditure of $8,000 per year into its newly-created Department of Relief and Corrections. It budgeted $3,000 to direct family relief and $5,000 to the Pisgah Welfare Home, a formerly private rescue home for fallen women. In the interest of efficiency the city transformed the home into an all-purpose institution "to receive all types of persons liable to become public burdens, misdemeanants, as well as dependents, men as well as women and children." In 1921 the League of Women Voters instigated an investigation which revealed that the Pisgah Home had indeed taken in such diverse people, with appalling results. "This motley group," said the report, "was thrown together without supervision, without industries of any kind, and without recreation," in "unsuited" buildings, with "entirely inadequate" equipment, under a matron "unqualified for social work of any kind." So bad were conditions that the report urged the city commission to close the home, which it promptly did, without renewing its former appropriations to any other welfare institutions.[21]

One group in particular—tuberculosis victims—suffered from lack of city welfare support. Tuberculosis constantly haunted Birmingham's

20. Quotations from *Age-Herald*, July 1, 1891; *News*, Oct. 11, 1902. See also *Age-Herald*, Sept. 3, 1891, Jan. 3, 1895, July 28, 1915; *News*, Feb. 8, 1900; Birmingham, Committee of One Hundred, *Report . . . Expenditures*, 46–48, 72–73. The Hillman became a county hospital in 1907, but in 1912 the secretary of the Associated Charities found it "hopelessly inadequate" for the needs of the entire county, with "every ward . . . constantly overcrowded, the accommodations for Negro patients being particularly inadequate," and the *News* reported that an average of twelve persons a day were turned away for lack of room. W.M. McGrath, "Conservation of Health," *The Survey* 27 (Jan. 6, 1912), 1501–1502; *News*, Apr. 11, 1911.

21. *Age-Herald*, July 14, 1915; Brooks, *A Half Century*, 12–13, 16. See also Birmingham, Committee of One Hundred, *Report . . . Expenditures*, 72–73.

smoky, unsanitary slums. In 1916, for example, it killed 356 persons in Birmingham, giving the city the highest tuberculosis death rate of any American city in the 100,000 class, except Denver, Colorado, where tuberculosis patients went to die. Birmingham's only institution for fighting the disease was the voluntary Anti-Tuberculosis Association, founded in 1910 by Dr. George Eaves, a Congregational pastor who had immigrated from England. Building a small sanitarium in the clear air on Red Mountain, in 1910 the association appealed to the city for $2,400 and received $200. By 1915 it had increased its city allocation to $3,800, but then, during the revenue crisis, the city cut it off entirely and failed to renew the appropriation later.[22]

In 1916 a United States health expert, Dr. Carroll Fox, declared that a state of tuberculosis epidemic existed in Birmingham and emphasized that local government must provide institutions and take vigorous preventive measures against the disease, rather than relying on inadequate charity organizations. The leaders of the Anti-Tuberculosis Association agreed completely and continually urged the city to take over the work. Four to five thousand people in the county were suffering from the disease, they said, and a tuberculosis hospital with 300 beds was an absolute necessity. The association, with its yearly income of approximately $10,000 from donations, could provide sanitarium beds for only thirty-three patients, all of them white.[23]

Yet tuberculosis was much more prevalent among Birmingham Negroes than among whites. From 1905 to 1915 Birmingham's average tuberculosis death rate per 1,000 population was 0.80 for whites and 3.90 for blacks. In 1915 Negroes, with 39 percent of the city population, accounted for 76 percent of the tuberculosis deaths. Tuberculosis of the lungs was the largest single cause of death among Birmingham blacks. But no medical institution in the city would admit tubercular Negroes. In 1915 Horace D. Slatter, a prominent Negro newspaper correspondent who had been stricken with tuberculosis wrote, "The colored person in Birmingham who gets any treatment for tuberculosis at all must pick himself up, bag, and baggage and go to far-off Colorado, away from friends and loved ones, simply because of his color." The Anti-Tuberculosis Association did have a few nurses who visited tubercular blacks in their homes, but the head of the association wrote,

22. *News*, Aug. 4, 1910, Apr. 5, 1914; *Age-Herald*, July 18, 1915, July 29, Aug. 3, 1916, Aug. 4, 1919.
23. *Age-Herald*, July 29, Aug. 10, Dec. 27, 1916, Aug. 4, 1919; *News*, Oct. 19, 1914, June 27, 1916.

"With regard to a sanitarium for negroes, nothing can be said until the resources of the association are greatly increased." No increase occurred by 1921, and it remained true, in the words of Horace Slatter, who died of tuberculosis in 1918, that "the very people who need help most to fight this disease are denied it because no arrangements are made for them on account of their color."[24]

Labor unions earnestly supported antituberculosis work and demanded that the city and county spend far more to provide adequate public institutions for tuberculosis patients. No group in fact spoke out openly against this work, but for most people it was a low priority concern. The four thousand tuberculosis patients and their families probably considered the need for government allocations to fight tuberculosis as urgent as the downtown businessmen found the need for first-class fire protection. But the welfare of tuberculosis patients did not seem to affect the prosperity of all Birmingham as directly as did the welfare of businessmen, and the patients lacked the businessmen's well-financed, politically-skillful interest group organization that enjoyed close personal rapport with government officials. And since most tuberculosis victims were poor and black, any antituberculosis expenditures would redistribute money, and this, in the view of the average taxpayer, made such expenditures seem much less legitimate. Thus in the bargaining for scarce city funds, tuberculosis victims and the few interest groups that supported them experienced little success.[25]

Birmingham also allocated meager funds for prison maintenance, which is included among services to persons because the level of expenditure affected the living condition of prisoners more than it did the level of property protection. Most years Birmingham had an uncommonly high number of arrests per capita, but its prison expenditures per capita were far lower than those of comparable southern cities, and periodic reports by city health officials and state prison inspectors condemned Birmingham prison conditions. In 1898 a Dr. Ledbetter found that each narrow city prison cell with four wooden bunks had held six to seven prisoners the night before his visit. Cell floors were flooded with water, human waste, and "mud apparently a quarter of an inch thick," and "the odor was terrific." Prisoners were "so thick" that "I had to elbow my way through," he said. "It reminded me of the stock pens,

24. *Age-Herald*, Nov. 22, 23, 1915, Aug. 4, 1919; Birmingham, *Reporter*, May 18, 1918; Birmingham, report of city health officer R.M. Cunningham, M.D., October 19, 1915, and report of W.A. Reynolds, registrar of vital & mortuary statistics, October 11, 1915, TS, BPL.

25. *Labor Advocate*, Oct. 18, Dec. 20, 1912, Sept. 12, 1913, Dec. 11, 1920.

though not so clean." In 1906 city physician Oscar Hayes reported: "In the South Side Stockade for negro men, the prisoners are huddled together like so many sheep, with no place to bathe except a small wooden trough some three or four feet from the ground, far too small for a man to get into. So far as the prisoner himself is concerned there is no sanitary system. He is never furnished with clean clothing; in fact he is only furnished clothing when those he has on wear out. No under clothing is furnished at any time. No provision is made for laundering of the prisoners' clothes. A great many prisoners are kept for more than a year in this condition." Until 1911, city prisoners on the street gang were kept in shackles day and night. Guards were so few and jails so flimsy that in 1911 the *News* reported street commissioner Frank H. Gafford as saying "that if the shackles were removed from the negroes it would be impossible to keep them from running away, inasmuch as the Southside jail was absolutely insecure." When the new city commission took office in 1911, it provided extra watchmen so prisoners need not be shackled while they slept. But as late as 1919 the state prison inspector said, "The city jail is not a proper place in which to confine human beings for a day."[26]

Thus departments serving the criminals, the destitute, and the sick suffered most from Birmingham's revenue scarcity, and by 1920 compared most unfavorably with similar departments in other cities. The revenue problems also handicapped the recreation, library, and health departments, which were designed primarily not to aid the sick and unfortunate, but rather to provide protection, civic conveniences, and cultural amenities to enrich the lives of all citizens. As of 1910 the library and recreation departments ranked lowest of all in comparison with other southern cities, but by 1920, having received much greater emphasis by the city commission regime, they had gained, though they too continued to lag far behind their counterparts elsewhere.

The impetus for increased allocations and activities for the health, recreation, and library departments came mainly from representatives of the upper- and middle-ranking economic groups. Prominent professional men provided leadership, as did some industrial corporation executives, who had come to Birmingham from more culturally developed cities, often from the North, and who wanted their adopted city to become a cultural center and a more attractive and progressive place to live. City commissioner James Weatherly, long a leading rail-

26. *News*, Dec. 8, 1898, Apr. 12, 1911, *Age-Herald*, Dec. 6, 1919; Birmingham, *Message of the Mayor*, 1906, p. 182.

road attorney and civic booster, articulated the creed of upper- and middle-ranking civic improvement leaders, saying that city government must provide more than the "actual necessities of the people," that it must also begin to provide the "comforts and conveniences of modern municipal life." The city must "be made beautiful and attractive and good to live in and good to look at." True economy in government "cannot mean simply the collecting of meager sums by taxation for meager needs." Rather it should mean "the practical and intelligent conservation and expenditure of revenue to accomplish the just and legitimate demands of modern community life."[27]

Among the just and legitimate needs of modern community life, according to civic improvement leaders, was a modern, efficient health department. It should collect data and provide technical services to improve the general level of health of the entire city and to protect all classes from epidemic or food contamination. Professional people spoke out most urgently for greater use of health experts and trained technicians. Until 1916 Birmingham's health department collected statistics and performed mostly bureaucratic and technical inspection services, but it did not provide any public nursing or health-education services. This probably accounted for its lower level of expenditure in comparison with other cities. A 1916 typhoid epidemic so alarmed citizens and officials that they called in Dr. Carroll Fox of the United States Public Health Service. He proposed a far-reaching plan to unify the city and county health services, dramatically increase city and county health expenditures, and employ many additional health officers, inspectors, technicians, and visiting public health nurses.[28]

The Board of Trade and the Chamber of Commerce enthusiastically endorsed the Fox plan and prominent businessmen lobbied for its adoption. The editor of the Birmingham *News* spoke of the "bad advertising the city of Birmingham had received from the typhoid epidemic" and told the city commission "you must find the money to do this." John C. Henley, Jr., of the Birmingham Publishing Company said that during the aftermath of the epidemic, while the usually apathetic public was aroused, was "the psychological moment to do something to protect the health of the city." President George Gordon Crawford of the Tennessee Coal, Iron, and Railroad Company earnestly supported the Fox plan and told the board of revenue, "In our several sanitary units

27. *News*, Apr. 1, 1912.
28. Birmingham, *Message of the Mayor*, 1907, pp. 161–69; *News*, editorial, Apr. 11, 1912; *Age-Herald*, July 22, Aug. 8, 10, 23, 25, 1916.

of the Tennessee company we expend annually several times the amount of money asked of you. We do it because it is a good thing and is a profitable venture because it keeps our employees in a healthy condition. However, if surrounding conditions are bad we are not getting all that we deserve from our investment." The *Labor Advocate* also urged acceptance of the plan to improve health standards among workingmen.[29]

The city and county tentatively approved the plan and borrowed Dr. F.E. Harrington from the U.S. Public Health Service for one year to organize the new program. But soon the leaders of Birmingham's burgeoning political anti-Catholic movement discovered that Dr. Harrington was a Roman Catholic, and they seized upon his appointment as an issue. Recalling the "heroic struggle" by which earlier Alabamians had driven out "carpetbaggers," they pledged to drive out "medical hierarchies and all other hierarchies in Alabama." The anti-Catholics controlled a majority of the board of revenue and blocked the county appropriations for the program. The city commission then refused to cooperate until the county contributed its share. Amid bitter factional wrangling the bright new program collapsed, and Dr. Harrington resigned after serving only half his year. The city commission finally did increase health appropriations significantly and implemented some new services, but the county did little.[30]

Thus top economic and civic leaders failed in a major effort to build an efficient, unified countywide professional public health service. Their program was demolished by an organization of middle- and lower-income people who actually stood to gain much from the new services, but who objected to the religion of one particular leader and who feared that the program was part of a plot to subject them to hierarchical control from outside the community. This illustrated a difficulty often encountered by civic improvement leaders. Any proposal to establish new government authority or activity would arouse much suspicion, would encounter carping criticism about trivial matters, and would provoke obstructive attacks on any vulnerable point. Thus when they undertook to promote such innovations, even the city's most prominent economic and social leaders were highly vulnerable to defeat.

Frustration also dogged all efforts to upgrade city recreation and library services. Civic leaders, particularly real estate men, were ashamed

29. *Age-Herald*, Aug. 10, Dec. 22, 1916; *Labor Advocate*, Sept. 2, 1916.
30. *Age-Herald*, Jan. 23, 1917. See also *ibid.*, Aug. 23, Nov. 24, Dec. 5, 6, 1916, Jan. 1, 19, 30, Mar. 3, May 11, Aug. 21, 1917.

of Birmingham's small "scantily improved" parks, and they urged the city to hire a renowned civic landscape architect to plan an extensive park system that would take advantage of the natural beauty of the rolling, wooded hills.[31] Moreover, the architect should design a civic center with a large civic auditorium "capable of caring for vast assemblages," because this would encourage "the religious, the musical and other aesthetic factors of the city" and would promote "rapid growth along business and commercial lines."[32] Beyond this, in 1908 civic leaders organized the Birmingham Playground and Athletic League to equip playgrounds, sponsor volunteer-staffed summer recreation programs, and urge the city commission to employ professional staff to continue and to expand the program.[33] In 1907 they organized the Birmingham Library Association to seek money from Andrew Carnegie and from local donors to build a $200,000 library.[34] And in 1912 they organized the Birmingham Zoological Garden Society to build a small zoo and to seek city support.[35]

No organized groups directly opposed the goals of these civic improvement leaders, but many expressed apathy, or quibbled about specific details, or asserted that other matters, such as education, should have higher claim upon scarce city funds. Organized labor was the most persistently outspoken of the doubtful groups, and labor's official statements served to illustrate the attitude of some middle- and many lower-ranking groups.

Labor unions apparently favored more parks, playground equipment, and supervised recreation, but they provided no leadership or systematic support for them. And when the park commission and the Chamber of Commerce asked the city to appropriate $20,000 to retain a civic landscape architect, the Trades Council "went on record as being opposed to spending $20,000 for an expert engineer to plan parks and civic center until the commissioners have established free textbooks in the public school." When the city zoo proposal came up, the *Labor Advocate* editorialized, "We are heartily in favor of a zoo or free menagerie for a city like this, but wait, we are not in favor of the expenditure

31. *News*, Apr. 13, 1913. See also *ibid.*, Feb. 11, 1911, for the report of leading realtor Hill Ferguson, chairman of the Chamber of Commerce committee on Civic Improvement.
32. *News*, June 28, 1913, July 31, 1911. See also *ibid.*, July 19, Aug. 17, Sept. 7, 1913.
33. *Ibid.*, Mar. 4, 17, 1908, June 5, 1913.
34. *Ibid.*, May 10, 1907, July 16, 1909, Feb. 17, Mar. 18, 1910.
35. *Ibid.*, Oct. 12, 1912.

of a single cent for this purpose until the city's entire public school system is on a free basis."[36] When the Chamber of Commerce sought city funds to build a civic auditorium, the Trades Council resolved that more schools, more free textbooks, and municipal ownership of utilities "are more essential to the well-being of the citizens of Birmingham than an auditorium," and said "we recommend that the members of the Chamber of Commerce ask that the public-spirited citizens of wealth finance such a proposition without asking the aid of the city of Birmingham."[37] As for a free city library, labor unions were heartily in favor, on one condition: no "tainted" Andrew Carnegie money, which had been "amassed by the employment of labor whom he treated unfairly and often inhumanely" should be used for the library, because "the acceptance by Birmingham of a donation from this archenemy of organized labor would be a direct affront to the working men of Birmingham."[38]

The outcomes of these questions provided only small comfort and encouragement for the civic-improvement leaders. The city did retain Warren H. Manning, an eminent civic landscape architect from Boston, and he published an elaborate forty-seven-page plan for a park system and civic center. But the city expanded its park area only slightly, and Manning's plans came to naught. The voluntary zoo association built a small zoo and eventually obtained a small appropriation from the city to operate it. The city also hired a full-time playground supervisor and appropriated funds for more playground equipment. But the supervised recreation program fell victim to the 1916 city retrenchment and was not reinstated until 1919, when it received only half of its earlier appropriation. And after 1916 regular park maintenance expenditures failed to regain their earlier levels. Instead, the city invested much of its recreation money in a commercial East Lake amusement park to which it charged admission, making it a self-supporting operation.[39]

By 1921 the city had not yet built the proposed civic auditorium, even though voters had approved two auditorium bond issues. Complex wrangles over location, architectural design, and the technical

36. *Labor Advocate*, Aug. 2, Oct. 25, 1912. When a zoo was established *without* city funds, the Trades Council and *Labor Advocate* endorsed it enthusiastically. *Ibid.*, Nov. 29, 1912.

37. *Ibid.*, Aug. 15, 1913.

38. *Ibid.*, Aug. 17, 1901, May 10, 17, 1907.

39. *News*, Feb. 10, May 7, 1914; Warren Henry Manning, *Warren H. Manning's City Plan of Birmingham* (Birmingham, 1919); *Age-Herald*, July 13, 1915, May 14, 1918; Birmingham, Committee of One Hundred, *Report . . . Expenditures*, 40–42; Birmingham, *Financial Report of the City of Birmingham, Alabama*, 1915–1921.

legality of the bonds continually thwarted the Chamber of Commerce auditorium committees. The matter illustrated again the difficulties that plagued any group which proposed new city activities of untested legality. Finally, the plan to seek Carnegie funds to build a large library was quietly dropped. Instead, the city established a small central library in a room of the city hall, with branches in suburban schools. In 1913 the *News* complained of "totally inadequate" facilities and said "the number of volumes is so far below actual requirements as to discourage reading." Still, by 1915 the library had a small professional staff and by 1920 the city's library expenditures, though far less than those of other cities, had grown significantly since 1910 (see table 7.1). In general, the civic improvement leaders had achieved some small beginnings in providing the "comforts and conveniences" of city life, but by 1920 the bare necessities still absorbed too much of the city budget to leave much for amenities.[40]

To Birmingham's Negroes fell only a few crumbs of the slowly developing amenities. The supervised playground movement began in 1908, but only in 1914, after the city had financed seventeen white playgrounds, did it open its first small park for blacks. And it made black volunteers mainly responsible for upkeep and improvement and allocated the Negro playground $300, or 2 percent of the $15,375 playground budget. The new zoo and library were closed to Negroes. During 1917 and 1918, therefore, blacks petitioned for a Negro branch library. The library board hesitated until the superintendent of schools sent it $3,400 which the Negro schools had earned through entertainments. With this money the board established a one-room Negro branch library in a former storeroom in the black business district.[41]

During the 1916 typhoid epidemic the health department opened a free vaccination bureau—for whites only. After three weeks, during which 338 new cases were reported and 15,000 whites were vaccinated, the authorities decided: "It is essential that the negroes be vaccinated. As the majority of the typhoid cases is amongst the well-to-do families who have negro servants, typhoid vaccination will do a great good and will remove a persistent source of infection." The city opened a separate Negro vaccination bureau and urged all white women to send their

40. The *Age-Herald*, Nov. 12, 1917, reviewed the history of the frustrating attempts to build an auditorium. One finally was built in 1924. Library reports in *News*, Oct. 26, 1913; Birmingham, Committee of One Hundred, *Report . . . Expenditures*, 44–46, 66–72.

41. *News*, June 24, Sept. 13, 22, 1914; *Reporter*, July 28, 1917, Oct. 5, 1918; *Age-Herald*, Oct. 27, 1918.

black servants. By the end of the epidemic, three weeks later, 25,000 whites and 600 blacks had been vaccinated. Most blacks, reportedly, were disinclined to avail themselves of vaccination, or unaware of the opportunity; and apparently only black servants sent by their employers took advantage of the bureau.[42]

The few Negro services to come from the civic improvement movement illustrated a pattern. White taxpayers considered it unfair to redistribute tax money from whites to blacks, and the white officials usually granted Negroes a new amenity such as a park or library only if the blacks themselves donated much of the money. And officials were likely to include blacks in protective services only to the extent deemed necessary to avert dangers to the white population.

EDUCATION

Public education was in Birmingham, as in most American cities of the time, the great growth sector of city expenditures, expanding from 20 percent of the general operating budget in 1890 to 43.8 percent in 1922. Education's growth in the face of the downward pressure of revenue scarcity did not indicate a clearcut victory or defeat for any interest group or set of groups. Rather, all groups of all social and economic ranks eagerly supported education growth because all of them anticipated benefits.

Social groups, ranging from the clubs of the social elite to the reform leagues of the evangelical Protestants to the political clubs of the Germans and Irish, enthusiastically sought better schools. And Negro leaders petitioned more persistently for better schools than for any other city service.[43]

Economic groups of all ranks also supported the schools. Public education distributed vital skills and income-earning ability more widely throughout the population, to the clear economic benefit of the lower ranks. But most upper- and middle-ranking groups found this to their advantage, as well, because it promised to enhance local productivity and economic development. In 1900, for example, the Commercial Club resolved: "It is our belief that no investment of the public funds

42. *Age-Herald*, July 3, 22, 25, 26, Aug. 11, 1916.
43. *Age-Herald*, Apr. 20, 21, 22, May 1, 1920 (social clubs); May 14, 1917 (Protestant activists); Mar. 2, 1899 (Germans); Birmingham, *State Herald*, Aug. 2, 1896 (Irish); *News*, June 11, 1900, Mar. 7, 1905; *Reporter*, Feb. 3, 1917 (Negroes).

brings to all our people such direct and immediate returns, and so directly affects the welfare of our city, as that money expended in the substantial improvement and extension of our public school facilities." Thus commercial and industrial entrepreneurs viewed school expenditures as an investment not only in the education of their own children, but also in the betterment of their entire labor force.[44]

The Tennessee Coal, Iron, and Railroad Company found that one of its greatest problems was the lack of skilled labor in the South, where most of the population engaged in agriculture and lacked the skills, the discipline, and often the simple literacy necessary for productive industrial employment. Improved public education could not solve the problem completely, but it was obviously a necessary beginning. Moreover, T.C.I. and other major industrial corporations earnestly promoted manual vocational training in Birmingham high schools, and they received eager cooperation from the board of education. In 1902 the board asserted that in Birmingham "the fundamental and dominant need must ever be that of intelligent labor," and it energetically developed one of the earliest and best public vocational training programs in the South. In 1904 Mayor Walter Drennen declared that the new business and manual training departments "will make the High School to Birmingham what the Georgia Tech is to Atlanta, and will return in skill to this district a thousand fold on the outlay." In 1912 T.C.I. financed a free mechanic arts night school in the Ensley public high school, and by 1914 the school enrolled 197 T.C.I. employees and 70 from other industrial plants.[45]

The board of education also developed part-time vocational courses specifically designed to teach concepts and skills needed by the young employees of the Stockham Pipe and Fittings Company, the Ingalls Iron Works, the American Cast Iron Pipe Company, the Avondale Mills, and the Birmingham Railway, Light and Power Company. And, in cooperation with Birmingham's largest department store, Loveman, Joseph and Loeb, the board developed a continuation school for department store employees. Such entrepreneurs recognized the value,

44. *News*, Oct. 12, 1900. See also *Age-Herald*, Sept. 22, 1894, Apr. 28, 1916. Though some of Birmingham's elite sent their children to private schools, many used the public schools. Birmingham, Board of Education, *Annual Report, 1907*, p. 20.

45. Justin Fuller, "History of the Tennessee Coal, Iron and Railroad Company, 1852–1907" (Ph.D. diss., Univ. of North Carolina at Chapel Hill, 1966), 272–73; Birmingham, Board of Education, *Annual Report, 1902*, pp. 37–38; *ibid., 1912*, pp. 55–58; *ibid., 1914*, pp. 37–38; Birmingham, *Message of the Mayor, 1904*, p. 9; *News*, Feb. 27, 1914.

not only of the special programs, but of the entire local public education system in upgrading the skills and productivity of their employees.[46]

Lower-ranking groups supported education even more energetically and vocally, for they saw schools as the ladder upward for their children. Organized labor's Trades Council and *Labor Advocate* devoted more space to discussions of education than to any other department of local government. From 1890 to 1920 they endorsed every proposed school tax and bond issue, and workingmen voted for them overwhelmingly. Labor concentrated especially on two proposals to reduce the cost of sending children to school: abolishing tuition charges and providing free textbooks. Tuition and book fees often deterred workingmen from sending their children to school. In 1897, when the board of education first charged tuition for the elementary school, white enrollment dropped 25 percent, but the next year it jumped back to normal when the board eliminated elementary tuition. The high school continued to charge $18 per year tuition, and the Trades Council campaigned against it continually until the city abolished it in 1910. The *Labor Advocate* immediately proposed that the city provide free textbooks for students, and in 1911 the Trades Council convinced the city commission to begin a free-textbook program in grades one and two. Enrollment in those grades shot up dramatically. In 1912 the Trades Council urged the commission to extend the free-book plan to grades three and four, and over the next two years the commission did so.[47]

Organized labor believed its program of "a completely free school system" with free textbooks from the first grade "to graduation" should have priority over any other new city services, and it announced adamant opposition to proposals for an auditorium or civic center until its program was enacted. But the 1915 "Citizens' Committee of 100" (composed 96 percent of men from upper- and middle-ranking groups) thought otherwise, saying that "free school books should never have been introduced" and recommending that the program be abolished and that tuition be reinstated. The Trades Council declared, "There could be no harder blow struck at the working man of Birmingham," and the city commission retained the book program and in 1918 ex-

46. Birmingham, Board of Education, *Annual Report, 1913*, pp. 78–82; *ibid.*, 1920, pp. 81–86.

47. *News*, Sept. 25, 1897, Oct. 3, 1911; Birmingham, Board of Education, *Annual Report, 1899*, p. 16; *ibid.*, 1913, pp. 45–46; *Labor Advocate*, Mar. 29, 1907, June 24, July 8, 1910, Aug. 21, 1914.

tended it to grade five.[48] But for two years it did charge a tuition fee which extracted $50,000 per year from pupils. In 1920 school board member W.J. Rushton, an ice manufacturer, again proposed to reinstate tuition and abolish the free-book program. The board refused, and the Trades Council began pushing for extension of free books to grades six and seven, an extension which occurred in 1926. Labor, in short, achieved some of its education program, and its enthusiastic support of school taxes and bond issues helped to maintain Birmingham's high appropriations for education, relative to other city departments.[49]

Education was also the city service of greatest interest to suburban residents. When the suburbs entered Greater Birmingham in 1910, the Birmingham superintendent of schools found most suburban school buildings "too small, poorly constructed, meagerly equipped, unsafe and unsanitary." In 1910 Old Birmingham's elementary schools were valued at $127.29 per enrolled pupil, the suburban elementary schools at only $65.15. The board of education and the city commission tentatively planned to build urgently needed new suburban elementary schools, but for years they were delayed by a lack of funds. In 1917, 1919, and 1920 the suburban residents' urgent desire for new schools contributed heavily to their willingness to vote for the new school taxes by which the city raised its property tax rate. And the suburbs reaped their reward. Between 1919 and 1922 the city commission, using much of the new revenue to finance school bonds, spent $962,601, or $71.86 per pupil, on new elementary schools in the suburbs, compared with $226,290, or $40.22 per pupil, in Old Birmingham, finally equalizing schoolhouse values. As for general elementary school operating expenditures, in 1910 the suburbs and Old Birmingham had received $22.67 and $28.86 per capita, respectively, but by 1920 they were equalized, with the suburbs slightly ahead.[50]

Although Birmingham maintained strong education expenditures, relative to other departments, even here it fell behind other cities in teachers' salaries and in construction of new school buildings. In 1914 the average Birmingham teacher's salary was only 70 percent of the average for Atlanta, Memphis, Richmond, and Nashville. In the decade

48. *Labor Advocate*, July 25, 1913; Birmingham, Committee of One Hundred, *Report . . . Expenditures*, 9, 55; *Age-Herald*, Jan. 20, 1915.

49. *Age-Herald*, Feb. 26, 1920; *Labor Advocate*, Apr. 2, 1921.

50. Birmingham, Board of Education, *Annual Report, 1910*, pp. 22–34, and foldout exhibit of expenditures; *ibid.*, 1920, pp. 35–44, and foldout exhibit on expenditures; *ibid.*, 1925, pp. 21–25; Birmingham, Board of Education, *The Birmingham School Building Survey, 1923* (Birmingham, 1923), 157.

1910–1920 Birmingham spent only $24.27 per pupil for new school buildings, compared with Memphis' $41.17, Atlanta's $42.93, and Richmond's $77.66. Only two other southern cities provided free textbooks, however. In this instance Birmingham had pioneered in the South, probably because of the pressure from organized labor.[51]

Birmingham's Negro schools were separate and inferior, suffering systematic allocation discrimination. In 1911, for example, city school appropriations per child of school age were $18.86 for whites and $2.81 (15 percent as much) for blacks. A much smaller percentage of school age blacks actually enrolled, and city expenditure per pupil enrolled was $24.13 in white schools and $8.04 (33 percent as much) in Negro schools. White teachers had thirty-six pupils enrolled, on the average; Negro teachers, fifty-eight. In 1911 white-school property was valued at $97.84 per pupil enrolled; Negro-school property, at $20.22. In 1922 the white-school enrollment was 131.5 percent of the normal capacity of the buildings; Negro-school enrollment, 264.2 percent. Since 1874 nearly all white school buildings had been brick, but the first brick Negro school building was built in 1910, and even after that most black schools were light, dilapidated frame buildings. The first white high school opened in 1883, but not until 1900, following persistent Negro petitions and a Negro promise to bear the entire cost through tuition, did a reluctant school board appoint one black teacher to start a Negro high school. In 1913 the editor of the Birmingham *News* toured the black schools and reported: "Only one negro school . . . is a modern, safe, proper building. The rest are shacks, with overflows into adjacent one-story tenement houses. All of the rooms are crowded, sometimes three children to a bench."[52]

Many whites believed the expenditures for Negro schools should be kept low; indeed, some whites, especially among the lower-ranking groups, wanted to reduce them further. Negroes, they claimed, paid very little school tax and were getting a free ride on white taxes, taking money urgently needed by white schools. Many white workingmen, moreover, saw the black worker as a competitor who would become more threatening as he became more educated. In 1897 the *Labor Advocate* warned that educating Negroes would cause them to "con-

51. Birmingham, Board of Education, *Annual Report, 1914*, pp. 18–19; Joseph Eli Allen, "A Study of the Financial Condition of the Public School System of Birmingham, Alabama" (M.A. diss., Univ. of Chicago, 1924), 65.
52. Birmingham, Board of Education, *Annual Report, 1911*, pp. 12, 16, and Exhibit A; *ibid., 1910*, p. 5; *ibid., 1925*, pp. 14, 17; Allen, "Financial Condition," 69; *News*, Sept. 4, 1900, Apr. 17, 1913.

tend all the stronger for equality," and that "if the whites resist all the stronger, there will be conflict, and if they relax in their contention for supremacy, there will be a state of things under which the present white generations would certainly not like to live." In 1906 Birmingham labor unions strongly endorsed legislative candidate Henry C. West, a labor spokesman whose platform included the plank: "This is a white man's country. I am opposed to negro education, because it is an established fact that an 'educated negro' is as a rule a worthless imp." In 1917 *Labor Advocate* columnist J.B. Wood, who had served as president and secretary of the Birmingham Trades Council and as first vice president of the Alabama State Federation of Labor, wrote: "The negro is a parasite; he pays no taxes, no school taxes." Moreover, "I have had daily demonstrations of the effects of education, i.e. book education on the negro. In the great majority of cases such negroes are insolent, overbearing, contemptuous of white men, not amenable to discipline, and with a lurking disregard for law." [53]

Few members of the upper- and middle-ranking groups ever opposed Negro education so openly; more often they deplored the city's failure to provide better black schools. Whites who employed Negro servants saw a direct benefit in raising the educational level of their servant class. In 1899, for example, board of education president Samuel Ullman, a Jewish merchant, reported that the board did all it could "to improve the possibilities of our colored children, recognizing that ... nearly all our domestic help are colored, and as such are in daily contact with our children; hence, the duty of raising their moral standard as indicated, as much as their educational standard." [54]

The industrial corporations, relying heavily on black labor, considered it in their self-interest to improve Negro schools to upgrade their labor force. Also better Negro schools could help attract black workers and keep them in Birmingham when northern opportunities tempted them to migrate. In 1901 the *Age-Herald* denounced a plan to reduce black school expenditures, saying, "If the negro is deprived of his much-appreciated schools, just so surely will he become the prey of immigrant agents, and he will begin to leave the state.... Can Alabama afford today to render her labor sour and discontent, and predisposed to seek other homes?" [55]

53. *Labor Advocate*, Sept. 25, 1897, Apr. 18, 1906, Mar. 17, 31, 1917.

54. Birmingham, Board of Education, *Annual Report, 1899*, pp. 11–12.

55. *Age-Herald*, June 6, 1901, Jan. 7, 1910; Horace Mann Bond, *Negro Education in Alabama: A Study in Cotton and Steel* (Washington: Associated Publishers, 1939, New York: Atheneum 1969), 240–43.

Even whites who supported black schools, however, gave them much lower priority than white schools, and Negro-school appropriations remained a mere fraction, often a declining fraction, of white-school appropriations. Consistent comparisons over time are difficult, but data on teachers' salaries show that in 1884 black teachers' salaries per school-age child were 49.3 percent of white teachers' salaries per school-age child, and that thereafter the percentage declined to 25.2 in 1894, 25.9 in 1907, and 16.9 in 1914. During World War I white leaders, hoping to promote Negro loyalty and stop Negro migration to the North, reversed the trend, boosting the percentage to 24.5 by 1920, and building some new black schools. In other words, in education as in other services, Negroes tended to achieve gains mainly when they were supported by the urgent self-interest of powerful white groups.[56]

CIVIC SERVICE PATTERNS

Civic service outcomes most strongly favored middle-ranking interest groups, especially the downtown businessmen, all in the upper 20 percent of the population. Businessmen saw to it that the downtown received good property services, even when the scarcity of revenue caused outlying areas to suffer neglect; they approved of letting the services to persons, particularly the more redistributive services, suffer most from the lack of funds; and they endorsed the relatively strong emphasis on education.

Upper-ranking groups, the top 1 percent of the population, had much less direct influence on allocation patterns than did the middle groups. Industrialists no doubt would have preferred better property services near their outlying industrial plants, but they did not demand them strenuously and did not get them. Indeed, they more frequently championed cultural amenities and better health services, with only minor success. But promotion of civic amenities was mainly an avocation of a few industrialist leaders; industrial associations did not put top priority pressure behind them nor consider their disappointments crucial. Such matters as taxation and regulation were more vital to the industrialists' economic well-being.

Lower-ranking groups, in the bottom 80 percent of the population,

56. *Age-Herald*, Aug. 29, 1894, Apr. 7, 1917; *Reporter*, Apr. 7, 14, Aug. 18, 1917; Birmingham, Board of Education, *Annual Reports* for 1884, 1907, 1914, 1920, 1925; Birmingham, Board of Education, *School Building Survey*, 157.

could not be completely ignored in allocation of services, but they had much less influence than the middle groups. They did exercise some leverage by obstructing expenditures for amenities to which they assigned low priority. But they had their greatest impact in their unswerving support for education. Even this success, however, was greatly facilitated by the middle groups' belief that wide dissemination of educational skills would benefit the entire local economy, and thus the middle rank as well.

A major reason for the success of the middle-ranking groups was that in service allocation, more than in any other policy area, the legislature and the city charter allowed local officials full authority to exercise their own discretion. Though the available city revenue was constrained by the state, the middle-ranking groups faced no outside constraint upon the allocation of that revenue, and they mobilized effective pressure for the services they considered crucial, reaping rewards commensurate with their political domination of the board of aldermen and the city commission. And steadily they established the precedent that the pattern they needed was legitimate and necessary and should persist. Thus, though the middle-ranking groups bore the heaviest direct tax burden, and to some extent imposed it on themselves to keep the city running, they at least had the greatest influence over how the revenue was spent.

VIII

Specific Public Improvements

$\mathcal{C}$ITY hall spent enormous time and effort paving streets and building sewers. Improvement ordinances, bristling with detailed legal descriptions of streets, sewers, and property lines, engrossed more pages in the city minute books than did any other city business. During some years the city outlays for such specific improvements were half as large as the entire operating budget of the general fund.

THE SPECIAL ASSESSMENT METHOD

The early town fathers used yearly general revenue to build simple dirt streets and ditches, but by the mid-1880s heavy downtown traffic generated, by season, blinding dust storms or treacherous, axle-deep mud. Citizens complained and merchants sorrowfully calculated dust damage to merchandise. Soon the mayors and aldermen began laying slag and macadam, and then granite "Belgian" blocks on the most heavily used downtown streets. The costs were far too great to be absorbed by the yearly general revenue, and at first the city financed them with long-term bonds to be paid off from future *general* property tax revenue. But the annual interest payments bit deeply into scarce general revenue, and gradually the city won from the legislature the authority to assess an increasing portion of the street improvement costs (after 1885 one-third; after 1891, one-half; and after 1895 the total cost) directly onto the owners of adjacent property. Under this system, which most American cities used, special assessment funds for specific improvements became entirely separate from general-fund revenue.[1]

1. Birmingham, *The Iron Age*, Jan. 10, 1884; Birmingham, *Code of Birmingham, Alabama, adopted February 19, 1890* (Birmingham, 1890), 37–39, 54–63; Birmingham *Age-Herald*, Feb. 19, 1891, Mar. 6, 1895.

The special assessment method was readily accepted by property owners, who realized that Birmingham, with its low property tax rate, could not otherwise finance street and sewer improvements. Since constitutional tax rate limits did not apply to special assessments, street and sewer building was the one city activity not restrained by the low general-fund revenue. The special assessment procedure quickly became routine. Property owners who wanted their street paved got petition signatures from the owners of more than 50 percent of the fronting property. The aldermen then had the city engineer survey the street and publish a detailed technical paving ordinance. After holding a hearing to allow dissenting property owners to protest, the aldermen confirmed the ordinance, secured bids, and let the contract. When the paving was done the aldermen apportioned the cost among the property owners according to the amount of abutting front footage each owned. The aldermen issued short-term public improvement bonds to pay the contractor, and the property owners could pay the city in cash or in ten-year installments, with an 8 percent carrying charge. The same procedures were used for sidewalks and sewers.[2]

Thus in the essential city-building service of creating a street and sewer system, the city government acted in effect as the agent of the property owners. The property owners relied on government rather than on some common voluntary association because only a city-wide engineering authority could create a unified system, only the city had sufficient bond-issuing ability, and only the city had the legal authority to collect efficiently, and if need be coercively, the apportioned payments.

Birmingham's public improvements and special assessments, unconstrained by state limits, could rise as high as property owners wished. And they were relatively high in comparison with other cities of similar size, probably because young Birmingham had had little time to build a basic street and sewer system and because it was growing and opening new residential sections more rapidly. In 1910 Birmingham collected $3.71 per capita in special assessments, compared with $3.92 for all American cities in the 100,000 to 300,000 population class, and compared with only $1.26 per capita in the other five southern cities in that class.[3]

2. Alabama, *Acts, 1898–1899*, pp. 1430–31; Birmingham, Minutes of the Mayor and Board of Aldermen, 1899–1911, *passim*.

3. U.S. Census, *Financial Statistics of Cities Having a Population of Over 30,000* for 1910, 1911. The Birmingham 1910 figures are actually from fiscal year September 30, 1910, to September 31, 1911. The 1910 fiscal year included the suburbs only part of the year.

Downtown streets required higher quality, more expensive improvements than did residential streets. When a new outlying residential street was opened, the city street force routinely graded an inexpensive dirt street and ditches, without any special assessment. If residential owners petitioned to hard-surface their street through special assessments, they usually chose plain macadam, composed of small crushed stone, mixed and packed with a tar binding substance, and often edged with stone curbing. Between 1900 and 1907 this typically cost $700 to $1,000 per block, depending on terrain and width. But such light macadam was inadequate for downtown business streets, where heavy traffic made necessary a stone-hard pavement. Before 1900 the city paved downtown streets with granite blocks, and after 1900 with vitrified brick or bitulithic macadam, a mixture of asphalt and crushed stone that hardened into a smooth, nonporous surface. Between 1899 and 1907 brick, stone, or bitulithic paving cost $5,000 to $7,000 per block, making the special assessments of merchants and downtown property owners six to seven times higher than those of residential property owners.[4]

However, the original granite-block paving of the thirty major downtown business blocks had been done before 1895, and at that time the businessmen had received a subsidy, since they had paid only one-third or one-half the cost, and the remainder had been paid through bonds secured by future general property taxes. Few citizens had objected to the original subsidized downtown paving, since all used the business streets. But after 1895 the subsidy was reversed. Because of heavy wear, most downtown streets had to be repaved long before 1921, and then the merchants and downtown property owners, bearing the entire cost, six to seven times as great as the cost of residential paving, subsidized everyone who rode or walked downtown. Moreover, the businessmen had to pay additional special assessments to provide both sanitary sewers and storm sewers. And the storm sewers, which were required only downtown, were five times as expensive as residential sanitary sewers.[5]

The merchants and downtown property owners bore these burdens without significant protest, making no serious effort to change the assessment procedure or to shift the burden away from themselves. If downtown improvement costs were higher than residential costs, so also were downtown property values higher than residential values, and by

4. Compiled from improvement ordinances in Birmingham, Minutes . . . Aldermen, 1899–1911; see also Birmingham, *Message of the Mayor and Annual Reports of the Officers of Birmingham, 1899,* p. 68; *ibid.,* 1907, pp. 103–12, 121.

5. Compiled by Judith H. Harris from street and sewer paving ordinances in Birmingham, Minutes . . . Aldermen.

roughly the same proportion. The high downtown values sprang from the benefits of central location and convenient access, and the paving and sewer assessments were reasonable business investments to maintain those benefits. As in the case of fire and police protection, most businessmen considered the quality of the downtown environment so crucial that they were willing to bear heavy burdens to maintain it. Residential property owners, who bore the entire cost of macadamizing their own streets, sometimes grumbled, but they too accepted the assessments as part of the normal cost of developing property, as an investment appropriate to the benefits, and they made no attempt to change the assessment method.

A major voice in street and sewer decision-making was exercised by real estate development companies such as the Birmingham Realty Company, which in 1903 owned 272 blocks inside Birmingham and which was promoting new residential areas, selling lots, and building and selling houses. Often Birmingham Realty alone owned a majority of the property involved in a specific improvement ordinance, and could have vetoed it. But instead it enthusiastically promoted such ordinances, reporting to its stockholders that paving a street raised the value of property on that street 40 percent and was also of "great benefit" to company holdings on other streets "in the vicinity of the streets improved." Thus their own assessments and those paid by residents on their new streets brought the company significant returns. In newspaper advertisements Birmingham Realty acknowledged that some property owners were "hostile to street improvements," partly because they "are unable to recognize the money value of it to themselves." It reassured them that "the Birmingham Realty Company, which has paid out more money for street and sidewalk improvements than any other company or individual in the city," had found "the almost uniform results" to be "an immediate and constantly growing demand for the property and a speedy enhancement of its value."[6]

The city government, in its street and sewer procedures, made itself the agent of a small minority of its citizens. In 1900 when Birmingham began its first major improvements in residential areas, only 13.6 percent of the heads of families owned their homes and had a voice in decisions about when and where to pave streets and build sewers. The 86.2 percent who rented had no legal influence on such decisions, which lay

6. Birmingham *News*, Apr. 8, 1908, Jan. 24, 1906, Feb. 23, 1907; George B. Kelley, engineer, *Map of Birmingham, Alabama, and Adjacent Suburbs* (Birmingham, 1903).

entirely with their landlords, often large real estate companies, or large industrial corporations that owned many blocks of cheap rent houses for workingmen. Such landlords made improvement decisions entirely according to their own calculations of financial return.[7]

The cheapest rent houses were unpainted Negro shacks packed into "quarters." There the realty companies and industries had no paving done. More important, under the special assessment system they could and did avoid building sanitary sewers in their Negro "quarters." City health officials demanded urgently and continually that sewers be extended into the "quarters" to eliminate the thousands of outdoor privies or "dry closets," which constituted "the greatest single menace" to city health and which were chiefly to blame for Birmingham's perennially high typhoid rate and occasional typhoid epidemics. But under the special assessment procedures the city simply did not force sewers onto owners who did not want to pay for them, and as late as 1918, 7,000 "dry closets" remained.[8]

In summary, the special assessment system gave to property owners and developers both the direct cost and the control of paving streets and building sewers. Downtown and residential property owners could procure a quality of improvements commensurate with their needs and property values, and they were not bothered with improvements for those who owned no property. Prosperous renters who would agree to pay more rent could probably obtain pavement and sewers, if landlords saw it as financially advantageous. But the poorest transient white workers and most Negroes got none. City officials, consciously functioning as agents of property owners and developers, prescribed only those improvements that promised tangible financial returns to owners.

In one important exception to the pattern, the Birmingham Railway, Light, and Power Company was obligated by its franchises to pay approximately one-third of the cost of paving any street on which it had streetcar tracks, but it had no voice in paving decisions. City engineers

---

7. Owner-occupied homes included those owned free or encumbered with mortgages. In 1910 and 1920, after the annexation of suburbs, 30 percent of homes were owner-occupied; 70 percent rented. U.S. Census, *Fourteenth Census, 1920*, II, *Population*, 1,288; *News*, May 6, 1905.

8. Birmingham *Age-Herald*, July 21, 1916. See also *ibid.*, July 28, 1916, June 3, 1918; *News*, Apr. 3, 1906, Sept. 17, 1910, Oct. 13, 1912; Morris Knowles, "Water and Waste: The Sanitary Problems of a Modern Industrial District," *The Survey* 27 (Jan. 6, 1912), 1487–89; John A. Fitch, "The Human Side of Large Outputs," *ibid.*, 27 (Jan. 6, 1912), 1532.

and aldermen candidly acknowledged that on paving questions they followed the wishes of the owners of the majority of abutting property, and that the street railway corporations had "the least influence of all the persons concerned in the paving." One city engineer said, "The street railways feel the pressure of paved streets more than any other factor of municipal life," and there were indeed times when the B.R.L. & P. protested against the mandatory paving costs and sought exemptions or extensions of time in which to pay. It obtained some extensions, but basically it was at the mercy of the property owners along its tracks. After 1915 the paving burden became increasingly onerous because the B.R.L. & P. faced serious competition from jitney bus companies that used the pavement but paid none of the paving costs. Such vulnerability was a significant example of the practical limits of the political power of the utility corporations.[9]

FAVORITISM AND REFORM

The basic pattern of improvement policy was noncontroversial, but occasional charges of corruption provoked bitter hostilities. Birmingham never suffered flagrant corruption on the scale that characterized some cities, but irate citizens often charged that city politicians, who annually let contracts worth $300,000 to $500,000, were corruptly favoring certain banks and contractors and were thereby departing from their proper role as efficient agents of property holders.

The greatest attention and outrage focused on the tangled web of transactions spun around alderman-banker Henry B. Gray. A graduate of an Atlanta high school, Gray had reported for the Atlanta *Constitution* before moving to Birmingham in 1886, at age nineteen, to become business manager of the *Age-Herald*. In 1895, after leaving the newspaper, he became president of the small People's Savings Bank and Trust Company, and in 1896 he was elected alderman on the regular Democratic ticket, opposing the Citizens' Reform movement. By 1898 he attained the chairmanship of the powerful aldermanic finance committee, and thereafter he switched expediently from faction to faction, allying quickly with each new mayor and persuading most of them to keep him in his key committee post. In mid-1907 Gray resigned from

9. *News*, Sept. 28, 1913; *Age-Herald*, Oct. 22, 1891; Birmingham, Minutes . . . Commissioners, X, 533 (Jan. 1, 1918); Birmingham *Post*, May 16, June 7, 1921.

the board of aldermen to become lieutenant governor of Alabama, but he and his bank maintained close ties with aldermanic politics; and when the Liberal Element caucus gained firm control of the city council in 1908, Gray aligned closely with them. While an alderman Gray was also treasurer of the Birmingham Board of Education for six years, chairman of the Jefferson County Democratic Executive Committee for four years, and treasurer of Jefferson County for four years, during which his bank held large county deposits without paying interest.[10] During most years after 1898 Gray's bank was also the official city depository, enjoying city deposits as large, in 1905 for example, as $344,000, which was three times the bank's capitalization, and which represented 38 percent of the bank's total deposits. Moreover, after 1902 Gray's bank gained an inside track on purchasing, sometimes without competitive bidding, the ten-year, 6-percent public improvement bonds issued to pay for street paving and sewers, and the bank customarily held the unused portions of the many separate public improvement accounts without paying interest on them.[11]

It later turned out that Henry Gray was involved in supplying pavement as well as credit for street improvements. From 1903 until the end of the aldermanic regime in 1911, one company—the Southern Bitulithic—captured more than two-thirds of all major paving contracts. Often the city engineer and the aldermanic street committee wrote paving ordinances with such explicit specifications for paving material that only Southern Bitulithic had a chance to meet them. The *News* reported a competitor saying "he didn't think it worth time to bid for street paving in Birmingham as the Bitulithic company and the aldermen were so thick." In 1907 an investigation revealed that Henry B. Gray owned $10,000 of Southern Bitulithic stock and was vice-president of the company. The company said there was no impropriety in this, because Gray had not bought the stock or attained the vice-presidency until five full weeks after he had resigned as alderman to become lieutenant governor. This failed to satisfy many citizens who knew that Gray as lieutenant governor continued to be a key leader in the dominant aldermanic faction, that his bank continued to be the depository and chief credit-supplier of the city council, and that Southern Bitulithic

10. Obituary of Gray, undated newspaper clipping in Hill Ferguson Collection, Personalities, vol. 12, BPL; *Birmingham City Directory* for 1898–1907; *News*, Jan. 28, 1905.

11. *News*, May 18, 1905, June 4, 1908. Bond purchases and loans of Gray's bank were compiled from Birmingham, Minutes . . . Aldermen, 1902–1907; Birmingham, Minutes of the City Council, 1907–1911.

continued to get a disproportionately large share of the major paving contracts.[12]

Gray's opponents pointed to his profitable mixture of business and politics as an example of how economic power could influence and corrupt politics; and indeed, Gray and other aldermanic politicians at times placed their own business interests ahead of the interests of property owners who were paying for pavement. But Gray's economic power, and the economic power of those who benefited from his influence, was never on a level with that of the upper-ranking firms of the city. His small savings' bank had one-fourth the capitalization of the major commercial banks. The Southern Bitulithic Company was a smaller concern than most of the downtown business houses. The other alleged beneficiaries of Gray's influence were mainly from middle- and lower-ranking business firms. A local hardware store allegedly received special consideration when the fire department bought hose. Allegedly for eleven years a politically-influential stable owner had a corner on selling mules to the street department. A certain "Mrs. Barfield" who ran a house of ill repute was allegedly seldom bothered by police, and on one occasion the cashier of Gray's bank arranged for her to make an unsecured $1,000 loan to police detective George H. Bodeker, who was soon elected chief of police by the Liberal Element. It was in the manipulation of such petty influence that Gray excelled, and through his manipulations many people of moderate economic power exercised undue political influence. From 1907 to 1911 Gray and his faction attained such efficiency in these operations that he gained a reputation as "the most powerful man in Birmingham."[13] His power, however, sprang originally not from great economic resources, but from political skills which he parlayed into considerable economic return.

The alleged corruption and favoritism of Gray and his aldermanic "cronies" became a major stimulus for the city commission reform movement of 1908 to 1911. City commission advocates said that unsalaried aldermen were unreliable agents of property holders, especially in letting improvement contracts, because they were tempted to get their reimbursement through petty payoffs. Under a salaried city commission, they promised, "Contracts will be scrutinized and sifted with a diligence

12. *News*, Nov. 19, 1907. See also *ibid.*, Nov. 23, 1907, Mar. 2, 1911; *Age-Herald*, Oct. 5, 1907. Data on contracts awarded Southern Bitulithic were compiled by Judith H. Harris from Birmingham, Minutes . . . Aldermen, and Minutes . . . Council. Major contracts were those worth more than $10,000 each.

13. *News*, June 1, 1910. See also *ibid.*, June 3, 1910, Jan. 13, 1914.

impossible when the work falls upon unpaid agents who have their own business affairs to look after." Such appeals stirred property holders who suspected that they were getting shoddy pavement and paying too much for it, and their concern was one important factor in the victory of the commission movement.[14] The new city commission, taking office in 1911, tried to live up to expectations. Using broader specifications for paving materials, it stimulated much sharper bidding competition, minimized opportunities for favoritism, and received significantly lower bids than had the aldermen. Through 1921, at least, there were no further complaints of favoritism in awarding contracts, and the property owners, continuing to control the location and timing of paving, felt confident that the commission served them efficiently.[15]

In 1911 the fate of Henry B. Gray and his bank symbolized the change and illustrated the political basis of Gray's economic power. Gray, working through the governor, almost packed the first commission with his allies, but a last-minute reversal placed anti-Gray men in control. The commission promptly withdrew city deposits from Gray's bank, where they were drawing no interest, and distributed them among other banks. Gray's bank had been prospering, and only one year earlier it had moved to a prominent main street location with a handsome façade of marble columns. But the city withdrawal undermined the bank so severely that Gray urgently asked the much larger American Trust and Savings Bank to buy him out and employ him as an officer. American Trust did absorb Gray's bank, but his standing had deteriorated so precipitously that they paid him nothing for good will and refused to make him a director or an officer. Gray retired permanently from banking and politics and became president of the Interstate Casualty Company.[16]

PUBLIC IMPROVEMENT PATTERNS

By 1895 Birmingham, like most American cities, had accepted the special assessment method of financing pavement and sewers, and the city officials customarily operated as obedient agents of the property holders who paid the bill. Downtown and residential property owners

14. *Ibid.*, May 12, 1910. See also *Ibid.*, Apr. 25, May 11, 1910.
15. *Ibid.*, Mar. 15, 30, July 24, 1912; Birmingham, Minutes . . . Commissioners, Q, 206 (Feb. 13, 1912).
16. *News*, May 6–10, 1911; Hill Ferguson Collection, vol. 40, pp. 110–11.

paid for improvements commensurate with their needs and avoided spending money on improvements for nonproperty holders. This pattern was especially favorable for real estate developers, who enjoyed exceedingly low taxes on undeveloped property, but who promptly received the city services they considered crucial—rapid extension of street improvements, sewers, and utilities. Such services did not depend upon general taxation and did not suffer from Birmingham's limited funds. The developers could obtain desired streets and sewers by investing in special assessments which they eventually recovered in payments from house buyers. And utility extensions were provided by private utility corporations that were eager to gain more user fees. Realtors and property owners objected to the system only when it appeared that aldermen were abusing their positions as agents and were seeking corrupt gain rather than competitive efficiency, and the advent of commission government in 1911 quieted that concern.

In sum, in the allocation of specific public improvements, as in the allocation of general civic services, members of middle-ranking groups tended to exercise the greatest influence.

IX

Social Regulation

W̲HENEVER a citizen of Birmingham took a drink of water or bought a drink of liquor, whenever he rode the streetcar to work or sought Sunday recreation, whenever he bought merchandise or sold it, indeed, whenever he breathed the smoky air, he was directly affected by the actions or inactions of local government in the spheres of social regulation (chap. 9), or economic regulation (chap. 10), or the regulation of utilities (chap. 11). Social regulation, the focus of this chapter, dealt with the definition and enforcement of public morality and with the prevention and punishment of criminality. And most controversy revolved around two separate but sometimes intertwined issues: first, the regulation of saloons, liquor, and Sunday recreation, and, second, the control of Negroes.

Pietistic Protestant activists carried the initiative on the first issue, demanding ever-tighter regulation of saloons and ever-stricter observance of Sundays. And thereby they generated bitter political battles with nonpietistic groups, especially with Roman Catholics, Jews, Germans, Irish, and Italians, and with saloonkeepers and theater owners, who resisted stricter government intervention.

On the second issue, most whites demanded vigilant government control of Negroes, who composed 40 percent of the city's population and whom whites considered an inherently inferior and troublesome lower caste. In 1889 the editor of the Birmingham *Age-Herald* declared: "The negro is a good laborer when his labor can be controlled and directed, but he is a very undesirable citizen." And most whites harbored similar notions, believing first, that the black was a useful, indeed necessary, menial laborer; but second, that he was an irresponsible and unreliable worker; and third, that he was unsocialized, menacing, prone to commit crime. Most whites therefore favored frankly discriminatory law enforcement to render Negroes more available as a pool of cheap labor, to overcome their alleged unreliability as workers, and to curb their alleged criminal tendency.[1]

The large coal, iron, steel, and machinery corporations of Birmingham depended heavily upon black workers to perform hot, heavy, dirty labor. By 1900, 55 percent of Alabama's coal miners and 65 percent of its iron and steel workers were black. And all employers relegated blacks to the menial, low-status, low-skilled, low-paying positions. In Birmingham in 1910 Negroes filled more than 90 percent of the positions in such occupations as iron mine operative, unskilled laborer in iron foundries, general unskilled laborer "not otherwise specified," helper in building and hand trades, laborer at road and street building, laborer on railroads, porter or helper in stores, and servant. In short, black workers formed the base of the Birmingham labor force.[2]

Birmingham employers and newspaper editors lamented that the very urban-industrial conditions that made the black worker so useful also served to increase his supposed irresponsible and menacing behavior. In urban-industrial society the Negro was no longer under the close personal supervision and discipline by which whites had controlled blacks in rural areas. As the *News* put it in 1913, "The Negro race is receiving little character training, little discipline, from the white race under the new economic conditions." Urban Negroes had paychecks, unsupervised free time, and easy access to liquor, knives, razors, and guns. Whites tended to characterize the entire black race by the highly-publicized behavior of a few criminal members, and many city whites came to fear "the menace of the liquor filled negro." In 1905 the *News* said: "Observant people know that the craps dive has done as much as any other influence to foster crime among the negroes. In fact, the tendency of negroes to leave the farm lands and drift to the cities where these very temptations are held out to them has become a serious problem with which the Southern people have got to deal."[3]

1. Birmingham *Age-Herald*, Dec. 8, 1889. Government control of Negroes was only a small part of Birmingham's pervasive system of racial caste controls, a system which relied heavily on social custom and social etiquette. But government activity, on which this study focuses, was also important. Government alone had the legal authority to use force or coercion, and, especially in dealing with the asserted irresponsible and menacing characteristics of the Negro, whites considered it necessary to use systematic coercion or the threat of coercion. Though extralegal force also played a role in the caste system, most uses of coercion against blacks required the support, or at least the acquiescence, of the legal authorities.
2. Paul B. Worthman, "Black Workers and Labor Unions in Birmingham, Alabama, 1897–1904," *Labor History* 10 (Summer 1969), 375–407; U.S. Census, *Thirteenth Census, 1910*, IV, *Population: Occupation Statistics*, 538–39.
3. Birmingham *News*, Sept. 22, 1913, Oct. 19, 1909, Jan. 3, 1905.

Many whites believed that the menace of the black was mitigated by sharp segregation of Negro and white residential areas, a practice which had developed quickly after Birmingham's founding in 1871. The segregated pattern persisted and intensified without benefit of government ordinances, but rather through custom and through planning by real estate companies and industrial corporations.[4] Also, from early in Birmingham's history, streetcars were segregated by custom and by rules of the private utility corporations rather than by ordinance.[5] But, despite the strict segregation, in a congested city Negroes inevitably lived, did business, and spent their leisure time in areas near white business and residential areas, thereby inspiring white apprehension.

White perceptions of personal danger from a Negro "menace" were in fact quite exaggerated. Birmingham's crime and homicide rates were often among the highest in the nation, but seldom did blacks attack whites. In 1921–22, for example, 59 percent of Birmingham homicides were committed by Negroes upon Negro victims, and in only 4 percent of Birmingham homicides did blacks kill whites. In fact, whites killed blacks far more often (12 percent of all cases) than vice versa, and in 25 percent of the homicide cases, whites killed whites. The few black attacks upon whites usually occurred during robberies by the Negroes, and the newspapers reported these cases vividly, causing them to loom large in the minds of whites.[6] Moreover, many whites feared that the violence among blacks within the nearby Negro communities would spill over into white areas. In 1914 the *News* warned: "When criminal negroes carve up, stab and kill other criminal negroes, they rapidly develop into human tigers. The taste of blood makes them reckless. They will readily, surely give vent to their hatred of some white men, and sooner or later kill white men." In 1909 a grand jury solemnly declared: "The white man's burden is the criminal negro. We are over-

<hr>

4. *Birmingham City Directory* for 1883, 1887, 1890, 1900, 1910, 1920. Several times between 1900 and 1920 Birmingham citizens or officials proposed residential segregation ordinances, but none was adopted, largely because of uncertainty as to how the United States Supreme Court would rule on the constitutionality of such ordinances. See Birmingham, Minutes of the Mayor and Board of Aldermen, L, 646 (May 1, 1907); *News*, Jan. 5, 1911, Aug. 17, 1913, July 13, 1914; *Age-Herald*, Mar. 18, 1916. In 1926 the City Commission passed a zoning ordinance which sought to reinforce segregated residential patterns. Birmingham *Post*, July 14, 1926.

5. *Age-Herald*, Feb. 16, 1899, Dec. 16, 1918; *News*, May 7, 1900, July 5, Sept. 21, Oct. 17, 1905, Apr. 7, 21, 1910.

6. Kenneth Barnhart, "A study of Homicide in the United States," *Birmingham-Southern College Bulletin* 25 (May 1932), 9–19; *News*, Nov. 12, 1913. See also *ibid.*, Sept. 25, 1905, Oct. 18, 1911, Sept. 22, 1913, July 13, Sept. 24, 1914.

whelmed with the amount of crime in this class of our citizenship."[7]

Whites therefore clamored for effective city and county control of Negroes. Nearly all whites endorsed certain customary law enforcement discriminations against Negroes. For example, the police, sheriff's deputies, and courts usually automatically accepted the word of any white against that of any black, and few whites questioned the practice. Negroes themselves were unable to offer significant political resistance to such discrimination, and such policies generated little political conflict. But four features of law enforcement against Negroes—the regulation of Negro saloons, the system of vagrancy law enforcement, the convict labor system, and the county fee system—did provoke white political conflict. The controversies did not pit the group to be regulated against the groups proposing regulation; rather they set white interest groups against other white interest groups, each seeking to shape government policy toward Negroes so as to provide certain benefits to itself or to avert certain supposed dangers.

SALOON REGULATION AND PROHIBITION

Birmingham's evangelical Protestant churches, especially the Methodists, Baptists, and Presbyterians, found liquor sinful on many counts: it undermined men's ability to behave rationally, it caused them to waste money and to deprive their families, and it produced drunkenness and violence. Saloons, moreover, were hangouts for the disreputable, vile centers of temptation and rowdy carousing. Beginning in the early 1890s the evangelical Protestants sought to use local government regulation to restrain such evils. By 1900 the Birmingham Pastors' Union had organized the Women's Christian Temperance Union, the Young People's Christian Union, and the Christian Endeavor Union to fight for stricter saloon regulation. In 1904 temperance leaders of Alabama organized the Anti-Saloon League, which spearheaded a much more militant statewide drive, especially after 1906, when the Reverend Brooks Lawrence, a Presbyterian minister from Ohio, came to Birmingham as a state superintendent of the league.[8]

In the 1890s the temperance organizations sought not prohibition,

7. *News*, July 13, 1914, June 11, 1909.
8. *Ibid.*, Dec. 10, 1900, May 6, Oct. 21, 1907; *Age-Herald*, Aug. 30, 1899; James Benson Sellers, *The Prohibition Movement in Alabama* (Chapel Hill: Univ. of North Carolina Press, 1943), 102–104, 114.

but rather government restrictions to curb such alleged evils as the dese-cration of Sundays by saloons that tempted citizens away from pious Sabbath leisure. In 1899 and 1905 pastors and temperance organiza-tions mounted campaigns for stronger Sunday closing ordinances and stricter enforcement. In mid-1905 they gained the cooperation of mayor George B. Ward, who summarily revoked the liquor license of any saloon that, according to police reports, had sold liquor on Sunday. Thereafter Sundays were quieter and drier.[9]

Antisaloon leaders claimed that another evil of liquor was that it dangerously intensified the irresponsible and menacing behavior of Negroes. Therefore, they said, the presence of a large black population made strict regulation of saloons doubly necessary. Many whites saw the Negro saloon as the "cancerous" sore where black criminality festered. In 1889, for example, the *Age-Herald* denounced Negro "dives" as "Deep, Dark, Damnable Dens of Degradation," that were "foul with the presence of prostitutes, thieves and murderers," and "where vice is flagrant and where evil doers hide and congregate to hatch iniquity." Also, in some saloons the separation of whites and Negroes was not strictly enforced, and white antisaloon leaders con-demned the relaxing of the color line in the already degraded social atmosphere of the saloon as a particularly egregious breach of public morality. Many of the "low Negro dives" harbored prostitutes who attracted white as well as black clients. Occasionally members of re-spectable white families were discovered in such "dives," which were therefore seen as a menace to the family morals of the entire community. Some disorderly "dives" pushed racial integration further, housing both white and black prostitutes. And in 1913 one grand jury discovered to its horror that, "while the filthy shacks in this row are supposed to be exclusively for whites, evidence of colored men having visited the white women has been obtained."[10]

In 1889, 1895, and 1907 Birmingham mayors B. Asbury Thompson, James A. Van Hoose, and George B. Ward, respectively, proposed a two-pronged program to eliminate, or at least to control, the Negro "dives." First, they would drastically increase the saloon license tax to at least $1,000 per year, in order to squeeze out the "low dives" that had little capital. Second, as a police measure, they would allow saloons only

9. *Age-Herald*, Apr. 8, May 4, 1899; *News*, May 30, July 6, 1905, Mar. 22, Apr. 2, 1906.

10. *Age-Herald*, Mar. 10, 13, 1889; *News*, Feb. 21, 1913. See also *Age-Herald*, Mar. 15, 1889, Feb. 19, Oct. 13, 1901; *News*, Oct. 23, 1907, Sept. 30, 1911.

in a special saloon "district" in the best-policed downtown areas. And the district boundaries would carefully exclude the shantytown Negro saloon and dance hall areas. Extra police would patrol the saloon district so that if any Negro "dives" moved into it rather than closing down, they would be, in Mayor Thompson's words, "properly restrained by policing."[11]

In 1895 and 1907 Birmingham churches and the Pastors' Union lobbied hard for these saloon-reform proposals, but the board of aldermen defeated them. From 1889 through 1911 (when the city commission replaced the board of aldermen), the prosaloon "Liberal Element" dominated the board. Several aldermen were saloonkeepers or liquor dealers, and the liberal faction had strong ties with the local Philip Schillinger Brewery, which owned several Negro saloons. Moreover all black saloons provided important markets for liquor wholesalers, and the Liquor Dealers' Association opposed any tightening of Negro saloon regulation. Until 1907 the prosaloon aldermanic faction kept the saloon license fee at $500 and allowed the liquor interests to operate saloons for either race anywhere in the city,[12] though they did require the brewery to move a few of its black saloons away from theaters or post offices in order to avoid an "affront" to white women.[13]

In 1905 Mayor Ward, elected on a progressive "Good Government," anti-machine platform, chose to make a dramatic issue of saloon reform, focusing particularly on Negro saloons. He proposed a central saloon district and a higher saloon license fee of $2,500 per year. In 1906 he said: "Birmingham has about eighty saloons catering to colored people. ... The number of these saloons should be arbitrarily reduced and the locations of the remainder shifted where they can be properly policed." He reported a police estimate that "80 percent of all arrests come from and are caused by these dives." Ward attributed the popularity of such saloons to their "side line of attractions" such as pool tables, gambling, music, and prostitution, and to "the rapid demoralization and breaking away from old fashioned ideas by our present colored population, male and female, especially the young." To undermine the "dives," Ward proposed "to rob the saloon of its social feature" by prohibiting games

11. *Age-Herald*, Dec. 22, 1889; *News*, Aug. 9, 1906, May 4, Aug. 30, 1907; Birmingham *State Herald*, Dec. 28, 1895.

12. See chapter 4, pp. 69–81 and *Age-Herald*, Dec. 24, 1889; *State Herald*, Dec. 28, 29, 31, 1895, Feb. 20, 1896; *News*, Aug. 8, Dec. 4, 1906, May 4, 6, June 20, Aug. 22, 23, 24, 30, 1907.

13. *Age-Herald*, Feb. 26, Apr. 4, 1899, Feb. 19, 1901, Jan. 2, 3, 1902; *News*, Jan. 5, 19, Mar. 16, 23, 1905, Jan. 10, 11, 1907.

of pool, dice, and cards, and by banning all women, music, and singing in saloons.[14]

The mayor had some limited success. In 1906 he prevailed upon the aldermen to ban games and music in saloons, and to close many, but not all, Negro poolrooms near saloons. By making astute informal arrangements with saloon men, the Schillinger Brewery, real estate men, and leaders of the prosaloon aldermanic faction, Mayor Ward in 1905 created a separate "red light" district in the midst of a lower-class Negro residential neighborhood and had the police transfer all prostitutes there. This program, he reported, "has reclaimed every other section of town from suspicion and contamination" and "has done more to prevent thievery, debauchery and murder; more to prevent insidious temptation; more to reduce licentiousness, incipient and chronic, than can ever be known by the public or the authorities." But he found that "the low class saloon is continuing to thrive," and he urged the board of aldermen to "commit itself firmly and boldly" to his entire program, including the high license fee and the central saloon district.[15]

The prosaloon majority on the board of aldermen refused to go this far, and in February 1907 when Ward ran for reelection, he made his saloon-reform program the chief plank of his platform. The Birmingham Pastors' Union enthusiastically supported Ward and took credit for his close 51.7 percent majority over the candidate supported by the liquor interests. But the prosaloon faction maintained a slim majority on the board of aldermen and in July and August 1907 again blocked Ward's proposals.[16]

Meanwhile, in February 1907 the state Anti-Saloon League had pushed a local option bill through the state legislature, insisting successfully that the county, rather than either the precinct or the city, be the unit for local option elections. In August 1907, therefore, the Pastors' Union, deciding that the whiskey-dominated board of aldermen would never approve saloon reform, dropped Mayor Ward's plan, broke with him politically, and demanded complete prohibition of all saloons. And soon they obtained enough petition signatures to call a county

14. *News*, Aug. 9, 1906.

15. Birmingham, *Message of the Mayor and Annual Reports of the Officers of Birmingham, 1906*, 16, 17; Birmingham, Minutes . . . Aldermen, K, 679 (June 7, 1905), L, 386 (Aug. 1, 1906); *News*, Aug. 16, Oct. 3, 4, Dec. 6, 1906, Sept. 13, 15, 18, Oct. 11, 1905; Jefferson County, Tax Assessment Map Books, Tax Assessor's Office, Jefferson County Courthouse, Birmingham.

16. *News*, Feb. 2, 19, Mar. 6, May 4, 6, June 20, Aug. 22, 23, 24, 30, Oct. 21, 1907.

local-option election for October 28, 1907. The Birmingham *News* agreed with the pastors that the aldermanic defeat of saloon reform had "destroyed" the "middle ground on the liquor question," and it campaigned zealously for prohibition.[17]

The antisaloon leaders concentrated heavily on "the negro phase of the liquor question," advertising prohibition as an effective means of controlling or eliminating the allegedly unreliable and menacing behavior of blacks. When opponents claimed that prohibition had not worked well in states that had tried it, such as Maine, the *News* replied that "a comparison of Maine with Alabama is neither fair nor reasonable. Alabama has a dangerous element to deal with which Maine has not. The negro becomes a criminal, a parasite, a public menace under the influence of the saloon."[18] At the height of their emotional campaign the prohibitionists centered their propaganda around "PICTURES OF NUDE WOMEN ON BOTTLES OF WHISKEY SOLD TO THE NEGROES," and the *News* urged citizens to "vote out the crime-breeding, sloth-producing saloons, including the menacing negro dives distributing among a dangerous element of the population whiskey bottles labeled with pictures of nude white women and insidious appeals to the basest instincts of idle and criminal negroes tempted to commit heinous offenses against unprotected women and girls."[19]

The *News*, moreover, told industrialists that "the solution of the unskilled negro labor problem in this district lies in the abolition of the saloon," which would eliminate the parasitical "crowds of black idlers who loiter about the resorts drinking liquor." But most Birmingham industrialists found this argument unconvincing, and they opposed prohibition, saying in a public letter: "Skilled, as well as ordinary labor is scarce and in demand all over the country, and we know that if a sweeping prohibition law should be enforced in this district, large numbers of our best workmen would leave." Moreover, "new labor, such as we need, will not come to a prohibition district." Prohibition, therefore, would be "a most serious blow to this community industrially, commercially and morally." Among the signers were the local heads of the Tennessee Coal, Iron, and Railroad Company; the Sloss Company; the Woodward Iron Company; the Dimmick Pipe Company; and the leading commercial-coal companies. Frank H. Crockard and Walker Percy

17. *News*, Aug. 31, 1907. See also *ibid.*, July 4, Aug. 20, 30, Sept. 20, 1907; Sellers, *Prohibition Movement*, 106–109, 114–15.

18. *News*, Sept. 28, 13, 1907.

19. *Ibid.*, Oct. 24, 26, 1907.

of T.C.I. and James W. McQueen of Sloss were so concerned that they personally took to the political stump, speaking at antiprohibition rallies.[20]

The saloonkeepers and liquor dealers, aided by a distillers' and brewers' "defense fund," discreetly organized antiprohibition efforts. The *Age-Herald* supported them, agreeing with industrialists that prohibition would retard the development of Birmingham. Ethnic groups such as the Irish and Germans had long opposed moralistic liquor regulation and firmly opposed prohibition. And most leaders and members of labor unions opposed prohibition as an infringement on individual rights. But some union members favored prohibition, and the Trades Council, after an intense debate, voted to take no part as an organization in the campaign. The *Labor Advocate* remained officially neutral, but it printed much more material against prohibition than for it.[21]

By September 10, however, the prohibitionists obviously held the momentum. The prosaloon aldermen, hoping to stem the tide, suddenly reversed themselves and enacted Mayor Ward's entire saloon-reform program. But it was too late. On election day Birmingham itself voted 55 percent against prohibition, but the suburbs and the outlying rural portions of the county voted 66 percent for it, overcoming the city vote and carrying the county with a 59 percent prohibition majority. On January 1, 1908, Birmingham became, against the will of a majority of its voters, legally dry. The keys to prohibitionist success had been the rural strength in the legislature and the county-unit plan which included the suburban and rural voters of Jefferson County in the decisive election.[22]

In a short time the state legislature, impressed by the prohibition strength even in urban Jefferson County, enacted a statewide prohibition law. But both prohibition laws proved too loosely drawn to be enforced effectively, and soon, to the dismay of many citizens, liquor was readily available to Negroes as well as whites in secret, illegal, totally unregulated "Blind tiger" saloons and locker clubs. At the same time, prohibitionists antagonized many voters by pressing for a constitutional amendment on prohibition. The amendment lost, and in February 1911, partly in reaction against it, the legislature passed local-option and

20. *Ibid.*, Sept. 18, 1907; *Age-Herald*, Aug. 25, 1907. See also *ibid.*, Oct. 21–28, 1907.

21. *Age-Herald*, Aug. 26, Oct. 5, 12, 1907; Birmingham *Labor Advocate*, Sept. 27, Oct. 11, 25, 1907; Sellers, *Prohibition Movement*, 115.

22. *News*, Sept. 10, 11, 19, 1907; election returns compiled from *ibid.*, Oct. 29, 30, 31, Nov. 1, 1907.

liquor-regulation bills which would permit counties to vote to allow saloons under a new strict-regulation, high-license system.[23]

In August 1911 Jefferson County held another local-option election, called by the antiprohibitionists. The vote against prohibition and for the strictly regulated, high-license saloon, was 63 percent in old Birmingham and 58 percent in Greater Birmingham, including the suburbs annexed in 1910. The county outside Greater Birmingham remained for prohibition by 52 percent, but the heavy city vote carried the county for the regulated saloon.[24]

Under the new system saloons were controlled by a local three-member excise commission appointed by the governor. The saloon license fee jumped from the $500 of 1906 to $3,000 in 1911. And in contrast to 1906, when Old Birmingham alone had had 132 licensed saloons, in 1911 the excise commission granted only 90 saloon permits in all Jefferson County, with only one "highly-recommended" Negro receiving a permit. The commission authorized some white saloons to build partial partitions to create separate black saloons, but it would allow no Negro-operated "dives" in the black quarters to serve as congregating points for unruly Negroes. The commission restricted Birmingham saloons to the most heavily policed central sections, and even there it prohibited saloons on all corners in the main business district and on all streets where "department stores and other shops frequented by women" were located. It also forbade the presence of women, of amusement and musical devices, and of gambling in saloons. In effect the 1911 system provided the type of discriminatory restrictions against Negro saloons and against the "social feature" of all saloons that Mayor Ward had sought before 1907. Only this middle position commanded the support of a majority of Birmingham voters; between 1871 and 1921 no other saloon restriction plan won a referendum majority inside the city limits.[25]

Birmingham and Jefferson County used this system until 1915, and would have continued it longer. But the Anti-Saloon League, working effectively in rural Alabama, gained control of the 1915 legislature and passed a new strict statewide prohibition law that closed all Birmingham saloons on July 1, 1915, against the wishes of a majority of Birmingham voters. The Birmingham evangelical Protestants had again

23. Sellers, *Prohibition Movement*, 118–28, 147–67; *News*, Oct. 29, 1910, Apr. 7, July 20, 21, Aug. 23, 1911.
24. *News*, Aug. 30, 1911.
25. *News*, Sept. 11, 13, Oct. 3, 4, 6, 14, 1911.

gained victory through their rural strength in the state legislature, which took the matter out of the hands of Birmingham voters and officials. Again, placing the law on the books was not a complete victory, because enforcement did not entirely eliminate the liquor traffic. But the law did restrict the traffic drastically, and Birmingham police statistics for the next five years showed a marked decline in criminal cases, in arrests, and especially in arrests for public drunkenness. And in 1916 even the *Age-Herald*, long-time foe of prohibition, praised the social control aspects of the law and hinted at a class difference in its impact, saying, "Those who, as Commissioner [George B.] Ward expresses it, 'enjoy a good drink of liquor as well as any healthy citizen,' usually are enabled to get it in Birmingham in a proper way and without violating the law. It cannot, however, be gotten in quantities to cause drunks, street brawls and fighting and shooting like unto the days of which no citizen of Birmingham is proud."[26]

PROHIBITION OF SUNDAY MOVIES

After the prohibition question was settled by state law in 1915, the Birmingham Pastors' Union and the Protestant activists focused on another moral issue: whether motion pictures should be allowed on Sunday afternoons. In 1915, after a four-year campaign, Birmingham's labor unions and several small theater owners had obtained permission from the city commission to show Sunday movies. Labor leaders said the movies provided worthwhile amusement which should be available to workingmen and their families on their one day of leisure. But the Pastors' Union, the Women's Christian Temperance Union, and several Sunday School organizations protested and launched an anti-Sunday-movie drive which forced the issue to a referendum in 1918. In response the Trades Council of organized labor resolved: "Whereas, morality being a question of individual conscience, we resent the attempt of the church interests to interfere with our individual liberty and denounce the same as savoring of government infringement of personal rights; that such action is merely 'churchanity' and not Christianity."[27]

During the referendum campaign a "Committee of Fifty of the Pas-

26. *Age-Herald*, May 25, 1916. See also *ibid.*, July 28, 1917. Sellers, *Prohibition Movement*, 174–89.

27. *Labor Advocate*, Feb. 16, 1918. See also *ibid.*, June 16, 1911, June 14, 1912; *Age-Herald*, Feb. 3, 10, Nov. 17, 24, Dec. 1, 24, 1915, Aug. 22, 1916, May 4, 1918.

tors' Union" claimed in a newspaper advertisement that on a list of pro-Sunday-movie petitioners they had discovered "every prominent Jew in the city," and "nearly every prominent Catholic." In addition, they alleged, the list contained the "owners of theatres," more than thirteen hundred people who were not registered voters and who therefore must represent "the loose, indifferent class of citizens," and many "convicted criminals, ex-saloon keepers, convicted aliens and other dangerous citizens of our community." Warning against "THE ENTERING WEDGE OF THE CONTINENTAL SABBATH," the pastors' committee proclaimed that "our fight in Birmingham is but one sector of the great battle for the preservation, or destruction, of the American Protestant Christian Sabbath as an institution for the conserving and preserving of our national moral life."[28]

The pastors' committee defined Christian morality as the basis of the American political order and went so far as to assert that non-Christians should not participate in political controversies over Christian morality. In a letter sent to all Jewish voters the committee pointed out that the Sunday movie issue "is a question touching a specific Christian institution, and that the adherents to the Christian religion are divided on this issue." If the Jews were divided on a religious custom, said the pastors, Christians would not feel called upon to take sides. Therefore, "we express the hope that in this particular election, to be held May 6, concerning a strictly Christian institution, our Jewish citizens will withdraw from this complication." In response the Jewish rabbi said simply, "I believe in Americanism which knows no religious distinctions in politics and public affairs." But the pastors replied, "We do not indorse your position that this is a question of politics, certainly not primarily so. It is different from any purely secular question. We do also believe in 'Americanism,' and therefore we contend earnestly for the Christian Sabbath as being fundamental to the Christian faith which has made 'Americanism' the synonym of the highest and holiest in the world of today."[29]

Most Roman Catholic priests and a tiny handful of Protestant pastors rejected this position and joined a pro-Sunday-movie committee. Among them were the Reverend Middleton S. Barnwell, rector of the Episcopal Church of the Advent, which was attended by many of Birmingham's social and economic elite; the Reverend Henry M. Edmonds, pastor of a theologically-liberal Independent Presbyterian

28. *Age-Herald*, Apr. 18, 1918.
29. *Ibid.*, Apr. 20, 26, 1918.

church in the elite residential section of South Highlands; and the Reverend George Eaves, a British Congregationalist pastor.[30]

But the "Committee of Fifty of the Pastors' Union" effectively mobilized Birmingham's majority of evangelical Protestants, especially in the suburbs, and produced a 54 percent majority against Sunday movies, without even calling on the aid of rural Jefferson County or rural Alabama. Thus by 1918 the pietistic Protestants had finally triumphed over every local group that opposed their moral regulations and had written all their major policy demands into law.[31]

VAGRANCY LAW ENFORCEMENT

To combat an alleged Negro proclivity for idleness, most whites endorsed strict enforcement of harsh vagrancy laws. But occasionally white workers, fearing that the laws threatened them as well, denounced antivagrancy activity.

Many white employers complained that their unskilled Negro laborers had excessively irregular work habits. In 1903, for example, Walker Percy of T.C.I. alleged: "Now, the ordinary Negro . . . works the least percentage of time. . . . They want to squander their money. The chief use they have for it is for three purposes—craps, women and whiskey. I do not believe anybody will deny that. They work for two or three days—just long enough to get money to shoot craps." Shelby M. Harrison, a writer for *The Survey* magazine, testified that managers of large companies had to keep from 50 to 75 percent more blacks on the payroll than they expected to have working on any given day. In 1906 the editor of the Birmingham *News* said, "Hundreds of idle negroes can be seen on the streets every day. They can all get work, but they don't want to work. The result is that they sooner or later get into mischief or commit crimes of one sort or another." And he urged: "Every one of the idle negroes should be forced to go to work or to be subject to the vagrancy laws. There is a great scarcity of labor in this city and district."[32]

30. *Ibid.*, Feb. 3, 1915, Jan. 6, 1916, Feb. 25, Apr. 29, May 6, 1918.
31. *Age-Herald*, May 7, 1918.
32. *Age-Herald*, Aug. 16, 1903; U.S. Congress, House of Representatives, *Hearings before the Committee on Investigation of United States Steel Corporation* (8 vols., Washington, D.C., 1912), IV, 2983; *News*, Oct. 27, 1906. See also *ibid.*, Aug. 29, 1907, Oct. 21, 1910; *Age-Herald*, May 21, Apr. 6, 10, 1917.

Seldom did industrial spokesmen, who desired mainly to defend and intensify strict controls, acknowledge that many of their black laborers were in fact steady, reliable, and highly productive. From 1916 to 1918, however, when wartime industrial opportunities in the north lured away many southern black workers, Birmingham industrialists did for the first time frankly avow that many of their most reliable and indispensable workers were Negroes. But such admissions, made only during an emergency effort to stem a black exodus, did little to counteract the popular stereotype, which industrialists had helped to create, of the Negro who worked as little and loafed as much as possible.[33]

As a remedy against the supposed Negro shiftlessness, employers frequently demanded stricter vagrancy law enforcement, and most middle-class whites endorsed this as a reform that would clean up the city and mitigate the menace of black crime. Periodically between 1890 and 1920 city police mobilized "to wage unrelenting war against the vagrants," under such slogans as "no idleness will be tolerated. . . . It is either a case of go to work or go to jail."[34] In 1906 the *News* described the procedure in one such campaign. The policemen on each beat "were instructed to make a visit to every saloon in their territory and to clean them out so to speak. Every negro who could not account for himself was ordered to be arrested. By this systematic plan none of the idlers will be overlooked, and in a short time the city will be rid of the vagrant negro." Police chief William E. Wier reported, "When the officers go into a saloon and several negro loafers are discovered they are either arrested or made to go to their work if they have a job."[35]

But the underpaid and undermanned police department could sustain such a drive only a short time before returning to a more normal routine. Reform-minded citizens, editors, and grand juries, therefore, continually exhorted the police to undertake more "bold" and "rigid" and "vigorous" vagrancy enforcement. In 1913 the *News* urged the city commission to "take in hand the Police Department, reorganize it if necessary, and strengthen it in every way possible by the additional employment of energetic, courageous, active men," because "the criminal negro class must be hunted out like tigers, and put behind bars."

33. *Age-Herald*, Nov. 28, 1916.
34. *News*, Dec. 12, 1913; *Age-Herald*, Sept. 26, 1906.
35. *News*, Sept. 28, 1906. For reports of other police campaigns against vagrancy see *ibid.*, Jan. 7, 1901, Sept. 26, 1905, Apr. 1, 1907, Dec. 18, 1909, Apr. 15, 1911, Oct. 21, Dec. 12, 1913; *Age-Herald*, Apr. 4, 1891, Oct. 7, 1893, Apr. 27, 1918, Dec. 17, 1920.

The *News* believed that "If Birmingham and Jefferson County can get rid of the vagrant," whose activities "have served too long to besmirch the good name of this district," then "this will be a community that will become as far-famed for its respect for the law as it now is for its indifference thereto."[36]

Birmingham's vagrancy laws covered most of the alleged Negro characteristics that whites wanted to control. An 1891 city ordinance deemed guilty of vagrancy "any person having no visible means of support, or being dependent upon his labor lives without employment, or habitually neglects his employment, or who abandons his family . . . , or who is a gambler or common drunkard or who habitually walks and rambles upon the streets at unreasonable hours of the night, or who habitually loafs and loiters about disreputable places." The vagrancy laws could be applied to whites as well as to blacks, and white gamblers and prostitutes were sometimes charged with vagrancy, but in practice the antivagrant drives against sheer idleness concentrated almost entirely on Negroes.[37]

In 1903 and 1907 the state broadened and strengthened its vagrancy laws, making penalties more severe and intensifying the labor control aspect. The *News* believed that under the tougher 1907 law "the number of available laborers in the industrial districts especially will be considerably increased and that alone would be a decided help in the solution of the serious labor problem."[38] As the emphasis on labor control increased, labor unions began criticizing vagrancy enforcement, especially since convicted vagrants were frequently leased to coalmining corporations. Still, the vagrancy laws exempted bona fide strikers, and so long as the laws were used mainly against unskilled Negroes rather than skilled white workers, the Birmingham Trades Council and *Labor Advocate* offered only sporadic criticism.[39]

Then during the labor shortages of World War I, employers and labor unions suddenly polarized in their attitudes toward vagrancy laws. In April 1918 the *Age-Herald* reported that twenty-five "prominent iron and steel manufacturers" appeared before the city commission to propose a new stricter vagrancy law to be enforced by a city employ-

---

36. *News*, Nov. 12, Dec. 21, 1913. See also *ibid.*, Dec. 7, 1906, Sept. 24, 1914.
37. *Age-Herald*, Apr. 4, 1891; *News*, Dec. 14, 1913.
38. *News*, Feb. 2, 1907. See also *ibid.*, Mar. 7, 15, 1907; *Age-Herald*, Sept. 29, 1903.
39. *Labor Advocate*, Dec. 23, 1910, Dec. 19, 1913, Feb. 6, 1914.

ment bureau. The industrialists told of an "acute labor shortage," with many plants "50 to 60 percent short of labor all the time." The *Age-Herald* alleged that high wartime wages enabled men "to work two or three days a week, and still support themselves," and that this resulted in a "large assemblage of men on the downtown streets." The proposed law declared that when any defendant "has been guilty of wandering or strolling about, or remaining in idleness during any working day in any calendar week, the burden of proof shall be upon the defendant to show that he is not a vagrant." The proposed city employment office would have two special police officers to enforce the law, in order to secure "continuous employment for all males" and "continuous operation of the industrial and other works in and around the City of Birmingham to their capacity during this time of emergency."[40]

A labor delegation bitterly opposed the ordinances. The local Machinists Union, which was striking for higher wages, said the proposed ordinance "was inspired by the larger employing interests of the District, and is directed solely at the men who refuse to work for the low wages paid by these concerns." Though the ordinance would not apply to men on strike, the machinists charged that it would help create a pool of strikebreakers. But labor opposition was to no avail. Employers appealed to patriotism and to the prosperity which full-capacity wartime production could bring Birmingham. One employer said it was "pro-German" to oppose such "progressive measures" as the vagrancy ordinance. The city commission passed the ordinances unanimously, and enforced them vigorously. By July 31, 1918, Henry J. King of the employment bureau reported, "Pool rooms have been deserted, few loiterers are seen in the streets during work hours, the negro section, where we once found scores loafing, now look[s] like a cemetery, and Birmingham is carrying out to the letter the 'work or fight' order."[41]

Once the wartime emergency was over, Birmingham briefly relaxed its antivagrancy activities. But in December 1920 police and county deputies launched yet another "war" on vagrants and promised that the "campaign" would continue "until every negro loafer, male and female, in Birmingham has been rounded up." By this method, reported the *News*, "it is expected that negroes actually responsible for crimes who

40. *Age-Herald*, Apr. 9, 1918; Birmingham, Minutes of the Board of Commissioners, Y, 62 (Apr. 11, 1918).
41. *Labor Advocate*, Apr. 13, 1918; *Age-Herald*, Apr. 12, 20, 27, May 4, July 18, 1918; *News*, July 31, 1918.

are yet at liberty may be caught in the dragnet spread for the idle class in addition to removing from the field of activity many of the idlers who have not yet committed crimes, but are ready to do so at the first opportunity." To these venerable goals and methods labor spokesmen raised no objection.[42]

CONVICT LABOR SYSTEMS

The convict labor system, another major feature of law enforcement against Negroes, stemmed in part from the determination of whites to control Negro vagrancy. Many whites considered forced labor the most effective punishment for the vagrant, who, said the *News*, "hates work worse than he fears imprisonment." Moreover, most whites believed that convicted lawbreakers rather than taxpayers should pay the expense of maintaining the police, court, and prison systems. Since most convicted Negroes were unable to pay fines, the city and county could recover their expenses only by forcing convicts to work during their imprisonment.[43]

During most years the city of Birmingham shackled its convicts in a chain gang and worked them ten hours a day cleaning and repairing city streets. Reports showed that Negroes comprised between 80 and 92 percent of the city chain gang, and after 1915 only black prisoners were employed on the streets. Most whites, including organized laborers, approved of working the city convicts on the streets. In 1910, however, some leading Birmingham professional men began protesting against the practice of shackling the prisoners together day and night. The "spectacle" of chained prisoners working in the streets, they said, was "shocking" to visitors and gave the city a bad image. In 1915 the city took the shackles off the prisoners, but it continued to work its Negro convicts on the streets.[44]

A second means of getting revenue from the labor of convicts was to lease them to coal-mining corporations. The city experimented with this briefly in 1897, 1905 and 1907, when it was desperate for revenue, but strong opposition from organized labor and from many middle-

42. *News,* Dec. 6, 1920.
43. *Ibid.,* Mar. 7, 1907.
44. *Ibid.,* Jan. 31, 1905, Jan. 29, 1908; July 2, 1910, Apr. 19, 28, May 2, 1911; *Labor Advocate,* Jan. 7, 1899, May 29, 1914; *Age-Herald,* May 16, 1915, Dec. 5, 1919.

class whites usually brought the experiment to a quick end and caused the city to return its convicts to the city street gang.[45]

The county leased convicts much more extensively than did the city. Between 1887 and 1891 the county commission experimented with using its convicts for road work, as the city did, but by 1891 the need for revenue led the county to resume leasing its convicts. Between 1891 and 1913 the county leased nearly all the able-bodied convicts, 80 to 90 percent of whom were Negro, to T.C.I., the Sloss-Sheffield Steel and Iron Company, and the Pratt Consolidated Coal Company. Because these corporations hired convicts not only from Jefferson County, but also from other counties in Alabama and from the state penitentiary, a large proportion of Alabama's convicts were funneled into the Birmingham mineral district. Between 1906 and 1911, the coal mines employed an average of 1,500 state and county convicts per year.[46]

The coal-mining corporations found convict labor cheaper than free labor. In 1903, for example, Erskine Ramsay, who from 1894 to 1902 had been chief engineer and assistant general manager of T.C.I., told Henry C. Frick of Pittsburgh that "the operation of the convict mines has been very remunerative" and that "the convicts mined the cheapest coal ever produced by the Company." In 1915 Milton H. Fies, who had served as coal-mining superintendent for three major Birmingham coal companies and who had supervised both free and convict miners, wrote: "It is an indisputable fact that coal cannot be produced by free labor within 20 cents per ton of what it can be produced by convicts."[47]

Some industry spokesmen denied that convict labor was necessarily cheaper than free labor. Even if that were so, however, convict labor was useful to employers, mainly because of its regularity. Convicts could not work three days and loaf four, nor "take off" for picnics, funerals, and excursions. Further, convicts were invaluable in suppressing unionism. During any strike the convict mines continued to produce their daily quota of coal. President George Gordon Crawford of T.C.I. acknowledged that convict labor helped to block unionism, and in 1911 he wrote: "The chief inducement for the hiring of convicts was

45. *News*, Apr. 8, 1897, Aug. 30, 1905; *Age-Herald*, July 22, 1908.

46. *Age-Herald*, Mar. 20, 1889, June 13, 1891, Mar. 11, 1893, Dec. 19, 1894; *News*, Jan. 10, 20, 1900, Dec. 15, 30, 1908, Nov. 28, 1912; *Labor Advocate*, Jan. 14, 1905; U.S. Congress, House, *Hearings . . . United States Steel Corporation*, IV, 2962.

47. Ramsay to Frick, Aug. 7, 1903, Erskine Ramsay Papers, BPL; *Age-Herald*, July 20, 23, 1915; *News*, Dec. 1, 1911. In 1903 Ramsay was vice-president and general consulting engineer of Pratt Consolidated Coal Company.

the certainty of a supply of coal for our manufacturing operations in the contingency of labor troubles."[48]

Variations in the rates paid for convicts suggested the crucial role of convicts in labor conflict. From 1891 through 1904 the Sloss company paid Jefferson County nine or ten dollars per month for able-bodied male convicts, and paid only the maintenance of women and boy convicts. In 1904, however, T.C.I. and Sloss, both beginning a bitter conflict with the striking United Mine Workers, submitted bids for double the customary ten dollars per month. T.C.I. got the 1905–1908 contract, paying the unusually high rates of $24.90 for able-bodied males sentenced to more than one year, $18.00 for males sentenced to less than one year, and $10.00 per month for women and boys. During those four years T.C.I. hired approximately 1,950 convicts from Jefferson County, averaging approximately 300 at any given time. But after the decisive defeat of the United Mine Workers in the great strike of 1908, the bids offered by all the coal-mining corporations dropped back to the pre-1905 level.[49]

Although the corporations found the convict lease system profitable and useful, many Birmingham interest groups opposed both the state and the county convict lease systems. The Birmingham Trades Council, the *Labor Advocate*, and the United Mine Workers bitterly denounced the state for channeling cheap forced labor into Birmingham to compete with free organized labor. In the 1890s both the *Age-Herald* and the *News* officially supported the position of organized labor and declared that most Birmingham citizens of all classes endorsed removal of the state convicts. Birmingham citizens objected to the state convict lease partly because it reduced the payroll spent in Birmingham and partly because of the many inhumane features of the system: the heavy work loads, frequent beatings, poor food, miserable sanitary conditions, and the appalling convict death rate.[50] But the objection most persistently and prominently mentioned by Birmingham citizens was that the state convict lease system made Jefferson County the "dumping ground" for the worst convicts of the entire state. The citizens and

48. Crawford to James G. Oakley, November 24, 1911, published in U.S. Congress, *Hearings . . . United States Steel Corporation*, IV, 3111–12. See also *ibid.*, 2982.

49. *Age-Herald*, June 12, 1891, Aug. 24, 1892, Mar. 11, 1893, Dec. 19, 1894; *News*, Jan. 10, 20, 1900, Dec. 15, 28, 30, 1908, Nov. 1, 1911, Nov. 28, 1912; *Labor Advocate*, Jan. 14, 1905.

50. *News*, Nov. 10, 1896, Apr. 11, 1911; *Age-Herald*, Feb. 12, 1889, Oct. 20, 1891, Nov. 26, 1892, Dec. 14, 1898, July 18, 1915, June 4, 1919.

press of Birmingham said that when these convicts were released after completing their sentences, they remained in Birmingham and joined the menacing class of "criminal negroes." In 1896 the *News* urged the legislature to "remove the baleful influences" of the convicts in the mines and thereby to "free Jefferson county from a curse that blights." And in 1914 the *News* said, "The cause of Birmingham's excess of criminal negroes has been frequently analyzed and enumerated. There is no need of repetition: the State's convict system is the chief one." Thus the lease system seemed to intensify rather than mitigate the black "menace."[51]

In most sessions of the state legislature between 1890 and 1920 the Birmingham representatives actively sponsored bills to remove the state convicts from the mines, or at least to reform the system significantly. During the period only one Birmingham legislator, Nimrod W. Scott in 1915, dared to vote directly against a bill to remove state convicts from the mines. But until 1927 Birmingham's efforts to evict the state convicts met perennial legislative defeat at the hands of the corporations, the revenue-hungry state officials, and the counties that "dumped" their convicts.[52]

Though the Birmingham city and county government could not overrule the legislature, the county board of revenue could take one major action against the system: it could quit leasing its own convicts to the coal corporations and could instead use the three hundred men to improve old county roads and build a network of new market roads into Birmingham's hinterland. This was consistently advocated by the *Labor Advocate*, the Trades Council, and the United Mine Workers, seconded by the *Age-Herald* and the *News.* If Jefferson County could demonstrate that it was more profitable to work convicts on roads than to lease them to the mines, it might convince the other counties and the state to remove their convicts from Jefferson's mines.[53]

51. *News*, Nov. 10, 1896, July 13, 1914. See also *ibid.*, Sept. 22, Dec. 21, 1913; *Age-Herald*, Jan. 15, 1889, Dec. 20, 1900, May 22, 1901, Feb. 11, 1903.

52. *Age-Herald*, Dec. 1, 1892, Jan. 31, Feb. 8, 10, 1893, Dec. 6, 1894, Jan. 31, Feb. 8, 1899, Feb. 11, Oct. 2, 1903, July 18, 1915, Sept. 8, 1919; *News*, Nov. 23, 1896, Jan. 11, 1897, Nov. 23, 25, 1898, Apr. 11, 1911; *Labor Advocate*, Mar. 10, Apr. 7, 28, 1911, Oct. 22, 1915, Sept. 27, 1919; Albert B. Moore, *History of Alabama* (University: Univ. of Alabama Press, 1934), 771, 814–17; Elizabeth Bonner Clark, "The Abolition of the Convict Lease System in Alabama, 1913–1928" (M.A. thesis, Univ. of Alabama, 1949), 68, 80–96, 105–13.

53. *Age-Herald*, Mar. 1, 1889, June 12, 1891, Aug. 29, 1892, Sept. 8, 1903; *News*, Aug. 10, 1906; *Labor Advocate*, May 28, Sept. 3, 1898, Nov. 19, 1904, Mar. 20, 1908, Feb. 23, Dec. 13, 1912.

Until 1913 the board of revenue always decided that it could not afford to heed such advice. The lease money from the three hundred convicts was the major, though not the only, source of revenue for the County Fine and Forfeiture Fund, which paid the court costs and fees of the county sheriff and other law enforcement officers. If the board diverted the county convicts to a new road program, the Fine and Forfeiture Fund would dry up and soon the board might have to levy unpopular new taxes to replenish it. And the board believed that the sentiment against the lease system and the desire for better roads were insufficient to generate approval of higher taxes.[54]

In late 1904, when the board signed a new convict lease contract, the *Labor Advocate* announced: "The Board of Revenue has acted and after much talk and palaver the corporations win and the people lose out."[55] Certainly the corporations had won, but the attitudes of many of "the people" had helped them win. As long as the people clung to the belief that the convicts must pay their own way, so long did the people offer an opportunity to any employer who was in a position to use coerced labor and who would guarantee the government a steady income from its convicts.

By 1912, however, dissappointment over the persistently low convict lease rates after 1908 had intensified, and the political opposition of organized labor and civic leaders had mounted. Moreover, in 1911 T.C.I., long the largest lessor of convicts, had decided to stop using convict labor altogether, mainly because political opponents had shut T.C.I. out of the 1911 bidding on state convicts. Thereafter, T.C.I. threw its weight against the convict lease system. With the largest coal-mining corporation out of the bidding, lease prices seemed likely to decline further.[56]

In early 1913, then, the board of revenue decided that it could risk the financial and political experiment of removing the convicts from the mines and putting them to work on the county roads. Board president Robert F. Lovelady warned that new equipment and preliminary arrangements would make the experiment expensive at first, but he promised: "We will try to get out of it all it is worth if the public gives us their patience and cooperation after it first begins. . . . We believe

54. *Age-Herald*, Aug. 23, 1906; *Labor Advocate*, Mar. 6, 1908; *News*, Nov. 3, 1911, Nov. 28, 1912.

55. *Labor Advocate*, Jan. 7, 1905.

56. *News*, Nov. 1, 1911, Nov. 28, Dec. 23, 1912; U.S. Congress, House, *Hearings . . . United States Steel Corporation*, IV, 3111–12, 3117; *Age-Herald*, July 23, 1915.

206

it will solve the convict problem and the road maintenance problem of the county."[57]

As of April 1913, the county assigned all new able-bodied convicts to the road gang. By April 1915 the board and two grand juries were enthusiastic about the improved condition of the convicts and the betterment of county roads. The board's engineer calculated that it was significantly cheaper to use convicts rather than free laborers on the roads, even when the board paid the convicts' court costs and fees to the Fine and Forfeiture Fund. Coal company spokesmen, such as president George B. McCormack of Pratt Consolidated Coal Company, challenged the board's accounting and asserted that the county was actually losing money by not leasing the convicts. He further declared that working convicts in mines was "infinitely better from every standpoint of health, humanity, and economy than working on the roads."[58] But the Birmingham newspapers and voters accepted the accounting of the board of revenue and showed no desire to return the county convicts to the mines. Thus the coal companies finally lost the Jefferson County convicts when the politicians and voters found another way to make the convicts pay their own way. Still, the ability of local government to rid Jefferson County of the convict lease system was limited. In 1915 editor Edward W. Barrett of the *Age-Herald* proclaimed that Jefferson County had "demonstrated what can be done by the general use of them [convicts] for road building throughout the state." But until 1927 the state and many counties continued to "dump" their convicts in Jefferson's coal mines.[59]

THE COUNTY FEE SYSTEM

The county fee system, the final major feature of law enforcement against Negroes, eventually provoked intense white opposition because it came to interfere with efficient utilization of black labor. Under the fee system most county law enforcement officers, such as the sheriff, the clerk of court, the justices of the peace, and the constables, received no salaries; rather they received fees according to the number of legal

57. *Labor Advocate*, Feb. 7, 1913.
58. *Age-Herald*, July 17, 19, 1915. See also *ibid.*, Mar. 25, 1914, Mar. 21, Apr. 4, May 30, June 22, Aug. 20, 1915.
59. *Ibid.*, Mar. 21, 1915, Aug. 29, 1916; Moore, *History of Alabama*, 771, 814–17.

notices they served and the number of arrests and court cases in which they participated. The sheriff received warrant and turnkey fees of at least four or five dollars, and often more, for each arrest made by his deputies, regardless of whether the arrest led to a trial or a conviction. (Judges and members of the county board, however, received flat yearly salaries instead of fees.) Until 1913 most fees were paid from the county convict-lease revenue, but in 1913, when the county stopped leasing convicts, it had to use other revenue. Thus until 1913 the lease and fee systems were in practice closely linked, but they were distinct systems, and one could be abolished while the other survived.[60]

Though the county paid fees for every arrest, it followed one procedure of payment if the arrest led to conviction, another if it did not. If a defendant was convicted, the judge assessed against him all the court costs, which included the fees of all law enforcement officers involved in the case, plus the fees of witnesses, at fifty cents or one dollar per day and three cents per mile for travel. In a typical case in which a Negro was convicted of gambling, the fine was usually ten dollars and the court costs ranged from thirty to seventy-five dollars. If the defendant could not pay cash, the judge sentenced him to about one-hundred days at hard labor to work out the fine and costs. Until 1913 the county promptly leased the convict to a coal corporation, which provided maintenance and paid the county approximately 40 to 96 cents per day. The county, however, credited only 30 to 40 cents per day against the convict's fine and costs. After 1913 the county used the convict on the road gang and credited 75 cents per day against his fine and costs. The earnings of the convict went into the County Fine and Forfeiture Fund, which also received all cash fines and all forfeited bonds. And from this fund the county paid the fees of the sheriffs and deputies, the court officers, and the witnesses. In a case which had resulted in conviction, the fund paid the fees in cash as soon as the convict had earned them.[61]

Arrests which did not lead to conviction, however, earned no income for the fund. If the county had immediately paid the fees for these cases

60. Alabama, *Code of Alabama, . . . 1897*, vol. II, *Criminal* (Atlanta, 1897), 224–37; Alabama, *Code of Alabama, . . . 1907*, vol. III, *Criminal* (Nashville, 1907), 435–55.

61. Alabama, *Code of Alabama, . . . 1897*, vol. II, *Criminal*, 213–21, 224–37, 263; Alabama, *Code of Alabama, . . . 1907*, vol. III, *Criminal*, 416–17, 422–26; *News*, Nov. 19, 1906, Mar. 21, May 1, 1907, Dec. 4, 1908, Mar. 8, 1909, Aug. 10, Sept. 4, Nov. 1, 20, 1911; Oct. 22, 26, 1912; *Age-Herald*, Mar. 20, 1889, Mar. 10, 1915; Birmingham, *Free Lance*, Jan. 16, 1909.

in cash, it would quickly have depleted the fund. For such fees, therefore, the county issued scrip, redeemable from the Fine and Forfeiture
Fund at some future date. And all witnesses received their fees in scrip,
regardless of whether their cases resulted in conviction or acquittal. The
fund redeemed scrip in the order in which it had been issued, and the
fund always ran several years behind, since only the income above
that necessary for the cash conviction fees could be applied to the non-
conviction scrip. Most witnesses sold their scrip immediately to scrip
buyers who paid twenty-five to sixty cents on the dollar for it, but the
sheriffs and other fee officers usually kept their scrip until it could
be redeemed, and many former sheriffs were still cashing in their scrip
years after they had retired from office.[62]

Thus the profit motive and the desire to ensure a future income
stimulated the sheriff and his deputies and constables to be vigilant in
making arrests. The law allowed the sheriff to employ as many deputies
as he thought necessary and to pay them according to private arrangement. The temptation was for the sheriff to employ as many deputies
as he could keep busy with fee-creating work, and to enlarge his force
when he thought additional deputies could generate sufficient new fees
to pay their wages and to leave the sheriff an increment of profit.[63]

The sheriff also profited from a food allowance of thirty cents per
day for each prisoner in the county jail. This was paid by the state.
Investigations in 1891, 1907, 1911, and 1915 revealed that the sheriffs
spent less than ten cents per day per man on food (typically two meals
of fat side meat, peas, and cornbread) and made at least twenty cents
per day profit on every prisoner.[64] Sheriffs habitually kept their "boarding house" jail filled far beyond its intended capacity. In 1907 sheriff
Elijah L. Higdon, reporting on his first eight months in office, acknowledged that in his jail, which had accommodations for 144 persons, "The
lowest number of prisoners that has been in jail at one time is 156, the
highest on any one day, 325."[65]

The jail cells were usually crowded with Negroes who would even-

62. Alabama, *Code of Alabama, . . . 1897*, vol. II, *Criminal*, 227, 263; *Age-Herald*, Mar. 20, 1889, Nov. 19, 1915; *News*, Nov. 19, 1906, Mar. 21, 1907, Dec. 4, 1908, Nov. 1, 1911, Oct. 14, 26, 1912; *Free Lance*, Jan. 16, 1909, Mar. 4, 1910.

63. *News*, Feb. 15, 1907, Sept. 4, Nov. 1, 1911, Oct. 13, 14, 19, 24, 1912; *Mayfield* v. *Moore*, 139 Ala. Rept. 417–20 (1903).

64. U.S. Congress, House, *Hearings . . . United States Steel Corporation*, IV, 2989; *Age-Herald*, Feb. 6, 1891, July 27, 1907, May 16, Sept. 24, 1915; *News*, Aug. 8, 1907.

65. *News*, Sept. 26, Nov. 27, 1907, Oct. 24, 27, 1912; *Age-Herald*, Jan. 22, 1902.

tually be acquitted, but who could not afford bail, and who therefore "boarded" in jail for months awaiting trial. If a man was convicted, the waiting time in jail did not count against his sentence. In 1915 reform-minded Jefferson County solicitor Hugo L. Black discovered that the waiting period was particularly long during the summer, because the criminal courts adjourned from June to October. Solicitor Black inaugurated reforms, including summer court sessions, to help alleviate the most obvious injustices of the system.[66]

Defenders of the fee system—chiefly its direct beneficiaries—argued that the many arrests generated by the system were absolutely necessary to control the criminal propensity of blacks. It saved tax money, they claimed, and promoted vigilant suppression of dangerous Negro dives and crime-inducing crap games.[67]

But many Birmingham industrialists and citizens of middle economic rank perceived distinct disadvantages in the system. They found it chaotic and corrupt, they believed it concentrated on trivial offenses while failing to deal with serious crime, and they said it disrupted Birmingham's industrial labor system. In 1894 reform-minded attorney Alexander T. London, chief counsel for the Elyton Land Company, began a public attack on the system, gradually building public sentiment against it by exposing the large profits made by fee officials. After 1900, London was joined by prison inspectors, local judges, and both the *News* and *Age-Herald*. Finally in 1910 the Chamber of Commerce launched a major campaign to abolish the fee system, although it remained silent about the separate but related county convict lease system.[68]

Such industrial spokesmen as Walker Percy of T.C.I. and James W. McQueen of the Sloss-Sheffield Company enthusiastically supported the antifee campaign, mainly because the fee-seeking officers often interfered with the free labor of Birmingham's industries. After defeating the United Mine Workers in the great coal strike of 1908, Birmingham's iron and coal corporations relied more heavily than ever on black workers. And the industrialists complained that the county-fee officers, instead of helping them control their Negro workers, actually harassed, disrupted, and drove away their black labor force, and therefore should

66. *Age-Herald*, Sept. 6, 1911, Dec. 20, 1914, May 16, 1915, Aug. 20, 1917; *News*, Nov. 27, 1907; *State Herald*, Nov. 27, 1896.

67. *News*, Sept. 26, 1907, Dec. 8, 1910, Feb. 8, 1911; *Age-Herald*, Sept. 29, 1915.

68. *Age-Herald*, Sept. 1, 1894, Jan. 22, 1902, Sept. 6, 1903, Oct. 31, 1904, July 26, 1907; *News*, Sept. 6, 1905, Nov. 14, 1906, Jan. 5, 1907, May 29, 1909, Oct. 21, 1910.

bear the blame for a severe labor shortage around Birmingham. In 1911 T.C.I.'s Walker Percy denounced "the disorganization of labor by indiscriminate arrests of working negroes for trivial offenses."[69] A Chamber of Commerce committee led by realtor Thomas H. Molton said, "Negro laborers are continually being annoyed by officers of the law invading the mines and furnace camps, night after night, looking for craps shooters, and those who are not arrested are demoralized through fear; consequently they work very irregularly. This evil can be modified only by the abolition of the fee system." The Chamber of Commerce and the industrialists did not oppose strict vagrancy law enforcement, however. Their complaint was that the county deputies concentrated on petty gambling among employed blacks, but that they ignored idle blacks, leaving them to the salaried city police force. The Chamber of Commerce report continued: "Negroes are allowed to loaf throughout this district, especially in the cities. The remedy for this is for the county and city officials to enforce the vagrancy law, which they can do by spending only one-hundredth as much energy as is spent in hunting down craps shooters. Should the vagrancy law be enforced the idle negroes would seek employment, which would insure better results at the mines, furnaces and other industries."[70]

Sheriff's deputies and constables probably found it more desirable to arrest employed men caught playing craps than to capture idle vagrants. Often if a valuable black employee was convicted, his employer would pay his fine and court costs immediately in cash (and probably dock his pay accordingly) in order to get him back on the job. In that case the sheriff or constable received his fee immediately, rather than having to wait until the costs had been worked out. Also often, according to custom, an officer who arrested a black for a petty offense would take an immediate "cash bond," which had no sanction in law and which never went beyond the officer's own pocket, and which therefore assured that he would drop the case, not even entering it on a docket. A black who had a good job and some cash on hand might well prefer to dispose of the matter in this way, outside the courts, for then he did not have to miss any work or bother his employer about bail, character testimony, or payment of fines and court costs.[71]

69. *News*, Feb. 8, 1911. See also *ibid.*, Jan. 6, 14, 1911, Oct. 24, Nov. 1, 1912; F. Ray Marshall, *Labor in the South* (Cambridge: Harvard Univ. Press, 1967), 74.
70. *News*, Oct. 21, 1910.
71. *Age-Herald*, Mar. 10, 1915; *Labor Advocate*, Jan. 13, 1911, Feb. 2, 1912; *News*, Jan. 14, 1911.

Some critics of the fee system, such as attorney John W. Altman, particularly denounced the deputies and constables for using Negro "spotters" to spy out Negro crap games for the deputies to raid. And in 1915 deputy sheriff Conrad W. Austin did acknowledge that "it had been the custom to pay spotters 50 cents per head for each person caught in a gambling raid." Moreover, in 1917 J. Campbell Maben, Jr., vice president of the Sloss-Sheffield Steel and Iron Company, charged that Negro spotters did not confine themselves to discovering crap games, but that they performed as decoys and deliberately worked up crap games and lured in victims for the deputies to raid. Other critics reported a widespread belief that deputies used this tactic, but no one produced direct evidence.[72]

By whatever methods, the deputies and constables did make frequent wholesale arrests of many black workers for gambling and other petty offenses. J. Campbell Maben, Jr., complained that "As the result of these practices, the larger industries are handicapped often for help. As the negroes are needed for coking the furnaces and other important operations, we must bail them out." A leading corporation attorney, Sidney J. Bowie, asserted that the industrialists found the system so disruptive and annoying that "it is a common practice for corporations to pay the constable in their beat to let the negroes play crap games. The corporation officials say this is the only way to keep their labor camps from being demoralized. They buy protection for their men."[73]

By 1911 all major Birmingham industrialists, even those who leased convicts from Jefferson County, opposed the fee system, which did not actually produce many extra convicts in relation to the arrests, fees, and harassment it generated. Also, coal corporations could hire convicts from other counties and from the state, and their proposal to abolish the fee system applied only to Jefferson County.[74]

The Birmingham *Labor Advocate* and its columnist R.A. Statham of the United Mine Workers were quite ambivalent toward the anti-fee-system reform movement, which they considered far less important than the movement to abolish the convict lease system. The *Labor Advocate* said the workingmen for whom it spoke had little to do with the fee system, and that they actually appreciated the system's tendency to

---

72. *News*, Oct. 19, 1912; *Age-Herald*, Sept. 29, 1915. See also *ibid.*, Mar. 17, 20, 1915, Feb. 2, 1917; U.S. Congress, House, *Hearings . . . United States Steel Corporation*, IV, 2990.

73. *Age-Herald*, Feb. 2, 1917; *News*, Mar. 5, 1912.

74. *News*, Oct. 25, 1910, Jan. 6, Feb. 1, 8, 21, Aug. 5, 8, 1912.

encourage vigilant law enforcement without cost to taxpayers. Statham had no sympathy with the industrialists' desire to relieve their under-paid black laborers from harassment, and he chided them for restricting their proposal to Jefferson County. The *Labor Advocate* said that as far as there actually was a labor shortage in Jefferson County, it should be blamed not on the fee system, but rather on the really crushing evil, the convict lease system, and on miserable housing conditions, high-priced company commissaries, and prohibition laws. The Birmingham Trades Council eventually did endorse the campaign for a constitutional amend-ment permitting abolition of the fee system in Jefferson County, but the *Labor Advocate* gave it only mild support.[75]

Birmingham's citizens of middle economic rank opposed the fee sys-tem more firmly, for they saw many clear disadvantages in it. Far from mitigating the menace of the criminal Negro, the system encouraged officers to concentrate on petty cases which clogged the courts and de-layed prompt justice to serious offenders. Also, potential witnesses, knowing they would receive a pitifully inadequate cash reimbursement for travel and lost wages, often evaded witness duty. Civic-minded people abhorred the chaotic corruption and "ghoulish graft" which gave inordinate profits to a few men. Walker Percy estimated the sheriff's net yearly income from fees to be between $30,000 and $50,000, and in 1907 the *News* reported a "general opinion" that "the office of Sheriff of Jefferson County is probably the most lucrative public office in the Southern States." The sordid and inefficient system did nothing to expedite good law enforcement, and it corrupted elections, because can-didates spent huge sums campaigning for the profitable office of sheriff. These characteristics, widely publicized after 1910 by the Chamber of Commerce and the Birmingham newspapers, stirred citizens of middle economic rank to fervent opposition.[76]

The movement to abolish the fee system in Jefferson County faced formidable obstacles, however, for the system was firmly entrenched in the legal and political system of Alabama. The 1901 constitution of Alabama had provided that the legislature could not substitute a salary system for the fee system in one county unless it did so in all counties. And in most Alabama counties the sheriff and his entourage of deputies dominated county politics and state legislative delegations.

75. *Labor Advocate*, Sept. 23, 1910, Jan. 13, 1911, Mar. 15, Aug. 9, Sept. 20, Nov. 1, 8, 1912, May 28, 1915; *News*, Aug. 26, Oct. 28, 1912.
76. *News*, Sept. 26, 1907. See also *ibid.*, Jan. 30, Sept. 4, Nov. 1, 2, Dec. 11, 1911, Oct. 13, 1912, Dec. 21, 1913, July 4, 1914.

In 1907 Jefferson County legislator Jere C. King introduced a bill to change from the fee to the salary system in all counties, but the Sheriffs' and Clerks' Association prevented the bill from reaching the floor. It became evident that only a constitutional amendment applying to Jefferson County alone could rid Jefferson of the fee system. In 1911 T.C.I. attorney Walker Percy was elected to the state legislature from Birmingham on a platform proposing such an amendment. And in Montgomery he obtained the necessary three-fourths approval of both houses for a constitutional amendment enabling the legislature to place Jefferson County alone on a salary system.[77]

In 1912 prominent Birmingham industrial, commercial, banking, utility, real estate, and professional leaders, with the reluctant cooperation of labor leaders, created an antifee-system league to organize a statewide campaign for the necessary referendum approval of the amendment. Corporation attorney Sidney J. Bowie initiated the league, and T.C.I. attorney Percy became state chairman. Other officers were Fred M. Jackson of the Cahaba Coal Company, W.P.G. Harding, president of the First National Bank, and John W. Altman, attorney for labor organizations and local businesses. On November 5, 1912, Jefferson County voters approved the amendment 9,144 to 1,186, and the voters of the entire state approved it 62,417 to 15,886.[78]

Even so, the fee system was to operate six more years in Jefferson County. The legislature did not meet again until 1915, and then it provided that Jefferson's new salary system should take effect only after the terms of the 1915 incumbents had expired in 1919. Until 1919 sheriffs, deputies, and constables continued to collect fees for each arrest in Jefferson County,[79] and industrialists continued to complain that fee grabbers harassed and demoralized their black labor force. In 1917, particularly, industrialists such as J. Campbell Maben, Jr., of the Sloss-Sheffield Company and James Bowron of the Gulf Steel Company ex-

77. *Ibid.*, Mar. 2, 1907, Mar. 24, 1910, Feb. 21, 1911, Oct. 1, 1912; *Age-Herald*, July 26, 1907, Sept. 20, 1910; "Constitution of Alabama, 1901," Art. IV, Sec. 96, in Alabama, *Code of Alabama, . . . 1923*, vol. I, *Political* (Atlanta, 1923), 299; Alabama, *Acts*, 1911, p. 47.

78. *News*, Aug. 5, 8, Oct. 13, 27, Nov. 6, 12, 16, 1912.

79. *News*, Nov. 28, 1911; Alabama, *Local Laws*, 1915, 374–75. In 1913, however, when the board of revenue put the convicts on the roads, it exploited a legal technicality to avoid reimbursing the Fine and Forfeiture Fund for those convicts, and the fee officers had to accept scrip, which the county treasury did not redeem until the legislature forced it to do so in 1915. *News*, May 11, Dec. 21, 1913; *Age-Herald*, Feb. 4, 14, 27, Mar. 20, July 11, 14, 22, 25, Nov. 19, 1915.

plicitly blamed "harsh treatment" by fee grabbers for provoking an "exodus" of black workers to northern wartime industry.[80]

Finally, in January 1919, when newly elected sheriff James C. Hartsfield succeeded sheriff Thomas J. Batson, Jefferson County's fee system expired—at least as far as the payment of the sheriff and the court officers was concerned. The courts actually continued to assess the fees against convicted defendants, but the county treasury rather than the officers received the fees. Fees paid in cash went directly into the treasury, and convicts who could not pay cash had to work out the fees on the county road gang. The county took charge of feeding prisoners and hiring deputies, and it paid the deputies and the sheriff flat salaries. No longer could arresting officers increase their incomes through wholesale arrests that did not result in convictions. The *Age-Herald* noted that with the fee system dead the number of prisoners in the county jail was one hundred, the lowest in years. But the old principle that convicted lawbreakers should pay the costs of the law enforcement system—either in cash or in work for the county—remained intact.[81]

SOCIAL REGULATION PATTERNS

The social regulation patterns of victory and defeat were complex, because social and economic groups were seldom neatly congruent and because social issues often provoked disagreement within economic groups. But one important generalization stands out: the groups that suffered the most severely-restrictive social regulation—Negroes, nonpietistic white ethnic minorities, saloonkeepers, and small movie operators—were predominantly of lower economic rank and social status. Certainly Negroes, the lowest-ranking group of all, underwent the most severe regulation. Reforms in control of Negroes did ameliorate a few of the most inhumane practices, but the basic thrust of the changes was to place the blacks more firmly and efficiently under the discipline of economically-powerful white groups. Other ethnic minorities found their traditional recreation curtailed, and probably the majority of all workingmen, even those of native white background, considered the general tightening of government social intervention, particularly the

---

80. *Age-Herald*, Feb. 2, 1917.
81. *Ibid.*, Nov. 19, 1915, Jan. 21, Aug. 2, 21, 1919; Alabama, *Local Laws, 1915,* 374–75.

imposition of prohibition, strict Sunday observance, and wartime vagrancy enforcement, to be disadvantageous.

The middle-ranking economic groups had no confining social regulation imposed directly upon their day-to-day economic activities. Of course, many men of middle rank opposed the new moral restrictions and ultimately suffered personal defeat. Still, businessmen who knew how to purchase liquor in the "proper way" probably experienced little curtailment of their drinking habits, at least until the advent of national prohibition. And the main adverse effect on the economic activity of the middle ranks was indirect, through the license-tax increase that followed prohibition. When it came to shaping social regulation of others, particularly Negroes, the middle-ranking groups had only moderate success. They supported the tightening of vagrancy law enforcement to clean up the business district, but enforcement was seldom rigorous enough to please them. They supported the battle against the fee system, but achieved their goal only in 1919. And their attack on the convict lease system succeeded at the county level in 1913, but they found themselves powerless to stem the importation of state convicts before 1928.

Upper-ranking industrialists found social regulation outcomes mixed. They suffered no major defeats and had no direct regulation imposed on their basic economic activities. Moreover, vagrancy law enforcement and the convict labor system helped them control and exploit black labor. And even when local opposition against convict labor became intense and deprived them of the county convicts, the rural-dominated state helped them keep the unpopular lease system alive. The industrialists did experience some minor setbacks, however. For example, the advent of prohibition in 1907 and the delay in ending the fee system seemed to produce an adverse effect upon the behavior, discipline, and recruitment of their labor force. And industrialists discovered, ironically, that when they needed government modernization, as they did in the case of the fee system, the cumbersome rural-dominated state political system that usually protected them could stand in the way of their progress. Still, on balance the industrialists gained more from government control of blacks than did anyone else, and by 1921 only they had been able to abolish a part of that control—the fee system—that they found directly detrimental to their economic activities.

X

Economic Regulation

$\mathbb{I}$N economic as well as social regu-
lation, the higher the economic rank of an interest group, the better it
tended to fare. Of course, the economic regulatory authority of local
government extended only to activities contained within city or county
boundaries. Thus many activities of the upper-ranking firms that produced for a regional and a national market were entirely beyond the
purview of the city or county. Still, such matters as the nuisances and
dangers created by railroads and industries, the payday and commissary
practices of manufacturers, and the actions of employers and workers
during strikes were potentially subject to local regulation, as were most
economic operations of middle- and lower-ranking firms. Within this
circle of local regulatory authority, interest groups contended sharply,
some seeking to shape regulation of others or of themselves so as to
gain certain benefits, others seeking mainly to avoid any government
regulation of themselves. In these struggles the economically stronger
contenders scored the most victories.

PEACEKEEPING DURING STRIKES

Birmingham and Jefferson County experienced fierce labor-manage-
ment conflict, which erupted into several bitter major strikes and many
smaller ones. And the peacekeeping activities of police, sheriff's deputies, courts, and state militia significantly influenced the strike outcomes
and the gains or losses of labor and management. During all strikes
from the 1890s through 1920 government officials defined their responsibility according to a customary formula: First, government must protect property. Second, laboring men had a right to organize unions.
Third, however, employers had a right to hire and fire whom they

pleased; thus, they had a right to fire all union men if they so chose. Fourth, during a strike any employee had a right to quit work, but no quitting worker had the right to interfere in any way whatsoever with anyone who desired to take his place and accept the employer's terms and wages.[1]

This policy, said government officials, was impartial, because it protected equally the freedom of strikers and nonstrikers to work or not work. In practice, however, the enforcement of the policy during strikes strongly aided management, which usually sought to continue operation using imported strikebreakers. Strikers usually sought access to the strikebreakers, hoping to induce them, through picketing, persuasion, or threats, to stop work and either join the strikers or leave town. And the supposedly neutral strike policy of local government helped management quarantine its strikebreakers from such union influence. Police and deputies usually ruled unlawful any activity by a striker that could be interpreted as an attempt to induce a nonunion man to leave work. Police and deputies arrested strikers not only for using violence, but also for picketing, for "hooting" strikebreakers, for jeering streetcars driven by strikebreakers, for congregating near places of work, for shouting "Scab!" or for simply attempting to talk with strikebreakers.[2]

The sternest antiunion enforcement occurred during the 1908 coal strike, when Jefferson County Sheriff Elijah L. Higdon ordered his deputies: "You will not allow any person or persons to loiter or congregate at or near the works of any employer of labor in Jefferson County. The situation has become such that assemblies however peaceful can only be looked upon as having the intention of intimidating the employees of the works from pursuing their usual peaceful avocations of life." Further, said Sheriff Higdon, "Picketing is also unlawful, when carried on to such an extent as to be an annoyance to any employer or to his workman, and I hereby charge you to break up said unlawful acts and if those who persist in the same continue, you will arrest them and bring them to the county jail." Moreover, "gathering around passenger trains, hooting and jeering at the passengers, at this time is an unlawful assembly."[3]

Many, but not all, nonunion citizens, particularly those of rural background, supported local government's antiunion right-to-work empha-

1. Birmingham *Age-Herald*, July 10, 1894, July 24, Aug. 12, 13, 1908; Birmingham *News*, July 10, 1908, May 23, June 21, 1913.
2. *Age-Herald*, July 10, 1894, July 16, 1908; *News*, May 20, 21, 31, 1907, Aug. 4, 1908, May 23, June 22, 24, 26, 1913.
3. *Age-Herald*, Aug. 6, 1908.

sis, partly because they found it congruent with individualistic rural tradition, and partly because they believed that continuous full production by the major local industries was crucial to the economic well-being of the entire city and that disruptive strikes injured all citizens, including workers. Strikes, moreover, frequently triggered violence on both sides. Houses were dynamited, trains loaded with strikebreakers were shot-up from ambush, and in frequent armed skirmishes, union and nonunion men were wounded and killed. The daily newspapers, nearly always siding with management, succeeded in blaming most of the violence on the strikers, portraying it as part of the union effort to intimidate nonunion workers. Consequently, much of the popular revulsion against the violence was directed against the strikers.[4]

Yet, despite the popular appeal of the antiunion doctrines, many citizens who were not union members and whose numbers cannot be determined were at times sympathetic to the cause of union strikers. During a major coal strike in 1894, for example, many Birmingham merchants contributed to the strikers' fund and extended credit to strikers. Such merchants identified more closely with the striking union men, who were their customers, friends, and sometimes kinsmen, than with the absentee-owned corporations, which ran monopolistic company commissaries and which sought to hold down the wages that workers spent in local stores. But during the next major coal strike, in 1908, few merchants sympathized with the union. William R. Fairley, national organizer of the United Mine Workers, was disappointed at the indifference and actual hostility of most merchants toward the strikers in 1908, and the *Labor Advocate* reported that to its surprise the "merchants have all the way through sympathized with the operators." At the height of the strike twenty-five prominent downtown businessmen called a mass meeting of 2,500 citizens to accuse strikers of "lawlessness" and "anarchy" and to issue veiled threats to lynch union leaders.[5]

Nevertheless, the union circulated a petition urging arbitration, which the companies opposed, and soon the union claimed to have 20,000 signatures. But the companies asserted that in fact only 600 had signed, and the union did back off from its claim of 20,000. And whatever the extent of citizen sympathy with the 1908 strikers, it had little effect

---

4. *Ibid.*, Apr. 14, 1894, Aug. 13, 1908; Birmingham *Labor Advocate*, Aug. 14, 28, 1908; Robert Ward and William Rogers, *Labor Revolt in Alabama: The Great Strike of 1894* (University: Univ. of Alabama Press, 1965), 90, 11–13.

5. *Labor Advocate*, Sept. 4, 25, 1908. See also *ibid.*, Aug. 21, 1908; *News*, Aug. 10, 13, 1908; *Age-Herald*, June 7, July 6, 18, 1894.

on the relevant policies of city and county officials, who intensified their antiunion activity as the strike progressed.[6]

The sheriff aided the corporations primarily by swearing in large numbers of special deputies who were paid and directed by the corporations. According to custom, any citizen who believed his life or property to be in danger could call on the sheriff for protection by special deputies, whose salary the citizen should pay. This custom enabled corporations to have all their regular guards and detectives deputized at the hint of a strike. And during a strike they could have the sheriff hire legions of armed special deputies, including such imported adventurers as "Texas Ranger sharpshooters," all of whom operated under company orders. Most sheriffs were happy to oblige, for, in addition to paying the special deputies $2.00 per day, the corporations customarily paid the sheriff $1.00 per day for each man he deputized. Thus during the 1908 coal strike, which lasted two months, Sheriff Higdon, who swore in 600 to 800 special deputies, made a profit estimated to be near $40,000. When critics reprimanded him, Higdon replied, "I did have a large force of deputies on duty during the strike; some put on at my own expense, the balance by request of the different mining corporations. These deputies were used to protect the property of the corporations, and I charged these companies the same price for these men that every other sheriff before me has charged for the same service. If the sheriffs who have preceded me were entitled to this money, I felt that I was. I gave the same service and took the same compensation, and, like the former sheriffs, expect to make what I can as sheriff legitimately." In effect, during each major strike from 1890 to 1921 the system enabled the corporations to use their economic power to hire small private armies clothed with law enforcement authority.[7] Even the abolition of the county fee system in Jefferson County in 1919 did not affect the sheriff's authority to swear in special deputies, whose compensation came not from fees, but directly from the corporations.

Labor unions complained bitterly against the use of special deputies, whom they called company "thugs," and on whom they blamed the violence which characterized the major strikes. Wherever the responsibility for initiating the violence lay, clearly much of it occurred in confrontations between deputies and strikers, and the deputies enjoyed the

6. *Age-Herald*, Aug. 19, 1908; *Labor Advocate*, Aug. 21, Sept. 4, 25, 1908.
7. *News*, Sept. 8, 1908. See also *ibid.*, Aug. 22, Dec. 4, 18, 1908, Feb. 15, 1911; *Age-Herald*, Aug. 4, 1908, Mar. 19, 1915: *Labor Advocate*, Jan. 10, 1913; *Mayfield* v. *Moore*, 129 Ala. Reports 417 (1903).

advantage of being able to make arrests and to declare any group an unlawful assembly and break it up.[8]

In the three great coal strikes of 1894, 1908, and 1919–1921, the pro-management actions of local government helped the operators mobilize enough strikebreakers to continue minimum operations and to render union victory impossible. But the strikes did diminish coal output significantly, and the operators could not finally break any of them without the intervention of the state governor and the state militia. During the 1894 coal strike, Governor Thomas Good Jones personally hired three Pinkerton detectives to spy on strikers, and he sent a military aide, Lieutenant James B. Erwin, to gather intelligence from the Pinkerton men and to help coordinate the importation and protection of strikebreakers. The governor also sent state militia to help protect strikebreakers and to help coal companies evict strikers from company houses. Under such pressure the strikers finally had to accept, very unhappily, a compromise settlement with a wage rate much below their minimum demand. But they did win some concessions, such as reductions in rent and the cost of supplies; they did gain a contract with T.C.I.; and the union did survive.[9]

In the 1908 coal strike, Governor Braxton Bragg Comer, an industrialist, dealt a decisive blow that completely broke the union. The United Mine Workers had organized 18,000 men, almost the entire mining force of the district; and despite the activities of sheriff's deputies, the strike was highly effective. After two months the coal companies began evicting the strikers from company houses, and the union set up tent colonies on land leased from sympathetic farmers. But Governor Comer, alleging that the tent camps lacked sanitation and police protection, ordered the militia to cut them down, leaving the strikers and their families without shelter. He also banned all public meetings of miners and declared that unless the union ended the strike immediately, he would call the state legislature into extraordinary session to enact laws allowing him to treat the strikers as vagrants. The governor's drastic actions forced the UMW officials to call off the strike in total defeat.[10]

Governor Comer and the operators employed virulent racial argu-

8. *Age-Herald*, May 15, 22, 1894, Nov. 1, 4, 1919; *News*, May 21, 1907, July 6, 10, 17, 18, 1908; Birmingham *Post*, Mar. 29, 30, 1921; *Labor Advocate*, July 1, 1899, Oct. 11, 1902, July 17, Aug. 14, 28, 1908, Nov. 8, 1919.

9. Ward and Rogers, *Labor Revolt*, 69, 77–84, 91, 105–15, 131–37; see folder of reports from T.N. Vallens and James B. Erwin to Governor Jones, Governor's Office Records, ADAH.

10. *News*, Aug. 24–28, 1908; *Labor Advocate*, Sept. 4, 25, 1908.

ments to justify his drastic intervention. More than half the Alabama miners were Negro, and the UMW had organized blacks as well as whites and had elected some blacks to union offices. Company propagandists alleged that the union tent colonies promoted social equality between the races, that the union had organized an interracial women's auxiliary, and that "impudent negroes" addressed union audiences in which southern white women sat. Comer declared that "the integrity of our civilization" was endangered when the union kept large numbers of Negroes in idleness. He and the companies addressed such racial propaganda not only to Birmingham citizens, but also to the entire state, using it to mobilize the state legislature and the rural voters behind the governor's drastic actions. Suppose, asked company spokesman Frank V. Evans, that Negro farm workers in the black belt "should leave the farms and pitching tents close by should there idly dwell, . . . interfering with the incoming of new laborers who desired to take their places; how long would the planters of Alabama permit that condition to exist?"[11]

In 1894 and 1908 the strikebreaking governors received close cooperation from the Jefferson County sheriffs, who formally requested state militia and thereby provided legal authority for state intervention. But this did not happen in the 1919–1921 coal strikes. During World War I organized labor, including the UMW, made significant gains in Jefferson County, and in 1919–1920 a labor Allied Committee campaigned energetically to register voters and to pay poll taxes, greatly increasing the labor vote and making the sheriff and city commission more mindful of labor's wishes. In fact, during the 1919 and 1920–1921 coal strikes, labor leaders commended Sheriff James C. Hartsfield for his evenhandedness and noted that he had protested against the intervention of the militia, but management spokesman Eugene L. Brown severely criticized county and city officials. The sheriff did provide the deputies that the companies requested, but labor spokesmen gave him credit for attempting to restrain the deputies and to prevent the companies from using them to intimidate strikers.[12]

Likewise, in 1919–1921 city government displayed a new, friendlier attitude toward labor. In 1920 General R. E. Steiner, who commanded the militia in the mineral district, forbade mass meetings of striking

11. *News*, Aug. 25, 1908; *Age-Herald*, Aug. 29, 1908. See also *ibid.*, Aug. 24, 26, 30, 1908.
12. *Age-Herald*, May 26, July 10, 1894, Nov. 1, 3, 4, 6, 1919, statement of Brown, Jan. 23, 1921; *News*, Aug. 4, 5, 1908; *Labor Advocate*, Nov. 8, 1919, Jan. 15, 1921; Wayne Flynt, "Organized Labor, Reform, and Alabama Politics, 1920," *Alabama Review* 23 (July 1970) 168, 177.

United Mine Workers. But the Birmingham Trades Council received permission from the Birmingham City Commission to use the main downtown park for a Sunday afternoon mass meeting to support the UMW. Borden Burr, general counsel of T.C.I., and James L. Davidson, secretary of the Coal Operators' Association, demanded that the city commission revoke the permit because it violated the spirit of General Steiner's order. But the commission reaffirmed the permit, saying that to cancel it would be an unwarranted invasion of the constitutional rights of the Trades Council. The council held the meeting, and several thousand determined workingmen convened to denounce General Steiner's denial of the right of assembly, to cheer the city commission "who respected the rights of the people enough to permit this meeting," and to adopt resolutions condemning the coal operators and the militia.[13]

Such actions by local officials greatly annoyed and inconvenienced the coal operators, even though the companies still received all the deputies they wanted. Again, as in 1908, the operators needed the aid of the governor and the state militia, and it was a measure of their power that again, despite the attitudes of local officials, massive and decisive state aid came from a sympathetic governor, industrialist Thomas E. Kilby. State militia helped weaken the strike, and finally the UMW and the coal operators agreed to submit to the arbitration of Governor Kilby. In March 1921 the governor one-sidedly ruled against recognition of the union, against wage adjustments, and against abolition of the subcontract system. He said the operators were under no obligation to reemploy strikers, and he refused to establish new machinery to adjudicate grievances. The governor's vigorous partisan intervention and decisions, so fiercely antiunion that they surprised many Birmingham citizens and newspapers, negated the UMW's local gains and defeated the cause of union labor in the coal mines of Birmingham.[14]

Thus in each of Birmingham's three major coal conflicts—in 1894, 1908, and 1919–1921—the coal operators had the good fortune to find in the governor's chair a man personally associated with capital and industry and against union labor. Moreover, the governors' statewide rural constituencies sympathized with the companies' racial propaganda and individualistic right-to-work principles, and this allowed the governors the freedom to exercise their strong personal antiunion beliefs and to intervene against labor with costly militia and drastic actions and decisions.

13. *Labor Advocate*, Oct. 16, 1920. See also *Age-Herald*, Oct. 8, 11, 1920.
14. *Labor Advocate*, Mar. 26, 1921; *Post*, Mar. 9, 20, 21, 1921.

CITY CONTRACT AND EMPLOYMENT POLICIES

Birmingham's labor unions, constantly seeking greater recognition and legitimacy, often asked local government to abide by union principles in its own contracts and employment policies. And the city sometimes complied, mainly when dealing with trades in which local unions had already been accepted by local management. For example, organized labor insisted that city printing be done only in union shops, and, with a few exceptions in 1906 and 1907, it was. But such compliance was relatively easy, because after 1900 all the daily newspapers regularly signed union contracts with the strong local typographical union. Also in 1900, when the city let contracts to build a new city hall and three new school buildings, the Trades Council persuaded the board of aldermen to require the contractors to employ only union labor, which most of them did already. Thereafter, most city construction and repair work probably went to contractors who employed union labor; only briefly in 1917 did organized labor complain severely about nonunion contractors obtaining city contracts.[15]

The story was different with regard to street railway workers. In 1907 and 1913 a large proportion of the streetcar employees of the Birmingham Railway, Light, and Power Company organized a union, affiliated with the Amalgamated Association of Street Railway Employees of the American Federation of Labor. Both times the B.R.L. & P. president quickly learned of the fledgling organization, and, before the union sought recognition or made any demands, he summarily discharged all known union members, provoking the remaining union men to strike. During both bitter strikes the company imported strikebreakers and the city and county rapidly employed several hundred extra policemen and special deputies to ride armed guard on the strikebreakers' streetcars, to patrol the streets, to break up prounion assemblages on street corners by energetically enforcing a "move-on" order, and to arrest men who jeered the "Scab" streetcars. In both battles the union was totally demolished, and it blamed defeat mainly on the intervention of local government. By 1916, however, the B.R.L. & P. had chosen a new president, more tolerant of unions, and when the streetcar men again organized, he promptly recognized the union and negoti-

15. Birmingham, Minutes of the Mayor and Board of Aldermen, I, 73 (Sept. 19, 1900); *Labor Advocate*, Dec. 8, 29, 1917, Mar. 3, 1906, Feb. 22, 1907; *News*, Nov. 26, 27, 1900.

ated a closed shop contract with it. The city government quietly accepted the decision, but clearly its support of the union principle extended only to those situations in which management itself accepted rather than resisted unions.[16]

City officials, moreover, adamantly opposed the unionization of any of their own departmental employees. In 1913 some Birmingham firemen sought to organize a nonstriking firemen's union to negotiate grievances, and the Trades Council supported the proposed union as "perfectly legitimate and praiseworthy." But the city commission declared that although it had no objection to unions as such, it would never allow its own authority and discretion to be diminished through the unionization of any city department, and that it would summarily discharge any fireman who joined such a union. The proposed union evaporated, and the fire chief, warning against future union escapades, summarily fired several veteran firemen who had helped organize the union.[17]

Organized labor had more success in gradually securing the eight-hour day for some city employees. In 1903 the *Labor Advocate* and the Trades Council began demanding the eight-hour day for policemen, and in 1906 the aldermen implemented it. Little was said about other employees until 1917, when labor's Co-operative, Citizenship and Educational Committee urged the eight-hour day for all city employees and all contracts let by the city. The commissioners elected in 1917 listened sympathetically but did nothing until December 1920, when they were entering a tough reelection campaign in which the newly mobilized labor vote was sure to be important. Then, after listening to vigorous objections from the Real Estate Exchange, the coal operators, several manufacturers, and a number of merchants, the city commission unanimously adopted an ordinance decreeing an eight-hour day for all work done or contracted by the city.[18]

Thus the local trade-union movement gained some government recognition and some mild use of regulatory power in favor of union principles. But such prounion government actions did not directly affect any of the upper-ranking groups that were resisting unions; rather,

16. *News*, May 20, 21, 25, 30, 31, June 6, 1907, June 15, 21, 22, 24, 26, 27, July 8, 1913; *Age-Herald*, Aug. 10, 22, 24, 1916; *Labor Advocate*, May 23, 31, June 7, 1907, June 27, July 4, 11, 1913; Aug. 12, 19, 26, 1916.

17. *News*, Mar. 14, 16, 20, 25, 26, Apr. 15, 1913; *Labor Advocate*, Mar. 21, Apr. 11, 8, 1913.

18. *Labor Advocate*, Dec. 25, 1920. See also *ibid.*, Jan. 31, 1903, Mar. 24, 1906, Sept. 1, 1917, Dec. 18, 1920; *Age-Herald*, Dec. 17, 18, 1920.

they were mainly formal ratifications of specific union positions already accepted by local management. For that reason, only the eight-hour-day ordinance, which had potentially wider ramifications, provoked serious protest from middle- and upper-ranking groups.

REGULATION OF LABOR AGENTS

During frequent periods of labor scarcity, labor agents swarmed into Birmingham, seeking, to the dismay of local industrialists, to entice workers to other states, often to the north. To discourage labor agents, the city government customarily levied a license tax of at least $500 per person upon them. In 1912 the agents became particularly troublesome, allegedly "crippling" the operations of several plants. Industrialists quickly induced the city commission to raise the tax to $2,000. And the News reported, "It will be the policy of the commission to harass the labor agents as much as possible and discourage their operation."[19]

Organized labor basically disliked labor agents, who sometimes recruited strikebreakers and who often lied about their companies' wages and conditions. But the agents were a source of job information, and union leaders had little sympathy with industrialists' intention of keeping local labor ignorant of alternative opportunities. Union leaders usually placed the ambiguous question low on their priority list and said little about it.[20]

During World War I, however, labor agents from northern industry focused especially on black workers, and some white labor leaders suddenly applauded the agents as fervently as industrialists denounced them. When the coal companies persuaded the city commission to raise the labor-agent tax to $2,500 per year, plus $5,000 bond, columnist R. A. Statham of the Labor Advocate said: "When you place this outlaw tax against labor agents you are denying the negro of a privilege of seeking aid to better his condition.... you want him here for exploitation, and to keep labor down on the level of slavery times." In 1916, at the beginning of the black migration, Statham had written, "I hope the negro will never come back. We white people who are held down to the level of the negro know how he is imposed upon.... The negro is seeking or being sought for new fields, and thank God, he is

19. News, Nov. 26, 1912. See also ibid., Dec. 10, 1912, Aug. 2, 1906; Age-Herald, July 24, 1901, Sept. 23, 1916.
20. News, Oct. 10, 1898; Labor Advocate, Dec. 6, 1912, Oct. 14, 1916.

accepting." But the city commission paid scant attention to such sentiments; wartime patriotism and the labor needs of Birmingham's payroll makers took precedence. The commission kept the labor-agent tax high, and the police and courts severely punished labor agents who had no licenses.[21]

REGULATION OF COMPANY COMMISSARIES AND PAYDAYS

Most of the coal, iron, and steel corporations of Birmingham paid their workers only once a month and operated a commissary check system that obliged most workers to trade at the company stores. When a man got a job, he had to work one month before his first payday and then the company withheld two-weeks' wages. Usually he needed money long before payday, and the company would give it to him only in the form of commissary checks, redeemable only in merchandise from the company store. If before payday an employee had to have cash instead of commissary merchandise, he had to sell his commissary checks to local speculative dealers, often saloonkeepers, at a discount which ranged from 20 to 40 percent. The speculators, or "scalpers," used the cheaply obtained checks to buy commissary merchandise, which they promptly sold at reduced prices. And this dismayed regular merchants, who denounced it as "unfair" competition.[22]

Birmingham merchants and labor leaders proposed not to abolish the commissaries, but to regulate them through two basic changes in the commissary-and-payday system. They wanted paydays twice a month, and they wanted the companies to stand ready to redeem their commissary checks *in cash* at no discount on the regular paydays. Then the checks would, they hoped, become completely negotiable, like good promissory notes. The employee could draw a check early, sell it at a small discount to any banker or respectable merchant, and trade where he found the best prices.[23]

Some coal and iron companies finally agreed to redeem their checks

21. *Labor Advocate*, July 26, 1919, Oct. 21, 1916; *Age-Herald*, Apr. 6, June 2, 1917, June 13, 1918, Oct. 4, 1919.

22. *Age-Herald*, Sept. 7, Oct. 19, 1895, Jan. 7, 1902, Aug. 16, 1903; *News*, Sept. 27, Dec. 29, 1912; John A. Fitch, "The Human Side of Large Outputs," *The Survey* 27 (Jan. 6, 1912), 1530; Justin Fuller, "History of the Tennessee Coal, Iron, and Railroad Company, 1852–1907," (Ph.D. diss., Univ. of North Carolina, 1966), 317–20; *Labor Advocate*, Aug. 5, 1910, Nov. 1, 1912, Feb. 10, 1917.

23. *Age-Herald*, Nov. 19, 29, 1892, Jan. 27, 31, 1915; Birmingham *State Herald*, Oct. 19, 1895; *News*, Jan. 19, 1900, Jan. 12, 1913; *Labor Advocate*, Feb. 3, 1917.

in cash, as well as merchandise, but only at a discount that ranged from 15 to 25 percent, which was "about what they thought they ought to make as fair profit in the commissaries." This, of course, did not change the basic practice to which labor and merchants objected: the company's insistence that all wages paid before payday go through its commissary, either directly or indirectly, there to render tribute, either in commissary profit or in a discount equal to the normal commissary profit. This normal commissary profit was a significant item, even for so large a corporation as T.C.I., especially during depression years. In 1899 T.C.I. operated fifteen separate company stores, with a gross merchandising business of $2,000,000 a year. In 1897 nearly one-third of T.C.I.'s total profit came from sale of commissary merchandise, and in 1894, 1896, and 1897 the company realized more profit from sales of commissary merchandise than from sales of pig iron. If the commissary profit was important for so large a concern as T.C.I., it was doubly so for many smaller coal-mining companies, some of which were described, only partially in jest, as grocery companies that operated a few coal mines in order to create a captive clientele of miners.[24]

Several times between 1890 and 1920 Birmingham merchants, labor unions, and newspapers urged the legislature to enact local laws requiring the coal and iron companies of Jefferson County to adopt the two-week payday and the transferable check redeemable at full value in cash on payday. The corporations opposed the measures. Frequent paydays were costly and time-consuming, they argued, especially since workers usually got drunk on payday and missed work afterward. And the commissary check system was the only way to handle improvident workmen. Moreover, T.C.I.'s Henry F. DeBardeleben candidly defended the commissary profits and discounts as a justifiable part of the return on investment in the development of Birmingham. Most Birmingham legislators supported the commissary and payday bills, but the corporations always sidetracked them. Commissary and payday policies remained entirely unregulated by local or state government.[25]

24. Age-Herald, Aug. 16, 1903; Labor Advocate, Nov. 1, 1912; News, Dec. 29, 1912; Jan. 5, 1913; Fuller, "History of the Tennessee Coal, Iron, and Railroad Company," 317–20, 376, 386–88; Fitch, "Human Side," 1529–30.

25. Age-Herald, Nov. 19, 27, 1892, Feb. 18, 1893, June 12, Aug. 29, 1894, Feb. 7, 1895, Aug. 16, Sept. 27, 1903, Jan. 27, 29, 31, 1915, Jan. 20, 1917; Labor Advocate, Aug. 5, 1910, Feb. 12, 1915; State Herald, Nov. 25, 1896, News, Feb. 2, 1897, Jan. 19, 1900, Sept. 27, 1912. A few Birmingham legislators such as state senator John T. Milner did not favor the bills. Age-Herald, Mar. 17, 1895.

In 1903 an arbitration commission included the two-week payday in a coal-strike settlement, but one year later the companies refused to continue the agreement. In

REGULATION OF SMOKE

Iron furnaces, coke ovens, and manufacturing plants filled the air above Birmingham with smoke. For years citizens welcomed smoke as a sign of active plants, good payrolls, and general prosperity. But by 1907 some middle-ranking downtown groups were complaining of " THE COSTLY SMOKE EVIL," which, according to the *News*, caused $3,000,000 annual damage to merchandise and property.[26] The chief downtown smoke-producer was the Sloss Company, which operated two iron furnaces and 288 coke ovens eight blocks from the main business district. In 1912 the *News* declared, "The Sloss furnaces and coke ovens are a dirty splotch upon the fair face of Birmingham. They . . . daily and nightly spew their noisome smoke and poisonous gases into the air. They are a dead weight around the neck of real estate values in their neighborhood. They are a blight to vegetation, a foe to health." Merchants suffered "a certain percentage of financial loss owing to the spoiling of their goods." In sum, said the *News*: "The Sloss plant is in the way of comfort, of development, of progress," and the company should "remove" it "to a more isolated site." But John Shannon, general superintendent of Sloss furnaces, asserted: "That plant represents a pay roll of exactly $2,000,000 per year. The Chamber of Commerce and the Business Men's League are always striving to get industries here. Here is a two million dollar one right on the ground. . . . If those furnaces should ever shut down it would take two million dollars right out of Birmingham."[27]

Nonetheless, in 1911 city commissioner James Weatherly, an enthusiastic advocate of the city beautiful, took the lead in "trying to create sentiment" for smoke regulation. And in December 1912 he persuaded his colleagues to enact a strict ordinance requiring mechanical smoke-reduction devices and regulating the number of hours per day that a firm could produce smoke. Soon two new special smoke inspectors arrested several manufacturers, including the vice president of Sloss, for smoke violations. The manufacturers, paying forfeitures rather than

---

1911 T.C.I. voluntarily adopted two-week payday, but the other companies protested and refused to follow suit; in 1918 federal government arbitrators provided for a two-week payday in Alabama coal fields, but none of these cases involved state or local government. *Labor Advocate*, Aug. 29, 1903, May 11, 1918; *News*, Nov. 17, 1911.

26. *News*, Mar. 22, 1907.

27. *Ibid.*, Oct. 6, 1912, Jan. 5, 1913.

standing trial, began mobilizing sentiment against the ordinance. The *Age-Herald* swung behind them, saying: "Better for people who cannot stand Birmingham smoke to move away than to handicap the pay roll makers; better for the commission itself to move out of town than to cripple the industries that are here; better anything almost than an idle furnace or factory. Be practical, Mr. Weatherly, and call off your smoke inspectors." The *Labor Advocate* agreed, saying: "Any hardship that is worked on the manufacturing plants in this district will react on the district itself in running some of the plants off and prevent new ones from coming."[28]

Rather than embarrass the commissioners by asking them to repeal the smoke ordinance, the manufacturers wrote technical amendments that would emasculate it, and in February 1913, over Weatherly's protest, they convinced the commission to pass the amendments. The smoke inspectors, finding the amended ordinance unenforceable, resigned, and effective smoke regulation in Birmingham ceased, barely three months after it had begun.[29]

To soften public anger, Sloss made a "compromise" contract with the city, agreeing that if it could keep its iron furnaces going, it would close down its coke ovens, which made the most objectionable smoke. In exchange the city would vacate certain streets that ran through the Sloss yards. The coke ovens ceased operation, but by 1915 Sloss wished to reactivate them and asked to be relieved of the contract. At first the city commission refused, but in April 1917, under pressure from wartime patriotism and the promise of more payrolls, it backed down and allowed Sloss to relight the ovens. The vacated streets remained closed.[30]

Meanwhile, in 1915 Birmingham legislator Dick R. Copeland sponsored a bill to prohibit cities from passing antismoke ordinances and thus to prevent them "from driving away corporations." The *News* denounced the bill as a "step backward," and the Birmingham city attorney lobbied against it.[31] Sloss attorneys lobbied for it, and it passed easily, relieving all Alabama manufacturers of any threat of city smoke regulation, and clinching the defeat of the merchants and residents who

28. *Age-Herald*, quoted in *News*, Jan. 29, 1913; *Labor Advocate*, Jan. 31, 1913. See also *News*, Aug. 3, 1911, Apr. 4, Dec. 1, 1912, Jan. 10, 23, 24, Feb. 5, 1913.

29. *News*, Feb. 26, Mar. 1, 1913.

30. *News*, Feb. 18, 19, Mar. 18, Dec. 25, 1913; *Age-Herald*, Sept. 8, Nov. 13, 1915, Apr. 18, 1917.

31. *News*, Sept. 12, 1915; *Age-Herald*, Aug. 10, 1915. See also *ibid.*, Sept. 3, 9, 16, 26, 1915.

had sought to use the power of government to mitigate the smoke menace. On such questions the economic power of major payroll makers counted heavily.[32]

REGULATION OF RAILROAD GRADE CROSSINGS

At dozens of locations in Birmingham the streets and the railroad tracks crossed each other at the same grade level, and as railroad and street traffic grew, they increasingly interfered with each other. Switching trains blocked streets and delayed traffic interminably, and all too often speeding trains toppled streetcars, demolished carriages, ground horses to death, and killed passengers and pedestrians. Angry citizens from many interest groups, especially merchants, real estate companies, and the street railway company, demanded that the city strictly regulate all the crossings and that it force the railroads to eliminate the worst ones.[33]

The most perplexing problems concerned the one-thousand-foot-wide railroad reservation that stretched one mile across the waist of the city (see map 1). In 1871, before the incorporation of Birmingham, the fledgling Elyton Land Company had sold the reservation to the South & North and the Alabama & Chattanooga railroads for one dollar, with the understanding that the railroads would hold the reservation "forever as a perpetual right-of-way for all railroad companies doing business in and through the said City."[34] The two railroads laid their tracks parallel through the east-west reservation, and the Elyton company and John T. Milner, chief engineer of the South & North, cooperated to plot the city streets, making Twentieth Street, which crossed the railroad tracks at right angles at the depot, the main business street. In the 1870s most residences clustered around the business district on the northern side of the railroads, but in the 1880s the Southside became the main residential area for all classes, with most wealthy residents gravitating to the fashionable South Highlands district. And at the same time more and

32. *Age-Herald*, Sept. 16, 25, 1915.

33. *Ibid.*, Dec. 3, 26, 1889, Aug. 17, 18, 19, 1899, Dec. 31, 1901; *News*, Feb. 9, 1907.

34. James R. Powell, "To the Stockholders of the Elyton Land Company" [Jan. 25, 1872], in *Birmingham City Directory, 1883*, pp. 10–11; Birmingham, *Franchises, Contracts, and Special Ordinances of the City of Birmingham, Alabama* (Birmingham, 1907), 14–16.

more railroad tracks cut through the city at its waist, obstructing the daily flow of traffic from the Southside residences to the Northside business district.[35]

Adding to the problem was a provision in the 1871 railroad deed that all odd-numbered streets, including the major Nineteenth and Twenty-first Street business arteries, must forever stop dead end at either edge of the railroad reservation. At the center of town only Twentieth Street was open across the railroads, and it was clogged daily with carriages, pedestrians, and streetcars bouncing over the tracks. In 1899 the *Age-Herald* said the railroads "effect a river dividing the town into about two equal parts," and "Passage across these parallel lines of railroad adjoining each other, is oftentimes as difficult and dangerous as passage of a river."[36]

As early as 1874 petitioners urged the city to open Twenty-first Street across the railroad tracks, and by 1889 Southside residents and Northside merchants were agitating to open both Nineteenth and Twenty-first Streets. But for the odd-numbered streets no legal street right-of-ways had ever been dedicated across the reservation; and the city, therefore, could neither open these streets at grade level nor make a strong case that the railroads should help finance viaducts over the tracks. Thus in 1890–1891 the city built, entirely at its own expense, a narrow bridge across the tracks at Twenty-first Street, but Nineteenth Street remained closed at the tracks. In 1899, when city officials obtained a new city charter from the legislature, they tried to include in it authority to extend odd-numbered streets across the tracks. But J.M. Faulkner, chief attorney for the Louisville & Nashville Railroad, fought the provision and had it excluded from the charter.[37]

Again in 1910, 1913, and 1916 several of the most prominent merchants and real estate men resolutely undertook to open Nineteenth Street, promising that success would enhance property values for ten city blocks, encourage the building of many permanent improvements, and relieve the chaotic traffic congestion on Twentieth Street. In 1916 the city commission suggested that the Nineteenth Street movement seek the support of the Chamber of Commerce, but Thomas H. Molton, leader of the movement, considered this futile. Molton was president of

35. Powell, "To the Stockholders," 14–15; Ethel Armes, *The Story of Coal and Iron in Alabama* (Birmingham, 1910), 225; *Age-Herald*, Aug. 25, 1899.

36. *Age-Herald*, Aug. 25, 1899; Birmingham, *Franchises*, 16.

37. Birmingham, Minutes . . . Aldermen, B, 53 (Feb. 18, 1874); *Age-Herald*, Feb. 26, 1889, Dec. 26, 1890, Feb. 9, 10, 1899.

a major real estate firm, and he had been a state legislator and a director, trustee, and president of the Chamber of Commerce. With bitter inside insight he reported that a Chamber committee had "unanimously indorsed" the previous effort to open Nineteenth Street, "but L. Sevier, one of the directors, objected saying the chamber should not go into politics. The endorsement was pigeonholed and has not since been brought out." Sevier was a counsel and executive of three railroads, and Molton interpreted the incident to mean that "The railroads have men on guard in the Chamber of Commerce and have had for 20 years. The Chamber of Commerce is a big, representative organization, but when it comes to railroads, the people simply are not in it. They will pigeonhole the resolution again." And indeed the chamber again failed to endorse the movement.[38]

Whether the chamber's silence was actually important in determining the outcome was never clear, but the railroads won, keeping the odd-numbered streets permanently closed across the tracks. As important, probably, as the railroads' ability to influence the Chamber of Commerce, were the property rights guaranteed in their 1871 deed from the Elyton Land Company. In 1871 the railroads had been the most powerful and indispensable economic institutions on the ground, and the early city boosters, seeking to promote economic development, had granted the railroads strategic locations and irrevocable property rights. And the power thus bestowed upon the railroads at the time of their greatest dominance enabled them, later, to resist efforts by other powerful boosters and developers to remove some of the increasingly dysfunctional features of the railroads' location.

As for the even-numbered streets, which were open at grade level across the railroad tracks, they became veritable "Death Traps," increasingly congested and dangerous. In 1899 a traffic count showed 161 railroad switches per day across Twentieth Street, including many "flying switches" in which cars were shoved across the streets without being attached to any engine that could control their speed or stop them.[39]

Gradually, the city gained some regulatory authority over the crossings. An 1887 charter amendment enabled the aldermen to enforce a five-minute time limit on blocking a street. But when aldermen ordained that locomotives must come to a full stop before crossing certain streets, the railroads said this was totally impractical and the city was never able to enforce the order. An 1899 charter revision gave the city, over the

38. *Age-Herald*, Apr. 5, 1916. See also *News*, Feb. 3, 1910, Sept. 3, 7, 1913.
39. *Age-Herald*, Aug. 17, 18, Sept. 23, 1899.

bitter objection of railroad lobbyists, authority "to require gates to be erected or watchmen to be kept, or both, wherever any railroad track crosses a public street." The railroads said gates would be "in the way," and the city did not require them, but it did force the railroads to keep flagmen at the busiest crossings. Frightful accidents continued, however, and realistic citizens and city officials realized that on the busy downtown streets the use of flagmen was at best a temporary makeshift measure and that a real solution would require, in the words of Mayor B. Asbury Thompson in 1889, that "at every street crossing these tracks must be either bridged or tunneled so as to unite our growing city, which is now practically divided by the railroads."[40]

The most urgent crossing problem was at Twentieth Street, which carried all streetcar traffic and most other traffic from the Northside to the Southside. In 1899 the city engineer declared that the only practical solution at Twentieth Street was to build a street underpass beneath the tracks, because the existing level of the street and buildings made a bridge or viaduct over the tracks unfeasible. James Bowron, treasurer of T.C.I. and widely-respected for his practical engineering ability, agreed with the city engineer and said the plan should be implemented at once. Bowron, who had been reared in England, told the aldermen: "In England no parliamentary committee would allow a surface crossing by a railroad. An Englishman is always surprised that such a menace to human life is allowed in America."[41]

The city engineer drew plans and Mayor Walter Drennen, backed by the aldermen, the newspapers, the downtown businessmen, and vice-president Robert Jemison of the street railway company, demanded that the railroads take "immediate steps" toward building the Twentieth Street underpass and several viaducts at other dangerous crossings. But the railroads refused to bear the expense, and long conferences, marked by persistent railroad delaying tactics, ensued. In 1906 Mayor George Ward told the aldermen, "As a rule delay is all they [the railroads] ask for and is what you will have to contend with," and in 1909 he summarized ten frustrating years of negotiations, saying, "The railroads have always been willing to confer, and would confer and draw plans. Action,

40. Alabama, *Acts, 1898–1899,* p. 1414; *Age-Herald,* Dec. 19, 1899. See also *ibid.,* Oct. 17, 20, 1899, Jan. 10, 11, 12, 1901; *State Herald,* Feb. 6, 1896; *News,* Feb. 9, 1907.

41. *Age-Herald,* Aug. 31, 1899. See also *ibid.,* Aug. 18, 19, 1899. There was ten times as much traffic on Twentieth Street as on the Twenty-first Street bridge, which was narrow, steep, and inconvenient.

however, has at each conference been extended to some future day."[42]

In 1907 and 1909 alderman John O'Neill, a leader of the Board of Trade, prompted the anti-railroad state legislature of Governor Comer to enact a law authorizing the city to require railroads to build and pay for viaducts over their tracks. But the law's constitutionality and the extent of railroad responsibility under it were uncertain; and city officials feared that if they tried to coerce railroads, they would provoke time-consuming court appeals, which, after years of delay, they might eventually lose. They continued, therefore, to try to negotiate a voluntary viaduct agreement with the railroads, using the law as a prod. Such negotiation, however, afforded the railroads infinite opportunity for "masterly inactivity," and it enabled them to demand concessions. In 1911, for example, the railroads consented to build one viaduct over the maze of tracks along First Avenue near the Sloss furnace on the eastern edge of Old Birmingham, but only if the aldermen agreed to close forever 28.5 blocks of streets near the viaduct, to pay all property damages caused by the viaduct-building and street-closing, to be responsible for any damage suits, and to pay the entire cost of the approaches to the viaduct. The owners of 179 lots that would be injured by the street-closing objected strenuously, and the city rejected the agreement rather than face the potentially heavy property damages.[43]

In 1911 the advent of city commissioner James Weatherly strengthened the city's negotiating team, for he was one of the leading railroad attorneys in the state, and, as counsel for the Southern Railway and the Birmingham Terminal Company, he had been involved on the railroad side of the viaduct dispute. Throwing himself vigorously behind the city's cause, Weatherly employed his intimate knowledge of the aims and vulnerabilities of railroads to harass his former masters. For example, after directing city attorneys and engineers to prepare technical and legal data on the many small encroachments committed by railroads in laying sidetracks and spur lines without obtaining proper city franchises, he threatened to bring lawsuits requiring the railroads to remove the encroaching tracks at "vital spots." With such tactics he finally worked out, after three more years of conferences, delays, and haggling,

---

42. *Age-Herald*, Aug. 19, 1899; *News*, May 1, 1909; Birmingham, *Message of the Mayor and Annual Reports of the Officers of Birmingham*, 1906, p. 16.

43. Alabama, *Acts*, 1907, pp. 736–38; *News*, Aug. 8, 1907, July 20, 1909, Apr. 6, May 19, 31, 1910, Jan. 11, 14, June 15, 1911; Birmingham, Minutes of the City Council, O, 234–35 (Jan. 18, 1911).

a new agreement for a viaduct on First Avenue near the Sloss furnaces. The city had to bear 25 percent of the cost and to close one short street for ten years, but Weatherly had finally overcome demands that the city close several streets permanently, and he finally got one viaduct built. The *News* rejoiced over "the first big fight the city has ever won against the railroads."[44]

In the meantime, commissioner Weatherly and the city engineers had developed a master plan of underpasses and viaducts, and Weatherly resolutely planned that the city would require the railroads to build one underpass or viaduct every year until they had eliminated all the bad grade crossings. But his master plan, like the city engineer's plan of 1899, called for an underpass at the crucial Twentieth Street crossing and at busy crossings at Fourteenth and Eighteenth streets, the other two major north-south arteries. To construct such underpasses the railroads would have to elevate their tracks several feet for more than one mile, building huge concrete walls to retain the fill to raise the tracks, and the L. & N. would have to build new freight yards and new passenger station tracks, platforms, and sheds. The railroads balked and eventually prevailed upon the state supreme court to rule that cities could only require railroads to help build viaducts over tracks, but not to elevate tracks, since elevation would injure railroad property rights too severely.[45]

Forced to work from a weak legal position, the city commission was unable to implement Weatherly's master plan and timetable. In 1917 they did get the railroads to help rebuild and widen the old Twenty-first Street viaduct, but the Fourteenth, Eighteenth, and Twentieth Street underpasses involved more than a decade's delay. For these streets the railroads held out for viaducts, which would leave the track level undisturbed. But the city could not accept this, because viaducts would be far less efficient for street traffic and because they would necessitate raising the street level above the existing storefront level for several blocks, making the city liable for three million dollars property damage.[46]

44. *News*, May 31, 1914. See also *ibid.*, Mar. 11, Oct. 17, 1912, Oct. 17, 18, 20, 1913, Mar. 5, 11, 24, 29, 30, 1914.

45. *News*, Sept. 14, Oct. 17, 1913; *Age-Herald*, Aug. 6, 1915; Statement of Birmingham City Commission, Mar. 1928, in folder on bonds, James M. Jones Papers, ADAH; Edward Wise, Jr., "Birmingham Grade Separation," *L. & N. Employees' Magazine* (Dec. 1930), 14.

46. *Age-Herald*, Mar. 15, 21, 1917; City Commission statement, Mar. 1928, Jones Papers.

To get the three downtown underpasses the city finally agreed, in October 1928, to bear 50 percent of the cost and to finance the entire cost of four million dollars by issuing city bonds. The railroads probably did not consider the agreement a defeat. One of their own engineers had written that at those streets "both railroad and street traffic have now developed to a point where a separation of grades is justified, even at heavy cost." In other words, the railroads had succeeded in delaying any outlay until it seemed in their own economic interest to invest in a more efficient system and more modern facilities. Work began in December 1928 and was completed in November 1932. To celebrate the opening of the underpasses, two parades marched toward one another from Northside and Southside and met for ceremonies at the Twentieth Street underpass exactly one-third of a century after the city engineer had declared the underpass an urgent necessity.[47]

Ever since 1899 a powerful combination of realtors, the Board of Trade, the leading professional men, the street railway company, the daily press, and the city officials had demanded that railroads eliminate the major downtown grade crossings. But so inherently difficult was a regulatory goal that called for the sacrifice of property rights and the renovation of costly physical structures that the railroads had been able to delay their first major grade separation outlay until 1914, their second until 1917, and their third until 1928. And every time they gave in, the railroads had probably decided that their own economic interest justified the investment, and in each case they finally forced the city taxpayers to bear a major portion of the cost.

BUILDING AND SANITATION CODES

Around the year 1900 Birmingham began enacting an array of building, electrical, plumbing, and sanitation codes and developing a bureaucracy of inspectors, technicians, and clerks. In the first instance the codes regulated builders and contractors, but they also affected realtors, property owners, and businessmen in general. Some members of these groups fretted about specific disadvantageous details, but soon all of them accepted the codes and the inspections as useful protective activities of

---

47. City engineer to railroads, June 28, 1927, Jones Papers, Edward Wise, Jr., "Grade Separation Work is Completed at Birmingham," *L. & N. Employees' Magazine* (May, 1933), pp. 4–6; A.J. Lamb, "New Facilities Opening at Birmingham," *ibid.*, (Jan. 1932), 23–24; Wise, "Birmingham Grade Separation," 14.

city government, and often, indeed, these groups were the key advocates of the codes.

The major impetus for adoption of Birmingham's first comprehensive building code came from the Southeastern Tariff Association (STA), which set fire insurance rates. In 1901 the STA drafted a seven-page, single-spaced, typewritten code and demanded that the aldermen enact it verbatim if Birmingham were to gain a first-class fire insurance rating. The aldermen promptly did so. In 1905, 1912, and 1913 the STA or the National Board of Fire Underwriters dictated stronger provisions, which city officials also enacted verbatim.[48]

In each case the merchants of the Board of Trade strongly endorsed the new codes, accepting stricter regulation of their own store buildings as useful for safety and as a legitimate price to pay for lower insurance rates. Organized labor, including skilled workers in the building trades, consistently endorsed stricter codes and tighter enforcement. The chief complaints came from contractors, who at first chafed at building permit fees and at inspection of their construction sites. Also in 1905 some realtors and property owners complained about a two-dollar permit fee for minor repairs and a requirement that they replace flues in many houses. But these minor irritations were easily settled, and leading realtors, such as Thomas H. Molton, quickly endorsed building inspection. The codes provoked no prolonged conflict; most affected groups approved them and found that they could live easily with the level of enforcement in Birmingham.[49]

In the downtown business district and in good residential areas the code was fairly well enforced, but by common practice it was ignored in areas of cheap rent houses, especially in Negro "quarters" where "long gray marches of little old rotten houses" and "tumble down shacks and shanties" were the norm. Occasionally civic leaders or women's clubs would demand that the city enforce "honest construction" of rent houses, prevent the use of "cheap flimsy materials," and induce "owners of these wretched quarters to patch them up, repair them and paint them." But the Real Estate Exchange denounced such proposals, and in 1917 listed among its accomplishments: "Defeated several drastic and

48. *Age-Herald*, Oct. 4, 1901; *News*, May 17, 1905, June 6, 1913; National Board of Fire Underwriters, Committee on Fire Prevention, *Report on the City of Birmingham, Ala., Supplement, 1913* (New York 1913), 11, 14.

49. *Labor Advocate*, Oct. 12, 1901, Apr. 30, 1915; *Age-Herald*, Oct. 4, Sept. 13, 1901; *News*, Aug. 29, Sept. 7, 13, 21, Oct. 5, 1904.

unreasonable housing 'reforms.' " By 1920 the city enforced neither construction nor maintenance standards in the "quarters."[50]

Only on the question of sanitation, which affected the health of the entire city, did owners of shabby rent houses come under significant regulatory pressure from city government. Most Negro quarters had no sanitary sewers and no indoor toilets, but only outdoor privies, the so-called dry closets, which the city sought to upgrade. However, the city did not force landlords to build sewers in the quarters (see chap. 8). In a few areas sanitary sewers already ran near Negro rent houses, but the landlords had refused to connect the houses to the sewers and install water closets. And the city provoked its one severe housing regulation fight when it insisted, after 1916, that the realtors connect these houses to sewers. Realtors resisted fiercely, arguing that the connections would "entail an expenditure of money almost equal to the cost of the houses themselves." But gradually, by 1922, the city forced them to install one water closet for every two houses or, in larger tenement houses, for every twenty people.[51]

WEIGHT AND MEASURE INSPECTION

Weight and measure inspection was the only city regulation of the actual business activities of most middle-ranking merchants. And in 1905 the Board of Trade and the Retail Grocers' Association jointly declared this inspection program "a good one." Although they quibbled a bit about the fees, most merchants came to consider such inspection a useful service which built trust among customers and prevented unscrupulous merchants from taking unfair advantage. In 1915 when the city, in an economy move, proposed to abolish the office of coal weight and measure inspector, the coal retailers objected, saying that the weight tickets he attached to each load of coal were vital to their business. Thus retail merchants found the main city regulation of their businesses mild, noncontroversial and valuable.[52]

50. *News*, Aug. 24, Dec. 28, 1913; *Age-Herald*, Jan. 7, 1920.
51. *Age-Herald*, Jan. 7, 1920. See also *ibid.*, July 25, Aug. 2, 1916; June 3, 7, 13, 1918; *News*, Mar. 2, 1920.
52. *News*, Jan. 19, 1905; *Age-Herald*, July 15, 21, 1915.

REGULATION OF FOOD AND MILK

But for retail grocers and milk and food producers, most of them in the lower economic ranks, city regulation became strict and comprehensive, partly because unsanitary food or milk posed such a clear danger to the health of all citizens, partly because voters expressed intense concern, and partly because the small producers lacked the resources to mobilize effective resistance.

The 100 to 150 dairies, in particular, felt and often resented the stern regulatory arm of the city government. In 1900 the city implemented its first tentative milk inspection, by 1905 it had developed an elaborate inspection system, and by 1910 it had adopted an official comprehensive dairy scorecard, approved by the U.S. Bureau of Animal Industry. Dairymen found the scorecard-carrying inspector probing into the health of cattle, the quality of water and feed, the smallest details of milkhouse and dairy-wagon construction, the sanitary conditions of the entire dairy premises, the methods of handling milk and washing utensils, and even into the health of dairy families and employees. In 1910, after the annexation of the suburbs, the inspector required a dairy to score at least 60 on a 100-point scale to receive a license to sell milk in Greater Birmingham. At first many of the annexed dairies scored far below 60, and under the inspector's pressure some improved rapidly and some went out of business. By 1915 the inspector reported that only 2 percent of the dairies scored below 60, and 87 percent scored above 70. Birmingham's minimum standards compared favorably with Boston's standard of 45 and Detroit's of 50.[53] Dairymen recognized the necessity of some regulation of their easily-contaminated product, but when the city tightened milk regulations in 1903, 1907, and 1911, the dairy association sought to repeal the more confining provisions and contested the constitutionality of the licenses and permits that gave the regulation teeth.[54]

In 1919 and 1920 the city health officer and the Jefferson County Dairy Association clashed in stormy hearings before the city commis-

53. *Age-Herald*, Sept. 21, 1899; *News*, Aug. 22, 1905, Feb. 11, Mar. 5, Sept. 2, Dec. 5, 1910; Birmingham, *Message of the Mayor, 1906*, pp. 157–64; Report of R.M. Cunningham, City Health Officer, Oct. 19, 1915, TS, 1915; E.M. Duncan to B.H. Rawle, chief, Dairy Division, U.S. Bureau of Animal Industry, July 6, 1914, and Ernest B. Kelly to E.M. Duncan, July 11, 1914, attached to report of R.M. Cunningham, BPL.

54. *News*, Mar. 22, June 5, 1900, Jan. 12, Apr. 20, 1907, Feb. 25, 1911; *Age-Herald*, Feb. 5, 1903.

sion, debating an ordinance that would reduce the allowable bacteria content of milk from 500,000 per cubic centimeter, the upper safe limit, to 50,000. Dairymen packed the chamber to hear their president and attorney denounce the ordinance as "radical" and "extreme," but the city commission adopted it. The dairymen did win a court injunction which forced the commission to grant them two years to conform gradually, but by 1922 they had to comply, and they continued to be the interest group that experienced the most continuous and coercive local regulatory governmental intervention into the routine details of their business operations.[55]

The city also developed regulation and inspection of other food producers and sellers, such as slaughterhouses, butchers, grocers, fruit stands, bakeries, and restaurants. After 1900 a city meat inspector examined every slaughtered animal and condemned the meat of diseased ones. After 1916, under a new comprehensive food code, the city regularly inspected all restaurants and food stores and published their scores. Federal health experts found the new ordinance and procedures excellent.[56]

Although most city food regulation was exercised in the interest of health, some regulation had little to do with health, and was actually exercised to promote the convenience of citizens and shoppers, or to curb alleged "unfair" competition with larger merchants. For example, to promote convenient market conditions for housewives, the city strictly regulated hours and places where truck farmers could peddle produce. In the name of fairness, the city set a minimum weight for bread loaves and refused to let bakers reduce the weight when costs rose. The city strictly regulated the size and locations of sidewalk fruit stands, most of which were operated by Greek and Italian immigrants. Most other merchants considered the fruit stands a nuisance, and in 1912 they prevailed upon the city commission to prohibit them entirely. And always the city placed a heavy tax on itinerant merchants or peddlers, partially in the name of consumer protection and partially to discourage "unfair" competitors.[57]

55. *Age-Herald*, Apr. 5, Nov. 19, 1919, Feb. 3, June 24, 1920, July 24, Aug. 18, 1921.

56. *Age-Herald*, Sept. 21, 1899; Birmingham, *Message of the Mayor, 1905*, pp. 235–38; W.M. McGrath, "Conservation of Health," *The Survey* 27 (Jan. 6, 1912), 1508; Birmingham, Minutes . . . Commissioners, V, 412–15 (Jan. 25, 1916); Carroll Fox, "Public Health Administration, City of Birmingham and County of Jefferson, Alabama."

57. *Age-Herald*, Sept. 3, 1891, Oct. 20, 1902, Apr. 18, 1915, Mar. 7, 1917; *News*, May 18, 19, 1905, Dec. 24, 1912, Feb. 7, 10, Mar. 11, 25, 1914; Birmingham,

CONTROL OF RENT AND FOOD COSTS AFTER WORLD WAR I

After World War I rent and food costs soared, and the response of the Birmingham City Commission indicated dramatically that grocers and food producers were more vulnerable to unwanted government interference and regulation than were real estate owners and agents. In 1919 both the Birmingham Civic Association and the United States District Attorney, Erle Pettus, urged the city commission to curb rent profiteers. The commission appointed a Fair Rent and Housing Board, but realtors and landlords quickly asserted that neither the commission nor its new board possessed legal authority to control rents, and the commission agreed. The chief activity of the Fair Rent and Housing Board was to hear complaints and publish reports documenting the rent increase. And the only response of the city commission was to adopt a resolution thanking the board for its "patriotic and unselfish labors." The city commission had no resources for dealing with the basic problem of rising building costs and a housing shortage. Not until the 1930s, when the national administration of President Franklin D. Roosevelt offered financial assistance, would Birmingham city government be in a position to do anything concrete about the housing shortage.[58]

In the case of high food costs, however, federal assistance was already forthcoming in 1919, when the war department made surplus food available to cities to distribute to citizens. And since this required only a small investment of city resources, the Birmingham city commission was able to cooperate fully, placing one of the first orders with the federal depot and selling large shipments of flour, sugar, canned vegetables, fruit, meats, and fish at cost through food distribution centers manned by city employees. The price was 20 percent below the original cost to the army and far below prevailing retail prices in Birmingham.[59] The Birmingham Retail Grocers' Association denounced "the principle involved" and told the commission that the sale would "hurt their business," even though "the individuals would save but very little." They asserted that "both the wholesale and retail groceries help to make Birmingham," and that "their point of view should be considered." The city commission listened politely, but then deliberately doubled its

Minutes . . . Aldermen, I, 621–23 (Aug. 24, 26, 1901). But for one fruit stand victory, see Age-Herald, Jan. 4–16, 1902.

58. Age-Herald, Aug. 14, 15, 1919, June 2, July 13, 28, 1920; Birmingham, Minutes . . . Commissioners, Z, 569 (Oct. 25, 1920).

59. Age-Herald, July 9, 10, 18, 26, Sept. 15, 1920.

standing food order. By December 1919 it had handled $100,000 of surplus food, and during 1920 it handled more large shipments. The program was far too popular politically to be stopped by the complaints of grocers.[60]

ECONOMIC REGULATION PATTERNS

With the partial exception of the railroads, who, after long delays, did have to install flagmen and two viaducts by 1921, the upper-ranking interest groups avoided all the adverse regulation proposed against them by middle- or lower-ranking groups. Moreover, the coal, iron, and steel corporations were able to invoke local and state police power to aid them in the regulation of labor during strikes.

The middle-ranking groups were seldom able to impose effective regulation upon upper-ranking groups. On the other hand, middle-ranking groups suffered relatively little adverse regulation of their own activities; most of them approved of the mild regulation that was directed toward them. Only on the question of rent house sanitation did a middle group, the realtors, strenuously object that city regulations were too severe, and only because the health of the entire city was at stake did government force the realtors to comply.

By contrast, several lower-ranking groups found themselves subjected to unwanted and confining economic regulation which was imposed at the request of combinations of upper-, middle-, and other lower-ranking groups. Many lower-ranking business groups were especially vulnerable because they produced and marketed food products, which required regulation for health reasons. But the relative economic insignificance of such groups was also a factor. Although they provided important economic services, they could not realistically claim to contribute heavily to the economic base of the city, nor could they deliver a believable threat that regulation, or even government competition, would hamper the prosperity of the entire district.

In sum, the greater the economic power of an interest group, the greater its ability to resist unwanted economic regulation and to use government regulation of other groups to its own advantage.

60. *Age-Herald*, July 9, 10, 1919, Sept. 5, 1920. See also *News*, Dec. 14, 1919, and *Post*, Sept. 26, 1921.

XI

Regulation of Utilities

I T is too palpable that forty or fifty men of this city have their grasps upon the throats of over 35,000 population," declared the Birmingham *Labor Advocate* in 1898. "It is too flagrant that corporations like the Birmingham Waterworks Company have their nets set, and that our municipal administration in the past has driven our people to them like so many partridges."[1] Many citizens echoed such dismay, complaining that city officials seemed unable, or, some thought, unwilling to force utility corporations to provide satisfactory rates and service. In Birmingham by 1901 the utility field was dominated by three major corporations: The Birmingham Railway, Light, and Power Company (created through consolidation of several gas, electricity, and street railway companies), the Southern Bell Telephone Company, and the Birmingham Water Works Company. Each stood among the city's upper-ranking firms, and the B.R.L. & P. ranked third in the county in property ownership, right behind the two largest iron and steel corporations. And critics frequently charged that city officials, far from regulating the utility giants for the benefit of the people, served as corporation puppets who expedited exploitation of the people. In 1911 the *Labor Advocate*, opposing a new electrical contract with the B.R.L. & P., said bitterly, "Birmingham is one of the worst corporation-ridden cities in the United States today."[2]

The utility corporation managers saw things quite differently. To them it seemed that local government should willingly cooperate to make easier the formidable task of mobilizing men and equipment to provide consistently good service and to earn a satisfactory return for investors. But from the managers' point of view it seemed that city

1. Birmingham *Labor Advocate*, Oct. 15, 1898.
2. *Ibid.*, Dec. 15, 1911.

officials were bent on harassing rather than helping the utility corporations. In 1906 Birmingham Water Works Company superintendent
Daniel J. O'Connell told his general manager in Pittsburgh that every
citizen with a minor complaint about a utility service would "run to the
Mayor or the Aldermen with their troubles," and consequently the
politicians "are always hammering at these corporations." According to
O'Connell: "The whole thing is a matter of cheap politics, and these
chaps [the aldermen] will make any kind of slaps at us that will in any
way help their political fortunes." Therefore, said O'Connell, "It seems
almost a waste of time to try to do anything with the members of this
Board of Aldermen here, as many of them will make you any sort of nice
promises and will walk right into the Board and vote 'Aye' on any proposition which is against the Water Company." Thus as the corporation
managers saw it, their influence with city officials was far less than it
should have been, and in fact, "cheap politics" was a major impediment
to efficient utility operation.[3]

In actuality the power relationships in utility regulation were more
complex than either the *Labor Advocate* or superintendent O'Connell
would admit. Utility regulation differed from other economic regulation
because utility services were so essential that local government itself
was responsible for making provision for them, either by building its
own plants or else by enfranchising public service corporations. In Birmingham from 1871 to 1921 and beyond, the city itself owned no
major utility plants, but relied entirely on franchises to private corporations.[4] The city sought to regulate the utility corporations mainly
through franchise or contract specifications concerning quality of service and maximum rates. But regulation through long-term inflexible
franchises and contracts often seemed ineffective, and the city and state
experimented with several supplementary regulatory procedures. Several
times the city seriously sought municipal ownership of one utility—the
waterworks. In 1911 the new city commission charter allowed citizens
themselves to vote on any new utility contracts, and the city conducted
several such referenda. In 1915 the state legislature created a state
public-service commission to regulate local utility rates and service. And

---

3. Daniel J. O'Connell to general manager J.H. Purdy, Nov. 17, 1906; O'Connell
to general manager W.S. Kuhn, Sept. 26, 1903, Aug. 27, 1904, B.W.W.C. Letterbooks.
4. There were two minor exceptions. When Birmingham annexed North Birmingham in 1910, it took over and briefly operated the very small North Birmingham
waterworks and electric plants, but soon abandoned them.

on several occasions the city sought to break the monopoly of a particular utility company by enfranchising a new company whose competition, the city hoped, would regulate the rates and service of the original company.

FRANCHISES AND CONTRACTS

Franchises and contracts, the basic instruments of regulation, were essentially long-term bargains between the city and the corporations. The relative bargaining power of the two at the time they negotiated a franchise largely determined whether the time limits, rates, and guarantees of service quality were nearer the preferred terms of city or corporation.

Early in Birmingham's history, when the city lacked such necessities as adequate water and a basic transportation system, the bargaining advantage lay with any corporation that possessed sufficient capital to offer to provide a utility service. The negotiation of the Birmingham Water Works contract of 1888 was an example. Back in 1872 the Elyton Land Company, seeing that a water supply was essential to the growth of its new town, had built a small plant to pump water from Village Creek, two miles away. But by 1887 Birmingham had outgrown this supply, and tapping a larger source would be costly because Birmingham was on a plateau between three river basins, with hills or mountains standing between the city and each river. The Elyton Land Company, still aware of the importance of having adequate water, proposed to build a new $500,000 waterworks, with large pumping stations, dams, reservoirs, and tunnels through Red Mountain and Shades Mountain to bring water eight miles from the Cahaba River, which could supply the potentially much larger city of the future. Before beginning work, the Elyton Land Company demanded a highly favorable, thirty-year contract for its subsidiary, the Birmingham Water Works Company. In the contract it listed permanent rates, which would immediately provide enough revenue to pay operating expenses and interest on the company's bonds, and which would soon, as population grew and unit costs declined, return handsome profits.[5]

5. Henry M. Caldwell, *History of the Elyton Land Company and Birmingham, Ala.* (Birmingham, 1892), 7, 18–21, 29–31; Birmingham *Iron Age*, Dec. 17, 1874; Birmingham *Age-Herald*, Nov. 5, 1890; Birmingham, *Franchises, Contracts, and Special Ordinances of the City of Birmingham, Alabama* (Birmingham, 1907), 421–27.

The city's bargaining position was weak. It critically needed a larger water supply, but the necessary outlay was far beyond its financial capacity, and the Elyton Land Company was the only institution with both the motivation and the financial resources to provide water. In 1888 therefore, the city accepted the contract offered by the company, to run until January 1, 1921. The company's principal attorney told one incorporator: "Now you have got your charter and you have got everything in the world that you could possibly want and a good deal more too."[6]

Birmingham's early street-railway companies enjoyed similar bargaining advantages and also obtained highly favorable franchises. The first street railroads were built by the Elyton Land Company and other land companies that were seeking to stimulate the development of their suburban residential sites by providing convenient transportation. City officials, eager to encourage capital to flow into any new service that promised to promote growth and enhance realty values, readily granted liberal, perpetual, street-railway franchises. Occasionally an alderman, such as merchant Sol Levi in 1891, would object, saying it was "about time for the city to use a little discretion," and "not be giving everything away," but until 1900 aldermen continued to grant liberal, perpetual franchises. In 1901 all the street-railway companies consolidated into the Birmingham Railway, Light, and Power Company (B.R.L. & P.), which thus held perpetual franchises to most of the streets suitable for street railways.[7]

The city was in a better bargaining position in dealing with early gas and electric companies, which were smaller, required less capital, and had local competitors. Consequently, most gas and electric contracts ran for shorter periods and gave the city authority to revise the rates every ten years.[8]

By 1900 Birmingham's enthusiasm for liberal franchises was disappearing. Citizens who found rates high and service bad discovered that the liberal long-term charters afforded no recourse against the companies. Also, by 1900 most of the revered local developers who had founded the utilities had sold out to absentee-owned holding companies that generated little local sympathy. Finally by 1900 Birmingham had acquired an adequate supply of the basic utility services and

6. O'Connell to J.H. Purdy, July 20, 1912, B.W.W.C. Letterbooks; *News*, Dec. 2, 1911.

7. *Age-Herald*, Dec. 3, 1891; Birmingham, *Franchises*, 55–69, 210–16; J.P. Ross, "Notes on Birmingham Public Utilities," TS, 1932, BPL.

8. Birmingham, *Franchises*, 222–26; Ross, "Notes," 1–8.

saw no urgent need to attract more capital to develop or extend them.[9] Accordingly, the city's bargaining stance stiffened. City officials, informed by the National Municipal League and by actions of other cities, began demanding that franchises be for definite short periods, never perpetual, that they reserve more regulative powers for the city, and that the corporations pay the city for any new franchise. In 1901 the B.R.L. & P. sought a franchise for a seventy-eight-block street-railway extension, and the aldermen, demonstrating the new attitude, insisted that the company pay $100 per block. The company agreed, but when it insisted on a lease for ninety-nine rather than thirty years, the aldermen stubbornly rejected the entire franchise.[10]

But by 1900 the city was already tightly bound by earlier contracts for most utility services. The street-railway contracts, for example, authorized the B.R.L. & P. to charge five cents per ride within old Birmingham and the nearby suburbs, but ten cents per ride to outlying suburbs such as Ensley and Wylam. By 1899 street railways in many large cities were instituting the universal five-cent fare, and the downtown merchants of the Birmingham Board of Trade demanded that the B.R.L. & P. do likewise, to encourage suburbanites to shop downtown. The board made the five-cent fare a major policy goal and marshaled strong support from the Chamber of Commerce, labor unions, the daily press, and the board of aldermen. Had these politically potent groups found any legal means of forcing the company to grant the five-cent fare, they would have done so. But a decade of agitation brought no progress, and in 1911 the president of B.R.L. & P. told the new city commission, which also demanded a five-cent fare: "your board has no power, authority, or control whatsoever over the rates of fare chargeable by a street railroad company." Further, the company's right to charge ten cents, "inasmuch as it grows out of a contract, is inviolable without the company's consent, and will be protected by the courts, both state and federal." He was right. The courts held the contract inviolable. Only after a competing street railway began serving the suburbs in 1913, did the B.R.L. & P. grant a five-cent suburban fare.[11]

Thus to many citizens it seemed that shrewd capitalists, getting in on

9. *Age-Herald*, Apr. 30, 1899, June 23, 1901; Ross, "Notes," 21–23; *Labor Advocate*, Nov. 9, 1901.

10. *News*, Feb. 22, 1900; *Age-Herald*, Apr. 21, Oct. 3, Nov. 13, 1901; *Labor Advocate*, June 1, 1901, Feb. 22, 1902.

11. *News*, May 6, 1911. See also *ibid.*, Jan. 4, 1900, Jan. 3, 1901, Oct. 18, 1907, Feb. 3, 1910, Nov. 2, Dec. 2, 1911; *Labor Advocate*, June 1, 1901; *Age-Herald*, Nov. 16, 1899.

the ground floor, had taken advantage of an innocent young city to obtain one-sided contracts which they used to control and exploit the people. Citizens took much less notice of ways in which the inflexible contracts at times worked to the corporations' disadvantage. Actually in the bargaining that shaped a long-term contract, both city and company were working in the dark, making agreements on the basis of their predictions of local population growth and economic conditions, predictions that could prove disastrously unrealistic. Unforeseen population changes or technological developments could be favorable to the company, enabling it to collect undue profits from the inflexible rates, but they might be unfavorable, bringing heavy losses. In Birmingham between the 1880s and 1915 the utility companies' gamble on rapid population growth paid off, and to citizens it seemed that the inflexible rates had become excessive and the profits exorbitant. But World War I reversed the situation. The city's population growth slackened after 1910, and the war stimulated enormous increases in operating costs, especially wages. Fixed rates which had seemed excessive suddenly became too low to keep the companies operating. The B.R.L. & P. street-railway system suffered severely, especially since competition from motorized "Jitney" cars and buses hit it at the same time. By 1919 its revenue was inadequate to pay operating expenses, taxes, and interest, and it went into receivership, as did street railways in many other American cities.[12] Thus the continuous power struggle between city and utilities occurred within a framework of long-term inflexible contracts, but it nonetheless changed constantly as new situations gave advantages or disadvantages to one side or the other.

CONTRACT ENFORCEMENT

The struggle and the city's supplementary strategies of utility regulation are best illustrated by the history of the city's thirty-year contention with the Birmingham Water Works Company. The 1888 contract made no provision for rate changes. During the first eight years the rates produced only enough revenue to pay operating costs, bond interest, and dividends averaging 3.3 percent yearly on the capital stock. But population and water consumption grew rapidly and unit costs declined,

12. *Age-Herald*, Feb. 10, 1915, Jan. 24, 1919; Birmingham, Minutes of the Board of Commissioners, Y, 631–40 (Aug. 22, 1919); Martin G. Glaeser, *Outlines of Public Utility Economics* (New York: Macmillan Company, 1917), 225–27.

and by 1895 and 1896 the company was paying dividends of 9 percent per year. Thereafter, no information on dividends is available until 1921.[13]

By 1898 Birmingham aldermen, believing that the growing population and water consumption entitled the city to reduced rates, enacted ordinances annulling the inflexible contract and setting new lower rates. To justify the annulment they referred to highly publicized and widely believed accusations that the company had often arbitrarily charged more than the contract rates and that it had failed to supply "clear" and "wholesome" water as called for in the contract. The *Labor Advocate*, supporting the aldermen, declared, "No one will deny that the Birmingham Waterworks company has violated its contract.... this king of monopolies has been unfaithful almost since the first day...."[14]

But the chancery court quickly overthrew the annulment. It found the alleged cases of overcharging to be weak and trivial, involving minor ambiguous contract clauses about boarding houses and mixed-use buildings. Arbitration or friendly lawsuits had already resolved these minor issues, and the company had complied strictly with the settlements. City officials and citizens were more confident of sustaining their allegations about impure water. The company provided unfiltered surface water which was often manifestly cloudy and muddy and it had a disagreeable odor and taste. But the 1888 contract did not technically define "clear" and "wholesome" water, and the company produced reports from chemists and experts who said that for surface water it was remarkably pure and that the occasional solid impediments, organic matter, and bad odors in the water were entirely harmless, though admittedly perhaps offensive to the consumer. The reports satisfied the chancery court, and it ruled that the contract was still binding and that the city had no right to regulate rates until the contract expired in 1921.[15]

City officials and citizens continued to denounce the muddy water, and the Jefferson County Medical Society pressured the company to filter it. The company resisted, asserting publicly that the water was essentially pure. Privately, the superintendent wrote company president W.S. Kuhn that to his intense dismay he could not overcome a "woody

13. Birmingham, *Franchises*, 421–27; Birmingham Water Works secretary and treasurer J.F. Graham to J.P. Mudd, Nov. 9, 1895; Graham to New York Security and Trust Company, Jan. 4, 1897; Graham to M.A. Hillman, Jan. 13, 1897; Graham to P.H. Earle, Apr. 12, 1897; superintendent W.J. Milner to B.J. Baldwin, Aug. 16, 1897, B.W.W.C. Letterbooks.

14. *News*, June 2, 7, 16, 1898; *Labor Advocate*, May 28, 1898.

15. *Age-Herald*, Jan. 10, 1899; *News*, Nov. 18, Dec. 13, 1897, June 2, 1898.

taste" and "peculiar smell" in the water. Samples that stood a few weeks "show a large amount of fibrous looking material in the water," he reported. He was glad that the most recent expert report continued to find the water pure, but he would "be better pleased when the water is free from the objectionable smell and taste." Despite its private worries, the company did not agree to filtration until 1902, and then only because a team of its own experts reported evidence of occasional typhoid contamination in the water. Thereupon, the company moved quickly to install a $300,000 filtration plant.[16]

The events from 1898 to 1902 established a pattern that was often repeated. On several later occasions city officials tried to annul the contract, charging failure to comply. Each time the courts adjusted minor disagreements and ruled that the company had essentially complied. And usually, under the pressure of attack, the company sought to allay complaints by making new improvements, which the courts interpreted as evidence of good-faith compliance.[17]

The company's installation of the filter system between 1902 and 1904 quieted indignation about impure water, but nearly all citizens continued to believe that the 1888 contract rates were unreasonably high, and that a "greedy" waterworks "octopus" was arrogantly amassing outrageous profits. Comparative data indicated that Birmingham's water rates were indeed considerably higher than those in similar southern cities, but the company said the special topographical problems of bringing water to Birmingham accounted for the higher rates. Whatever the cause of the high rates, the Board of Trade, the Chamber of Commerce, organized labor, and city officials agitated continually and vigorously to lower them, but for years they accomplished nothing.[18]

The company acknowledged in effect that the contract rates were higher than necessary, because it repeatedly offered to reduce the rates if the city in turn would add one crucial provision to the 1888 contract—the right to use meters on domestic consumers. The contract, it turned out, was not as one-sidedly advantageous to the company as most

16. B.W.W.C. superintendent to general manager W.S. Kuhn, Oct. 17, 24, Nov. 20, 1901, B.W.W.C. Letterbooks; *Age-Herald*, Oct. 21, 1899, Dec. 4, 10, 1901; *Report of Geo. H. Benzenberg, of Milwaukee, Wis. and Geo. W. Fuller of New York, Upon the Water Supply of the Birmingham Water Works Co., of Birmingham, Ala.* (Birmingham, June 4, 1902); Birmingham, *Message of the Mayor and Annual Reports of the Officers of Birmingham, 1904*, p. 14.

17. Birmingham, Minutes of the Mayor and Board of Aldermen, K, 331–33 (May 4, 1904); *News*, June 14, 22, 23, 1904, July 5, 1906, June 27, 1914.

18. *News*, Dec. 13, 1897, Nov. 3, 1900, June 23, 1905, Feb. 7, July 11, Sept. 20, 1906, Jan. 23, 1907, Mar. 14, 1912.

citizens (and the 1888 waterworks attorney) believed. It explicitly authorized the company to use meters on large commercial and industrial consumers, but not on domestic users. For houses and apartments the contract listed flat rates, graduated according to the number of rooms and water outlets, but not according to actual usage. These rates, dictated in 1888 by the company, were quite high for most normal users, but the company soon realized that they did not cover the cost of supplying water to wasteful users. The company argued that the right to use meters extended, by implication, to wasteful domestic consumers, but the courts disagreed, declaring the flat rates to be maximum rates, regardless of usage. Thus the contract, through oversight, provided no efficient way to discover or penalize wasteful users. By 1896 the company found that excessive waste through unrepaired leaks in service pipes and water closets was increasing the daily pumpage 20 to 25 percent. Superintendent W.J. Milner told the company president, "the only remedy for this is meters. Nothing else will avail."[19]

To make matters worse, after 1900 several dry summers sorely taxed Birmingham's water supply, and by 1905 superintendent O'Connell wrote that the uncontrolled waste would almost immediately force the company to make costly investments in new pumps and reservoirs. But, he added, "If we can make a contract with the City, whereby we can get the right to meter, I am satisfied that we can cut at least two million gallons of water per day out of our pumpage, and of course under such conditions, we would be in good shape for the next couple years."[20] The company noted that the Atlanta municipal waterworks had instituted domestic meters and had thereby cut its daily pumpage to approximately half the Birmingham average. But a contract to allow domestic meters, which the company sought continuously from 1895 to 1915, was difficult to obtain. The company frequently offered to forego its firm legal right to charge the high domestic flat rates, and, for good measure, it proposed to reduce the rent on city fire hydrants, if the city would authorize the company to use domestic meters. In 1902, for example, it offered a plan which would, according to studies by the city and the Commercial Club, cut the monthly water bills of nonwasteful domestic consumers by 50 percent.[21]

19. Birmingham, *Franchises*, 421–27; *Age-Herald*, May 30, June 1, 1895; W.J. Milner to Jas. T. Woodward, Aug. 31, 1896, B.W.W.C. Letterbooks.
20. Superintendent to Purdy, July 8, 1902, O'Connell to Purdy, Nov. 9, 1905, B.W.W.C. Letterbooks; *News*, Dec. 13, 1897.
21. W.J. Milner to Jas. T. Woodward, Apr. 6, 1898; O'Connell to Kuhn, May

The aldermen rejected all such proposals, even though the Chamber of Commerce urged them to accept the 1902 plan as a reasonable compromise. Most citizens believed that the company already had a stranglehold on the city, and they resisted any concession that might give the company greater power over consumers. Even though the existing flat rates were high, at least the consumer could use water liberally and still know ahead of time exactly what his bill would be. Despite the company's promises, many distrustful citizens feared that under the meter system, with no guaranteed maximum monthly charge, their bills would skyrocket.[22]

Many government officials admitted privately, and some publicly, that the meter system would be more equitable, but fierce pressure from voters convinced them that to adopt it would be political suicide. A frustrated superintendent O'Connell reported, "I can go and talk to the Mayor, or to either one of the Committees, personally, and they are not in favor of a Municipal Plant, and are not opposed to giving us the right to meter services to prevent water waste, and every time the subject comes up before the Board of Mayor and Aldermen, they invariably vote the other way. I have about made up my mind that it is a never ending case of cheap politics, and I suppose we are to put up with it, and perhaps by steady work, finally wear it out."[23] But not until the city commission replaced the aldermen in 1911 was he to make any progress.

MUNICIPAL OWNERSHIP

Meanwhile, many citizens and organizations, frustrated by the deadlock, came to demand municipal ownership of the waterworks. Back in 1894, in the depth of depression, the company stockholders had tried to sell out to the city at a price much above the prevailing market value of the stocks. The city had tentatively agreed, but had been unable to finance the purchase, and the purchase had fallen through.[24] After

---

13, 1904; O'Connell to Purdy, Nov. 27, 1905, Mar. 10, 1906, Jan. 8, 1912, B.W.W.C. Letterbooks; *News*, Dec. 3, 1902, July 3, 1914.

22. *Age-Herald*, June 1, 1895, Aug. 10, 1901, Dec. 2, 3, 4, 1902; *Labor Advocate*, Dec. 6, 1902.

23. O'Connell to Purdy, Oct. 16, 1906; O'Connell to Kuhn, Feb. 19, 1904, B.W.W.C. Letterbooks; *Age-Herald*, Aug. 10, 1901.

24. W.J. Milner to C.A. Jones, 1894, B.W.W.C. Letterbooks; *Age-Herald*, Jan. 21, Feb. 22, Apr. 7, 8, 27, Nov. 15, 1894.

economic recovery began, the company made no more offers to sell. But by 1897 the *Labor Advocate* was saying that "Municipal ownership of these public necessities is the only salvation of the people, and of Birmingham," and by 1902 the Board of Trade and daily newspapers strongly agreed. Voter sentiment for municipal ownership became so strong that the board of aldermen continually reiterated their commitment to it, and every mayor, candidate for mayor, and city commissioner went on record favoring it. In 1907 reformers organized a Municipal Ownership League, and most local politicians, civic leaders, and prominent downtown businessmen joined. In a referendum in 1914 an eight-to-one majority of voters favored municipal ownership of the waterworks.[25]

Waterworks superintendent O'Connell looked upon the municipal ownership movement as amusing but essentially harmless "cheap politics," and he dismissed aldermanic resolutions for it as "pure 'Buncomb.'" In 1907, 1911, and 1915 the company did take special notice when the city sponsored legislative bills giving the city the right to condemn and buy the waterworks plant. But, each time, corporation friends in the legislature—Jefferson County senators Nathan Miller in 1907 and Hugh Morrow in 1911, and Jefferson County representative John Weakley in 1915—helped company lobbyists defeat or emasculate the bills.[26]

Even at times when the ability of the company's friends to kill the bills seemed in doubt, the superintendent remained calm because he knew that, contrary to the belief of many citizens, the measures would not allow the city to purchase the plant for less than a fair appraised price. And his confidence that the municipal ownership schemes would fail stemmed from his very realistic knowledge that the city, in its strained financial condition, simply could not market the necessary bonds to finance such a large purchase. In many years the city's chronic revenue shortage forced it to issue bonds to cover part of the yearly operating expenses, and such bonds, added to bonds for schools and public buildings, practically exhausted the city's borrowing ability. O'Connell noted all this carefully. In 1910, for example, he sent his general manager newspaper clippings about a new city bond issue and

25. *Labor Advocate*, Jan. 15, 1897; *Age-Herald*, Dec. 4, 1902, Jan. 8, 1903; *News*, Feb. 7, 1906, Jan. 23, 1907, Sept. 22, 1914.

26. O'Connell to Purdy, June 17, 1909, July 12, 1907, Mar. 27, 1911; superintendent H.H. Horner to A.M. Lynn, Aug. 9, 26, Sept. 27, 1915, B.W.W.C. Letterbooks; *News*, Mar. 2, July 25, 1907.

commented "all of which is perfectly satisfactory, as the more bonds issued, the better we are satisfied." In 1912 city attorney Romaine Boyd, an earnest advocate of municipal ownership, substantiated O'Connell's analysis, telling citizens: "As a matter of fact the problem of municipal ownership is really a financial one rather than a question of legal difficulty." So long as the city failed to solve its financial difficulties, O'Connell could rest assured that the dream of municipal ownership was futile.[27]

INDUSTRIAL WATER

The Birmingham Water Works Company supplied industrial water at much cheaper rates than domestic water, but during the contention over domestic rates and municipal ownership, the industrialists sought to get the city or county to provide a separate free industrial water supply.

For industrial and commercial water consumers, the 1888 contract included a sliding scale, descending from thirty cents per 1,000 gallons for small consumers to eight cents per 1,000 gallons for large ones. And actually, after 1894, the company charged most large industries four cents, which was only half the lowest contract rate. In 1905 a waterworks official explained: "We adopted the policy of supplying the largest of the manufacturing plants at practically cost, we figuring that it would be to the interests of the Birmingham district, as well as to our own interest, to encourage the location of new industries, we to make our profit in supplying an additional amount of water for domestic use."[28] Thus through economic leverage the largest industries won especially favorable rates, and the 1888 contract gave neither government nor citizens any voice in the matter.

But the industrial corporations, not entirely satisfied, sought government aid. In 1905 they proposed that the city and county taxpayers finance dams and canals to bring an independent supply of industrial water to Birmingham from some branch of the Warrior River, twenty miles away. A shortage of industrial water was retarding the development of Birmingham, they argued, and a new industrial water supply

27. O'Connell to Purdy, June 27, 1910. See also O'Connell to Kuhn, July 10, 1903; O'Connell to Purdy, Feb. 21, 1907, Sept. 23, 1910, B.W.W.C. Letterbooks; *News*, July 4, 1912.
28. *News*, July 20, 1905. See also *ibid.*, Dec. 13, 1897.

would boost growth phenomenally. The Commercial Club orchestrated a newspaper and civic club campaign for industrial water and solicited money from industries, businessmen, and government to finance engineering surveys. But the careful surveys showed that the Birmingham Water Works Company was in fact providing more than adequate industrial water, and that it had a vastly greater potential supply which it could easily tap as industrial needs rose. Thereupon, the industrialists, acknowledging that the supply was actually adequate, began to argue that the industries needed cheaper, or subsidized, water, and eventually their slogan became "Free water for factories."[29]

The Birmingham Water Works Company opposed the independent industrial water idea, but did not grow greatly alarmed about it. The company published occasional statements asserting, accurately, that it could and would expand its water supply to provide adequate water at cost for Birmingham industry. Privately, the company superintendent said: "I do not think they [the industrialists] honestly believe there is any shortage of water, but they do not want to have to pay for the water supply." But, he added, ". . . of course this water will only be free to them [the industrialists], for it is certain it will not be free to the tax payer who has to pump it from its source to Birmingham." And he confidently predicted: "I have no idea that the tax payers of the City of Birmingham or of Jefferson County, would ever agree to vote bonds for any scheme that had for its object the furnishing of water to manufacturing plants, or any other concerns for that matter, at their [taxpayers'] expense."[30]

By 1908 the Tennessee Coal, Iron, and Railroad Company, which clearly preferred to have local government finance an industrial water supply, recognized that the prospects for that were nil. T.C.I. thereupon spent $1,500,000 to dam a portion of Village Creek and build a reservoir to provide its own water. Waterworks superintendent O'Connell wrote: "Personally I am very glad to see these people going into this work, as I am satisfied that they will give us enough additional consumers in a very few years to use more water than we are now furnishing them and at much better rates." The other industrial corporations, with less capital resources, continued to rely on the Birmingham Water Works Company. Thus on the matter of water for factories, the industrial cor-

29. *News*, Jan. 14, 19, 31, Feb. 1, Aug. 22, 1905, Apr. 13, 14, 1906, Nov. 5, 6, 7, 1908.

30. O'Connell to Purdy, Apr. 7, Sept. 15, 1906, B.W.W.C. Letterbooks; *News*, July 20, 1905, Nov. 16, 1908.

porations had enough leverage to obtain very favorable rates, but not enough political power to induce local government to provide free or heavily subsidized water.[31]

In 1911 the Birmingham City Commission replaced the aldermanic city council and immediately attacked the entire waterworks question, as well as several other utility controversies, with new vigor. The commission framed yet another ordinance annulling the 1888 waterworks contract and enacted a 33-percent rate reduction. To the surprise of everyone, the company accepted verbatim the new rate schedule (though not the annulment) on the condition that the city give the company the right to use meters on domestic consumers. Two of the three commissioners agreed and in 1912 signed a new supplementary waterworks contract.[32]

Birmingham's new city commission charter, however, provided that by petition of 1,000 voters any new or revised franchise might be subjected to a referendum. And the third commissioner, James Weatherly, opposed the 1912 contract, organized a petition campaign, and called a referendum. "When the waterworks company comes to us with gifts," warned an opponent of the new contract, "it is time for us to get up and fight." Commissioner Weatherly said the devious company was anxious to make a new contract because it knew it had violated the old one and feared that the city could nullify it in the courts. Weatherly promised that if the voters would reject the new contract, he would initiate court proceedings to cancel the old contract and then buy the company cheaply.[33]

The waterworks officials actually had no fear that the 1888 contract could be nullified. Their continuing paramount objective was simply to make enough rate concessions to win the right to use meters on domestic consumers. Also, they urgently hoped to calm the hostility of their customers, hostility which had become a distinct business and political liability.[34] But so intense was the hostility that voters rejected

31. O'Connell to Purdy, Sept. 23, 1909, B.W.W.C. Letterbooks; *News*, Jan. 28, 1908, July 5, 1911, May 23, 1912.
32. Birmingham, Minutes . . . Commissioners, P, 534–35 (Oct. 31, 1911), Q, 237 (Feb. 27, 1912), Q, 672–78 (July 3, 1912).
33. *News*, July 12, 1912. See also *ibid.*, Aug. 27, 1912.
34. O'Connell to Purdy, June 22, 1912. See also *ibid.*, Jan. 18, Feb. 6, July 15, 1913, B.W.W.C. Letterbooks; *News*, July 3, 1914.

the new contract by an overwhelming ten-to-one ratio (3,055 against, 291 for). The company was determined to have its customers discover by experience how they would fare under the new meter rates in the defeated contract. It therefore challenged the constitutionality of the referendum and claimed that the new contract was valid despite the negative vote, since a majority of the city commission had signed it. As the company expected, the resulting court cases dragged on for two years, during which the company resolutely implemented the provisions of the new contract, setting meters on domestic consumers and rendering bills according to the new meter rates. The courts finally ruled that the referendum was constitutionally valid, and that the company must return to the old flat rates provided for in the 1888 contract. The company did so in July 1914, expecting accurately and a bit gleefully that the return to the higher flat rates would provoke consumers to complain indignantly to the city commission, particularly to commissioner Weatherly. To increase Weatherly's discomfort, the company published figures indicating that during the two years under the new rates, domestic consumers had saved $164,000.[35]

Meanwhile, Weatherly had kept his promise to institute quo warranto court proceedings to annul the 1888 contract. Privately, the company's lawyers considered Weatherly's case contemptibly weak, which indeed it proved to be. Weatherly's most serious charge, that the company's water was responsible for several typhoid cases, backfired when city health officials showed that the actual culprit was a small suburban North Birmingham waterworks plant which the *city* had operated since the 1910 annexations.[36] The state circuit court firmly upheld the 1888 contract. Weatherly appealed to the state supreme court, but the prospects for a reversal appeared so slim that he joined the other two commissioners in reopening serious private negotiations with the company. Finally, in February 1915, the company and a unanimous city commission agreed on a new supplementary contract establishing rates and meter rights almost identical with those in the defeated 1912 contract.[37]

Weatherly's intransigient three-year opposition won him one popular, face-saving concession—a clause in the 1915 contract giving the city the right to buy the company at any time, at a price to be agreed upon

35. *News*, Sept. 10, 1912, July 3, 1914; O'Connell to Purdy, July 18, 20, Sept. 10, 1912; H.H. Horner to Lynn, July 4, 1914, B.W.W.C. Letterbooks; *News*, July 3, 1914.
36. Horner to Lynn, Feb. 16, June 26, 1914, B.W.W.C. Letterbooks.
37. *News*, June 27, 1914; *Age-Herald*, Feb. 23, 1915.

by a jointly appointed board of appraisers. Citizens and newspapers rejoiced, believing municipal ownership was finally at hand, but the company remained confident that the city's financial condition would prevent it. New waterworks superintendent H.H. Horner wrote, "we think our troubles here are over now and that we will have a good long season of peace and quiet in the operation of our business, . . . and this is something very much to be desired after the turmoil we have had here."[38]

Two months after the new contract went into effect, the city commission instituted the first step in purchase proceedings, but superintendent Horner did not take it seriously. He noted that an important election was coming up, and "as the Water Works question is always a popular one, they think that this will gain votes for the three Commissioners. I believe that this is the reason for passing this resolution at this time; in fact, three or four of the City Hall employees have so advised me." And indeed, after the election, purchase proceedings ceased. Horner reported that one commissioner "advises me that he wants municipal ownership, but that he does not see how the city can possibly get the money now to buy the Water Works, or any other utility."[39]

By 1920 the city still had not purchased the plant. As January 1, 1921—the expiration date of both the 1888 contract and the supplementary 1915 contract—approached, the *News* observed: "It was originally planned to purchase the water works plant by the issuance of bonds as soon as the present contract expired, but the condition of the city treasury at the present time and the unsteady condition of the bond market, will probably cause an abandonment of the plan to buy the plant." The city was unable to sell school bonds or road bonds, and rather than attempt a purchase it drew up a new thirty-year contract which gave the city an option to purchase the plant at any time on six months' notice. It established a base valuation of the plant and provided a method of calculating the value of any new improvements. The contract, drafted almost entirely by the city's attorneys, removed all legal obstacles to municipal ownership of the waterworks, and the city commission promised that just as soon as the city's financial condition improved, it would buy the plant. But not until 1951 did the city do so.[40]

38. Horner to Lynn, Feb. 25, 1915, B.W.W.C. Letterbooks; *Age-Herald*, Feb. 23, 24, 1915.

39. Horner to Lynn, June 8, Dec. 27, 1915, B.W.W.C. Letterbooks.

40. *News*, Aug. 26, 1920, Jan. 2, 1921; *Age-Herald*, Jan. 8, 1921; Birmingham, Minutes . . . Commissioners, Al, 43–48 (Jan. 19, 1921).

THE STATE PUBLIC SERVICE COMMISSION

Meanwhile, the year 1915 had brought not only a new waterworks contract, but also a new state public service commission to regulate local utilities. By 1915 the utility corporations had become completely disgusted with the necessity of submitting contracts to popular referenda. Birmingham voters had seized upon the referendum device to express their hostility to corporations, and had returned majorities of 90 and 68 percent against two contracts which had been approved as reasonable compromises by a majority of the city commission. Utility officials found it appalling that complex, carefully negotiated contracts should be placed at the mercy of a "hoodlum element" of voters who, according to Daniel O'Connell, could not look at contracts "from a cold-blooded business standpoint" because "their whole idea is to 'get even' with you whenever the opportunity presents itself."[41]

The corporations found that city commissioners with such an electorate behind them were wary and vexatious when they bargained over utility contracts. The commissioners, realizing that any contract they signed might have to stand the test of an emotional, politically embarrassing referendum campaign, cast a jaundiced eye upon every clause proposed by a utility company. And often they refused to include clauses that they acknowledged to be fair and reasonable, simply because they feared that suspicious citizens might easily misunderstand or distort the meaning of the provisions and call a referendum.[42]

In 1915 the utility corporations decided that they would prefer to deal with a state regulatory agency rather than a locally elected city commission and a referendum-prone electorate. Accordingly, they sponsored a legislative bill to transfer regulatory authority over local utilities to a state public service commission. The *Age-Herald*'s legislative reporter wrote that "the corporations are exerting every nerve to secure its enactment," and, he noted, "one of the main reasons for the existence of the bill is the fact that utility corporations in Birmingham have been relentlessly assailed within the past year or two." The Birmingham City Commission, seconded by the newspapers, the Merchant Association, the Board of Trade, and the labor unions, fought the bill, which would, they said, rob the city of home rule. But the corporations

---

41. O'Connell to Purdy, Sept. 2, 1912, B.W.W.C. Letterbooks; *News*, Dec. 1, 1911, Jan. 30, Sept. 10, 1912.
42. Horner to Lynn, May 11, 1915, B.W.W.C. Letterbooks.

formed a strong alliance with prohibitionist leaders and effectively stirred up rural resentments against big cities. The *Age-Herald* reported that the bill "has behind it all those who believe that Birmingham is already too powerful and that its wings and spurs should be trimmed." The measure passed, and in 1920 a supplementary Public Service Commission Act further eroded local jurisdiction and increased the state commission's authority on utility issues. And Lee Bradley, the chief attorney of the B.R.L. & P., later acknowledged that he personally had collaborated closely with the attorney general in drafting the 1920 act.[43]

The transfer of utility negotiations from the passions of local politics to the calm professional atmosphere of the state public service commission office in Montgomery was a clear political victory for the Birmingham utility corporations. As a result they received far more sympathetic hearings and more favorable rulings. They found it a timely victory, because the wartime inflation beginning soon after 1915 caught utilities in a fierce cost-price squeeze, and they frequently appeared before the state commission seeking higher rates.

The experience of the waterworks company between 1915 and 1921 illustrated the situation. The 1915 supplementary waterworks contract seemed at first a good bargain for both sides. Citizens enjoyed substantial savings, and when domestic meters were installed, the company's operating expenses declined as expected. In 1915 and 1916 net income, after operating expenses and bond interest, remained relatively stable at 7 to 8 percent of the $1,500,000 capital stock. But World War I inflation reversed the situation, pushing operating costs much higher. In 1919 net income was less than 3.7 percent of capital stock; in 1920, 4.7 percent. The city commission's own consulting engineers warned that if the city bought the plant it would have to raise rates to break even. In 1920 the company, over the city's protest, persuaded the state public service commission to override the 1915 contract and raise domestic meter rates 37 percent, from 20 to 27.5 cents per 1,000 gallons, still 2.5 cents cheaper than the old 1888 contract rates for commercial users.[44]

The state law required the city commission to incorporate these rates in its new 1921 waterworks contract. The state commission designed the rates to earn a 7.15 percent return on the basic valuation of the plant,

43. *Age-Herald*, Sept. 21, 23, 1915. See also *ibid.*, June 16, 17, 19, 1915, July 16, 1919; Birmingham *Post*, July 8, 1921.
44. Birmingham Water Works Company account books, 1919; *Age-Herald*, June 26, 29, 1917, Nov. 30, Dec. 31, 1920.

a valuation which the city had accepted as reasonable. If earnings rose above 7.15 percent, the rates would be reduced, but in actuality earnings stabilized at slightly less than 7.15 percent. Since approximately 70 percent of the plant value had been financed with 5 percent bonds, in 1921 the 7.15 return on total valuation enabled the company to pay the bond interest, plus a 9.5 percent dividend on the common stock; and by 1924, 16 percent on the common stock—both much higher than dividends before 1920. The company had every reason to be happy with regulation by the state commission, which shielded it from irate local attacks, enabled it to plan on a stable income, and allowed its stockholders to earn higher dividends.[45]

The other utility corporations also fared well before the state public service commission. By 1921 the commission had granted two telephone rate increases and three successive street railway-fare increases, from five cents to eight cents per ride. And it allowed the first streetcar increase, in 1918, immediately after a Birmingham referendum had rejected the increase by an eight-to-one margin. Clearly, all the increases would have suffered defeat had they depended on local referendum approval.[46] The Birmingham City Commission appeared before the state commission to fight all the rate increases except the first one for street railways, but invariably it lost. And citizens denounced the legislation which had "shorn" local officials of their power in utility questions and reduced them to "but little more authority than the average chief clerk in an office."[47]

Members of the Alabama Public Service Commission defended their sympathetic attitude toward the corporations, arguing that in the long run it would prove beneficial to the very voters who opposed it. One state commissioner was Blucher H. Cooper, a former Birmingham alderman and an earlier leader of the Birmingham municipal ownership movement. Cooper became convinced that "poor service was high at any rate," that people would be willing to pay well for good service, and that "to refuse adequate compensation for adequate service brings

45. Account Books, B.W.W.C. 1919–1923; statement of Birmingham Water Works Company earnings in James M. Jones Papers, ADAH; Alabama, *Biennial Report of the Alabama Public Service Commission, 1919–1920*, pp. 230–36; *Age-Herald*, Jan. 8, 1921.

46. On the telephone rates, see *Age-Herald*, Oct. 27, 1918, Jan. 15, 1921; on the street railway fares, see *ibid.*, July 24, 1918, Sept. 3, 1919, Dec. 31, 1920; *Post*, Aug. 1, 1921.

47. *Age-Herald*, Sept. 11, 1917. See also *ibid.*, Oct. 10, Dec. 13, 1920; *Post*, June 6, 18, 1921.

conditions that hurt the community far more than the stockholders." Continuous good service was possible only when rates were set properly to allow a fair return on capital, he said. Establishing and administering such rates was highly technical, and could not be done efficiently through inflexible contracts or erratic "home rule" referenda. Only a state regulatory agency had the financial resources and technical assistance to regulate local utilities efficiently, he believed, and in the long run local consumers would benefit by the removal of utility decisions from their direct political control.[48]

Academic public utility experts tended to agree with the Alabama state commissioner,[49] but most Birmingham citizens disagreed. The local consumers saw only that companies had clung tenaciously to advantageous old contract rates until 1915, and then, when the rates no longer suited the companies, that they had wriggled out of their long-sacrosanct contracts, obtained a change of venue, and escaped entirely from the political control of the people. Certainly after 1915 the direct political power of the local citizens vis à vis the utilities declined, and few consumers accepted the view that in the long run they might be better off for it. They suspected, perhaps justifiably, that the public service commission, removed from local pressure, would too readily accept the corporations' self-serving formulas for calculating fair rates of investment return.

COMPETITION

Between the 1880s and 1921 the other utility corporations experienced a pattern of contention similar to that of the water company. They too resisted attacks on their contract rates and on the quality of their service, they too despised referenda on new contracts, and they helped engineer the shift from local to state regulation. But in one way the experience of the B.R.L. & P. and Southern Bell was significantly different. Neither faced a movement for municipal ownership; instead, both had to cope with a city strategy of promoting new corporations to help regulate the established companies through competition. Citizens and city officials learned through frustrating experience that utility corporations were impervious to most regulation by ordinance or lawsuit, and by 1900 they were convinced that the one realistic and effective

48. *Post*, Sept. 15, 1921.
49. Glaeser, *Outlines of Public Utility Economics*, 294.

way to fight the power of a big utility corporation was to encourage competition from another big corporation.[50]

The old established utility corporations resourcefully fought enfranchisement of competitors. They raised complex technical objections in city committee hearings, creating long delays and seeking to discourage financial sponsors of new companies. The B.R.L. & P., which held perpetual street-railway franchises to almost every downtown street, generated tedious court contests over the question of whether the city could allow another company to enter the business district on some of those streets. Sometimes such delays actually led to the financial downfall of potential competitors.[51]

But on several occasions city officials eventually overrode all opposition and granted franchises to new utility corporations. After the consolidations of many early street-railway companies into the B.R.L. & P. in 1901, however, only two such potential competitors ever began actual operation in Birmingham. The Tidewater Railway Company operated a street railway line from 1912 to 1915, and the small independent, locally owned People's Home Telephone and Telegraph Company functioned from 1900 to 1912.

The new competitors suffered constant economic difficulties and faced the unrelenting opposition of the old companies. The new Tidewater street-railway routes tapped a less-developed market than that already absorbed by the B.R.L. & P., and the Tidewater lacked feeder lines and could not provide transfers to the many sections where it had no lines. It did, however, force the B.R.L. & P. to grant a five-cent fare to the suburb of Ensley, and this achievement powerfully reinforced the popular belief that competition was the one truly effective means of regulation. The People's telephone company offered lower rates than the established Southern Bell Telephone Company, but obtained only one-third as many subscribers and steadily lost money. Eventually, both challengers failed and merged with the larger established companies.[52]

Thus the new companies and the city discovered that most economic advantages lay with the established companies. As the owners of the People's telephone company finally acknowledged, telephone service was a natural monopoly. Academic economists, also, were beginning

50. *Labor Advocate*, May 25, 1901; *News*, Jan. 28, 1907, Dec. 7, 1910, Jan. 15, 1913, Feb. 15, 1914.

51. *News*, Jan. 22, 1901, Apr. 14, May 8, 19, Dec. 3, 4, 5, 6, 1910, Jan. 9, 1913, Feb. 5, 15, 1914; *Age-Herald*, May 10, 16, 25, 1901.

52. *News*, Apr. 28, 1906, Mar. 22, 1912; *Age-Herald*, Sept. 2, 1916, *Labor Advocate*, June 20, 1913.

to speak of all local utilities as "inherently monopolistic," since a utility provided an indispensable service which, because of economies of scale, could be most efficiently produced by a single large supplier. Establishing a competitor might prove actually disadvantageous to the consumer, since two competitive utility companies would probably engage in wasteful investment in duplicate facilities and would, in the long run, provide less efficient, more costly service than would one large company.[53]

The competition between the People's and the Southern Bell telephone companies was an extreme example of this inefficiency, since their basic service was communication. The companies provided no means of placing telephone calls from People's subscribers to Southern Bell subscribers, or vice versa. To call someone on the other system, a subscriber had to run to the house of a neighbor whose telephone was on the other system. Businessmen found this especially inconvenient and costly. Sixteen hundred of them subscribed to both systems, paid double rates, and received less convenient service than a single system would have provided.[54]

Even for services such as transportation, electric power, or water, the development of competition would probably in the long run decrease efficiency and increase costs to the consumer. A new competitor might force some concessions for consumers for a time, but eventually consolidation would become necessary to provide more efficient service, and usually the new company, operating at a disadvantage, would be absorbed by the established company.[55] Thus unless a city was able and willing to purchase and operate its own utility plants, its original corporation franchises for each basic utility service were likely to create local corporate monopolies, despite all efforts of the city to the contrary. And so long as the city and citizens clung to the belief that competition was the most effective means of regulating utilities, so long were they doomed to suffer continuous frustration because of the constant tendency toward consolidation and monopoly.

Citizens' frustration reached a boiling point when consolidating companies adroitly circumvented stern legal prohibitions against merger. The Tidewater Railway Company charter explicitly forbade transfer

---

53. *News*, Mar. 22, 1912; Glaeser, *Outlines of Public Utility Economics*, 204.
54. *News*, Sept. 20, 25, 26, 28, 1911, Mar. 22, 1912.
55. Martin Glaeser, professor of economics at the University of Wisconsin, declared that competition "involved social waste and that the inevitable outcome of competition would be consolidation." *Outlines of Public Utility Economics*, 204.

of the franchise to any competitive line, but in 1914–1916, when the company was losing money, it blithely went into receivership and sold itself at "forced sale" to its bondholders, who promptly sold the company to the B.R.L. & P. Company. The city commission protested, but the state supreme court upheld the transaction.[56] Likewise the People's telephone company franchise stated that if the company entered into any transfer or sale "to any competing company," the franchise would become null and void. But by 1912 the company was losing money and businessmen were clamoring for a merger into one efficient system. The city commission itself decided that nothing could be gained by resisting consolidation, so it arranged to cancel the People's contract and allow the People's company to sell its physical properties at auction. At the auction Southern Bell, the only bidder, acquired the People's property.[57]

Outraged citizens denounced the "telephone steal," which seemed to prove that the city commission preferred to help corporations rather than to defend the interests of the people. The political "infamy" of the "steal" lingered for years, and in 1915 Arlie Barber, the small drugstore owner, found it a potent issue when he ran against commissioner Alexander O. Lane, who had voted for the deal. Barber stumped the city shouting, "The deal robbed you, the people of Birmingham, of $650,000. It was plain highway robbery," and newspaper writers said such charges "made a deep and abiding impression" that helped Barber overwhelm Lane with a 63 percent majority.[58]

To labor union leaders the telephone case, in which corporations actually got city commissioners to help them violate the explicit provisions of a utility franchise, seemed but one dramatic "tip-of-the-iceberg" example of a much broader pattern of corporation control of Birmingham. A leading labor organizer, J.B. Wood, asked a mass labor meeting: "Why the Telephone Steal? Whom did it benefit and why? What bearing did it have upon the administration of the government since it was effected? If the city is governed by the Country and Southern Clubs, Why?" And Clement R. Wood, the young socialist lawyer, told the meeting, "The whole course of action of the Commissioners shows to any fair-minded observer that their action in regard to all the main

56. *News*, Sept. 1, 1914; *Age-Herald*, Sept. 2, Oct. 5, 21, Nov. 3, 1916, Jan. 19, 1917.
57. Birmingham, Minutes . . . Aldermen, H, 421–25 (Apr. 18, 1900), Minutes . . . Commissioners, Q, 355 (Apr. 2, 1912); *News*, Aug. 16, Sept. 26, 1911, Mar. 22, Aug. 3, 1912.
58. *News*, Oct. 17, 1915; *Age-Herald*, Oct. 19, 1915.

questions that have come before them has been to the interest of a few corporations and not of the people. . . . Their attitude throughout has been such as to justify the reasonable conclusion that they could not see any interest but that of the corporations, and could not act but for their benefit."[59]

Thus the citizens' repeated frustrations in attempting to regulate utilities helped create a popular image of a small behind-the-scenes "Country Club" power elite that pulled hidden strings to manipulate obedient city officials. But this image was based on distorted perceptions. Defenders of the commissioners were nearer the mark when they said that in the telephone episode the commissioners had fought for the best possible deal for local businessmen and consumers, and had in the end made the most realistic arrangement possible within the constraints of a private enterprise utility system. The power exercised by Southern Bell stemmed from the inherently monopolistic nature of its service, not from some behind-the-scenes ability to manipulate compliant commissioners.[60]

The distinction was significant. If the corporations had indeed been able to augment their economic leverage with an ability to control puppet politicians, they could have avoided the many intense and costly struggles over rates and service that in fact characterized Birmingham's history. The waterworks, for example, would have gained its urgently desired metering right more expeditiously, and all regulation outcomes would have been more one-sidedly advantageous to the companies. Moreover, if the utility corporations had become dictators of local government they could have triumphed consistently in other policy areas as well, and would not have found themselves paying relatively higher taxes than most other upper-ranking groups, or paying burdensome street-paving and repair costs. In short, the corporations found the leaders of the local political system to be not willing political puppets, but troublesome customers.

Some citizens alleged that utility corporations simply bought city officials through bribery. In some cities of the period corporations may have employed large-scale bribery, but in Birmingham it seems unlikely that corruption played a significant role in corporation influence over policy. To be sure, the waterworks company was not above attempting to use improper influence on aldermen, but it usually found it ineffective. Superintendent O'Connell candidly noted situations where he thought

59. *Labor Advocate*, June 20, 1913.
60. *News*, Sept. 25, 1911, Mar. 22, 1912, Oct. 17, 1915.

graft might be useful, saying of one bothersome alderman, "If I had some real cheap sort of law work, I would employ the old gentleman, and in that way keep him in line, but I may be able to work it through somebody else." But O'Connell's exasperation with the alderman's subsequent actions indicated that O'Connell was not able to "work it." The tone and content of O'Connell's frequent political comments indicated that he found most aldermen, commissioners, and mayors perversely uncooperative. Even Henry Gray, the reputed aldermanic boss, proved unreliable, and O'Connell reported, "Gray I have no confidence in whatever. He is a candidate for Lieut. Governor, and with him it is anything for votes." Corruption, while no doubt used on occasion, was simply not an efficient or reliable method of influencing political outcomes.[61]

The mistaken image of city officials as corporation puppets or bribed lackeys sometimes led people to hope futilely that they could subdue the utilities through political movements to throw out the puppets and elect stern honest statesmen who would take orders only from the people. But the fact was that few local leaders could have fought the utilities as resourcefully and tenaciously as did the three much-maligned commissioners who signed the telephone deal. The notion that the utilities won because the commissioners had become devoted corporation servants only obscured the more fundamental monopoly power of any established, privately-owned utility corporation, power which would persist and confront any new commissioners.

UTILITY REGULATION PATTERNS

Since the utility corporations provided essential services and since they were dependent on city contracts which set the rules for their daily or monthly transactions with masses of citizens, they were more vulnerable to government regulation than were other upper-ranking economic groups. Indeed, they considered themselves the targets of obstructive government harassment. Still, they were able to frustrate much of city government's effort to regulate them. They avoided municipal ownership, delayed costly improvements in quality, and absorbed competitors, and until 1915 they maintained old contract rates, then they got the rate-setting authority transferred to a sympathetic state

61. O'Connell to Kuhn, Sept. 26, 1903; O'Connell to Purdy, Nov. 26, 1905, B.W.W.C. Letterbooks.

commission which awarded steady rate increases. But such success did not derive basically from corruption or manipulation of puppet politicians; it stemmed rather from Birmingham's inability or unwillingness to establish public ownership, from the resulting dependence of citizens and government upon the capital and the indispensable services of the utility companies, and especially from the monopoly positions which the companies inexorably developed.

In sum, though the utilities had special vulnerabilities which forced them to engage in continual regulation skirmishes, their overall experience conformed to the pattern that interest groups of great economic power were usually able to resist unwanted regulation.

XII

The Birmingham Pattern

IN Birmingham, 1871–1921, the
overall distribution of political power followed this pattern: within
each government function—extraction, allocation, and regulation—the
higher the economic rank of a seriously contending group, the better its
overall record of political success. In every policy area the best record
of success was compiled by either the upper- or the middle-ranking
groups, never by the lower-ranking groups. Thus political power was
concentrated in the top 20 percent of the population. And when the
large industrial corporations vied against the downtown commercial
interests in a policy area that both considered vital, the corporations,
which embraced the top 1 percent of the population, usually defeated
the commercial interests, which encompassed the next highest 19 percent. This is not to say that on every issue the highest-ranking group in
earnest contention always won. On occasion lower- or middle-ranking
groups defeated upper-ranking groups, or at least denied them clear
victory. But within each broad government function and each policy
area, the consistent pattern was that among the groups which found the
issues highly salient, greater political success went to groups of greater
economic power.

The Birmingham pattern differs from both the power elite pattern
described by Floyd Hunter for mid-twentieth-century Atlanta and the
pluralist pattern described by Robert Dahl for mid-twentieth-century
New Haven. In contrast to the situation in Hunter's Atlanta, in Birmingham the upper-ranking economic groups were not politically
monolithic.[1] True, on many issues they united, having similar political

1. Floyd Hunter, *Community Power Structure: A Study of Decision Makers*
(Chapel Hill: Univ. of North Carolina Press, 1953; Garden City: Doubleday Anchor
Books, 1963), 64–76, 107–109, 240–44. Page references are to the Anchor edition.

goals. But on other issues they divided and fought one another, as they did, for example, when the street railway opposed the regular railroads on the viaduct question, or when the iron and steel manufacturers opposed the waterworks company on the question of a government-financed industrial water supply, or when the Tennessee Coal, Iron, and Railroad Company stopped leasing convicts and sought to force other corporations to stop. Moreover, on such important issues as annexation, commissaries, smoke, railroad grade crossings, convict labor, and utilities, middle-ranking commercial groups, which were also well up the economic pyramid, fiercely attacked upper-ranking industrial groups, though on other questions the industrial and commercial interests joined forces. Social issues and social interest groups further complicated the picture, cutting across class lines, pitting leaders from the same economic ranks against one another, and frequently dividing the economic elite. In short, in Birmingham there was no small consensual elite of economic and social notables that worked together behind the scenes to control the entire local political process. Nor were economically powerful groups equally interested in or influential in all policy areas and government functions; groups with dominant influence on some issues had none on other issues.

All this is consistent with Dahl's New Haven model, but Birmingham's pattern also differed significantly from New Haven's. Dahl concluded that "To reconstruct these decisions is to leave little room for doubt that the Economic Notables, far from being a ruling group, are simply one of the many groups out of which individuals sporadically emerge to influence the policies and acts of city officials." He reported no consistent pattern of relationships between economic power and political power, but rather said, "Almost anything one might say about the influence of the Economic Notables could be said with equal justice about a half dozen other groups in the New Haven community."[2] In Birmingham, by contrast, a quite consistent pattern of relationships between economic power and political power emerged: political power was roughly proportional to economic power. And it could justly be said only of the upper-ranking economic groups that in every policy area which they found highly salient, they compiled a better record of success than did any other groups.

2. Robert A. Dahl, *Who Governs? Democracy and Power in an American City* (New Haven: Yale Univ. Press, 1961), 72; see also 63–84.

CHARACTERISTICS OF
THREE GOVERNMENT FUNCTIONS

Although an overall pattern of power distribution emerged, each government function—extraction, allocation, and regulation—generated its own pattern of distribution of political power, its own configuration of interest group contention, and its own procedures, agencies, and hierarchies of decision-making.

The extraction of revenue frequently stimulated sharp interest-group conflict, and most fundamental decisions were made at the state level. All groups felt the direct yearly impact of taxation, and tax variations tended to strike the entire membership of each economic interest group in a common way, making group action especially relevant. Sometimes groups sought mainly to minimize their own burdens—to prevent assessment increases, to hold property- or license-tax rates down, to abolish the street tax—and in such negative efforts they did not necessarily confront opposing groups. But since everyone realized that the city needed more revenue, contention often intensified into aggressive efforts to shift revenue burdens onto other specific groups—to annex industries, to raise utility-license taxes, to "equalize" assessments on business and industrial property—and this created direct group confrontations. Taxation decisions directly involved local aldermen and county commissioners, but since the all-important property tax was tightly constrained by state restrictions, most fundamental decisions about tax changes were made at the state level, by the legislature, the governor, constitutional conventions, or the statewide electorate.

By contrast, allocation of services often produced not confrontation between interest groups, but a general consensus for long-established precedents and common-sense guidelines, and the distribution of available local revenue was done almost entirely by local officials, without significant state constraints. Growing education appropriations were supported by a broad consensus. The allocation of services to property was governed by noncontroversial priorities established by businessmen. Services to persons suffered the greatest neglect, partly because articulate groups concurred on other priorities, partly because the poorest citizens who most desperately needed such services were inarticulate, unorganized, and often disfranchised. Finally, specific improvements went routinely, through widely accepted procedures, to those who paid for their own.

Government regulation, on the other hand, produced the most sharply focused interest-group confrontations; and many, but not all, regulation controversies were ultimately decided at the state level. Often a specific regulation proposal was an attempt by one interest group or a coalition of several groups to use the power of local government to help control some other group—to inspect dairies, to prohibit saloons, to reduce utility rates, to control industrial smoke—and the target group usually resisted. Thus regulation proposals and policies were often quite congruent with group interests, and they stimulated energetic group mobilization. And the outcomes reflected the balance of power among groups demanding and resisting regulation. The city's traditional regulatory powers sufficed to regulate some groups, usually the economically weaker ones, but any bold new regulatory departure, especially if it aimed at economically-powerful groups, required new authority from the state, which became the agency of ultimate decisions.

THE RECORD OF THE UPPER-RANKING GROUPS

The top 1 percent of the population which owned and managed the firms of the upper-ranking economic groups generally found extraction and regulation highly salient, allocation less so. They did find some local services of value, but, unlike many middle- and lower-ranking groups, they did not depend so heavily on any local housekeeping service that they found it necessary to exert constant pressure to maintain or improve it. They devoted their most intense efforts to resisting the only local government activities that could seriously affect their economic well-being—tax increases and regulatory intervention. And in general they succeeded, avoiding new burdens more consistently than any other group.

The upper-ranking groups succeeded partly because local powers of taxation and regulation were weak and restricted and partly because the top groups could often induce state coalitions and authorities to stifle new regulations and to perpetuate ineffective tax machinery. Often, also, the economically-powerful groups held the advantage of defending the status quo, with their favored positions frozen in property rights, contracts, or constitutions, and often old tax patterns had come, through long usage, to seem normal. In addition, the upper-ranking groups were aided in translating economic power into political power by campaign contributions; by occasional corruption (which they recognized, however, as inefficient and unreliable); by the ability to employ attorneys and experts to do research, devise strategy, speak, and lobby; and sometimes, but not always, by the friendly support of the daily press. Finally, and perhaps most important, upper-ranking groups succeeded because they could convince many citizens that the economic growth and prosperity of all Birmingham depended on the unhindered development of the large industries which formed the economic base. These industries competed in regional and national markets, and many people believed that local tax and regulatory burdens might undermine the industries' ability to compete and to bring money into Birmingham. Such beliefs did not, however, apply to utility corporations, whose markets were local. And consequently utilities, which were also more dependent on local government franchises, were much more vulnerable to local taxation and somewhat more vulnerable to regulation.

The upper-ranking groups usually experienced less success obtaining positive government actions or service allocations than in avoiding adverse actions. On the whole, of course, positive actions were less important to them than to most other groups, but on occasion such a proposed service as a subsidized industrial water supply could be vital to industrialists. Also some corporation executives coveted improvements in local education and in civic amenities. On the issue of education they achieved some success, because their goal dovetailed nicely with concerns of many other local groups. On amenities they achieved only minor and disappointing success, and on industrial water, none. Thus when upper-ranking leaders did seek positive government services, they often experienced frustration because they had to work with weak and restricted governments. But the upper-ranking groups found the impotence of local government in providing positive services less debilitating than did other groups and they found the advantages of dealing with weak governments on regulatory and taxation policies to outweigh the disadvantages on service allocations.

One positive local government activity—favorable police control during strikes—was, however, crucially important to industrialists. And this assistance, more regulatory than allocative, the industries obtained, though they had to rely heavily on county and state authorities. Thus the industries not only avoided adverse regulation, but they also used regulatory police power as a positive instrument of labor control.

Time brought gradual change within this general pattern of upper-ranking success. Between approximately 1900 and 1921 the middle- and lower-ranking groups managed to erode somewhat, but not to overwhelm, the powers of resistance of the upper-ranking groups. The city annexed and taxed industries, state tax commissioners boosted corporation assessments, the city and state raised utility taxes, and the city gradually pressured the railroads into beginning to build viaducts. Usually such changes were closely related to the statewide "progressive" political reform movement, especially to the reform administrations of governors Joseph F. Johnston and Braxton Bragg Comer. Since basic change almost always required state action, it could come only when a state administration assembled a reform-minded anticorporation legislature that would break through the bottlenecks at which upper-ranking groups usually defended their positions. Still, progressive governors did not always oppose industrialists. Indeed, progressive governors Comer and Thomas E. Kilby intervened decisively in support of industry in Birmingham's two most crucial coal strikes, even when, by 1919, labor unions had undermined industry's control of local peace-keeping activities. Also, Comer strongly supported the state convict-labor system, and Kilby, though speaking against it, endorsed compromises that perpetuated it, thus helping to keep it available to industry long after Birmingham sentiment had turned strongly against it. Moreover, statewide progressive leaders helped Birmingham's upper-ranking groups abolish the county fee system and create the state utility regulation commission, thus supporting progressive-type reforms designed and initiated by leaders of the top groups themselves.

Thus despite some erosion, by 1921 the upper-ranking groups retained greater ability to shape policy than any other groups. They continued to thwart most, if not all, progressive-type regulatory proposals aimed against them by middle- and lower-ranking groups, and on occasion they turned the progressive impulse to their own ends. When they agreed to pay higher city property taxes, after 1914, they were able to insist upon the method which was least costly to them. They still prevailed consistently on the issues they considered absolutely essential; they still obtained from the political system everything they really needed from it.

THE RECORD OF THE MIDDLE-RANKING GROUPS

In contrast to the top industrialists, the middle-ranking economic groups, containing the next highest 19 percent of the population, were more locally oriented and depended heavily on positive government

275

services to nurture and expand the local market. Their prosperity was intimately bound up with the fortunes of the city itself, and they had a broader and more intense interest in the entire range of local government policies than did most upper groups. The middle groups found allocation by far the most crucial of the three government functions, and they exercised the dominant influence over allocation, maintaining the crucial downtown services at a satisfactory level, even when other services had to be neglected to do so. The business district maintained top priority, partly because it contributed conspicuously to the growth and prosperity of the entire city, and partly because it generated the most visible need for services. Downtown priorities, once established, seemed normal and were reinforced by developing civic pride. Also, downtown businessmen possessed the time and money to develop highly-effective pressure-group associations; and they attained heavy overrepresentation in local government offices, primarily because they had the time, money, skills, and visibility to run for and occupy elective office. Allocation patterns, however, were necessarily influenced by revenue patterns, and the businessmen exercised less than complete control over city services because the scarcity of revenue depressed the level of all allocations, including those for downtown services.

For middle-ranking groups, therefore, extraction also was critical, both for its impact on allocation possibilities and on their own tax payments. On tax policy the real estate interests, a middle-ranking group, did very well; but in a partial exception to the overall pattern of power, the merchants and other local businesses bore an unusually heavy burden through the license tax, a burden forced on them in part by the successful resistance of lower-ranking residents to property tax increases. The exception was only partial, because the license tax itself was regressive, hitting lower-ranking businesses harder than those of middle rank. Moreover, middle-ranking businessmen grudgingly accepted the burden, because they knew they received the greatest allocation benefits. Also, they gradually undermined the strict constraints on the property tax and finally achieved license tax reduction.

Political scientist Theodore J. Lowi has suggested that in contemporary American city and national government, extraction and allocation, considered together, are redistributive, or at least potentially so, and that they tend to pose class battles between "money-providers" and "service-demanders," or between haves and have-nots.[3] But in Birming-

3. Theodore J. Lowi, *At the Pleasure of the Mayor: Patronage and Power in New York City, 1898-1958* (New York: Free Press, 1964), 143, 137-48; Lowi,

ham before 1921 the potentially redistributive services such as charity, welfare, prisons, and hospitals were extremely undeveloped, and the poorest have-nots, especially Negroes, were so unorganized and so completely excluded from government counsels that they could seldom create class battles over the budget. The middle-ranking groups considered redistribution by local government illegitimate, and they saw to it that as little as possible occurred. Businessmen believed that taxpayers, like stockholders in a corporation, should receive benefits roughly proportional to their contributions. Service-demanders should be money-providers, and the major money-providers should have the largest say in what services were provided. And in fact, Birmingham budget discussions and outcomes conformed closely to those principles.

In Birmingham the combined extraction and allocation patterns especially favored real estate developers. The developers paid unusually low property taxes, but revenue scarcity produced little inconvenience for them, because the services on which they most depended, such as street-paving and rapid utility extensions, were financed not through general revenue, but through user fees and through special assessments which they passed on to buyers.

Government regulation was important to middle-ranking groups, though perhaps less crucial than allocation and extraction. Middle groups generally avoided adverse regulation or shaped mild regulation of their businesses so as to be actually beneficial. But they were less successful than upper-ranking groups. Real estate interests, for example, finally had to bow to some regulation imposed in the interest of city health. And middle groups made little progress when they directly confronted upper-ranking groups, trying to impose government regulation on corporation commissaries, industrial paydays, industrial smoke, railroad grade crossings, convict labor, and utilities. Still, in regulation, as in the other two functions, middle-ranking groups consistently gained strength vis-à-vis other groups as time passed. After 1900 they instigated much new regulation of lower-ranking groups, and especially under the city commission after 1911, they achieved some success in regulating upper-ranking groups. Basically, as the institutions of city government gradually developed more authority and power, the middle-ranking groups that dominated them gained leverage in relation to other groups.

"American Business, Public Policy, Case-Studies, and Political Theory," *World Politics* 16 (July 1964), 703–15; Wallace S. Sayre and Herbert Kaufman, *Governing New York City: Politics in the Metropolis* (New York: Russel Sage, 1960; Norton 1965), 514.

THE RECORD OF THE LOWER-RANKING GROUPS

The lower-ranking economic groups, containing the bottom 80 percent of the population, found all three government functions salient, and they exercised some influence over outcomes in each. But in none did they have the best record of success; and in general, with some significant exceptions on specific issues, in each they tended to exercise the least influence. Government extraction was a serious matter to citizens of small means, who felt keenly the bite of city taxes and fees. The tax structure was regressive, burdening lower-ranking groups relatively more heavily than others, and the few changes achieved by the lower groups were not great enough to overcome the imbalance. The assessment system continued to give the greatest breaks to higher-ranking groups, and the license tax remained regressive. But on some specific issues which they found especially pressing and on which they mobilized effectively, the lower groups did succeed, getting rid of the regressive street tax and school tuition, and in 1916, obtaining a more equitable license-tax schedule. Moreover, their determination to keep property taxes low helped to shape the overall tax structure. Ironically, their goal was congruent with the desire of upper-ranking groups and real estate interests to keep the property tax levying machinery weak and ineffective, and together they forced onto the middle- and lower-ranking businessmen the unusually high license tax burden.

Allocation of local services was a matter of consequence to most lower-ranking groups, whose quality of life often depended heavily on city services. Certainly they had some influence on the allocation of services most vital to them, but they exercised much less sway than did middle-ranking groups. They shaped the pattern most significantly by resisting property tax increases unless the money went for schools, and they could take partial credit for the steady growth of education appropriations. But the growth did not come in opposition to other groups, and it was facilitated by the belief of upper-ranking groups that improved education of the labor force would benefit everyone.

In the regulatory arena, lower-ranking groups had mixed experiences. They demonstrated the least ability to impose regulation on higher-ranking groups, and they themselves were the most vulnerable to unwanted regulation of their business or their life styles. Still, the pattern is not neat; much of the economic regulation imposed on such lower-ranking business groups as dairymen and grocers undoubtedly benefited wage earners, who ranked even lower in the economic scale. Moreover, social regulation victories and defeats cannot be attributed neatly to upper, middle, or lower ranks, because the ultimately successful pietistic Protestant organizations recruited from all three ranks. Nevertheless, the pattern of losses is significant because all the business groups and by far the majority of individuals who suffered the imposition of unwanted new regulations were from the lower ranks. Intensification of all types of government regulation was a characteristic of the progressive and municipal reform movements, and it is significant that in Birmingham, the lower the economic rank of an interest group, the more intense and comprehensive were the types of progressive social and economic regulation to which it finally had to bow. The regulation of Negroes, the lowest-ranking socioeconomic group of all, provided the most extreme example; the central thrust of several reforms was to place the blacks more firmly and efficiently under the discipline of economically-powerful white groups.

POSITIONAL ANALYSIS

In Birmingham from 1871 to 1953 businessmen from middle-ranking groups consistently dominated city offices, a pattern which contrasts with the findings of most positional studies of other cities. Several studies have found that during the early years of their cities, in the nineteenth century, the very top economic leaders often held public office, presiding over a monolithic power structure, but that beginning around 1900, economic leaders withdrew from or were shut out of formal local government office, and have remained out ever since. In a pioneer positional study of "Cibola" (Ypsilanti, Michigan) from 1823 to 1955, sociologist Robert O. Schulze interpreted this as a "bifurcation" of the community power structure into "two crucial and relatively discrete power sets, the economic dominants and the public leaders." The Schulze bifurcation thesis was essentially supported by studies of "Wheelsburg" (Lansing, Michigan) and of Chicago. And Robert A. Dahl found that during the 1840s in New Haven, an oligarchy of old patrician political leaders was displaced by self-made industrialists, the "entrepreneurs," who in 1900 were in turn displaced by "ex-plebes" of "working class or lower middle class families of immigrant background." But historian Samuel P. Hays, in his positional study of municipal reformers in Pittsburgh, reported a directly contrary finding: that around 1910 Pittsburgh economic leaders used municipal reform innovations to move themselves directly *into* "the inner circles of government," and that economic leaders "brought into one political system their own power and the formal machinery of government, and dominated municipal affairs for two decades." Both social scientists and historians have acknowledged that patterns could vary widely from city to city, but the social scientists have tended to consider the bifurcation pattern dominant, while political historians have been most influenced by Hays's thesis that, in municipal reform cities at least, the early twentieth century brought forth not a withdrawal of economic leaders from government, but a reassertion of their political dominance.[4]

In Birmingham the top 1 percent of the population in the upper-ranking economic groups neither dominated city positions in the early years (only to withdraw after 1900) nor reentered city positions through the municipal reform movement. Rather, the next highest 19 percent of the population in the middle-ranking groups dominated throughout, and the triumph of the municipal reform city commission movement in 1911 dramatically increased their proportion of city offices. The domination by middle-ranking groups was weakest in the 1880s and 1890s, when immigrant groups and wage earners achieved their strongest representations. And from 1890 through 1911 the board of aldermen, though business-dominated, leaned toward the Roman Catholic and immigrant Liberal Element on social policy. In 1910 and 1911 the annexation of heavily Protestant suburbs and the adoption of the city commission system ended immigrant and Roman Catholic representation in city offices and demolished Liberal Element control over city social policy. But big businessmen and top industrialists did not take control of the commission. For the first six years the typical commissioner came from higher economic and social rank than had the typical alderman, but thereafter the commission was dominated by suburban Moral Element business and professional people, who came, on the average, from the same middle economic ranks as had the aldermen before 1911.

4. Robert O. Schulze, "The Role of Economic Dominants in Community Power Structure," *American Sociological Review* 23 (Feb. 1958), 3–9; Donald A. Clelland and William H. Form, "Economic Dominants and Community Power: A Comparative Analysis," *American Journal of Sociology* 69 (Mar. 1964), 511–21; Donald S. Bradley and Mayer N. Zald, "From Commercial Elite to Political Administrator: The Recruitment of the Mayors of Chicago," *American Journal of Sociology* 71 (Sept. 1965), 153–67; Dahl, *Who Governs?* 11–62; Samuel P. Hays, "The Politics of Reform in Municipal Government in the Progressive Era," *Pacific Northwest Quart.* 55 (Oct. 1964), 167; Melvin G. Holli, *Reform in Detroit: Hazen S. Pingree and Urban Politics* (New York: Oxford Univ. Press, 1969), 157–81.

But the Birmingham evidence indicates that the positional pattern of a city, whatever its shape, might not be congruent with the actual distribution of political power among groups. Since entrenched positions and state decisions were so important in the overall pattern of political outcomes, positional analysis of Birmingham offers at best an imperfect picture of the political power structure, and used alone it would be highly misleading. On many issues the overrepresented middle-ranking groups had much less sway over policy outcomes than did the upper-ranking groups that held only a small minority of local offices. Often state constraints and weak local authority deprived local officials of the ability to implement the policy wishes of the middle groups. And sometimes officials bowed to the desire to nurture the top growth-producing groups. Only on such government activities as allocation of services, on which local officials had a free hand and on which the desire to stimulate growth reinforced the policy goals of the local businessmen, did the middle-ranking groups actually influence policy-making to the extent that they dominated elected positions in local government.

Since state intervention in local policy was so important, the usefulness of the positional method is improved by extending it to delegations to the state legislature, something which few positional studies of political power have done. The occasional appearance of representatives of upper-ranking groups on the legislative delegations provides a hint of their political power at that level, as does their domination of the state senatorship until 1915. Even this, however, fails to indicate the great extent to which legislative bottlenecks and alliances with rural interests enhanced the local political power of upper-ranking groups.

Positional analysis does reveal that the major cleavage in local electoral politics was defined not by economic interests, but by social groups, particularly ethnic and religious groups, and by such issues as saloon regulation and Sunday observance, which touched deeply-held life style traditions and moral attitudes. Such issues were highly salient in local electoral politics, because local officials, whose ability to change economic policy was severely limited, clearly did have the authority and the police power to produce either lax or severe regulation of saloons and Sundays. Moreover, easily observed socioreligious characteristics of candidates reliably indicated their positions on social issues. Economic characteristics of candidates, on the other hand, stirred less controversy. Many voters, impressed by the business-like duties of aldermen, mayors, and commissioners, and concurring in probusiness policies of allocation, considered it appropriate that a majority of officials be businessmen of the middle rank. And since most voters concurred in electing business-men, controversy could focus upon the social characteristics and policies of the assortment of business-oriented candidates.

THE BIRMINGHAM PATTERN AND OTHER CITIES

What can a study of the distribution of political power in one city suggest about other cities? Certainly many cities experienced to some degree the factors that helped produce the Birmingham pattern: state constraints, weak city powers, entrenched rights, established precedents, the legitimacy of business concerns in the public mind, the widespread desire to promote growth, the reluctance to handicap payroll-creators, the superior organizational ability of business, and the business orien-tation of daily newspapers. But some of these factors operated more intensely in Birmingham than elsewhere, and in some outcomes Bir-mingham deviated from the norm for other cities. Moreover, in defining and explaining the Birmingham pattern, this study has often focused sharply on the deviations. How representative, therefore, was the Bir-mingham pattern? To the extent that other cities departed from it, which characteristics were probably associated with the departure, and what types of cities were likely to diverge the furthest?

Two southern characteristics distinguished Birmingham from most northern cities. First, after 1890 Birmingham systematically disfran-chised blacks, thereby excluding roughly one-third of its citizens from the electoral process, and, in comparison with northern cities, thereby diminishing the electoral leverage of lower-ranking economic groups. In northern cities, therefore, lower-ranking groups packed more ballot power. But even in Birmingham lower-ranking white groups comprised a majority of the electorate; the disfranchisement of blacks cannot alone account for the lower groups' weak influence in Birmingham.

Second, in Birmingham and other southern cities, the immigrant and non-Protestant groups were much smaller and less influential than in most northern cities. In Birmingham, however, these groups were stronger than in most other southern cities. And the Birmingham pattern of saloon and Sunday regulation—permissive before 1908, thereafter increasingly restrictive—corresponded both with the declining propor-tion of Catholics and immigrants in the relevant electoral units and with the rising progressive reform spirit. Northern cities with immigrant and Catholic majorities often developed powerful immigrant-based machines which successfully resisted Protestant reform efforts to impose strict Sunday and saloon regulation. Even in such cities, however, immigrant and Catholic citizens had to contend with the threat that rural voters, often more Protestant, would impose state regulation or state prohibition. And by 1920 all were subjected to nationwide prohibition. Still, in cities in which immigrants and Catholics embraced a majority, they won more social regulation victories than they did in Birmingham. Thus those cities departed from Birmingham's tendency to impose most social regulation defeats on groups of lowest socioeconomic status.

But it does not necessarily follow that in such cities middle- and upper-ranking economic groups fell from power completely, or that they lost all influence over policies of taxation, allocation, and economic regulation. Past decisions and patterns, business legitimacy, state constraints, and state coalitions might still have helped middle- and upper-ranking groups to maintain political leverage in salient economic policy areas. Also, many ethnic political leaders were themselves businessmen, sympathetic to business priorities. The ethnic ex-plebe mayors and political leaders who, as Robert Dahl reported in *Who Governs?*, took over New Haven politics after 1900, were certainly of lower economic rank than were New Haven's late-nineteenth-century industrialist mayors, but clearly the five lawyers, the realtor, the garage company president, the printing business official and the undertaker among the ex-plebe mayors also had business interests and sympathies.[5] In cities like New Haven the self-styled "respectable" or "better" elements no doubt deplored the takeover of city hall by nobodies of immigrant background, who reputedly cultivated questionable alliances with liquor and vice interests. But it would require detailed decisional analysis of the patterns of taxation, allocation, and economic regulation, before and after the ethnic takeover, to determine the extent to which upper- and middle-ranking groups lost political power on vital economic issues.

Some characteristics unique to the state of Alabama caused Birmingham to deviate significantly from the norm of other cities. The state was overwhelmingly rural and it imposed severe constraints upon city authority. But this was only an extreme case of a widespread phenomenon; few cities of the era entirely escaped state interference. All cities derived their powers from state legislatures, and most struggled against legislative intervention, contended with state debt limits, demanded stronger regulatory powers, and campaigned urgently, with only partial

5. Dahl, *Who Governs?*, 40, 14.

success, for "home rule."[6] In many cities, therefore, state intervention could affect local power distribution, since groups that lacked influence with local voters and officials might shape policy by mobilizing statewide coalitions and influencing legislators and state officials.

Alabama shaped the Birmingham pattern most drastically through its tight property tax restrictions which penalized middle-ranking businessmen and aided industry and real estate interests. In most other cities merchants probably fared better, but for each city only careful studies of tax incidence and of tax controversies and decisions could reveal the distribution of political power in the policy area of municipal revenue.

Alabama's tax restrictions also created singularly severe shortages of revenue in Birmingham and placed cruel constraints upon the allocation of services. But most American cities in most historical periods have struggled with revenue deficiencies. Though perennially in crisis, Birmingham's revenue and allocation systems were basically similar to those of other American cities. And a political system often reveals much about its underlying power relationships by the way it responds to crises, since crises force officials to decide what must be preserved and what and who shall bear the brunt of sacrifice. Birmingham's deviations from the typical city patterns helped to indicate which Birmingham groups exercised strong and which weak influence over extraction and allocation outcomes, and the deviations might also suggest which groups in more typical cities were most vulnerable to tax increases or service sacrifices, and, by contrast, which groups held the most secure positions. Birmingham singularly neglected charities, hospitals, and prisons, which were particularly important to the poor and disadvantaged. But did the typical city pattern from which Birmingham deviated represent failure or success of the poor and disadvantaged? To delineate the pattern of power in the other cities it would be especially important to measure the extent to which lower-ranking groups shaped the more normal allocation pattern. And in instances of strong lower-ranking influence, it would be significant to discover the factors which facilitated lower-ranking success.

In sum, the Birmingham pattern from 1871 to 1921 was produced by a combination of some factors unique to that Alabama city and of other factors common to most rapidly growing commercial and indus-

6. Charles N. Glaab and A. Theodore Brown, *A History of Urban America* (New York: Macmillan, 1967), 172–74, 187–89; Sayre and Kaufman, *Governing New York City*, 558–98.

trial cities. Few cities completely escaped even the factors most unique to Birmingham, but probably the less dependent a city was on heavy industry, the less committed to rapid growth as a route to general prosperity, the less hampered by state intervention, the less bound by entrenched property rights and long-term contracts, the less dominated by a single ethno-religious tradition, and the less restrictive of the right to vote, the more likely that city was to depart from the Birmingham pattern. But even cities which escaped most of Birmingham's special traits also shared many of its common features, and historians of urban politics could profitably measure other cities against the Birmingham pattern, as well as against Floyd Hunter's Atlanta pattern and Robert Dahl's New Haven pattern.

After 1921 the pattern in Birmingham may have changed significantly; that would be a matter for further study. After 1921 Birmingham and other cities experienced the impact of the automobile, the Great Depression, the New Deal, the assumption by federal, state, and local government of greater responsibility for welfare activities, and the recognition of the legitimacy of labor organization; and such developments may have altered the distribution of political power. But as of 1921, with the years of rapid city-building and municipal reform just completed, the pattern still held. Political power was concentrated in the top 20 percent of the population, in the hands of the upper- and the middle-ranking economic-interest groups. But these groups did not create or obey a single united power elite. On some issues, to be sure, most of them cooperated to pursue common goals, but on other issues they clashed sharply and publicly in pursuit of conflicting goals, with some economic leaders defeating others. Moreover, many of the wealthiest businessmen did not deem all issues worthy of serious attention. Thus contention was pluralistic. But the distribution of political power was not so pluralistic as to be patternless, without any systematic relationship between economic and political power. Rather, in Birmingham groups of high, medium, and low economic status, when they imperatively needed and tried to shape local policy, usually experienced political success roughly proportional to their economic rank.

Appendix

Financial statistics on the general revenue and departmental expenditures for the city of Birmingham have been compiled for every year for which any systematic information was available in federal census publications and in the partially extant official financial reports of Birmingham. The selected years reported here were the most significant in terms of developing patterns and changing trends. The basic data came from the following federal publications: U.S. Census Office, *Report on Wealth, Debt, and Taxation at the Eleventh Census: 1890*, Pt. II, *Valuation and Taxation*, Vol. 15 (Washington, D.C., 1895); U.S. Department of Labor, *Statistics of Cities* for 1899, 1900, 1901, and 1902 (Washington, D.C., 1899–1902); U.S. Bureau of the Census, *Statistics of Cities Having a Population of Over 30,000* for 1904, 1905, 1906, and 1907 (Washington, D.C., 1906–1910); U.S. Bureau of the Census, *Financial Statistics of Cities Having a Population of Over 30,000* for 1909, 1910, 1911, 1912, 1914, 1915, 1916, 1917, 1918, 1921, and 1922 (Washington, D.C., 1913–1924). The categories reported here derive from the census classifications, which were relatively consistent over the years, but revenue and expenditures for specific assessments and for municipal industries have been excluded from general revenue. Census reports before 1904 were less detailed, and the census data for those years have been reclassified, using the more detailed, but sometimes incomplete information from official Birmingham city reports. Therefore the data before 1904, and especially before 1899, are less reliable and are based on less detailed information. The data for 1873, 1881, and 1885 are fragmentary and come entirely from city reports published in the Birmingham *Iron Age*, Jan. 14, 1875, Mar. 30, 1882, Jan. 14, 1886. Other city reports were Birmingham, *Message of the*

Mayor and the Annual Reports of the Officers of Birmingham for 1897, 1898, 1899, 1904, 1905, 1906, and 1907 (Birmingham, 1897–1907); Birmingham, *Financial Report of the City of Birmingham, Alabama* for 1912–1921. (Birmingham, 1912–1921). Per capita values are based on population estimates arrived at by dividing the city population growth between decennial censuses into ten equal increments. Between 1900 and 1910, however, the population estimates were adjusted to take into account the annexation of Avondale in 1908 and of the rest of Greater Birmingham before the census of 1910.

Table A.1 Birmingham General Revenue

Year	Total Gen. Rev.	PROPERTY TAX Total	Real & Pers.	County & State Aid	LICENSE TAX Total	Liquor	Business	Street Tax
			(In Thousands of Dollars)					
1873	15.4	5.1	n/a	n/a	5.7	n/a	n/a	—
1881	17.7	4.0	4.0	n/a	8.6	n/a	n/a	0.5
1885	57.6	18.0	16.7	1.3	22.0	n/a	n/a	2.7
1890	261.1	89.7	80.5	9.2	93.9	n/a	n/a	n/a
1898	243.4	89.5	74.5	14.9	94.9	37.1	57.8	17.2
1900	389.9	172.9	152.0	20.9	134.9	46.8	88.2	12.0
1904	527.6	234.4	205.6	28.7	189.4	57.7	131.7	6.1
1907	826.8	328.5	267.4	61.1	320.3	113.1	207.2	—
1909	855.4	420.8	330.5	90.3	276.7	—	276.7	—
1911	1,467.2	870.7	641.0	229.7	375.8	—	375.8	—
1915	1,844.3	1,228.4	938.9	289.4	438.8	65.2	373.6	—
1916	1,917.9	1,194.2	913.2	281.0	426.0	—	426.0	26.2
1920	2,920.2	1,677.5	1,065.9	611.6	787.4	—	787.4	—
1922	4,265.1	3,035.1	2,224.4	810.7	777.8	—	777.8	—
			(In Dollars per Capita)					
1881	5.75	1.29	1.29	n/a	2.77	n/a	n/a	.17
1885	4.22	1.32	1.22	.10	1.62	n/a	n/a	.20
1890	9.98	3.43	3.07	.35	3.59	n/a	n/a	n/a
1898	6.77	2.49	2.07	.42	2.64	1.03	1.60	.48
1900	10.15	4.50	3.96	.54	3.51	1.22	2.30	.31
1904	11.08	4.92	4.32	.60	3.98	1.21	2.77	.13
1907	15.17	6.03	4.91	1.12	5.88	2.08	3.80	—
1909	13.76	6.77	5.32	1.45	4.45	—	4.45	.00
1911	10.68	6.33	4.66	1.67	2.73	—	2.73	—
1915	11.79	7.85	6.00	1.85	2.80	.42	2.39	—
1916	11.90	7.40	5.66	1.74	2.64	—	2.64	.16
1920	16.20	9.30	5.91	3.39	4.37	—	4.37	—
1922	21.75	15.47	11.34	4.13	3.97	—	3.97	—
			(Percentage Distribution)					
1873	100	33.3	n/a	n/a	36.9	n/a	n/a	—
1881	100	22.4	22.4	n/a	48.3	n/a	n/a	2.9
1885	100	31.2	28.9	2.3	38.2	n/a	n/a	4.8
1890	100	34.3	30.8	3.5	36.0	n/a	n/a	n/a
1898	100	36.7	30.6	6.1	39.0	15.2	23.8	7.1
1900	100	44.4	39.6	5.4	34.6	12.0	22.6	3.1
1904	100	44.4	39.0	5.4	35.9	10.9	25.0	1.1
1907	100	39.7	32.3	7.4	38.7	13.7	25.1	—
1909	100	49.2	38.6	10.6	32.3	—	32.3	—
1911	100	59.4	43.7	15.7	25.6	—	25.6	—
1915	100	66.6	50.9	15.7	23.8	3.5	20.3	—
1916	100	62.3	47.6	14.7	22.2	—	22.2	1.4
1920	100	57.4	36.5	20.9	27.0	—	27.0	—
1922	100	71.2	52.2	19.0	18.2	—	18.2	—

n/a Not available.

Table A.1 (cont'd)

DEPARTMENT EARNINGS

Year	Total	Fines	Con. Labor	Ed.	High-way	San.	Inspec-tion	Misc.
			(In Thousands of Dollars)					
1873	2.4	1.5	n/a	0.9	—	—	—	2.2
1881	4.4	3.6	n/a	0.8	—	—	—	0.2
1885	8.9	6.0	n/a	3.1	—	—	—	5.9
1890	38.2	n/a	n/a	n/a	n/a	n/a	n/a	39.3
1898	32.5	10.0	6.1	10.0	n/a	1.9	4.5	9.2
1900	60.8	29.9	13.6	7.1	1.8	2.7	5.6	9.2
1904	87.7	24.7	20.0	11.5	1.6	.4	29.5	10.1
1907	153.8	49.9	30.4	18.4	22.2	1.0	31.9	24.2
1909	130.9	37.0	36.9	17.0	12.6	1.5	26.0	27.0
1911	161.4	61.3	41.2	1.8	16.4	.8	39.9	59.3
1915	133.3	47.0	30.4	3.0	13.8	.9	38.3	43.9
1916	223.1	62.7	21.9	50.2	11.6	7.8	68.9	48.5
1920	355.1	159.0	20.7	36.1	17.6	39.3	82.4	100.3
1922	367.9	177.4	n/a	n/a	n/a	n/a	n/a	84.2
			(In Dollars per Capita)					
1881	1.44	1.18	n/a	.26	—	—	—	.08
1885	.65	.42	n/a	.23	—	—	—	.44
1890	1.46	n/a	n/a	n/a	n/a	n/a	n/a	1.50
1898	.90	.28	.17	.28	n/a	.05	.12	.26
1900	1.58	.78	.35	.18	.05	.07	.15	.24
1904	1.84	.52	.42	.24	.03	.01	.62	.21
1907	2.82	.92	.56	.34	.41	.02	.57	.44
1909	2.11	.60	.59	.27	.20	.02	.42	.44
1911	1.17	.45	.30	.01	.12	.01	.29	.43
1915	.85	.30	.19	.02	.09	.01	.24	.28
1916	1.38	.39	.14	.31	.07	.05	.43	.30
1920	1.97	.88	.11	.20	.10	.22	.46	.56
1922	1.86	.90	n/a	n/a	n/a	n/a	n/a	.43
			(Percentage Distribution)					
1873	15.6	9.7	n/a	5.9	—	—	—	14.3
1881	25.1	20.5	n/a	4.6	—	—	—	1.4
1885	15.5	10.1	n/a	5.4	—	—	—	10.3
1890	14.6	n/a	n/a	n/a	n/a	n/a	n/a	15.0
1898	13.4	4.1	2.5	4.1	n/a	0.8	1.8	3.8
1900	15.6	7.7	3.5	1.8	0.5	0.7	1.4	2.4
1904	16.6	4.7	3.8	2.2	0.3	0.0	5.6	1.9
1907	18.6	6.0	3.7	2.2	2.7	0.1	3.9	2.9
1909	15.3	4.3	4.3	2.0	1.5	0.2	3.0	3.2
1911	11.0	4.1	2.8	0.1	1.1	0.1	2.7	4.0
1915	7.2	2.5	1.6	0.2	0.7	0.0	2.1	2.4
1916	11.6	3.3	1.1	2.6	0.6	0.4	3.6	2.5
1920	12.2	5.4	0.7	1.2	0.6	1.3	2.8	3.4
1922	8.6	4.2	n/a	n/a	n/a	n/a	n/a	2.0

n/a Not available.

Table A.2 Birmingham Departmental Expenditures

Year	Total	Gen. Govt.	Police	Fire	Inspec- tion	San.	High- ways
			(In Thousands of Dollars)				
1873	17.4	4.5	2.5	1.1	n/a	n/a	4.3
1881	16.4	2.9	2.9	0.7	n/a	0.4	4.9
1890	224.7	9.1	46.6	36.9	n/a	29.3	22.6
1898	187.9	20.2	33.1	39.2	2.4	10.7	30.2
1900	270.9	32.5	43.7	48.7	2.7	14.9	37.8
1904	372.2	35.7	57.3	73.2	6.1	17.3	66.2
1907	579.3	55.5	76.1	127.8	12.9	61.9	70.3
1909	646.1	55.7	79.9	138.7	16.4	59.6	84.0
1911	1,401.3	121.9	197.6	237.2	34.3	87.7	143.4
1915	1,485.1	103.7	174.5	234.1	28.0	122.1	157.9
1916	1,359.0	120.1	143.7	184.2	31.3	105.5	181.9
1920	2,308.1	142.1	219.7	353.9	37.7	229.5	210.1
1922	3,396.5	202.1	821.7	(c)	(c)	260.4	295.5
			(In Dollars per Capita)				
1881	5.31	.94	.95	.22	n/a	.14	1.59
1890	8.58	.35	1.78	1.41	n/a	1.12	.86
1898	5.23	.56	.92	1.09	.07	.30	.84
1900	7.05	.84	1.14	1.27	.07	.39	.98
1904	7.82	.75	1.20	1.54	.13	.36	1.39
1907	10.63	1.02	1.40	2.35	.24	1.14	1.29
1909	10.40	.90	1.29	2.23	.26	.96	1.35
1911	10.20	.89	1.44	1.73	.25	.64	1.04
1915	9.49	.66	1.12	1.50	.18	.78	1.01
1916	8.43	.74	.89	1.14	.19	.65	1.13
1920	12.82	.79	1.22	1.96	.21	1.27	1.17
1922	17.32	1.03	4.19	(c)	(c)	1.33	1.51
			(Percentage Distribution)				
1873	100	25.7	14.2	6.2	n/a	n/a	24.9
1881	100	17.6	17.9	4.2	n/a	2.6	30.0
1890	100	4.1	20.7	16.4	n/a	13.1	10.0
1898	100	10.7	17.6	20.8	1.3	5.7	16.1
1900	100	11.9	16.2	16.0	1.0	5.5	13.9
1904	100	9.6	15.4	19.7	1.6	4.5	17.8
1907	100	9.6	13.1	22.1	2.2	10.7	12.1
1909	100	8.6	12.4	21.5	2.5	9.2	13.0
1911	100	8.7	14.1	16.9	2.4	6.3	10.2
1915	100	7.0	11.8	15.8	1.9	8.2	10.6
1916	100	8.9	10.6	13.6	2.3	7.8	13.4
1920	100	6.2	9.5	15.3	1.6	9.9	9.1
1922	100	6.0	24.2	(c)	(c)	7.7	8.7

n/a Not available.
(c) Included in Police column.

Table A.2 (cont'd)

Year	Ed.	Prison	Lib.	Health	Hos. & Char.	Rec.	Misc.
			(In Thousands of Dollars)				
1873	4.0	n/a	—	—	0.4	—	0.7
1881	3.2	0.7	—	—	0.1	—	0.5
1890	43.4	11.7	—	n/a	6.5	2.5	16.3
1900	48.9	13.8	—	8.5	4.3	1.6	13.6
1904	78.4	14.6	—	10.8	5.2	4.6	2.5
1907	136.1	15.5	—	9.5	6.9	3.6	3.0
1909	159.2	14.8	1.8	12.7	7.1	10.2	5.9
1911	421.7	27.8	4.5	36.2	9.5	11.6	67.8
1915	528.7	30.6	14.8	16.0	12.2	24.6	37.9
1916	508.3	23.1	14.1	15.5	1.6	14.2	15.6
1920	896.3	35.4	30.4	38.5	8.8	65.3	40.7
1922	1,487.2	53.1	46.3	(a)	(b)	114.6	115.5
			(In Dollars per Capita)				
1881	1.03	.23	—	—	.04	—	.17
1890	1.66	.44	—	n/a	.25	.10	.62
1898	.89	.16	—	.08	.06	.02	.26
1900	1.27	.36	—	.22	.11	.04	.35
1904	1.65	.31	—	.23	.11	.10	.05
1907	2.50	.28	—	.17	.13	.07	.06
1909	2.56	.24	.03	.20	.11	.16	.10
1911	3.07	.20	.03	.26	.07	.08	.49
1915	3.38	.20	.09	.10	.08	.16	.24
1916	3.15	.14	.09	.10	.01	.09	.09
1920	4.97	.20	.17	.21	.05	.36	.23
1922	7.50	.27	.24	(a)	(b)	.58	.59
			(Percentage Distribution)				
1873	22.7	n/a	—	—	2.1	—	4.2
1881	19.4	4.4	—	—	0.7	—	3.1
1890	19.3	5.1	—	n/a	2.9	1.2	7.2
1898	16.6	3.1	—	1.5	1.1	0.4	5.0
1900	18.0	5.1	—	3.1	1.6	0.6	5.0
1904	21.1	3.9	—	3.0	1.4	1.2	0.7
1907	23.5	2.7	—	1.6	1.2	0.6	0.5
1909	24.6	2.3	0.3	2.0	1.0	1.6	0.9
1911	30.1	2.0	0.3	2.4	0.7	0.8	4.8
1915	35.6	2.1	1.0	1.1	0.8	1.7	2.5
1916	37.4	1.7	1.0	1.1	0.1	1.0	1.2
1920	38.8	1.6	1.3	1.7	0.4	2.8	1.8
1922	43.8	1.6	1.4	(a)	(b)	3.4	3.4

n/a Not available.
(a) Included in Sanitation column.
(b) Included in Prison column.

Table A.3 Birmingham per Capita Departmental Expenditures
Compared with Those of Five Other Southern Cities, 1910, 1920

	Total	Gen. Govt.	Police	Fire	Inspec- tion	San.
1910		(In Dollars per Capita)				
Birmingham (1911)	10.20	.89	1.44	1.73	.25	.64
Louisville	13.00	1.20	1.92	1.59	.09	1.13
Atlanta	10.93	.78	1.55	1.30	.13	1.55
Memphis	12.24	.86	1.53	1.40	.24	1.12
Nashville	9.14	.58	1.09	1.30	.14	.84
Richmond	9.99	1.27	1.21	1.27	.18	1.05
5 cities combined*	11.36	.97	1.53	1.40	.15	1.16
Birmingham as % of 5 cities combined	89.8%	91.8%	94.1%	123.6%	166.7%	55.2%
1920		(In Dollars per Capita)				
Birmingham	12.82	.79	1.22	1.96	.21	1.27
Louisville	20.05	1.30	2.77	2.45	.18	1.56
Atlanta	20.07	.84	2.28	2.00	.24	2.73
Memphis	21.85	.85	2.62	2.74	.26	1.87
Nashville	16.92	1.03	1.97	2.29	.32	1.00
Richmond	21.44	1.70	2.50	2.43	.61	2.48
5 cities combined*	20.24	1.16	2.47	2.38	.31	1.99
Birmingham as % of 5 cities combined	63.3%	68.1%	49.4%	82.8%	67.7%	63.8%

*Total expenditures of the 5 cities divided by total population of the 5 cities.

Table A.3 (cont'd)

	High-ways	Ed.	Hosp., Char., Prison	Lib.	Health	Rec.	Misc.
1910			(In Dollars per Capita)				
Birmingham (1911)	1.04	3.07	.27	.03	.26	.08	.49
Louisville	1.50	3.38	1.05	.29	.25	.38	.24
Atlanta	1.50	2.32	.90	.14	.35	.34	.06
Memphis	2.26	2.88	.41	.13	.40	.88	.11
Nashville	1.36	2.62	.42	.16	.21	.36	.06
Richmond	1.23	2.34	.60	.01	.28	.43	.13
5 cities combined*	1.57	2.78	.74	.16	.30	.46	.13
Birmingham as % of 5 cities combined	66.2%	110.4%	36.5%	18.8%	86.7%	17.4%	377.0%
1920			(In Dollars per Capita)				
Birmingham	1.17	4.97	.25	.17	.21	.36	.23
Louisville	1.55	6.06	2.02	.40	.80	.60	.36
Atlanta	1.95	6.24	1.69	.18	.87	.52	.53
Memphis	3.98	5.77	1.35	.35	.46	1.55	.05
Nashville	2.48	4.72	1.09	.25	.32	1.22	.22
Richmond	1.68	7.51	1.07	—	.61	.57	.28
5 cities combined*	2.23	6.15	1.51	.30	.65	.83	.31
Birmingham as % of 5 cities combined	52.5%	81.0%	16.6%	56.7%	32.3%	43.4%	74.2%

*Total expenditures of the 5 cities divided by total population of the 5 cities.

Bibliographical Essay

This essay, necessarily selective, makes no attempt to list every source used in this book. Scholars desiring such a list may consult the author's "Economic Power and Politics: A Study of Birmingham, Alabama, 1890–1920" (Ph.D. diss., University of Wisconsin, 1970), 595–616.

The two most important sources for this study were government documents and Birmingham newspapers. Voluminous government records are extant, and many that have not survived in their original form were published and preserved in the newspapers. The most systematic record of government deliberation and action lies in the official handwritten or typewritten minutes of the Birmingham Board of Aldermen, 1871–1907, the Birmingham City Council, 1907–1911, and the Birmingham Board of City Commissioners, 1911–1921, bound in ledger volumes and stored in the city clerk's vault in the Birmingham City Hall. Though essential, the minutes are often frustratingly formalized and cryptic. More descriptive are the periodic, often annual, reports of mayors, treasurers, auditors, boards of education, superintendents, engineers, inspectors, health officials, and other city officials, boards, and committees. Most of these are available in the Birmingham Public Library's Department of Southern History and Literature. Records of the Jefferson County Court of Commissioners, the Jefferson County Board of Revenue, and the Jefferson County Tax Assessor are available in the Jefferson County Courthouse. For the frequent decisions that involved state agencies, the published reports of governors, state auditors, tax commissions, public service commissions, and courts were essential.

Daily and weekly newspapers were the richest sources, adding flesh, blood, and spirit to the bare bones in the official records. Weeklies were read systematically for the period 1874 to 1888, and at least one daily was read for each day for which one was available from 1888 to

1921. For times of sharp controversy or heated political campaigns, several newspapers were read. The newspapers lavished great attention, reportorial and editorial, upon city hall, courthouse, and statehouse. They covered every political campaign extensively, actively taking sides in many; they provided the most complete local election returns and lists of winning and losing candidates; they published verbatim many government reports; and they carried detailed formal accounts of all local government meetings and actions. These they supplemented profusely with chatty behind-the-scenes gossip, informative background essays, muckraking investigative reports, and columns and editorials both informative and polemic. Moreover, they reported extensively on interest-group meetings, statements, resolutions, and gossip, they printed lists of association officeholders, and they frequently interviewed group spokesmen.

For the period 1874–1887 the most important newspaper was the weekly Birmingham *Iron Age* (title varied slightly under different owners and editors). Relatively complete files are available in the excellent newspaper collection of the Alabama State Department of Archives and History. Also valuable for the period from 1879 to 1881 are the department's files of the *Weekly Independent*, sometimes called the *Jefferson Independent*.

In 1888 two daily newspapers, the morning Birmingham *Age-Herald* and the evening Birmingham *News*, launched long, successful, highly-competitive careers. Each was shaped by an able, forceful owner-editor who controlled his paper for many years.

The *News* was founded in 1888 by the editor who would mold it, Rufus N. Rhodes, a thirty-two-year-old Tennessee attorney. Before moving to Birmingham, Rhodes had served as city attorney of Clarksville, Tennessee, as a Tennessee legislator, and as secretary to United States Senator James E. Bailey. Rhodes ran the *News* for twenty-two years, until his death in 1910. Then Victor H. Hanson, publisher, and Frank P. Glass, editor, bought the *News*, controlling it through 1921 and beyond, perpetuating much of Rhodes' style and philosophy, though dropping his advocacy of prohibition.

The *Age-Herald* was born in 1888 of a merger of the short-lived daily *Herald* and the long-established weekly *Iron-Age*. During its first decade, the *Age-Herald* had several owners and editors, most of them associated financially with local Democratic Liberal Element politicians. From 1895 to 1897 it was associated with the state free-silver Democratic faction of Governor Joseph F. Johnston, changing its name during these years to the Birmingham *State Herald*. Then in July 1897 Edward W. Barrett, a thirty-one-year-old Georgia journalist, moved to Birmingham, bought control of the paper, restored the name *Age-Herald*, and presided as owner-editor for the next twenty-five years. Before moving to Birmingham, Barrett had served eleven years as Washington correspondent for the Atlanta *Constitution* and four years as political secretary to the speaker of the United States House of Representatives, Congressman Charles F. Crisp of Georgia.

Both editors continued their active interest in national politics after their arrival in Birmingham, both serving frequently as Alabama delegates to the national Democratic party conventions. Locally both were business-oriented civic boosters, enthusiastically cooperating with the Chamber of Commerce, in which they often held office. Both promoted and praised Birmingham's rapid economic growth, championed civic improvement, and demanded more efficient and effective government services. Both the *News* and the *Age-Herald* clearly aligned with the "business progressivism" defined by George B. Tindall in "Business Progressivism: Southern Politics in the Twenties," *South Atlantic Quarterly* 62 (Winter 1963), 92–106. But the two newspapers also differed significantly. The *News* was in general more reformist and moralistic in spirit, embracing the 1890s Citizens' Reform movement that the *Age-Herald* opposed, endorsing prohibition between 1907 and 1910 while the *Age-Herald* remained wet, supporting "progressive" governor Braxton Bragg Comer while the *Age-Herald* opposed him, leading the drive for city-commission government, which the *Age-Herald* endorsed but did not actively promote. Also the *News*, though staunchly probusiness, was more likely to use anticorporation rhetoric, to denounce corporation political campaign funds, and to urge regulation of corporations. During strikes both papers consistently supported management, but the *Age-Herald* was more intensely hostile to unions, the *News* slightly more sympathetic. Both newspapers are conveniently available on microfilm at the Birmingham Public Library and the University of Alabama library at Tuscaloosa.

A less influential Birmingham daily, the *Ledger*, was similar to the *News*, but more persistently prohibitionist, and in 1920 it was absorbed by the *News*. The Birmingham *Post*, affiliated with the Scripps newspaper chain, was founded in 1921 and quickly emerged as an influential daily with extensive local coverage.

The weekly Birmingham *Reporter*, edited by Oscar W. Adams, presented the point of view of the Negro business and professional class. Issues for 1915 to 1921 are available at the Alabama Department of Archives and History. The Birmingham *Labor Advocate*, edited by J.H.F. Moseley, was published weekly after 1891 and was, except for a few brief periods, the official organ of the Birmingham Trades Council. It devoted much attention to local politics and government, presenting a moderate trade unionist point of view. It is available on microfilm at the Wisconsin State Historical Society, Madison, Wisconsin. The German-language newspaper, the Birmingham *Courier*, edited by Emil Lesser, was published weekly from 1893 to 1912, consistently presenting a Liberal Element point of view. The extant issues for 1899 to 1903 are held by the Alabama Department of Archives and History.

Indispensable statistical data were found in the United States census reports on population, occupations, manufacturing, religious bodies, and financial statistics of cities; in the United States Geological Survey reports on mineral resources; in published congressional hearings on the coal, iron, and steel industries; in the *Birmingham City Directories*, 1883, and 1887–1953; in a *Social Directory* (Birmingham: Roberts & Son, printers, n.d. [c. 1909]); in Alabama Industrial Development Board, "An Economic Survey of the Metropolitan District of Birmingham," prepared by John A. Maguire, statistician (mimeo., Birmingham, 1932); in William Battle Phillips, *Iron Making in Alabama* (2d ed., Montgomery, 1898; 3d ed., University, Alabama, 1912); and in the January volumes, 1880, 1890, 1895, 1900, 1905, 1910, 1915, and 1920, of R.G. Dun & Company, *Reference Book (And Key) Containing Ratings of Merchants, Manufacturers and Traders Generally, Throughout the United States & Canada*, available at the Business Library, Dun & Bradstreet, Inc., New York, New York.

Some manuscript collections proved valuable, but city politicians, communicating face-to-face or over the telephone, tended to leave much less working political correspondence than did state and national politicians. Still, on such issues as annexation and the adoption of commission government, in which the governor played a crucial role, much correspondence from concerned Birmingham citizens found its way into the Governor's Office Records at the Alabama Department of Archives and History. Especially valuable are the collections for the administrations of Governors Braxton Bragg Comer and Emmet O'Neal. Also at the ADAH are the papers of James Marion Jones, Birmingham city commission president from 1925 to 1940. They contain some information on the years before 1921.

The library of the University of Alabama holds the diaries, letters,

and three-volume typescript autobiography of the prominent industrialist, James Bowron. Bowron's exceptionally clear and forceful writ-
ings provide unique insights concerning industrial development and the
human side of life in Birmingham.

The Southern History Department of the Birmingham Public Library
has the extensive Hill Ferguson Collection, containing a useful genea-
logical and biographical section, "Personalities: a Collection of Material
on Birmingham and Alabama Men and Women Arranged in Dictionary
Form," including scrapbook material and typescript essays, compiled
and written by Hill Ferguson, president emeritus, Birmingham Historical Society. A much smaller collection of similar material, relating
mostly to real estate, is Robert Jemison, Jr., "Miscellaneous Data from
Robt. Jemison, Jr. Re. Developments and Personal References Re. a
Few Friends and Citizens of Birmingham." The department also holds
the Erskine Ramsay Papers, which contain several valuable letters.

The Birmingham library has also acquired the papers and letterbooks
of the now defunct Birmingham Water Works Company. The letterbooks contain carbon copies of thousands of letters from the company
superintendents in Birmingham to the company presidents in Pittsburgh.
Between 1900 and 1921 the superintendents wrote every few days,
transmitting voluminous technical information and commenting frequently on local politics and the company's relationship with local
government. Finally, useful statistical and descriptive material was found
in the typescripts of the Southern Bell Telephone and Telegraph Company, "Commercial Survey, Birmingham, Alabama, 1914," and "Commercial Survey, Birmingham, Alabama, 1927," made available by the
office of the Southern Bell Telephone and Telegraph Company in
Birmingham.

Birmingham city maps are available at the Birmingham City Hall,
in the Birmingham Public Library's Southern History Department, and
particularly in the library's Rucker Agee map collection.

Many contemporaries of late-nineteenth and early-twentieth-century
Birmingham—informed citizens, journalists, and social scientists—made
valuable studies and wrote insightful analyses of Birmingham. In 1910
Ethel Armes, a talented journalist and later a perceptive social critic,
published *The Story of Coal and Iron in Alabama* (Birmingham, 1910).
Sponsored by the Chamber of Commerce, permeated with a booster
spirit, and financed by local subscriptions (which seem to have influenced
the coverage accorded to individuals and families), the book is nonetheless very accurate and readable, containing an enormous amount of

carefully researched information about the men and firms that developed early Birmingham. A more general account by a prominent Birmingham publisher and historian is John C. Henley, Jr., *This is Birmingham: The Story of the Founding and Growth of an American City* ([Birmingham]: Southern Univ. Press, 1960).

Staff members of *The Survey* magazine and several prominent social reformers conducted an intensive study of Birmingham and published "Birmingham: Smelting Iron Ore and Civics; A Social Interpretation of the New Industrial Frontier of the South," *The Survey* 27 (Jan. 6, 1912), 1449–1556. The issue included penetrating, highly-critical essays by Ethel Armes, John A. Fitch, Morris Knowles, W.M. McGrath, Alexander J. McKelway, Graham Romeyn Taylor, and Shelby M. Harrison. Other valuable contemporary accounts were Henry M. Caldwell, *History of the Elyton Land Company and Birmingham, Ala.* (Birmingham 1892; reprinted Birmingham, 1926); Institute for Government Research of the Brookings Institute, *Taxation of the State Government of Alabama*, vol. IV, Pt. 3 of *Report on a Survey of the Organization and Administration of the State and County Governments of Alabama*, submitted to the governor, B.M. Miller (Washington, D.C., 1932); Warren Henry Manning, *Warren H. Manning's City Plan of Birmingham* (Birmingham, 1919); and J.P. Ross, "Notes on Birmingham Public Utilities," (typescript, 1932, Birmingham Public Library).

The Birmingham Public Library contains an array of other city and county histories, company histories, organizational histories, biographies, and civic booster publications. They were a mine of biographical information for positional analysis, and that information was rendered more accessible by an unpublished typescript compilation by the Birmingham, Alabama, Library Board and the Works Progress Administration, "Alabama Biography: An Index to Biographical Sketches of Individual Alabamians in State, Local and to Some Extent in National Collections," a Works Progress Administration Project, completed in 1956, available in the library's Southern History Department.

The scholarly literature on the analysis of political power is surveyed in chapter 1. The only general scholarly history of Birmingham is Martha Carolyn Mitchell Bigelow, "Birmingham: Biography of a City of the New South" (Ph.D. diss., Univ. of Chicago, 1946). Covering the years 1871 to 1910, it provides much useful information on early economic and social development. Paul B. Worthman has published two valuable articles on workingmen in Birmingham: "Black Workers and Labor Unions in Birmingham, Alabama, 1897–1904," *Labor His-*

tory 10 (Summer 1969), 375–407; and "Working Class Mobility in Birmingham, Alabama, 1880–1914," in *Anonymous Americans: Explorations in Nineteenth-Century Social History*, edited by Tamara K. Hareven (Englewood Cliffs, N.J.: Prentice-Hall, 1971), 172–213. Blaine A. Brownell has published two enlightening articles on Birmingham during the decade following the conclusion of this study: "Birmingham, Alabama: New South City in the 1920s," *Journal of Southern History* 38 (Feb. 1972), 21–48; and "The Notorious Jitney and the Urban Transportation Crisis in Birmingham in the 1920's," *Alabama Review* 25 (Apr. 1972), 105–18. The Birmingham coal strike of 1894 is the focus of Robert David Ward and William Warren Rogers, *Labor Revolt in Alabama: The Great Strike of 1894* (University: Univ. of Alabama Press, 1965). Interesting impressionistic accounts of Birmingham appear in George R. Leighton, "Birmingham, Alabama: The City of Perpetual Promise," *Harper's Magazine* 175 (1937), 225–42, and in Irving Beiman, "Birmingham: Steel Giant with a Glass Jaw," in *Our Fair City*, edited by Robert S. Allen (New York: Vanguard, 1947). Kenneth E. Barnhart, "A Study of Homicide in the United States," *Birmingham-Southern College Bulletin* 25 (May 1932) is a statistical study that focuses on a comparison of Birmingham homicide rates with those in other cities. Among the many theses and dissertations on aspects of Birmingham history, the following were most helpful: Joseph Eli Allen, "A Study of the Financial Condition of the Public School System of Birmingham, Alabama" (M.A. diss., Univ. of Chicago, Dept. of Education, 1924); Justin Fuller, "History of the Tennessee Coal, Iron and Railroad Company, 1852–1907" (Ph.D. diss., Univ. of North Carolina at Chapel Hill, 1966); Jere C. King, Jr., "The Formation of Greater Birmingham" (M.A. thesis, Univ. of Alabama, 1935); and Lillian Estelle Worley, "Urban Geography of Birmingham, Alabama" (Ph.D. diss., Dept. of Geology and Geography, Univ. of North Carolina, 1948).

The two most important monographs on the iron and steel industry are H.H. Chapman, W.M. Adamson, H.D. Bonham, H.D. Pallister, and E.C. Wright, *The Iron and Steel Industries of the South* (University: Univ. of Alabama Press, 1953); and George W. Stocking, *Basing Point Pricing and Regional Development: A Case Study of the Iron and Steel Industry* (Chapel Hill: Univ. of North Carolina Press, 1954).

Any Alabama scholar has the good fortune of being able to rely on many excellent studies of Alabama politics. The following were indispensable for placing Birmingham politics within the state context:

Horace Mann Bond, *Negro Education in Alabama: A Study in Cotton and Steel* (Washington, D.C., 1939; New York: Atheneum, 1969); Elizabeth Bonner Clark, "The Abolition of the Convict Lease System in Alabama, 1913–1928" (M.A. thesis, Univ. of Alabama, 1949); James F. Doster, *Railroads in Alabama Politics, 1875–1914* (University: Univ. of Alabama Press, 1957); Hallie Farmer, *The Legislative Process in Alabama* (University: Univ. of Alabama Press, 1949); Walter L. Fleming, *Civil War and Reconstruction in Alabama* (Chicago: S.J. Clarke Pub. Co., 1906; New York: Peter Smith, 1949); Wayne Flynt, "Organized Labor, Reform, and Alabama Politics, 1920," *Alabama Review* 23 (July 1970), 163–180; Allen Johnston Going, *Bourbon Democracy in Alabama, 1874–1890* (University: Univ. of Alabama Press, 1951); Francis Sheldon Hackney, *Populism to Progressivism in Alabama* (Princeton: Princeton Univ. Press, 1969); Allen Woodrow Jones, "A History of the Direct Primary in Alabama, 1840–1903" (Ph.D. diss., Univ. of Alabama, 1964); Malcolm Cook McMillan, *Constitutional Development in Alabama, 1798–1901: A Study in Politics, the Negro, and Sectionalism,* "The James Sprunt Studies in History and Political Science," vol. 37 (Chapel Hill: Univ. of North Carolina Press, 1955); Albert Burton Moore, *History of Alabama* (3 vols., Chicago, 1927); Thomas McAdory Owen, *History of Alabama and Dictionary of Alabama Biography* (4 vols., Chicago, 1921); and James Benson Sellers, *The Prohibition Movement in Alabama,* "The James Sprunt Studies in History and Political Science," vol. 26 (Chapel Hill: Univ. of North Carolina Press, 1943).

The wider "New South" context of Birmingham history is synthesized superbly in two volumes of the ten-volume *History of the South,* edited by Wendell Holmes Stephenson and E. Merton Coulter. In *Origins of the New South, 1877–1913* (Baton Rouge: Louisiana State Univ. Press, 1951), C. Vann Woodward brilliantly defined the contours within which scholars of post-Reconstruction Southern history have worked for a generation. And in the early chapters of *The Emergence of the New South, 1913–1945* (Baton Rouge: Louisiana State Univ. Press, 1967), George B. Tindall provided a stimulating synthesis and analysis of Southern Progressivism. The excellent bibliographies in these two volumes are the best guides to the extensive literature on the South since Reconstruction.

The best general accounts and analyses of American urban history in the late nineteenth and early twentieth centuries are Blake McKelvy, *The Urbanization of America* (New Brunswick, N.J.: Rutgers Univ.

Press, 1963); Charles N. Glaab and A. Theodore Brown, *A History of Urban America* (New York: Macmillan, 1967); Sam Bass Warner, Jr., *The Urban Wilderness: A History of the American City* (New York: Harper, 1972); Zane L. Miller, *The Urbanization of Modern America: A Brief History* (New York: Harcourt, 1973); and Howard P. Chudacoff, *The Evolution of American Urban Society* (Englewood Cliffs, New Jersey: Prentice-Hall, 1975).

Index

Index

Lower-ranking economic (*cont.*)
on board of aldermen, 80; members
of, on board of education, 89; members of, on board of revenue, 90; members of, among state legislators, 92;
members of, nominated by Citizens'
and Democratic factions, 69; most
vulnerable to reform regulation, 278–
79; and municipal revenue patterns,
124-25, 144-45; and Negro education, 172–73; and overall pattern of
power, 270; overall record of, 278–
79; portion of population in, 52–53;
and positional analysis, 280; provide only one mayor, 59; and social
regulation patterns, 215–16; support
public education, 168, 170–71; tend
to exercise least influence, 278; underrepresented on board of aldermen,
62–63
Louisville & Nashville Railroad, 15,
232, 236
Lowi, Theodore J., 276–77

Maben, J. Campbell, Jr., 212, 214
McCartin, John M., 123, 154
McCormack, George B., 207
McDonald property tax rate lawsuit, 140,
142
McDonald, Thomas C., 140
McLendon, David E., 88
McQueen, James W., 194, 210
Manning, Warren H., 166
Manufacturers' Record, 116
Master Builders' Association, 42
Mayors: positional analysis of, 59–61;
typical characteristics of, 61; voter
cleavages in election of, 63; winners
compared with losing candidates, 61
Meat inspection, 241
Merchants: on board of aldermen, 1907,
79–80; on board of education, 89; on
city commission, 88; early examples
of, 22–23; found Board of Trade, 42;
found Commercial Club, 41; among
middle-ranking groups, 47–48, 53;
among state legislators, 92
Mercy home, 159
Metal manufacturers: and annexation,
107, 109–10; described, 20; as interest group without a local association, 43; among upper-ranking groups,
47, 53

Middle-ranking economic interest
groups: and annexation, 111–12; defeated on home rule tax amendment,
139; defined, 47–48, 52–53; dependence of, upon development of local
market, 275–76; dominate board of
aldermen, 61–62; dominate office of
sheriff, 90; and economic regulation
patterns, 243; exercise greatest influence on allocations, 149; and fire
protection, 150; and general civic service patterns, 174–75; lead charity
organizations, 157; members of, on
board of aldermen, 79–80; members
of, on board of education, 89; members of, on board of revenue, 90; members of, on city commission, 88–89;
members of, nominated by Citizens'
and Democratic factions, 69; members of, among state legislators, 92;
members of, among state senators, 93;
and municipal revenue patterns, 124–
25, 144–45; and Negro education,
173; and overall pattern of power,
270; overall record of, 275–77; overrepresented in local offices, 95; portion of population in, 52, 53; and
positional analysis, 280; power of,
grows over time, 277; provide most
mayors, 59; and public health plan,
163–64; reasons for influence of, in
general civic services, 175; and services to persons, 162; and social regulation patterns, 215–16; support public education, 168
Middleton, S.A., 152
Miller, Nathan L., 93–94, 108, 254
Milner, John T., 13, 93, 228n, 231
Milner, W.J., 252
Mineral reserve land, assessed valuation of, 115–17, 133
Minor revenue sources, 96n, 121–24
Molton, Thomas H., 211, 232, 238
Moody, Dwight L., 37
Moody, John, 116
Moore, Walter, 80
Moral Element, 70–72; aldermen of,
characterized by economic and social
affiliations, 75–79; annexation in-
creases power of, 83–85; dominates
city commissioners from suburbs,
85–86; policy positions of, 71; and
positional analysis, 280; and saloon

Twentieth-Century America Series

DEWEY W. GRANTHAM, GENERAL EDITOR

Each volume in this series focuses on some aspect of the politics of social change in recent American history, utilizing new approaches to clarify the response of Americans to the dislocating forces of our own day—economic, technological, racial, demographic, and administrative.

VOLUMES PUBLISHED:

*The Reaffirmation of Republicanism: Eisenhower and the
    Eighty-third Congress* by Gary W. Reichard
*The Crisis of Conservative Virginia: The Byrd Organization
    and the Politics of Massive Resistance* by James W. Ely, Jr.
Black Tennesseans, 1900–1930 by Lester C. Lamon
Political Power in Birmingham, 1871–1921 by Carl V. Harris

This book has been manually composed on the Linotype in eleven-point Garamond No. 3 with one-point line spacing. Windsor type was selected for display. The book was designed by Jim Billingsley and set into type by Heritage Printers, Inc., Charlotte, North Carolina. It was printed offset by Thomson-Shore, Inc., Dexter, Michigan and bound by John H. Dekker and Sons, Inc., Grand Rapids, Michigan. The paper on which the book is printed bears the watermark of S. D. Warren and is designed for an effective life of at least three hundred years.